Western Art and the Wider World

Paul Wood

WILEY Blackwell

This edition first published 2014

Registered Office
John Wiley & Sons, Ltd, The Atrium, Southern Gate, Chichester, West Sussex, PO19 8SQ, UK

Editorial Offices
350 Main Street, Malden, MA 02148-5020, USA
9600 Garsington Road, Oxford, OX4 2DQ, UK
The Atrium, Southern Gate, Chichester, West Sussex, PO19 8SQ, UK

For details of our global editorial offices, for customer services, and for information about how to apply for permission to reuse the copyright material in this book please see our website at www.wiley.com/wiley-blackwell.

Library of Congress Cataloging-in-Publication Data is Available for this Title

Hardback: 9781444333916
Paperback: 9781444333923

A catalogue record for this book is available from the British Library.

Cover image: George Nuku and Tracey Tawhiao, TE AO: *The Light*, installation in Chapelle du Calvaire, rue St Roch, Paris, 2012. Photo: Tracey Tawhiao
Cover design by Simon Levy Design Associates

Set in 11/13pt Dante by SPi Publisher Services, Pondicherry, India
Printed and bound in Great Britain by TJ International Ltd, Padstow, Cornwall

1 2014

Western Art and the Wider World

For Charles at the beginning, and Roberta at the end.

Contents

Illustrations

Acknowledgments

The debts I have incurred in researching and writing this book are many and various. I must first collectively thank the Arts Faculty and the Department of Art History of the Open University. Also the team at Wiley Blackwell, including, in the USA, Jayne Fargnoli, Julia Kirk, Allison Kostka; in England, Lisa Eaton, Caroline Hensman, Felicity Marsh, Leanda Shrimpton. I gratefully acknowledge the permission of the Open University, Tate Publishing, Yale University Press, and the editors of *Visual Culture in Britain* to reproduce parts of previously published material.

I would also like to thank the following individuals who have helped me in a variety of professional and personal ways. Without them this work would not have been possible (none, of course, are in any way responsible for its faults): Michael Baldwin, Fionna Barber, Emma Barker, Peter Berry, Barbara Conway, Tom Crow, Whitney Davis, Renate Dohmen, Steve Edwards, Briony Fer, Jason Gaiger, Charlie Gore, Bob Graham, Suman Gupta, Charles Harrison, Sean Heneghan, Michael Howard Maia Jessop Nuku, Robert and Abigail Katz, Heather Kelly, Peju Layiwola, Nick Levinson, Siobhan McDermott, Andrew McNamara, Pam Meecham, Howard Morphy, Ademola Olayiwola, Duro Oni, Bruce Onobrakpeya, Richard Parkinson, Gill Perry, Alex Potts, Mel Ramsden, Carol Richardson, Ann Stephen, Leon Wainwright, Linda Walsh, David and Roberta Wood, Kim Woods.

Old Wolverton, March 2013

Introduction

It took me a long time to wake up to the wider world, most of my life in fact. I have no doubt there will be critics of this book who will claim I never have, that I remain locked in the twilight zone of a Western worldview. It is true that this book is not written according to the principles of some of the most radical outcrops of contemporary theory. At various points in the text I discuss postcolonial perspectives as well as identity politics, but the book has not, on the whole, been composed from those points of view. Apart from the Conclusion, where I do explicitly address contemporary academic debates, the rest of the book consists of a more factually inclined historical narrative. That empirical history is, of course, leavened throughout with discussion of ideas. How could it be otherwise in a field whose very fabric is woven out of the threads of different beliefs, opinions, and theories? Neither is the narrative continuous. I jump around, pretty much as I have thought fit as I have been writing, and very much conditioned by my own knowledge, including the gaps in it.

I often wondered whether this book would be a failure. Apparently Iris Murdoch said that all books are, insofar as they all fall short of the perfect idea that set them going. I know that in my own case the book as it stands has some of the qualities of a sketch, a study for a much longer, much more complete, much more finished text that I shall probably never write. When I first had the idea to try and write about that borderline territory where the arts of the Western tradition encountered others, my project met with conflicting responses. Some welcomed it and thought it would potentially be very useful, especially in the practical context of education, of trying to broaden curricula and help students to an awareness of things they might in principle be interested in but not really know how to find out about. That is, indeed, the spirit in which I have written the book, for the most part. Its originality, insofar as it can claim any, lies in its capacity for juxtaposition,

Western Art and the Wider World, First Edition. Paul Wood.

for bringing things together that often lie apart, for making connections, for trying to look at meanings from different sides. Despite the fact that it has involved a lot of reading, it is not the fruit of years spent in the archive in search of that elusive nugget that will prove X could have known Y in 1492, or 1917. It is not that sort of research, though I do hope it will be useful and informative. Others, however, when informed of my project, said it should never see the light of day, that it marked a retrograde step, that it was the last thing we need at this time. These were people who felt that, at the very moment when the hegemony of the Western canon of art was finally being challenged, I was trying to return it to center stage. In short, that I was engaged in a conservative rearguard action to restore a repressive status quo. I leave it to the judgment of others whether I have done that. But it is certainly not what I set out to do. Having said that, I am forced to recognize that, particularly in this field of study, there will be those whom I can never satisfy.

The book has had a long and intermittent period of gestation. I teach in a university art history department, and the day-to-day demands to produce teaching materials and courses, not to mention the need to administer them, all conspire against the time one can devote to research. Actually, I am quite strongly opposed to the separation of teaching and research. I recognize that the demands are not congruent; but at the same time, driving a wedge between them contributes to the kind of compartmentalized academic specialization that I have come to believe is not only the bane of much contemporary scholarship, a passive drag on enterprise and openness. I fear it is an active cause of the failure to ask wide-ranging and difficult questions, questions without clear answers; of doing things that might not please those who police the criteria for what scholarship is, or for what it passes to be in the present, increasingly corporate climate of academe.

I have been lucky to work for an institution that has allowed me more space than most would to rove across boundaries and give myself an autodidactic education in the worldedness of art while remaining connected to the business of communicating with people who are not specialist academics. When I try to think about where this book came from, I keep returning to two things, both of which happened quite a long time ago now. One is that, at an indeterminate point sometime in the 1990s, after I had finished working on the first volume of the anthology *Art in Theory* with my late colleague Charles Harrison, I found my skepticism increasing with the widespread tendency in the field of the "new art history" to disparage the canon. I wasn't even sure what the canon was, but as a result of working through *Art in Theory* I knew that modernism was a lot more complex, difficult, and interesting than most of its detractors recognized. At around this time, because of some work I had done on art and revolution, I was invited to a conference in Greece. Once the conference was over, I took the opportunity to travel to as many ancient sites as I could. I remember one particular early morning on the Acropolis in Athens. I may as well have been an eighteenth-century Grand Tourist. The day was perfect, the air was clear (though the city below was bathed in a haze of smog), the sky was blue, and the marble was white. At first I was almost the only person there. Over the next few hours a tide of humanity engulfed the monument, most of them Italian teenagers whose main concern was to have themselves photographed with their friends in front of it. Both things were significant: the ancient monument and what the modern culture was making of it. Less than a year later, and again because of some other work I had done (this time not on revolutionary Russian art but on the radical conceptual art of the late 1960s, Art & Language amongst others) I was invited to speak in Australia. Before I went to Australia, although I had been told by others who had been what a marvelous place it is, I myself had little idea what to expect beyond blue skies and cricket. Not long after I arrived, I went to an exhibition at the Museum of Contemporary Art in Sydney and saw paintings by Rover Thomas and Emily Kngwarreye. I had no idea what I was looking at. I had encountered Aboriginal art. It was the start of a long road of discovery in which I traveled not only through many books and art galleries but to Arnhem Land and the Central Desert. Somewhere between those two unexpected confrontations in Greece and Australia, between the Parthenon and Uluru, a current arced across the gap that has made this present circuit around the world possible. I still don't know whether it was the right thing to do or whether I have been walking upside down ever since.

There are many other things I could talk about. From about 1999 to 2004 I worked in the team at the Open University that produced the course Art of the Twentieth Century. As part of that collective I tried to ensure that a dimension of engagement with the world, reaching beyond the conventional narratives of the Western modern movement, was included in the course material. Even though, once it had appeared, all I could see were the gaps, I still believe that series of books offers the most open introduction to the subject currently available.[1] It remains part of their achievement that issues such as the discourse of "primitivism," certain aspects of non-Western art (including Aboriginal art), and the effects on art of contemporary globalization, all received some address. In subsequent years, again with colleagues in the art history department of the Open University, I was able to work on Renaissance Venice, on eighteenth-century European encounters with the Pacific, on the manifold questions surrounding the case of the "Benin bronzes" from West Africa, and even on the art of Ancient Egypt. Some of that research and scholarship has found its way, in modified form, into the present book. Some of it has not found a place here. But taken together, it has meant that I have been able to build up a portfolio of knowledge about various aspects of the relationship of Western art to the wider world that, while idiosyncratic, has allowed me to remain open and to keep on moving through the field without becoming restricted to one orthodox academic specialism.

I take this as a positive; though doubtless there are many other more conventional scholars who would question such an improvised approach. In my defense, I can only say that I have always found "both/and" preferable to "either/or," and that I believe the collage method in its manifold forms still to be the appropriate method of our times. Writing the book has often felt like a long and narrow way, but for all that, I have been unable to resist occasionally turning off the high road, seduced by the old sign at the end of a crooked alley, or having to reverse out of a cul-de-sac, before carrying on with the journey. "Journey," by the way, is one of those terms that has become utterly corrupted through its use by corporate administrations to manage their fiefdoms. (Others include "transparency" and "value.") What I have in mind is less the academic administrator's mirage of a successful "learning journey" from A to B according to well-planned guidelines than a Situationist *dérive* through the hinterlands of adjacent interests.

The critical reader may feel that this approach courts superficiality and eclecticism. And to a degree it does. It is an impossible dream to become an expert on everything. Indeed it is probably wrongheaded altogether. But the closures of specialization are also always lying in wait. Navigating this Scylla and Charybdis is something you either manage or not, and you will not know if you have been successful until later. I had this brought home to me by a diagram. A few years ago I wrote a paper for a conference on the European avant-garde and modernism. The main preoccupation of the conference, held in Poland, was to bring to light the work of marginalized and obscured Eastern European avant-gardes, lost to sight not just because of the fascist obliteration of the avant-garde but also the subsequent Soviet occupation with its patchily enforced doctrine of Socialist Realism. My contribution, I have to confess, was a little adjacent to these concerns and, following arguments by Whitney Davis, James Elkins, David Summers, and others, I reckoned it was time to "move the goalposts" further, and to open our concerns onto a wider world art history.

After the conference, almost as a joke to give some visual impact to the published version of my paper, I decided to construct a diagram, part homage and part ironization of Alfred Barr's famous flowchart of the development of abstract art. This took as its central thread a line extending down the page from classical antiquity, to the Renaissance, to the academy, then on to modernism and finally to postmodernism / globalization. The arrows between academy and modernism and between modernism and postmodernism / globalization were crossed through to indicate a relationship less of direct inheritance than a complex continuity-in-contradiction. Aligned on either side of this central line were various "others" including Medieval, Byzantine, Pacific, China, Japan, Prehistory, Africa, and more. These were connected to the Western tradition by a series of either continuous or broken arrows to indicate the points at which their legacies had been assimilated into the Western tradition. The exception was postmodern / globalization, which stretched its arms back to encompass everything.

Clearly the image is flawed. But the point is that it is flawed in more than one way. As printed, on a flat surface, it has the effect of situating the Western tradition as a kind of mainstream, very much in the way that the critics of my project mentioned earlier in this Introduction, had feared would happen. The simple placement of the Western tradition in the center of the page, others arrayed to right and left, reproduced the very relation of dominance and subordination that the enterprise was intended to get away from; much as the Mercator projection of a world map centers the Atlantic between Europe and North America, marginalizing the actually much larger Pacific region. Likewise the arrows, signifying the West's developing interests in its Others, all pointing in one direction. These problems are obvious at a glance. But the more serious point is that "correction" is impossible. It should in principle be possible to imagine the thing in three dimensions, perhaps in virtual space on a computer screen, so that it could be commutated around or viewed from different positions. Thus one could potentially position an East Asian tradition as central, with others feeding into it, including the Western tradition. Except of course, and quite precisely, that it doesn't work like that. You would come up with something. But it would not match the Western tradition. I am guessing, but I think there would be far fewer arrows. This is the double-sided point. You cannot be an expert on everything. You cannot draw the flow diagram from every conceivable point of view (that is, I cannot). But even if you could, it most likely would not work as a set of equivalents. Because the traditions have not, in history, been equivalent in their relations with each other. This is not to say that individual cultural traditions have not been internally complex and evolved. But because of the path world history has taken, it does have implications for intercultural relations; the more so when "culture" is winnowed down to "art."

One is faced with a choice, then. What does one do? Abandon the enterprise of thinking about a world art history altogether or keep calm and carry on, aware of the contradictions? It is understandable that certain contributors to recent roundtable discussions on these topics edited by James Elkins, those whose cultures have for many years been faced by the necessity to resist Western domination, have argued for the former.[2] I have chosen to do the latter, writing openly from my perspective within the Western tradition; which I persist in believing is not wholly an organ of hegemony. In the Introduction to *Art in Theory*, written over twenty years ago now, we commented that in the then contemporary intellectual conjuncture, reason and history had begun to be "contested as the relevant criteria of intellectual commitments."[3] We disagreed with that trend then. I still do. David Summers' ambitious book *Real Spaces*, subtitled *World Art History and the Rise of Western Modernism*, has been criticized for imposing "Western" spatial coordinates including north, south, east and west on the art and architecture of other cultures, in an effort to construct a viable intercultural account of what has motivated the production of art in a world-historical context.[4] The level of cultural relativism implied by that criticism is not something I espouse. I do not adhere to what has been unhappily dubbed "radical particularism." I know that in studying art in a world context it is important not to impose Western definitions of art on the practices of other societies. But while acknowledging the continual requirement for translation, for better or worse (and while recognizing they may not be absolutes), I continue to try and operate with concepts such as reason and history. I continue to value facts, accuracy, and criteria of testability. I acknowledge that I may not always succeed, but I think that if those criteria are abandoned and radical relativism is accepted, we are in a Babel; a Babel, moreover, in which the weakness of reason opens the door to power as the arbiter of what has to be believed.

In 2012 I sat on a panel at the Clark Institute in Williamstown, Massachusetts, to discuss avenues of possibility in the rethinking of postmodernism, the art, that is, of the late twentieth century. Despite the best efforts of the Chair of the panel, Thomas Crow, to broaden a sense of the centers of work involved to include England and California, among others, the discussion kept on coming back to developments in New York. However wide-ranging the discussion it never seemed able to escape the gravitational pull of New York. Some were, or seemed, happy with this; some weren't. Esther da Costa Meyer, speaking from the floor, challenged the preoccupation of the debate as it had unfolded, and in so doing challenged the composition of the panel, which she felt might be contributing to the metrocentrism of the discussion. I agreed. But on reflection, what seemed to be happening was a variant of the problem with the diagram. Changing the point of view wasn't going to equalize or solve everything. All you would end up with was another string of priorities with no particular connection or fruitful relation back to the first one. At this point Tom Crow made an interesting point. Resisting the idea of simply broadening out the panel's composition – or by implication of my "diagram" example – of rotating the points of view, he recalled an adage from the old left-wing History Workshop debates by Raphael Samuel, Eric Hobsbawm, E.P. Thompson and others: that in seeking to rewrite history you should "Dig where you stand." There are two ways of taking this. It can be an excuse for intellectual orthodoxy, a tacit acceptance of discipline boundaries and specialization. And that is the way it works most of the time. But I think it was intended as an argument against intellectual eclecticism. What Raphael Samuel originally meant, and what Tom Crow intended in quoting him, was to evoke the possibility of digging down and uncovering all sorts of criss-crossed hidden root systems, informing, even producing, the place where we stand. I have taken this to heart. I have no doubt that Tom Crow was thinking of something quite different when he made the point, something more confined and manageable. But I too have tried to dig where I stood. And where I stood was in the Western tradition of art and art history. I remain alarmingly ignorant of much of that tradition, let alone of other traditions in the world. But I have tried to dig down and uncover some of its points of contact with other types of art. I have done so not so much in order to function within that tradition of art history writing but to answer to present needs. History Workshop was not just about academic history; it embodied a political project. I would not go so far as to dignify the present book with claims for a coherent political project. I am not sure there is a coherent political project in the world today. But I have written it as a possible contribution to thinking about some aspects of art and culture in history and in relation to the world today, that I feel matter. Somehow.

Books have to begin somewhere, and this one begins with the Renaissance. I have begun there because that is where most conventional histories of Western art over the extended modern period begin. The half millennium that stretches from the invention of perspective in the mid-fifteenth century to the "crisis of modernism" in the mid-twentieth is quite closely congruent to the beginning of the period of European exploration and the onset of full-blown globalization. What is the nature of the connection, or the nature of the disconnection, between our present and that past, is an open question which I address at the end of the book. But the interaction between Europe and the wider world did not, of course, commence with the Renaissance. There had been contacts, embracing the full spectrum from art to war, in antiquity. Aeschylus in his *Persians*, Herodotus in his *Histories*, Strabo in his *Geography*, all reach beyond the West. Thereafter, the collapse of the Roman Empire and the subsequent rise of Islam much reduced the contact of East and West across the vastness of Eurasia; contact did continue, but was mediated for the most part by Jewish and Arab merchants. The Crusades had an ambiguous impact on East–West relations, but it was the rise of the Mongol Empire during the thirteenth century, and the consequent temporary weakening of Islam in the Middle East, that most facilitated the reopening of contact between the different ends of the Eurasian landmass. The most vivid account of the cultures of the East at this period that has come down in Western literature is that of Marco Polo, known to us as his *Travels* but at the time titled *Description of the World*.

The Venetian merchant Marco Polo travelled in East Asia (if indeed he did; the veracity of his journey is sometimes disputed) between 1271 and 1295, and the story of his travels was written down in the very early fourteenth century by the professional romance-writer Rustichello of Pisa. Not that Marco Polo was the first. His uncle and father had travelled in the east during the 1260s before returning to Italy and taking him with them on a second trip. Others had preceded them, including John of Carpini and William of Rubruck in the 1240s and 1250s. As far as art goes, William had famously lamented the inadequacy of his words to describe the decorated carts of the Tartars: "for I would right willingly have painted all things for you, had my skill been in that direction."[5] Later he noted how the people of Cathay "write with a brush like painters use, and a single figure comprises several letters, signifies a word."[6] As an early example of something which was to take on greater significance later, in artistic exchanges between West and East, he also noted how the Khan, on inspecting their Bible "asked with much curiosity what meaning the images had."[7] But both Carpini and Rubruck were Franciscan clerics, on religious missions and motivated by religious ends, and their accounts have none of the density, the sheer thickness of description, that comes through in Rustichello's version of Marco Polo's merchant's tale.

Before glancing at that, it is salutary to be reminded of the nature of the world into which Marco Polo advanced. The besetting sin of Western history, philosophy, religion, and art throughout the extended modern period has been the assumption that they were bringing enlightenment, civilization, and progress to a static world that lacked all of them. Nothing could be further from the truth, and one of the undoubted benefits of contemporary globalization is the way that it has quite rapidly dispelled the myths of Western cultural superiority (even as Western science and technology actually did move into a position of superiority, thus projecting world history onto the course it has taken over the last two hundred and fifty years). In his *Rihla*, or "Book of Travels," the Islamic jurist Ibn Battuta recounted his travels throughout North Africa, the Middle East, India, China, and sub-Saharan Africa between 1325 and 1354, barely a generation after Marco Polo. In his account of Ibn Battuta's travels, Ross Dunn underlines how "drastically different" his experience of the world was from that of Marco Polo. Marco Polo was an "oddity," an "alien visitor into lands few Europeans had ever seen and whose people knew little, and cared to know little, about Europe." By contrast, Ibn Battuta moved within "dense networks of communication and exchange" which, by the fourteenth century "had linked in one way or another nearly everyone in the hemisphere with nearly everyone else." This was the Dar al-Islam, which stretched from the Atlantic to India and Southeast Asia, with extensions further east into China, as well as south into sub-Saharan and east Africa. Although Ibn Battuta encountered people whose local ways of life were strange to him, he functioned within a shared culture that offered "not simply a religious faith" but "a coherent, universalist model of civilised life."[8] This flourishing, cultured, and in places very rich world, was the world which the European Christian Marco Polo traversed, essentially as a stranger.

Isolated he may have been, but Marco Polo had a clear eye and a good memory. The account of his journey to Cathay contains nothing explicitly about "art." The word had not yet accrued its modern meanings in medieval Europe and neither did it have currency in the worlds through which he travelled. But many of his descriptions contain a powerfully visual element, and I want to draw this Introduction to a close by noting some of what he says about the wider world he encountered: partly because of how his descriptions put some foundation underneath comments about East–West trade and cultural impact later in my narrative; partly because at the very end of the book I briefly discuss a work of contemporary art which draws on Polo's words for its own powerful meditation on history, cultural crossings, and contemporaneity.

The early part of his *Description of the World* is concerned with Marco Polo's journey towards Cathay, traveling first through the Middle East and then across central Asia. On the first page, they are at a port on the Black Sea coast, "a busy emporium" where "spices and cloths are brought from the interior." The "choicest and most beautiful carpets in the world," along with "silk fabrics of crimson and other colours, of great beauty and richness," are sought by merchants from "Venice and Genoa," as well as Pisa and other places.[9] Further on, in Baghdad, they see pearls that are "imported from India into Christendom" as well as "many fabrics of cloth of gold and silk," all "richly decorated with beasts and birds." This litany of pearls, precious stones, rich textiles, of craftsmen engaged in leather and metal work, of women "embroidering silk of all colours with beasts and birds and many other figures" continues across Persia and only slackens across the deserts of central Asia where descriptions of crops and social customs come more into play. When they reach China, the description of imperial power conveys the complete opposite of what became the norm in later centuries: "all the kings of Christians and of Saracens combined would not possess such power or be able to accomplish so much as this Kubilai, the Great Khan." Polo's descriptions of visual arts are for the most part of what subsequently in Western culture became relatively downgraded as the "decorative arts," though occasionally he notices a "vast hall" decorated with "admirably painted portraits of all the kings" or "chambers all decorated with pictures." But his descriptions of Chinese cities present an image which, far from being completely alien, is often made out of comparison with his own experience of Venice, albeit to China's great advantage. Thus the Chinese streets are "so broad and straight"; the "building sites throughout the city are square and measured by the rule"; the "whole interior of the city is laid out in squares like a chessboard." The contrast with Venice could scarcely be more pronounced. Yet at the same time, the Chinese city has "many fine hostels which provide lodging for merchants coming from different parts: a particular hostel is assigned to every nation", all of which seems reminiscent of the Venetian *fondacos*. Elsewhere, bridges over city waterways are "covered with handsome roofs richly decorated and painted in red," and "all along the bridges on either side are rows of booths devoted to the practice of various forms of trade and craft." The description could easily be of the Rialto, in Venice. So, in among the exotica, the silk and the ginger, the cinnamon and the coal-heated bath houses, Marco Polo is describing a functioning society, a civilization, boasting crafts, guilds, arts, and architecture; just like Europe but more so.

With the end of the *pax mongolica* and the resurgence of Islamic power across central Asia, trips like Marco Polo's ceased. But the trading relations that subtended them continued. The traffic along the "Silk Road" bringing the luxury products of east and south and central Asia westwards continued into the Renaissance period. Venice remained one of the key sites for this exchange, both material and cultural. As art in the West began to develop along the lines of what we still think of as "art" today, the kinds of things described at the end of the thirteenth century by Marco Polo continued to be the traces of the wider world with which that art interacted.

In the chapters that follow I trace the development of this interaction in a broadly chronological sequence. There are, however, many overlaps. The beginning of each chapter tends to retrace features of the previous one, often focusing on a different aspect of a formation in order to ground the narrative for its development in the subsequent section. Thus Chapter 2, the bulk of which concerns European encounters with the "New Worlds" of the eighteenth century, begins by stepping back to the late Renaissance period to look at the initial "discovery" of America. Chapter 3, which concludes its discussion of modernist primitivism with a brief survey of the mature modernism of the mid-twentieth century, is succeeded by Chapter 4, which begins by stepping back to re-encounter the early twentieth-century avant-garde's rather different relationship with the wider world.

So the chronological progression is not always continuous, but I have found it helpful to retain the framework. Overall, I have tried to offer as comprehensive a picture as I can of the complex interaction of the developing canon of Western art with aspects of the cultures of the wider world over the last five hundred years and to do so taking account of both the ideas which animated those interactions and, where relevant, the retrospective criticism of those ideas and beliefs which have emerged in the present day. Such an enterprise can never be "complete." I am sure there are many silences, many things I have overlooked, many things relevant to the account of which I remain completely ignorant. But I do not think that, taking all things into consideration, I would change the fundamental structure of what I have written. If my thinking were to change substantially, and if as a result I were to change the framework of the book, it would not be the same work. As I said at the beginning of this Introduction, there will be those who disagree. But now, for better or for worse, this is where it rests.

Notes

1 Gaiger, ed., 2003; Edwards and Wood, eds, 2004; Wood, ed., 2004; Perry and Wood, eds, 2004.
2 See Elkins 2007; see, for example, pp. 202–207.
3 Harrison and Wood 2003, p. 8. The sentence occurred on p. 9 of the original edition of 1992.
4 Summers 2003.
5 "The Journal of Friar William of Rubruck" in Komroff, ed., 1928, p. 60.
6 Komroff 1928, p. 152.
7 Komroff 1928, pp. 141–142.
8 Dunn 2005 quotations from the Preface and Introduction, respectively, pp. ix, 6, and 9.
9 *The Travels of Marco Polo*. I am using the Penguin Classics 1958 edition, translated by R.E. Latham, partly because it is an easily accessible modern translation of Polo's text (for which no original exists) and partly because it is the edition used by Fiona Tan for her art installation *Disorient* at the 2009 Venice Biennale, which I discuss at the end of the book. For brevity's sake, I list all my quotations from Polo's *Travels* in the present footnote, in the order in which they appear: pp. 15–16, 21, 32, 66, 136, 139, 99, and 141.

References

Dunn, Ross E., 2005, *The Adventures of Ibn Battuta: A Muslim Traveller of the 14th Century*, University of California Press, Berkeley, Los Angeles, London, rev. edn. First published 1986.

Edwards, Steve and Paul Wood, eds, 2004, *Art of the Avant-Gardes*, Yale University Press, New Haven.

Elkins, James, 2007, *Is Art History Global?* Routledge, New York and Abingdon.

Gaiger, Jason, ed., 2003, *Frameworks for Modern Art*, Yale University Press, New Haven and London.

Harrison, Charles and Paul Wood, 2003, *Art in Theory 1900–2000: An Anthology of Changing Ideas*, Blackwell, Oxford. First published 1992.

Komroff, Manuel, ed., 1928, *Contemporaries of Marco Polo*, Jonathan Cape, London.

Perry, Gill and Paul Wood, eds, 2004, *Themes in Contemporary Art*, Yale University Press, New Haven and London.

Summers, David, 2003, *Real Spaces: World Art History and the Rise of Western Modernism*, Phaidon, London.

The Travels of Ibn Battuta, 2002, Tim Mackintosh-Smith, ed., Picador Macmillan, London.

The Travels of Marco Polo, 1958, trans, R.E. Latham, Penguin Classics, Harmondsworth.

Wood, Paul, ed., 2004, *Varieties of Modernism*, Yale University Press, New Haven and London.

1

Renaissance and Old World

Introduction: The Status of the Renaissance

Stato da mar. The Venetian "empire of the sea." Sea of words. The Renaissance is a sea of words. But surely, you say, the Renaissance is nothing like that? Water is entirely the wrong figure. The Renaissance is a cornerstone, a keystone, it bears the weight of the Western canon, more than anything it provides a foundation for who we are. A few years ago, a TV series on the Medici put the received wisdom in a nutshell when it was claimed that "the whole of Western culture pivots on the extraordinary period we have come to know as the Renaissance."[1] Dissolve again into the sea of words … "Renaissance." Rebirth. Of what? "We." Who is that?

Two writers, more than any others, marked out the ground of what we might call the normative sense of "Renaissance": Giorgio Vasari writing in the sixteenth century and Jacob Burckhardt writing in the nineteenth. The arguments of both have been challenged, denied, proved false or at best partial, pulled this way and that, worn away by waves of modern scholarship. As is the way of such things, the texts themselves, let alone the paintings and sculptures, cities and libraries to which they refer, have become part of what we talk about when we talk about the Renaissance.

Both defined their Renaissances against something else. Vasari, who wrote about art, set it against "the dead tradition of the Greeks," that is, against Byzantine painting, with its "staring eyes, feet on tiptoe," and "absence of shadow."[2] Burckhardt, who didn't, or at least not in his principal book, set it against the Middle Ages, In his view, people then were conscious of themselves only as members of wider groups, whereas in the Renaissance, for the first time "man became a spiritual *individual*, and recognized himself as such."[3] Neither of these claims

Western Art and the Wider World, First Edition. Paul Wood.

now command assent in progressive inquiry, but their power has been such that perspective and humanism (which is what Vasari and Burckhardt, respectively, were championing) continue to bear down on anyone who would engage with the Renaissance even now, half a millennium after it happened.

In a recent collection of debates about the status and meaning of the Renaissance today, James Elkins has commented on its strangely doubled identity. On the one hand it retains the kind of exemplary status gestured to above – he calls it an "anchor" for our broader sense of what "Art" is, and of what is at stake in our dealings with it.[4] But on the other hand, almost no one outside the ranks of specialists in the field engages with it anymore; and in particular, people whose interests lie with modern art, especially younger people, seem to have little or no interest in it, knowledge of it, or curiosity about it. It is regarded, at best, as having nothing to do with art now and, at worst, as symbolizing that litany of values concerning authority, taste, religion, the canon – in a word, conservatism – that modern and contemporary art are set against. The fact that tens of thousands will attend a temporary exhibition by an "Old Master," or that there is a permanent throng of tourists around the *Mona Lisa* in the Louvre, not to mention the fact that there is a mass audience for *The Medici: Godfathers of the Renaissance* and *The Da Vinci Code* only serves to reinforce the point. For most people outside of a shrinking scholarly specialism, the Renaissance seems to lie on the other side of a river of history separating a critical consciousness of modernity and globalization from the academic, Eurocentric past; and on the rare occasions that it washes up on our shore, it does so, unmistakably, as kitsch.

Yet the Renaissance is in the process of being rewritten, in ways whose implications are more far-reaching than at any time since the formation of the modern discipline of art history in the nineteenth century. The term arrived at its modern meaning, as signifying a period, in the nineteenth century. The French historian Jules Michelet used it to indicate a stage in his history of France; others, including the English writers John Ruskin and Walter Pater used it in relation to Italian art. But the definitive identification of the term with Italy was made by Burckhardt in his classic study translated into English as *The Civilization of the Renaissance in Italy*. In that book Burckhardt dealt with the state, the individual, and the wider culture rather than with art as such, although he did discuss art in other works. Nonetheless art was the principal focus for others, including Heinrich Wolfflin's *Renaissance and Baroque* and Walter Pater's *The Renaissance*, both of which appeared in the second half of the nineteenth century. This is not to say that in the field of art practice the Renaissance canon went unquestioned. Quite the reverse; it is one of those historical ironies that at the moment when the Renaissance was being inscribed in the new academic field of art history it was the object of fundamental challenge in the emerging French avant-garde. Less radically in some ways, in England a reaction had set in against the over-valorization of the "High" Renaissance art of Leonardo, Raphael, and Michelangelo, as the self-consciously chosen name of the "Pre-Raphaelite Brotherhood" testifies. They were already, in 1848, looking back to the "primitives" of the fourteenth and fifteenth centuries for a vigor they felt had begun to be lost in that work which the subsequent academic tradition of the seventeenth, eighteenth, and early nineteenth centuries venerated above all else. The term "Renaissance" in its modern sense might not have been used until Burckhardt but for three centuries the same names crop up again and again wherever in Europe art was seriously debated.

This is an important point, for in that long period the tradition we think of as the "Western canon" was formed. It emerged in discussion and criticism, it was negotiated, tested, reinforced, and revised in a long process of debate. It did not emerge fully formed and stereotypical, a motionless gallery of dead white European males waiting to be knocked off their pedestals by a generation of radical art historians at the end of the twentieth century. In this sense, figures such as Burckhardt and Wölfflin are not only initiators of an art historical tradition that is now under such far-reaching criticism by contemporary scholarship, they are in the true sense of the word canonizers. They articulate something long in process. In that process, even the principal actors, whose names recur again and again, are represented as vivid exemplars. At least before the sclerosis of the academy had really set in, Raphael, Michelangelo, Titian, and others were there to be emulated, challenged, championed, *learned from*, and not merely parroted by rote.

For a long time, certainly extending into the middle of the twentieth century and the period often referred to as the crisis of modernism, despite fluctuating fashions, the Renaissance was widely accepted as the benchmark of Western art and culture. Many nineteenth- and twentieth-century modernists (including figures as diverse as Degas and Cézanne, Picasso, and Rothko), whose art took overt issue with the heritage of the academy, nonetheless repeatedly measured themselves against a range of "Old Masters" whom they particularly admired. Despite modernism's rejection of most of the norms of Renaissance art, especially the fundamental commitment to verisimilitude, the Renaissance remained the implicit standard of value against which subsequent Western art was measured. The coining of the term "modern masters" in the early twentieth century to refer to figures such as Matisse is an example of this kind of thinking. The case of the avant-garde was, however, double-edged. Although a sense of the achievement of the Renaissance masters may have continued to inform the thinking of artists whose own work looked very different, modernist painting and sculpture drew on techniques and models that could not have been further from the Renaissance example. I shall look at some of this later on, particularly problems attendant on the concept of "primitive art," and its relation to ideas of authenticity and expression that were so central to the modern movement.

All I am trying to establish at the moment is some of the complexity of the relationship of modern Western art to previous Western art, as well as to the arts of the rest of the world. To fill out a sense of the dual status of Renaissance art today that Elkins alluded to, that uncanny mix of persistent presence and almost complete eclipse, one needs some understanding of this multifaceted internal history of Western art itself, of what has been at stake in the shifts from Renaissance to academy, from academy to the modernist avant-garde, and from modernism to postmodern and contemporary art. Part of the problem of thinking about Western art in relation to the wider world concerns the changes Western art itself underwent, often in response to that wider world, knowledge of which came about through mechanisms of power which were themselves far removed from the world of art. It is important to bring capitalism, industrialization, and imperialism into the picture while resisting the reductionist impulse to conflate art and learning with the exercise of temporal power as such. The post-Renaissance Western tradition of art has been both continuous and conflicted against itself. Part of our problem with the Renaissance today is the way it has been invoked within the overarching cultural tradition as an originary point of Western modernity. A certain view of the individual in the active life of society, and a certain kind of verisimilitude in the representation of it, have been jointly invoked as the standard against which not only subsequent Western but *all* other cultures were to be measured. It is especially this latter assumption that has now come to be questioned. In fact, that is to understate the situation. That assumption is now regarded as the unacceptable symptom of a Eurocentrism which is not only an inappropriate object of continued endorsement in the present period of increasing globalization but is now widely seen as having been historically complicit in the advance and management of Western imperialism too.

It would be stating the obvious to acknowledge that globalization is responsible for the decentering of the Western canon. People who have had that canon rammed down their throats for several hundred years, while their own cultures have been systematically disparaged if not physically destroyed, are unlikely to feel well-disposed towards claims about universal aesthetics and disinterested knowledge. Rightly so. But there is another side to this: those neophiliacs whose project is to manage contemporary globalized art by cutting it free from tradition risk a form of historical amnesia that is closer to the protocols of globalized management in general than it is to any kind of informed resistance to its depredations. For my own part, I feel it is important to treat these questions carefully, above all to avoid an all too easy reductionism whereby European art is denied any measure of relative autonomy and is merely presented as either the unwitting tool or the willing servant of power. At a point when the claims of the Western canon are coming under greater scrutiny than at any time since its formulation, it is useful to investigate the changing sense that canon made of its others, both positively and negatively. It follows that the vaunted "rebirth" of that tradition from its roots in pagan antiquity is a suggestive site of encounter with received meanings and interpretations.

This work is already in train, in the form of a wide range of new approaches to Renaissance art history. In historical representation, consciously or otherwise, the horizon of the present is always drawn around the continent of the past. A period gets the Renaissance it deserves – or needs. For Burckhardt in the nineteenth century, the impetus to researching the Renaissance was a conviction of its status as "a civilization which is the mother of our own."[5] Contemporary historians, by contrast, are inclined to explore differences between the fifteenth and sixteenth centuries and our own times. Not only has our map of the societies and cultures that produced Renaissance art been substantially redrawn and expanded, our sense of what counts as "Art" itself has been subject to redescription. In a way that echoes the de-centering of painting and sculpture from the contemporary practice of the arts, our sense of Renaissance cultural practice is now moving away from an exclusive focus on painting, sculpture, and architecture. Now, painting and sculpture are being re-embedded in a matrix of ritual and building, mechanical reproduction, design and consumption, from which the modern system of the arts as it was developed in the late eighteenth century, detached them. Furthermore, the geographical boundaries of the Renaissance are being expanded, and not only from Italy to other areas of northern, central, and eastern Europe. Claire Farago has argued that "the kind of art historical practice I would like to see in Renaissance studies goes all over the world and deals with all kinds of practices, representational systems, cultural conditions."[6] Such an expanded field, which Farago had begun to explore as early as the 1990s in her book *Reframing the Renaissance*, would take as its subject "a world of cultural interactions."[7] The internal hierarchical distinctions of the canon no less than its export have come to seem out of tune with our own cultural hybridity in the epoch of globalization.

It would be hard to argue with claims for the relevance of an understanding of Renaissance art to the subsequent Western tradition. How the latter could signify without at least some apprehension of the former is difficult to conceive. What is at issue is the terms of that understanding, most particularly as it relates to that tradition's relation to a wider world than has usually been considered. As new historical inquiry has begun to shed light on the diversity of Renaissance experience, the consequences for a sense of European cultural identity are considerable.[8] John Martin has argued that

> earlier histories – grounded in the liberal and conservative myths of the gradual but heroic emancipation of the individual – have given way to histories that explore the varied constructions of the self in different time periods and different cultures. Not only is it no longer possible to view its history as one of continuous development, but individualism is itself not a uniquely Western phenomenon.[9]

Changing Histories

The principal geographical site and the main historical emphasis of normative Renaissance art history were respectively Italy, especially Florence and Rome, and the recovery of the art and learning of classical antiquity. Redirecting our gaze on the first of these has an effect on the second. One important focus for new approaches has been the city state of Venice, which has the effect of directing our gaze further east than has been usual in thinking about the Renaissance. In Renaissance studies, the concept of the "East" was conventionally taken to refer to the territories of the Eastern Orthodox Church, that is to the Byzantine Empire centered on Constantinople (as distinct from the legacy of the Western Empire, the domain of the Catholic Church centered on Rome).[10] More recently, however, this sense of the "East" has been extended to refer to a range of Asian societies stretching from Turkey to China. This introduces a tension between the Christian legacy of Byzantium and the impact of these other societies, most of which were Islamic.[11] In the case of Venice, the greatest influence in addition to Byzantium came from the Ottoman Turks and the Mamluks, who in the fifteenth century ruled the territories of present-day Egypt and Syria.

The relationship of these societies to the more conventionally understood heartlands of the Renaissance in Italy needs careful handling. Important as it is to draw them into the circle of historical explanation, it is just as important not to overstate their significance. For a long time, indeed for most of the time that art history has been practiced, their impact on Renaissance art was far from being a main consideration, if it was acknowledged at all. One exception to this rule was Rudolf Wittkower who had published articles on the impact of non-European civilizations on the art of the West during the 1930s, 1940s, and 1950s. His final series of lectures, at Berkeley in 1964, was on the same subject, addressing amongst other things "the problem of cultural exchange" between East and West. Wittkower died before he could work up the lectures into book form, and it is symptomatic of the wider situation that the material was not published until 1989. By then, Wittkower's wide-ranging interest in the influence of China and India, the ancient Near East, Egypt, and Turkey on European art might have commanded more widespread interest than they had at the time of their inception. But the fact that they so obviously grew out of an earlier mode of scholarship than the "new art history" of the time seems to have prevented them from having much resonance in revisionist histories. The beginnings of a postcolonialist interest in de-centering the Western canon would not have found much stimulation in claims such as Wittkower's assertion that "despite the complexity of non-European influences on European art, one point should be made quite clear. The impact of foreign civilizations never had the power to deprive Europe, after its consolidation, of its typically occidental mode of expression."[12] Like so many before him, Wittkower assigned that characteristic "mode of expression" to Greece in the fifth century BCE. For all that, however, Wittkower perceived that "seen as a whole, the history of European art has been and still is insular, or rather pen-insular (if we look upon Europe as a peninsular of the Asiatic landmass)."[13] At the time at which he was writing, few had been willing to do that. One who had was Raymond Schwab, who also noted of Europe that "she is a small promontory of Asia."[14] But his tantalizingly titled *Oriental Renaissance* of 1950 is in fact about a later period and concerns the impact of newly translated oriental texts on Romanticism in the late eighteenth and early nineteenth centuries.[15]

Wittkower remained a diffusionist, and explicitly argued against the idea of centers of "independent, autonomous creation" and for "the diffusion of ideas, concepts, techniques and forms of art."[16] But it is important to recognize that this is not saying, as so many others had, that European art stood at the head of world culture and that all other cultures were in a secondary position with respect to Europe. If anything, the reverse was true for much of history, which, in Wittkower's view, had witnessed the continual exchange of "forms, designs and styles" as well as "concepts and motifs," that is to say, of both techniques and subjects, through "historical roads of migration, transmission and dissemination."[17]

Wittkower says little about the different social orders involved in his survey, nor about the relation of art to its society, concentrating instead on the transmission of designs or particular motifs from one civilization to another. Thus he discusses the use of Kufic script as a decorative element in haloes, or on the Virgin's robe, in various trecento and quattrocentro Italian paintings, and the impact of Egyptian obelisks or pyramids on town planning in Renaissance Rome. This continuing focus on formal analysis and iconography marks a considerable distance from the preoccupations of some of the most prominent new approaches to Renaissance art history, which tend to invoke a broader sociopolitical context as well as to adopt a more overtly critical stance with respect to preceding intellectual history.

An example of this new temper can be found in Lisa Jardine and Jerry Brotton's pioneering *Global Interests*, which begins with a frontal attack on Burckhardt's claims about the concept of the individual as the distinguishing feature of Renaissance civilization. For them, this is "a retrospective construction of nineteenth century ideology" intended to universalize a historically local construct.[18] In their view, this construct, namely "Renaissance Man," is set up to be "psychically whole, clean, possessed of integrity and essentially humane," all of which is supposedly counterposed to its antithesis, the "dark, dirty, exotic Eastern Other, as the negative to which humane individualism has been opposed."[19]

Taken in isolation, this can read as a peculiarly exaggerated stereotyping of its own. But to ameliorate it somewhat, to understand what motivates the rhetorical opposition, two factors have to be taken into consideration. The first is that the argument is being polemically counterposed against a long-standing, virtually silent orthodoxy in Euro-American art-historical thought. Thus, the overstatement is at least partly for effect; the text is driven by a kind of righteous anger against an academic status quo which in their view has covertly employed notions of the "individual," the "human," etc. to bolster specifically Western constructions of those ideas against others, and has done so, moreover, in an age of imperialism to which the supposedly impartial scholarship has actually been client. To that extent the stance is of a piece with the tradition of "new art history" going back to the aftermath of 1968 which concerned itself initially with a critique of the universalizing pretensions of modernism – attacking those submerged idealist presuppositions by drawing out the actual, material contradictions structuring social relations. In order of adoption, so to speak, these were, initially social class, subsequently gender, which became the privileged site of the "new art history" *tout court*, and then, with increasing force as the Cold War ended and the process of globalization accelerated, "race" and ethnicity. By the final years of the century, these tropes had found their way into Renaissance art history where, in a slightly comical rerun of the early anti-modernist social history of art, Vasari took on the role of a Renaissance Greenberg, and figures such as Burckhardt – and even more so, Hegel – were pilloried as the intellectual sources of all that was wrong in orthodox art history.

The second consideration is rather different. It represents, so to speak, a critique of a critique, rather than of orthodoxy as such. Edward Said's *Orientalism* of 1978 was the text which more than any other opened the door for the postcolonialist, proto-global rewriting of the assumptions of the Western canon. Said's focus was on literature, but his argument was soon – although by no means immediately – adapted to the visual arts. For Said, following Michel Foucault, European culture had systematically constructed a discipline by which it was "able to manage – and even produce – the Orient politically, sociologically, militarily, ideologically, scientifically and imaginatively,"[20] the upshot of which was "the idea of European identity as a superior one in comparison with all the non-European peoples and cultures."[21] For the most part, Said ascribed this European sense of "positional superiority" to the period following the eighteenth century and its key intellectual component of the "Enlightenment"; he writes, for instance, that "taking the late eighteenth century as a very roughly defined starting point" orientalism can be understood as the principal Western "corporate institution for dealing with the Orient."[22] But in places he also identified it more broadly as "the period of extraordinary European ascendancy from the late Renaissance to the present."[23] For Jardine and Brotton this is to get something significantly wrong about the Renaissance. Their rereading of the relations between Renaissance societies and the Islamic societies to the east leads them "to reject the appropriateness to this period of Said's vision of Western Europe's construction of the Orient as an alien, displaced other, positioned in opposition to a confident, imperialist Eurocentrism."[24] For Jardine and Brotton, during the Renaissance period the world of Islam, in particular the Ottoman Empire, was *part of* the networks of both trade and diplomacy through which Europe in the late medieval and early modern period organized itself, and not some alien other, outside of and inferior to Europe. Rather, as they explicitly state, "in the fifteenth and sixteenth centuries, East and West met on much more equal terms."[25]

In what is perhaps a distant echo of the historical materialism that continued to resonate in some of the revisionist scholarship that otherwise sought to go beyond the more ossified or even Eurocentric features of the critical tradition associated with Marxism, Jardine and Brotton in their various books always tend to emphasize the broadly economic dimension over the more purely cultural. For them, despite the anti-Islamic rhetoric which marked so many Western Christian pronouncements during the Renaissance, and despite, too, the very real military challenge to Christendom posed by the Ottoman Empire, an underlying truth is told by the continuation of trade and exchange. Thus, the Venetians might have been collectively excommunicated for it by the pope, but their resumption of trade with the Turks barely six months after the fall of Constantinople told its own story. In this expansive vision, Jardine describes the various items visible in Crivelli's *Annunciation with St Emidius* of 1486 as bespeaking "a world which assembles with delight rugs from Istanbul, tapestry hangings from Arras, delicate glass from Venice, metalwork from Islamic Spain, porcelain and silk from China, broadcloth from London", all amounting to "a vigorously developing worldwide market in luxury commodities."[26] For Brotton, this new vision of the Renaissance is one that foregrounds a surprising "level of global awareness and cultural mobility";[27] surprising, that is, to those accustomed to a parochial view of the Renaissance in which all its references are internal to European antiquity and the Christian tradition. There is a powerful sense in which this changed perspective brings the Renaissance alive. Far from being forced to erect an ideology of timeless aesthetic values to make sense of the art because the world which subtended it is so remote from our own, something different emerges. The argument is that our world of consumer-driven competitiveness, and the inbuilt tension between expansiveness and openness on the one hand and petty nationalism and religious bigotry on the other, "is a world which was made in the Renaissance."[28]

Venice

I want now to look in more detail at some of the interactions between Renaissance art and the Islamic cultures to the east by discussing the case of Venice.[29] From its earliest days until the twelfth century, Venice had stood at the western limit of the Eastern Christian empire, centered on Byzantium. The first permanent Venetian trading post was established there in 1082, though commercial links had existed long before that. As Venice grew stronger, particularly from the beginning of the thirteenth to the end of the fifteenth centuries, the city became the principal maritime power of the region. Its naval dockyard, the Arsenal, was the biggest industrial complex in late medieval Europe. As the Byzantine Empire declined and that of Venice expanded, the relation of power between the two states gradually changed. Crisis point had been reached in 1204. In that year the Venetian doge succeeded in diverting the Fourth Crusade from its destination in the Holy Land to Constantinople. After a siege, the city was ruthlessly sacked. As a consequence, huge amounts of booty made their way to Venice, ranging from jewels, metalwork and both bronze and marble sculptures to porphyry columns and sheets of marble for use in the decoration of buildings.

This was a time before Columbus' voyages to America, before the Portuguese opened a sea route to Asia, when the eastern Mediterranean remained, as it had been since antiquity, one of the most active centers of world economic and cultural development. Throughout the late medieval period Venice and Genoa competed for domination of this European trade with the East. The Genoese watchtower, built in the mid-fourteenth century, still stands in Galata, in modern-day Istanbul. In late medieval Constantinople, it overlooked the junction of the Golden Horn and the Bosphorus, leading north to the Black Sea and Trebizond, one of the western ends of the Silk Road. As already noted, when we think of the term "Renaissance," we tend to think first of a rebirth of the art, architecture, literature, science, and philosophy of antiquity. Venice, however, was different. Alone among major Italian cities, Venice had no antiquity. The creation of refugees fleeing from the barbarian invasions in the fifth century after the collapse of the Roman Empire, there are no significant classical ruins or inscriptions in the Venetian lagoon. Perhaps because of this, the impact of the Eastern trade was greatest on Venice. Venice more than anywhere else was the gateway through which the manufactured goods of Europe spread out to the East and a vast range of stuff from the East – spices and carpets, metalwork and perfumes, colors, shapes, and ideas – entered the European consciousness.

A recurring figure in recent studies of Venetian culture is that of the collage; in another variant, it is the palimpsest. In both cases, the intention is clear: the figures are meant to bring out the *layering* of Venetian culture, of Venice as a place of marked juxtapositions. Neither is this a wholly retrospective construct. At the end of the fifteenth century, the French ambassador Philippe de Commynes remarked that "most of the people are foreigners." And this perception of a society in which northerners – Flemish and Germans – Dalmatians, Greeks, Muslims, Jews, and mainland Italians mingled with indigenous Venetians, was sharpened in the sixteenth century by the Venetian writer Francesco Sansovino: "Peoples from the most distant parts of the world gather here to trade and conduct business," people who "differ among themselves in appearance, in customs and in languages."[30]

Even the fabric of Venice was different. With its power based on the *stato da mar* (the "empire of the sea"), the city was itself literally built on the water. The palaces of the wealthy merchants that stood aside the Grand Canal and other waterways were highly distinctive. Until the end of the fifteenth century, the dominant elements were a mixture of Gothic and Islamic. Thus the façade of the Ca' d'Oro, begun in 1421, presents a diverse collection of Gothic arches and tracery, topped by Islamic-inspired cresting along the roofline. The pointed "ogee" arch is itself a hybrid. Found in English Gothic, though less usual in continental Europe, it also occurs in Asian architecture. Deborah Howard has argued that "the intention behind the introduction of the ogee arch and its adoption as a trademark by the Venetian merchant class was to allude to a mental image of the Orient"[31] – a "mental image" composed out of a myriad individual memories of trade in the East, of characteristic Islamic forms in mosques and markets, in ornaments and furniture, descriptions in travelers' tales, even the double-curves found in the hulls of the galleys themselves. The colored marbles set in circular mounts on the façade of the palace of the diplomat Giovanni Dario echo designs he would have seen on diplomatic missions to the Mamluk court in Cairo.

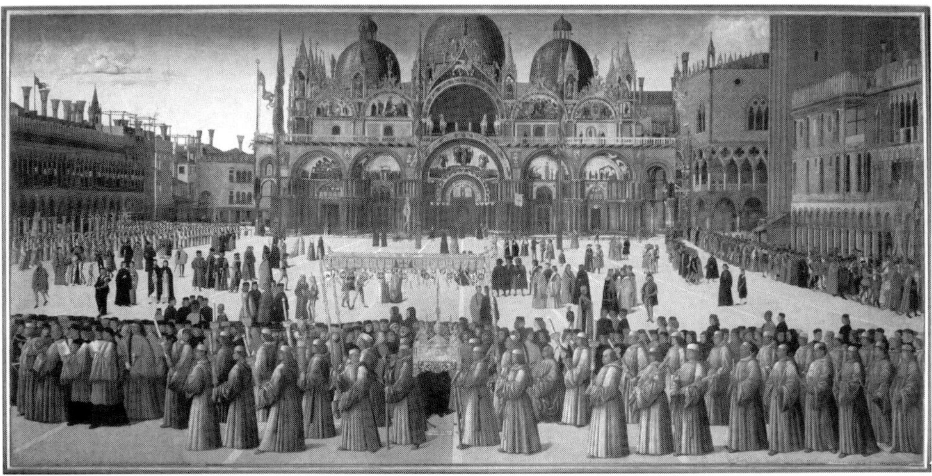

Figure 1.1 Gentile Bellini, *Procession in the Piazza San Marco*, 1496, oil on canvas, 367 × 745 cm. Accademia, Venice. © 2013. Photo Scala, Florence – courtesy of the Ministero Beni e Att. Culturali.

This layered architectural heritage is to be seen most vividly in the two great buildings which stand adjacent to each other on the main ceremonial space of St Mark's Square (Figure 1.1). The Basilica of San Marco and the Palazzo Ducale marry Gothic tracery and arches with, respectively, Byzantine domes and mosaics, and colored tiles in an Islamic lozenge pattern. The Basilica of San Marco is the single most important transmitter of Byzantine influence into Venetian culture. It was first established in the ninth century to house the relics of Venice's patron saint, St Mark, which were transferred to the city from Alexandria in 829. Both in its external architectural form and its interior, San Marco is distinct from the conventions of Italian and northern churches alike, with their characteristic decorative schemes either of fresco or stained glass. San Marco began to assume its present form in the late eleventh century, based directly on the plan of the Church of the Holy Apostles in Constantinople, that is, a Greek cross with five domes marking each arm and the central crossing point. Thereafter it was in a continuous process of expansion and embellishment until the fifteenth century and beyond. Mosaic decoration had started in the late eleventh or early twelfth centuries, but a surge of work followed in the wake of the capture of Constantinople. In addition to the four life-size bronze horses of classical antiquity shipped over and set above the main entrance, the domes, arches, and vaults of the interior were decorated with mosaics by artists brought from Constantinople, often working with glass tesserae actually brought back for the purpose. The effect is to suffuse the dimly lit interior with an atmospheric golden glow, as if the biblical scenes occupy a different realm elevated above the mundane world of the human spectator. Mosaics depict episodes from both the Old and New Testaments, including some related to Egypt, where, according to tradition, St Mark preached.

Traces of centuries of interaction with the East abound elsewhere throughout the city, even including a few surviving sculpted images of turbaned porters and a camel and carved fragments of decorative Islamic script. All of which forms a marked contrast to the rational composition of the façades of the classically influenced *renovatio* movement which emerged in the early sixteenth century.[32] The specific character of Venice as a physical space is thus inscribed by the sedimented experience of cultural otherness, manifest in both form and color: ogee arches, gothic pinnacles, asymmetrical façades, overhanging balconies, narrow twisting streets, colored marble, and painted plaster.[33]

Apart from the physical, built environment of the city, something else contributes to making Venice different: the organization of Venetian society. In contrast to Florence, with its strand of individualism, Renaissance Venice was a corporate society, with a related tendency to social conservatism – factors which had an influence on Venetian art in areas such as official portraits and the pictorial organization of public pictures showing scenes of Venetian life. Venetian society was hierarchical. At the top were the patricians, with a legally enshrined monopoly on political power, amounting to no more than about 4 to 5 percent of the total population. From them a doge was elected, almost always a senior figure, head of state for life but prevented from accumulating wealth and power on the model of, say, the Medici. Below the patricians was a larger, but still numerically small, layer of citizens, the *cittadini*, comprising approximately 8 to10 percent of the population. And below them were the vast majority, well over 80 percent, the *popolari*. These distinctions have now been shown to be more fluid than was once thought.[34] Nevertheless, in an age of great social upheaval and almost continuous wars, both small and large, the city state, according to its own officially sanctioned "Myth of Venice," remained stable and survived for a thousand years, from the end of the Roman Empire to Napoleon.

Underlying this stability was economic power. Controlling a trading empire that was based in the eastern Mediterranean but stretched into northern Europe and Asia, Venice enjoyed great wealth. Within the overall framework of prosperity, the key to continuing stability lay in critical points of flexibility within the hierarchy. Thus, at the top end of the *popolo* there was room for movement into citizenship with its accompanying status. Of more particular significance for the arts is the fact that, despite political power as such being reserved for the hereditary patrician class, the citizens played an extremely powerful role as a kind of permanent civil service. Among the institutions for which they were responsible were the *scuole*: lay – albeit deeply religious – confraternities, in the larger cases extremely wealthy, and responsible for a wide range of activities approximating to what we would think of as social services. There were five of the important *scuole grandi*, and some hundreds of smaller ones, *scuole piccolo*, of varying size and influence. Several of these were linked either to trades (including the painters), or to foreign groups in the city. The meeting rooms within the buildings which were home to the *scuole* provided an important source of work for artists. As well as providing many commissions for artists, the *scuole* played an important role in maintaining that social cohesion which, allied to naval supremacy, underwrote Venetian power and prosperity.

In the wake of the Crusade of 1204, Constantinople was actually retaken by the Greeks from Venetian domination after less than sixty years, and a new dynasty secured: the Palaiologans. But Byzantine power had been fatally eroded. Under pressure from the expanding Ottoman Turks, the Byzantine Empire contracted over the next two centuries, as its eastern outposts fell one by one. During 1438–1439, John VIII Palaiologus led a Byzantine delegation to Italy to a great conference held in Ferrara and Florence that was aimed at reuniting the Eastern and Western Christian churches against the common Islamic enemy. After months of debate, even when the unification had been agreed in principle and the Byzantine delegation had returned to Constantinople, it was rejected and never implemented in practice. Without the reinforcement of a military alliance, however, the unification of the churches would have had little effect. In the event, barely a decade and a half later, the whole of Christendom was convulsed by news of the final collapse of the Byzantine Empire. Constantinople fell to the Ottoman Turks, under the leadership of Mehmet II, in 1453. In the second half of the fifteenth century, after 1453, the Ottomans emerged as not only the one serious imperial rival to Venice in the eastern Mediterranean but as also, for the next hundred years, a real challenge to the hegemony of Western Christendom as such. Yet, despite calls for a new crusade to repel the infidel, there was in fact no collective military response by the Christian powers of western Europe. The relative fragmentation of the West meant that no coordinated resistance could be organized, and despite much ideological breast-beating – and, of course, its concomitant, a demonization of the "enemy" – realpolitik prevailed. In a remarkably short period of time, Venetian trade was resumed with the Ottoman Empire, now based in Constantinople, or Istanbul as it came to be known.

New Light on Perspective

Having for so long been absent from our sense of what the Renaissance was, to have the Ottoman Empire brought into the web of cultural influence marks a significant advance in art historical thinking. At the same time, though, it is equally useful to be reminded of the deep differences which existed between the cultures of Catholic Italy and Islamic Istanbul. In a recent study, challengingly titled *Florence and Baghdad*, Hans Belting has sought to draw out the connections between that cornerstone of Renaissance artistic innovation, namely perspective, and Islamic science. Once again, an extant form of understanding is being challenged. The development of single-point perspective in Florence around 1430 has conventionally operated like a signpost pointing in two directions, one forwards and one back.

On the one hand it has been seen as setting the terms of the Western tradition forwards into the future by enabling a criterion of "lifelikeness" against which all other representations could and would be judged. This certainly sat with the West's increasing sense of its own superiority over the rest of the world in political, moral, and military terms. Within the West itself, even the far-reaching challenge of modernism did relatively little to dethrone lifelikeness as a kind of default setting in the culture at large for what pictorial art should be doing (something that photography reinforced). On the other hand, Renaissance perspective has been seen, not least by its fifteenth-century advocates themselves, as building on the prior achievements of Giotto and others in the fourteenth century, and beyond them, on the examples of partial perspective to be found in the surviving art of antiquity.

Ancient paintings and mosaics (not to mention sculptures) are replete with lifelike representations of individual human beings as well as images representing spatial recession in things like buildings, paths, and landscape generally. What they appear to lack is a coherent spatial armature in which the various mimetically rendered things can be disposed in relation to each other. It is this latter that the work of Brunelleschi and Alberti is widely held to have provided, going beyond the more or less lifelike representation of particular figures – animate or inanimate – found in ancient art, to the arrangement of those figures in a coherent spatial unity.[35]

Belting argues differently. For him there is no line from antiquity, via the trecento, to fully achieved Renaissance single-point perspective. Belting argues that although the artists of antiquity and the trecento did make spectator-oriented representations, they did *not* have true perspective: "the mathematical method for systematically representing three dimensions on a flat surface was not invented until two generations later [than the trecento artists]."[36] Belting's point is that the earlier artists could not have done this for the fundamental reason that antique mathematics had not developed the capacity to articulate a true theory of perspective. The revolutionary aspect of Beltings claim is that "perspective art is based on a theory of Arab origin, a mathematical theory having to do with visual rays and the geometry of light."[37]

This represents a departure not only from the conventional sense of Renaissance perspective having built on the proto-perspective of antiquity but also from the conventional sense of the scale of the contribution of Islamic science to the European Renaissance. It has long been acknowledged that some of the lost science of antiquity – lost that is, during the "Dark Ages" and the medieval period in Europe – had been preserved in Arab culture and that this found its way back into European thought via Islamic scholarship from the thirteenth century onwards. For Belting, however, the Arab contribution far exceeds the mere "translation" of the already existing knowledge of antiquity. Instead, the theory of perspective as it came to be applied in the visual arts depends on crucial mathematical *innovations* made by Arab theorists. To put the point polemically, Renaissance art could not have happened when it did without the prior contribution of Islamic science.

The crucial figure in Belting's story is Abu Ali al-Hasan Ibn al-Haytham, a mathematician who worked in Baghdad and Cairo in the late tenth and early eleventh centuries of the Christian calendar, and who was subsequently known in the West as Alhazen. His book, called in the West *Optics*, though according to Belting originally translated under the title *Perspectiva*, was composed between c.1028 and his death in 1040, and was translated into Latin in Islamic Spain around 1200. His innovation consisted in establishing that rays of light traveled from objects to the human eye and that they could be measured. Almost four hundred years is, however, a long time, and Belting accounts for the delay in the reception of Alhazen's ideas in the West in terms of the great difference between European and Islamic culture. As he says, "The Arab *theory of optics* was known at European universities by the thirteenth century, but it did not become a *theory of pictures* until the fifteenth century."[38]

The fact that the theory of optics was developed in a culture which was largely disposed against pictures caused a problem in its application within a culture that did give a prominent place to visual imagery of the world. In fact, as Julian Bell has pointed out, Belting does seem to overstate the degree of iconoclasm in Islamic culture.[39] But for all that, the use to which the theory was put within Islam militated against its easy transposition to the West, for in Islam it became a way of generating not lifelike pictures but complex geometrical patterns. These were held to signify God's creation not mimetically but abstractly. The idea of abstraction as something which can be cognitive rather than simply decorative is a concept which is still hard to grasp from within a conventional Western worldview – where the tendency to regard the non-figurative as "merely" decorative has been used to underwrite the whole modern distinction between the meaning-bearing "fine" arts and the "lesser" arts of design and craft. This was certainly an issue which preyed upon the minds of artists seeking to develop an abstract type of modernist painting in the early twentieth century. The capacity of abstraction to convey meaning would not have been an issue in Islam. Belting's contention is that the Italian mathematician Biagio Pelacani of Parma was able to bridge the gap between Islamic mathematics and the requirements of picturing by his treatment of the concept of space; that is, the space between objects. By making ostensibly "empty" space into "a quantitative dimension that provided reliable data from the external world," in the sense that objects and their distance from each other became measurable, Pelacani's work meant that matters of "size" and "proportion" "became the cornerstones of visual perception."[40]

Such elements are clearly of crucial relevance to the development of a method for generating spatial illusion on a two-dimensional surface, and as Belting points out, Pelacani's work was known in the circle around Brunelleschi. However, Belting also has to confess that his argument connecting the development of perspective in Florentine art with Arab mathematical theory "lacks a contemporaneous document specifically linking Alhazen, Pelacani and the debate on perspective in Florence."[41] This is a pity, for Belting's argument does have the effect of "worlding" the Renaissance, of relating the technical achievement of perspectival representation to a dense web of cultural exchange rather than seeing it as the result of an autarchic lineage which effectively separates the West from other social formations. But by the same token, at the very moment when it draws two hitherto separated worlds together, Belting's argument in its very fabric also has to acknowledge these two worlds' apartness. The Arabic world and the Western world are both drawn together and held apart in Belting's thesis. There is little of the sense that a superficial cultural difference is being undercut by a shared economic reality, and that that is what really matters. Quite to the contrary, the two worlds coexist *in* difference. Western theory took the Arab theory and "reconceived it" to the point that the effect was to "revise its meaning completely."[42] Belting's construct is not one which minimizes or glosses over difference. It is built out of a recognition of real differences in which the key thing is relations and transformations between the different elements. Thus it provides an effective counterpoint to other new histories which have responded to a long tradition of Western insularity by emphasizing material exchange between hitherto separated worlds. Belting's new account of the intellectual roots of Renaissance perspective manages both to enrich the mix of cultures while yet preserving a sense of their difference.

A Portrait

Yet, across the space of cultural difference, eyes could look both ways. Western eyes – and fingers – could observe and touch and desire silks and carpets and ornamented metal ware or porcelain, for the most part without any real grasp of either the social relations that produced such things or of their meanings in themselves. Not that that is necessarily a bad thing; picking something up and running with it is an important part of the way the world works. Looking the other way, some Eastern eyes at least could be entranced and intrigued by the potential power of perspective. For perspectival representation reaches beyond the status of mere device (just as Islamic ornament reaches, for those who do grasp its cultural and spiritual matrix, beyond the merely decorative). Perspective allows the artist to set figures within the overall ground of the image, thus producing the semblance of a spatial unity within which particular things can have a credible virtual existence. What "credible" means here can go all the way to the attribution of mental and emotional states to those figures in relation to each other in their virtual worlds. Perspective is a technique, a trick if you like, but it can open up an imaginative world whose possibilities are infinite. In the conditions where Islamic power encountered European trade in the eastern Mediterranean, some eyes were capable of seeing across the cultural divide, capable of seeing the cultural power of the other as potentially fruitful in a different world.

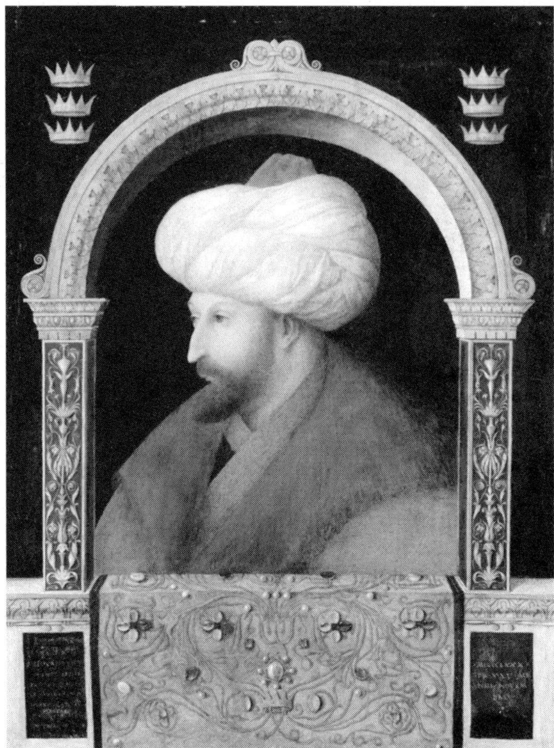

Figure 1.2 Gentile Bellini, *Portrait of Mehmet II*, c.1480, oil on canvas, 70 × 52 cm. National Gallery, London. © World History Archive / Alamy.

One of the most intriguing portraits to have survived from the Renaissance period depicts the Ottoman sultan Mehmet II, the conqueror of Constantinople. Painted from life around 1480, its author was the Venetian painter Gentile Bellini (Figure 1.2). These are curious conjunctions. They prompt questions such as What is an Italian painter doing in a Turkish court? and Why does an Islamic monarch want to have his portrait painted by a Western, Christian artist? There is a sense in which this modest picture figures not just a man, but the relation of two cultures.

Gentile Bellini, elder brother of Giovanni Bellini and son of Jacopo Bellini, had become head of the family workshop after the death of his father in around 1470. This was the leading workshop in the city, and Gentile's organizational skills led to him becoming the most powerful artist in late fifteenth-century Venice. One historian calls him "the principal impresario": he received the most important commissions for the decoration of the Grand Council Chamber in the Palazzo Ducale in 1474 as well as others for the *Scuole grandi* and was given a knighthood from the Holy Roman Emperor.[43]

Mehmet II had ascended to the Ottoman throne for the second time in 1451 aged 19. His original tenure as an adolescent had been unsuccessful and his father had to come out of retirement and reassume power. After his father's death, Mehmet did not fail again. He immediately began building his military power, and a policy of expansion rapidly led him to the siege of Constantinople in 1453. The city was by then almost all that remained of the former Eastern Empire. The large Ottoman army and navy, estimated at between eighty thousand and one hundred thousand men faced a defending force of only about seven thousand. Despite the imbalance of forces, the siege lasted fifty-five days, but on May 29, 1453, a date perceived as one of European history's turning points, Constantinople fell to the Turks. Mehmet the Conqueror was 21 years old, and the analogy with Alexander the Great, who was credited with having led the cavalry charge that decisively won Byzantium for the Macedonian Empire at a similarly young age, was not lost on his contemporaries.

News of the fall of Constantinople, which reached Venice a month after it happened, and Rome a week later, in July 1453, set off a panic in Christian Europe. Nonetheless, the immediate reaction, to unite in a crusade to retake Constantinople from Islam, foundered on the reefs of internecine squabbling and self-interest on the part of individual states. Before the end of the year, Venice had concluded a treaty which established a permanent embassy in Turkish Constantinople and secured the continuing domination of Venetian trade in the eastern Mediterranean (for which collective excommunication by the papacy for betraying Christendom was deemed a fair price to pay). The peace lasted a decade but was then followed by a draining fifteen-year war between Venice and the Ottomans which broke out in 1464. This history has a bearing on Bellini's portrait. By 1478 Venetian wealth and trade had become so adversely affected as a result of war that peace negotiations were initiated. The experienced diplomat Giovanni Dario travelled to Constantinople charged with acceding to as many demands as were necessary to preserve Venetian trade in the region. The terms of the treaty concluded on January 25, 1479 were harsh for Venice, including financial reparations for the costs of the war and the payment of an annual rent for trading within the Ottoman Empire.

On the positive side, the permanent ambassador, or *bailo* in Constantinople was re-secured. Mehmet meanwhile had built up the city from the impoverished and depopulated shell it had been after the conquest a quarter of a century earlier into a new capital of sixty thousand to seventy thousand inhabitants. The question of the Western construct of the barbaric oriental despot is relevant here. Recent research has shown that, rather than being a constant of East–West relations, this notion crystallized in the late sixteenth century.[44] For well over a hundred years, from the fall of Constantinople until the last quarter of the sixteenth century, fear of the Turks was mixed with admiration for their social system, which seemed to grant them in equal measure irresistible military power and enviable cultural riches. The same Mehmet who was responsible for thousands of executions and was in one report described as "feared and dreaded, ruthless and cruel … a second Nero and far worse" also reputedly spoke several languages, wrote poetry, and possessed considerable knowledge of the literature and philosophy of antiquity.[45] An eyewitness subsequently cited in a contemporary Venetian chronicle reports that before the siege of Constantinople, Mehmet enjoyed daily readings from "ancient historians such as Laertius, Herodotus, Livy and Quintus Curtius and from chronicles of the popes and Lombard kings."[46] Kritovoulos of Imbros, a Greek scholar, recounts how he "used to read philosophical works translated into Arabic from Persian and Greek and discuss the subjects which they treated with the scholars of his court."[47] What matters here is less a question of the objective truth or otherwise of the claim than how Mehmet's identity is being constructed. At about the same time Vespasiano da Bisticci writes of Federigo, Duke of Urbino that "he was ever careful to keep intellect and virtue to the front, and to learn something new every day," going on to catalog his patronage of the arts, architecture, and music as well as his deep knowledge of both classical authors and the scriptures.[48] Half a century later, no less ambiguous a figure than Henry VIII is recorded as frequently receiving Sir Thomas More into his private apartments, "and there sometime in matters of astronomy, geometry, divinity, and other such faculties, and sometimes of his worldly affairs, to sit and confer with him."[49] The point is not, therefore, that Mehmet's learning was incompatible with brutality (nor indeed Henry VIII's) but that Mehmet's identity is being fashioned as a Renaissance prince rather than as an alien despot.

One of Mehmet's most important projects was the construction of a new palace complex – the Topkapı Palace – from which the Ottoman Empire was administered. Although many Christian churches were taken over and converted into mosques, the Orthodox Church had been reestablished, and a degree of multiculturalism with Christians and Jews existed within the overall Islamic culture of the city. Mehmet continued his personal fascination with the West – partly, it would seem, for its intrinsic interest, partly for strategic ends: building up a knowledge of contemporary Italy with a view to its eventual incorporation into the empire.[50] According to the then widespread view of world history as rooted in the Book of Daniel, the four pagan empires of Babylon, Persia, Greece, and Rome were to be followed by a fifth empire uniting the world. In the late fifteenth and early sixteenth century it was not unusual for Renaissance scholars to worry that with Christendom prey to internecine warfare, this empire would be Islamic. In 1521 a report by the Venetian ambassador stated that the sultan "holds in his hands the keys to all of Christendom," and as late as 1576, it was still being lamented that "the fall of such an empire by the hands of men is therefore the vainest thing to think of."[51]

In discussions with the Venetian delegation during the peace negotiations of 1478–1479, Mehmet's interest in Western culture, contemporary as well as classical, seems to have been a topic that arose – including his grasp of the tradition whereby rulers reinforced their power through the circulation of images of themselves on coins and medals. As an experienced Venetian diplomat, Giovanni Dario was fully conversant with the artistic situation in Venice, and one of the requests that emerged from Constantinople in the summer of 1479 was for a "good painter" to make medals and to paint the Sultan's portrait.[52] After 1453, Venice had lost a string of important colonies in the eastern Mediterranean, with consequent damage to its overseas trade. For both military and commercial reasons, Venice needed to secure its accommodation with the Turks, and complying with Mehmet's artistic desires – both in terms of palace decoration and the dissemination of his own image – was going to be a useful means to this greater end. One is reminded of Michael Baxandall's observation that "in the fifteenth century, painting was still too important to be left to the painters."[53] In short, the Venetian government would have done all they could to satisfy Mehmet's desire to propagate his image. Within a month of receiving the request, a painter was on his way. The leading artist in Venice at the time, in charge both of the decoration of the Grand Council chamber in the Palazzo Ducale and of producing the official portrait of the doge, was Gentile Bellini.

Portraits of the doges were displayed in a frieze above the Venetian history paintings in the council chamber of the Palazzo Ducale. In keeping with the corporate spirit of Venetian life, the point of them was less to celebrate the individual and his achievements than to represent the individual as part of a collective – the head of a family, officer of a *scuola*, the first among equals within the inner circles of Venice's aristocracy. Gentile's portrait of Doge Giovanni Mocenigo, completed just before the summons to Constantinople, shows him facing left, in profile, his elevated status conveyed by the flat gold ground, the gold collar and *cornu* embossed with geometric designs. Following an established formula, only the doge's face is lightly modeled, conveying just sufficient information for the painting to qualify as a portrait rather than a stereotype. There seems little doubt that Gentile Bellini's ability to fulfill contemporary requirements for an individuated likeness combined with a classically legitimated sense of the gravity of office led to his being chosen for the mission to Constantinople in 1479.

In some ways, the surprising thing about Gentile Bellini's year-and-a-half long sojourn in the Ottoman capital is what he did not do. Despite the emergence of a form of public painting in Venice, Gentile produced no images of contemporary Ottoman architecture or social life. He did, however, make several studies of individual Turkish people in daily costume which formed the basis for many subsequent depictions of Turks and other orientals in Western art. This sense of building up a repertoire, albeit a limited one, of exotic "types," proved to be important. In this regard, Gentile was the best knownWestern artist involved with the Ottoman court, though not the only one. A little earlier, around 1460, Mehmet had approached Sigismondo Malatesta to borrow the services of one of the artists who had been involved in the modernization of buildings in Rimini. Matteo de' Pasti, who had collaborated on this work with the well-known architect and theorist Leon Battista Alberti duly set off to Istanbul to assist in work on the new Topkapı Palace. However, he was arrested en route by the Venetians in Cyprus for having in his possession maps of Italy.

More successful was the Venetian-born Costanzo da Ferrara. Having been sent there by the King of Naples, he was in Istanbul during the late 1470s.[54] The principal work of Costanzo's to have survived is his portrait medal of Mehmet of c.1480. This image of a powerful man provides an interesting instance of the way images of "orientals" entered art, often built up from a single actual observation. Costanzo's model was an earlier portrait medallion that had been designed by Pisanello of the Byzantine emperor John VIII Palaiologos, made at the time of the previously mentioned Council of Eastern and Western Churches held at Ferrara and Florence in 1438–1439. The portrait of Mehmet is modeled on Pisanello's image of the Byzantine emperor, not least through its use of exotic headgear to signify "otherness." The reverse of the medal, however, shows an equestrian image of the sultan also derived from Pisanello, whose work includes a sheet of drawings, apparently made from life, of the Byzantine emperor's entourage. They show the emperor standing, clad in a full-length cloak, some details of its embroidered hem, and another image of the emperor wearing the characteristic Timurid hat, mounted on horseback.[55] This observed image, adapted for the circular proportions of Pisanello's medal was then in turn used as compositional basis for the equestrian portrait on the reverse of Costanzo's medal of Mehmet forty years later. Subsequently, this image became transformed into a generic representation of an "Ottoman rider" by no less a figure than Dürer during his first visit to Venice in 1495. Rosamond Mack has remarked of this kind of borrowing that "artists tended to adapt a small repertory of authentic images to a variety of representational uses," concluding that what they reveal, despite the level of commercial contacts between East and West is "a limited vision of the Orient."[56]

Gentile Bellini also produced a portrait medal of Mehmet, either during his time in Istanbul or shortly after his return. It is slightly smaller than Costanzo's albeit very similar in format, and it gives a somewhat less robust image of the sultan. The outstanding work to survive from Gentile's mission to Constantinople, however, is his oil portrait of Mehmet, dated in its inscription at the bottom right to November 25, 1480. By this time Mehmet the Conqueror – the title he had assumed on capturing Constantinople a quarter of a century before – was 50 years old and in ill health. He had retired within the confines of the palace and was principally preoccupied with its decoration and with the cultivation of a garden. He is represented in the painting in the bust-length profile familiar from the medals and also from the contemporary portraits of the eminent in Venice. The image, however, has a pensive, scholarly air, more marked even than Gentile's medal and quite dissimilar to Costanzo's thicker-set, somewhat belligerent-looking figure. In all three, the sultan is depicted wearing the distinctive Ottoman *tāj*, the turban in which a length of white material is wound around a stiff, ribbed cap of red felt. He also wears a similar garment, a kind of shirt with a cross-over collar, under a deep-red kaftan with a broad fur collar. In the painting, the archway in which he is framed is Western in style, with decoration suggestive of classical candelabra and tracery. But draped over the lintel is an opulent oriental fabric decorated with jewels. Apart from the date, the legible part of the inscription reads "Victor Orbis" – conqueror of the world. The significance of the crowns, for all the prominence of their placement, is unclear. On the reverse of Bellini's portrait medal there are three of them, which are usually taken to refer to the three components of the Ottoman Empire – their own original territories in Asia, Greece (including Constantinople),

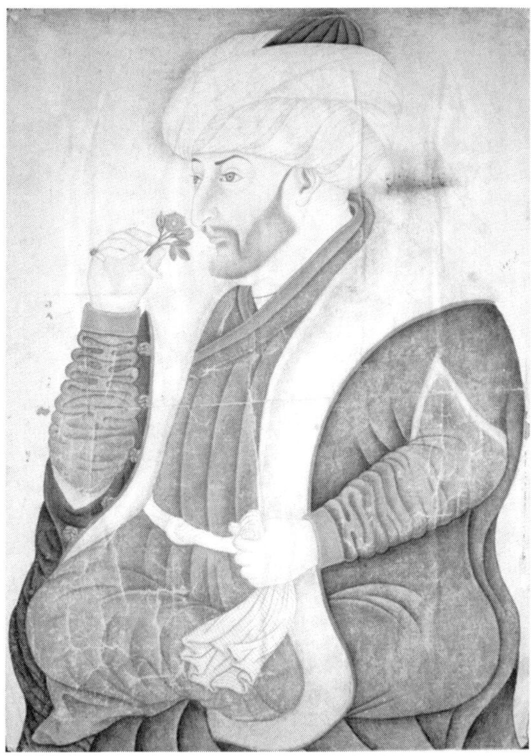

Figure 1.3 Attributed to Shiblizade Ahmed, *Portrait of Sultan Mehmet II* c.1480, opaque pigment on paper, 39 × 27 cm. Topkapı Sarayi Muzesi, Istanbul, H 2153, fol.10a. Photo Werner Forman Archive / The Bridgeman Art Library.

and Trebizond (as already mentioned, the gateway to the Silk Route into central Asia, captured by Mehmet from Venetian control within a decade of the end of Byzantium, in 1461). More recently, however, it has been suggested that the six crowns in Bellini's oil portrait represent the six previous Ottoman sultans, with Mehmet himself symbolized by the seventh crown, made of pearls, at the bottom center of the jeweled textile right at the front of the painting.[57]

Bellini left Constantinople in January 1481. Mehmet was dead within a year, and his iconoclastic successor sold or destroyed the Western-style figurative art he had commissioned for the Topkapı Palace. Legend has it that the sultan's portrait was bought for a knock-down price in the marketplace by an observant Venetian merchant and subsequently transported home. Interestingly, however, Bellini's portrait did leave a few traces in Ottoman art. There survives a portrait attributed to Shiblizade Ahmed from the same time (Figure 1.3) which appears to draw on the same pose – the profile portrait, the cross-over collared shirt, the fur-collared Kaftan, the *tāj* – as well as to employ Western shading to suggest volume in areas such as the handkerchief and turban, as well as the face, in contrast to the Ottoman convention for flat, unmodeled planes. Where this picture departs from Bellini's

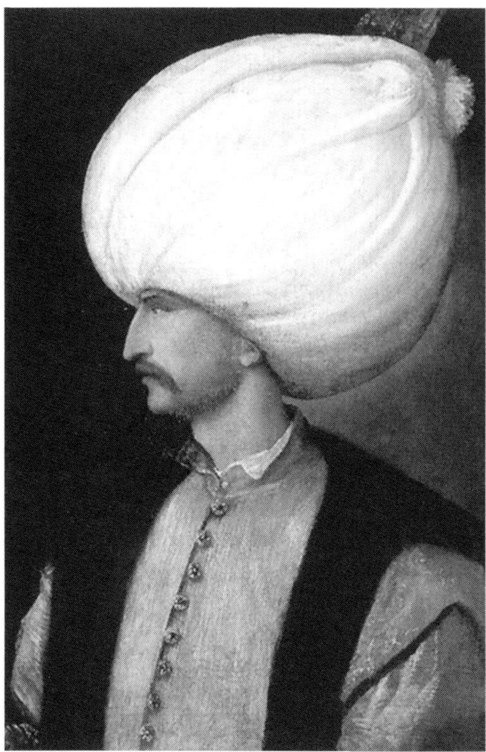

Figure 1.4 Titian (studio), *Portrait of Suleiman the Magnificent* c.1530–1540, oil on canvas, 99 × 85 cm. Gemaldgalerie, Kunsthistorisches Museum, Vienna. © World History Archive / Alamy.

portrait is the inclusion of the oriental cross-legged sitting posture, and the enigmatic device of having the Sultan smell a rose. This is an image which recurs in later Ottoman portraits but whose precise meaning is unclear. One possibility is that it refers to the grace of paradise; another is simply that Mehmet was renowned for the pleasure he took in the cultivation of his garden.

Be that as it may, this story of the image of the Ottoman sultan is inseparable from the larger story of two societies and their interaction, economic, cultural, and military. A generation later, when the pressure of the Turks on Christendom reached its highest point, the studio of Titian produced another profile image of a Turkish sultan: Mehmet's descendant Suleiman the Magnificent (Figure 1.4). Probably based on studies by European envoys to the Ottoman court that were intended to be used to illustrate the many printed books on the threat of expansionist Islam, the painted portrait is an arresting image. Headgear had become the principal visual signifier of the oriental, and here it reaches a crescendo. The fact of its authorship by the most eminent workshop of the day, its unstable mix of authority and otherness, of majesty and caricature, says much about the ambiguous power of *El Gran Turco* in the European imagination of the time.[58]

Some History Paintings

Venetian trade, together with the colonies of merchants established throughout the eastern Mediterranean, meant a constant interplay and importation of ideas and stories as well as objects, stuffs, and raw materials into Venice itself. The result of the merging of thousands of individual responses was a distinctively inflected society bearing witness to "the profound cultural impact of centuries of trade with the Islamic world."[59] Towards the end of the fifteenth century, and in the early years of the sixteenth, an "oriental mode" appeared in Venetian pictorial art.

Much of this work involved exotic locations, but it also included representations of the heart of the city, or rather its hearts, plural: the political and religious focus around the Piazza San Marco, with the Palazzo Ducale and the Basilica, and the economic and commercial center of the Venetian empire at the Rialto. We have already touched on the nature of Venetian society, and the way in which a collective ethos held sway. Although nineteenth-century claims about the emergence of a modern sense of the individual as a key to the nature of the Florentine Renaissance are now regarded with skepticism by contemporary historians, the Venetian relationship of the individual to the collective does seem to have been distinctive.

The ethos of the ordered totality, enshrined in the myth of Venice, encompassing a multiplicity of distinctions, but encompassing and subsuming them nonetheless, is what underwrites the very particular representation embodied in Gentile Bellini's *Procession in the Piazza San Marco* of 1496 (Figure 1.1). Bellini's piazza is dominated by the façade of the Basilica of San Marco, in front of which a procession makes its way from right to left. It might be said that the top half of the picture testifies to the force of the Byzantine and the Gothic in Venice. The domes of the church and the golden mosaics of its portals speak of Byzantium. But interspersed with the East is the North – in the form of the Gothic pinnacles at either end and between the pointed arches. The Gothic theme continues in the arches of the Doge's Palace, visible to the right of the Basilica, and Islamic influence is apparent in the pink and white lozenge-shapes of its decorative tile work.

Bellini's picture was originally painted for the meeting room of the Scuola Grande di San Giovanni Evangelista, whose members process across the front of the square. The organized quality of the painted representation stands unequivocally for the ordered nature of Venetian society – its diversity rendered equal in the sight of the church. The doge is one of a crowd, halfway along the right-hand side of the square. The other *scuole* have finished their procession and are drawn up in orderly fashion to the left. The middle of the picture offers nothing less than "a demographic cross-section of Venice."[60] Along with ladies, gentlemen, and citizens in recognizable costumes can be seen a group of German merchants in the middle distance to the right of the canopy, four Greek merchants in their distinctive black-brimmed hats standing in the middle of the square to the left; and in the distance, in front of the Basilica to the right are three turbaned Turks. In the row of first-floor windows along the far left of the square, well dressed women, two of them apparently veiled in Islamic style, look out from balconies over which are draped more than thirty rich oriental carpets.

The real subject of the picture is, however, none of this urban spectacle. Or rather it is all of it, in balance with a single defining motif of divine intervention in the secular domain. The point of the commission as a whole, of all nine paintings in the scuola's great *albergo*, or meeting room, is to commemorate the miracles of the True Cross. Throughout Renaissance Europe, and nowhere more so than Venice, holy relics marked the borders of the mundane and the divine, in fact the miracles they performed *were* the proof of the presence of the divine in the material world below. The Scuola di San Giovanni Evangelista possessed a fragment of the True Cross, donated in the previous century by the Grand Chancellor of Cyprus, who had in turn received it from the Patriarch of Constantinople. The depicted scene recounts an instance of the miraculous work of the relic and thus provides the underlying meaning of Bellini's picture: the divine at work in the cosmopolitan life of Venice.

Something similar holds for another picture in the same cycle in the Scuola's meeting room, painted by Vittore Carpaccio two years earlier. Here Carpaccio depicts another miracle, this time in the economic and commercial heart of Venice, the Rialto, adjacent to the busy Grand Canal (Figure 1.5). Once again the key to the picture is displaced to the margins, the sacred being embedded in the flow of secular life. At the far left, in the first floor loggia, an exorcism is taking place. A possessed man is being healed by the miracle-working fragment of the True Cross as commercial and social life rolls on with barely a blink. Another varied cast of characters is discernible. Along the bank of the canal, just before the bridge, can just be seen the columns of an open loggia where the merchants met. Outside it, two white-turbaned figures in long robes, one white, one orange, can just be made out. In the foreground, at the far left, in black-brimmed hats and sumptuous brocade robes stand figures thought to be Armenian or Greek merchants. And unmissable, right in the center foreground and acting as a kind of counter-focus to the decentered miracle, is a working man, albeit no ordinary workman: a distinctively attired African gondolier.

The black gondolier was probably a slave.[61] Venice had traded in slaves since at least the tenth century, probably earlier.[62] Most were Christians, often described as "Tartars" or "Circassians" from the area around the Black Sea. After the fall of Constantinople, there was a decline in this trade (not that the traffic died out – the slaves were simply taken over by the Ottomans), and an increase in the use of black slaves from Africa. These numbers increased further in the sixteenth century as European attitudes turned against the enslavement of fellow Christians, and increasing Ottoman power militated against the use of Moslem slaves. It has been calculated that in the late fifteenth century perhaps 1,500 African slaves were being traded annually at Venice.[63] By 1600, however, Venetian slavery had died out – not least because of competing demand from Portuguese, Spanish, Dutch, British, and French colonies, as well as the Muslim states. After that time, freed slaves

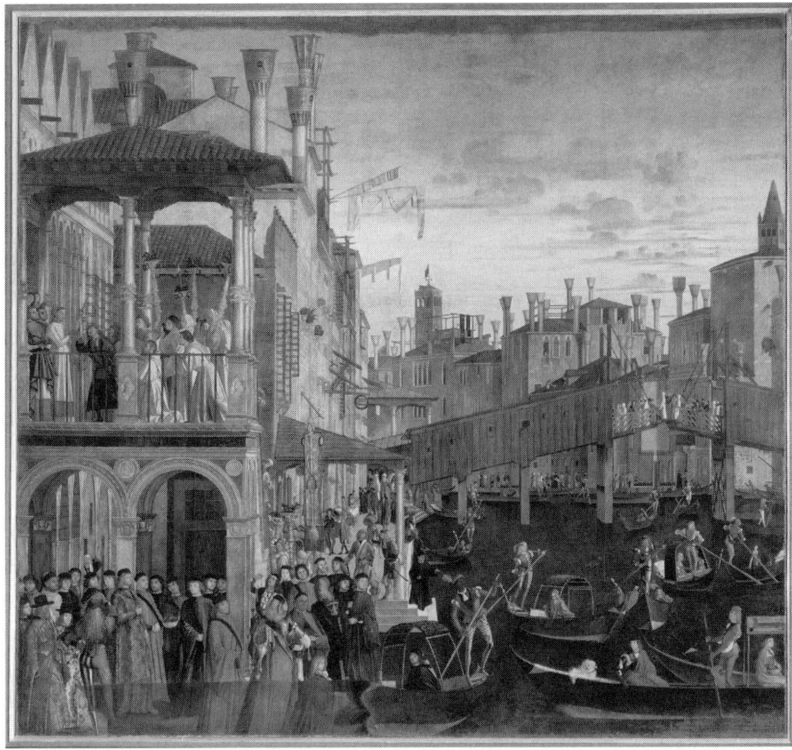

Figure 1.5 Vittore Carpaccio, *Miracle at Rialto* (*The Exorcism*) 1494, oil on canvas, 365 × 389 cm. Accademia, Venice. © 2013. Photo Scala, Florence – courtesy of the Ministero Beni e Att. Culturali.

continued to live in Venice, mostly though not exclusively working as domestic servants. Although Africans were never as numerous as other communities such as Jews, Turks, and Germans, the imagery of black people entered into Venetian popular culture and has never really left it.

In the Scuola di San Giorgio degli Schiavoni, the *fondaco* of the merchants from Dalmatia, between 1502 and 1508, Carpaccio painted three scenes from the life of St George as part of an overall scheme of nine pictures. Whereas the two paintings from San Giovanni Evangelista represent the diversity of Venetian society itself, these pictures form part of an overtly "oriental mode" in Venetian art. The narrative mode as a whole functioned to represent the myth of Venice back to Venetians themselves, a visual counterpart to the historical chronicles which narrated the city's foundation and prosperity.[64] In the late fifteenth century, contemporary political developments seem to have stimulated artists to address a newly pressing theme, namely the "Other" to Venice's imperium in the shape of expansionist Islam. In these works certain Venetian artists "attempted to reproduce an Islamic setting, with figures dressed in Muslim garb, exotic animals – camels, monkeys and giraffes – and, on occasion, architecture of Islamic inspiration."[65] In contrast to

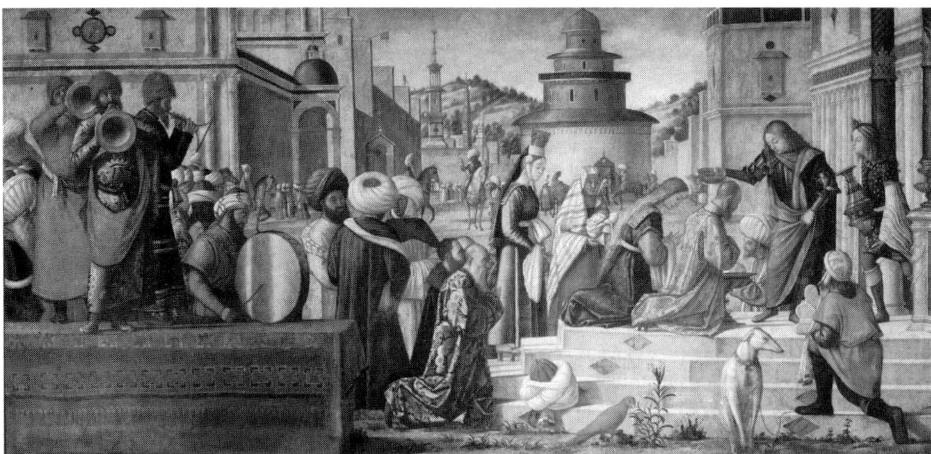

Figure 1.6 Vittore Carpaccio, *St George Baptising the Pagans (Selenites)*, c.1507–1508, oil and tempera on canvas, 141 × 285 cm. Scuola di San Giorgio degli Schiavoni, Venice. © The Art Archive / Alamy.

Bellini's portrait of Mehmet II, or the individual costume studies of Costanzo da Ferrara, these pictures involve a conscious attempt to imagine an oriental culture and society. (See Figure 1.6.)

The representation of the world of Islam takes a specific form, however. One curious feature of this development is that Venetian artists seem to have shied away from representing contemporary Ottoman society as such. Whereas verbal reports on Ottoman society abounded, and although Ottoman figures can be found in Venetian art – sometimes situated in the heart of Venice itself – there are no images of the lived environment of the Ottoman world. What there are, though, are plentiful images of the early Christian world of the Holy Land. And in the late fifteenth and early sixteenth centuries the Holy Land lay not in Ottoman territory but in the empire of the Mamluks, the other eastern Mediterranean Islamic culture based in Syria and Egypt. So Venetian artists, representing the trials and victories of the early Christian church imagined them against a partly factual, partly made-up background of known architecture and non-Christians in Mamluk costume.

Thus, Carpaccio's *Triumph of St George* shows a miscellaneous crowd of Mamluk figures witnessing the triumph of the Christian knight against a background of buildings based on woodcut images of the Dome of the Rock and the Church of the Holy Sepulchre in Jerusalem. Traditionally, the St George story was set in the Eastern Empire, which included Palestine. The dragon motif was established in the thirteenth century *Golden Legend*, wherein the killing of the dragon results in the conversion of the people to Christianity. It does not take an enormous leap of the imagination to read the dragon that is about to succumb to George's *coup de grâce* as a figure for the pagan unbelief that the church is poised to overcome. This reading is reinforced

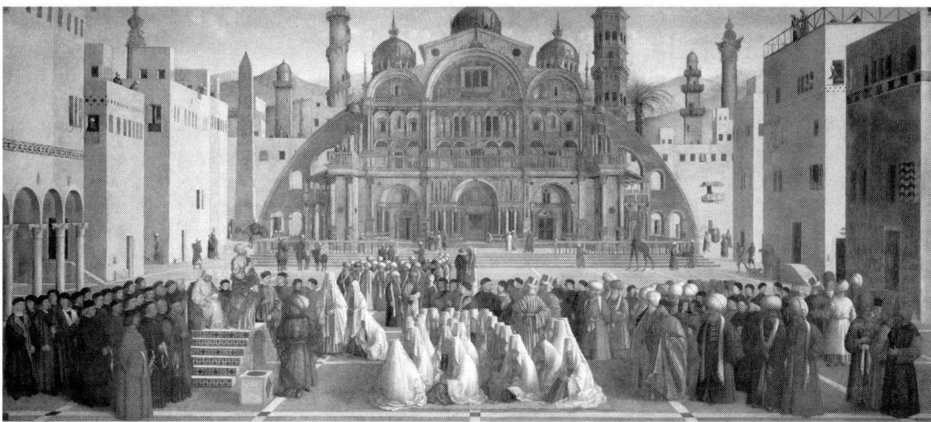

Figure 1.7 Gentile Bellini, *St Mark Preaching in Alexandria* 1504–1507, oil on canvas, 347 × 770 cm. Pinacoteca di Brera, Milan. Photo: akg-images / Erich Lessing.

in the final painting of the series, *St George Baptising the Pagans*. To the left, musicians wearing the Mamluk *zamt*, a tufted bonnet, stand on a plinth covered in an Islamic carpet, while to the right, conspicuously bare-headed figures are baptized into the Christian faith, their elaborate Mamluk headgear cast aside at the foot of the stairs they have mounted.

The meeting house of the Dalmatian confraternity of St George was in a building owned by the Knights of St John of Jerusalem, a crusader organization. The Dalmatians had been in the frontline of the Venetian struggle against the Turks in the Adriatic, and their presence in Venice marked them as, essentially, refugees from Ottoman expansion. The occasion of the commission to decorate the meeting room was their receipt of an important relic of St George in honor of their exploits under the flag of Venice. This was a gift from the commander of the Venetian forts in Dalmatia before they fell to the Turks in 1499, who in turn had received it from no less a figure than the Patriarch of Jerusalem. It can readily be seen, therefore, how the St George legend of the defeat of pagan unbelief by the action of a virtuous Christian knight becomes a resonant motif at a point where Venetian Christian culture perceives itself threatened by the apparently unstoppable expansion of the Islamic Ottoman Empire.

A similar cluster of concerns underwrites the enormous painting by Gentile Bellini of *St Mark Preaching in Alexandria* (Figure 1.7). This picture turned out to be Gentile's last, and although the design and most of the actual work is his, some of the foreground figures and the buildings to right and left of the central square were completed after his death by his brother Giovanni. The Scuola Grande di San Marco had been rebuilding their premises after a fire in 1485, and Bellini put himself forward to decorate the albergo as early as 1492. The commission, however, was not finalized until 1504, by which time Bellini had behind him the success of his *Procession in the Piazza San Marco*. The new painting was intended to evoke that earlier triumph, and was indeed "specifically cited as the standard which he promised to surpass."[66] The added ingredient in this commission, of course, is that St Mark is the patron saint of Venice itself. Preaching to the infidel (and, indeed, dying for the cause) represents a powerful ideological message in early sixteenth-century Venice.

This was not the first work to dramatize St Mark's attempts to win over the infidels in a plausibly Egyptian setting: precedence goes to works of the late 1490s by Cima da Conegliano and Giovani Mansueti for the Silk-Weavers Guild. But in the grandeur of its conception it does represent a culmination of the orientalist mode in Venetian painting. Taken in conjunction with the *Procession in the Piazza San Marco*, it represents a kind of mapping of Venice onto its Other: St Mark's Square onto the Alexandrian plaza, the Basilica onto the imaginary pagan temple. It is as if by assimilating the exotic – and threatening – to the familiar, the all-too real threat of the Islamic Other could be negotiated and absorbed at the level of the imagination.

In his pioneering work on Venetian orientalism, Julian Raby investigated a number of possible sources for this complex imagery of Islamic society that was fashioned by Venetian artists. "Fashioned" is an appropriate term because they are not the product of direct experience. In addition to the "type and costume" studies made of Ottoman Turks by Bellini himself and Costanzo da Ferrara, another important visual resource was provided by the German woodcuts of Erhard Reeuwich. These accompanied Bernhardt von Breydenbach's *Peregrinationes*, an account of his pilgrimage to the Holy Land in 1483, published three years later in Mainz. Yet another possible source of oriental imagery is provided by an arresting picture by an anonymous artist now in the Louvre. The city of Damascus was an important trading center situated at the end of an Asian caravan route, as well as a staging post for Western pilgrims en route to the Holy Land. In *The Reception of an Ambassador in Damascus* (Figure 1.8), both the clothing and the architecture show that the painting represents a Mamluk scene. The turbans are not Ottoman: they include the bearskin-type hats of the military, the large often white turbans lacking the Ottoman *tāj* in the middle, and the elaborate horned, so-called waterwheel turban – used, for example, by Mansueti in his St Mark series of paintings. Despite the Mamluk clothing, however, the location of the *Reception* long remained unidentified, and was in fact mistaken as being Cairo because of its compatibility with a verbal description of such a reception there. Now, though, the dome and minarets of the Umayyad Mosque have been identified, and other features such as the bathhouse in the center, with glass tiles in its dome, the walled garden and rooftop terraces all bespeak first-hand knowledge of such a scene. It has indeed been suggested that the mosque was viewed from the Venetian merchants' *fondaco* itself. Local color is provided by the authentic costumes, the Mamluk insignia on the walls and gateway, and not least by the camels and palm tree. The focus of the scene is an official reception by the Mamluk viceroy of Damascus (shown seated on a low platform with two other dignitaries behind him) of a Venetian ambassador (standing in a red gown with other black-clad Venetians to the left of the gateway).

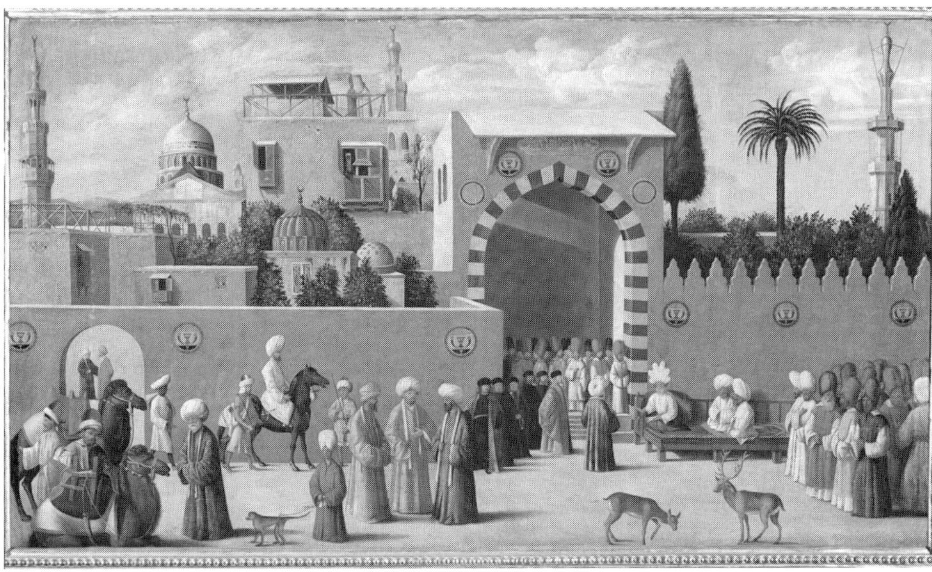

Figure 1.8 Anonymous, *The Reception of an Ambassador in Damascus*, between 1488 and 1516, oil on canvas, 175 × 201 cm. Musée du Louvre, Paris. Photo: akg-images / Erich Lessing.

The Damascus *Reception* was for long believed to be an important source for the Venetian oriental mode of Carpaccio, Cima, Mansueti, Gentile and others. However, recent research indicates it may follow, rather than predate these works. The precise relationship of the pictures remains a matter for interpretation, a salutary reminder of the uncertainties still attendant on Renaissance art history, and of the often provisional nature of historical knowledge.

However the question of sources is eventually resolved, it does appear that Venetian artistic orientalism depended on a relatively limited repertoire of images, some representing quite distant "translations" of some actual, original observation. Gentile Bellini's *St Mark Preaching in Alexandria* is one such example. In it Bellini adapts three figures in his bottom right corner from the anonymous Louvre painter, as well as the palm tree in the right middle distance and many of the Mamluk turbans. His white veiled figures are derived from the Reeuwich woodcuts. The man standing directly before St Mark, apparently paying close attention to his preaching, is in Ottoman costume. At the very front of the composition in a bright red gown stands Gentile Bellini himself, wearing a gold chain given him by Mehmet II. The picture is thus a composite put together to produce the effect of an oriental scene. Many of the architectural details are topographically accurate: the pillar in the right hand background is the Column of Diocletian in Alexandria, known as "Pompey's pillar" and marking the site of a pagan temple destroyed by early Christians; the top of the famous Pharos lighthouse, one of the Seven Wonders of the World appears at the far left; the obelisk to the left of the central temple had been brought to Alexandria by the Roman emperor Augustus from Heliopolis.[67]

One of the defining features of the picture, rather than its circumstantial detailing, is of a somewhat different order: it is an imaginative recycling of Bellini's own previous masterpiece. The composition of the piazza flanked by the receding orthogonals of the side buildings; the band of figures across the foreground, parallel to the picture plane; but above all the fantastic temple dominating and defining the scene as "Other" are all adapted from the *Procession in the Piazza San Marco*. The façade with its arches and domes unmistakably evokes the Basilica of San Marco, shorn of its Gothic tracery but with the addition of enormous curving buttresses. Probably drawing on a visual memory of Hagia Sophia, which Gentile would have seen in Constantinople a quarter of a century earlier, as well as on the Venetian San Marco, this formidable synthesis serves to situate the scene in a realm at once exotic and familiar. In sum, the giant picture with its hundreds of figures and colossal architecture aspires to nothing less than a displaced affirmation of Christian Venice's sway over the realm of the infidel, imagined moreover, at precisely the moment when that actual hegemony was threatened as never before.

Later

The great trading empire on which Venetian wealth was based came under increased pressure in the late fifteenth and early sixteenth centuries from relentless Ottoman expansion. Soon, the Ottomans had even vanquished the Mamluks, taking Cairo in 1517. It was in response to this developing threat to their *stato da mar* that Venice expanded into the north Italian mainland, the *terra firma*. This shift marked both the beginning of a decline in Venice's orientation eastwards and a corresponding increase in engagement with the classical heritage associated with a more conventional sense of the Italian Renaissance.

In art, these changed priorities are manifest in the work of the Venetian school of the sixteenth century: Giorgione, Titian, Tintoretto, Veronese – the "great masters" who came to be ranked with Michelangelo, Raphael, and others in the subsequent academic construction of the Western canon.

To be sure, tokens of a wider world continue to appear in that art, Venetian, Florentine, northern European alike. Rudolf Wittkower added to his discussion of the formal and thematic influences of non-European art on the art of western Europe a third category, which also bears upon the mutual interaction of European art with other cultures. This was "the European image of non-European civilisations." That is to say, the long-established practice on the part of European artists of depicting, within the armature of Renaissance perspective (which as we have already seen was itself the product of cultural interaction), "non-European objects, plants, animals and humans in order to show life in faraway countries."[68]

Some of these we have seen in the "orientalist" mode of Venetian art in the late fifteenth and early sixteenth centuries. That time, and that place, was arguably the

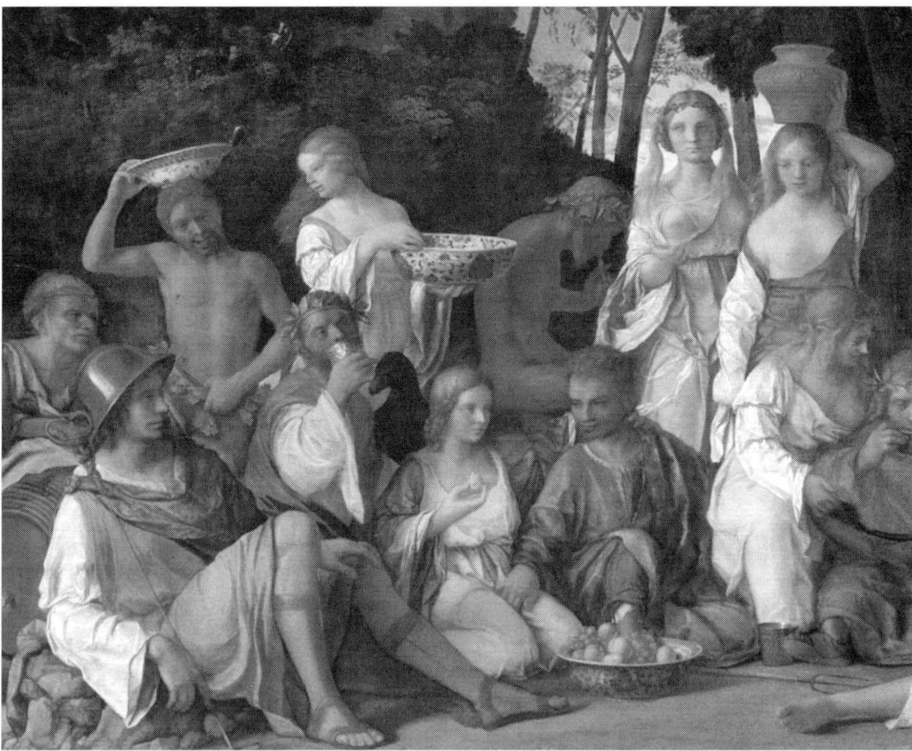

Figure 1.9 Giovanni Bellini and Titian, *The Feast of the Gods* (detail), 1514, oil on canvas, 170 × 188 cm. National Gallery of Art, Washington, DC, Widener Collection 1942.9.1.

nearest such an "orientalist" tendency came to the mainstream of Western art before the modern period, when because of the specificities of the Venetian situation, Europe's Other briefly occupied a place which forced it onto the agenda of a major European art form. Beyond that, images of black Africans are frequently to be found in European Renaissance art, often in the guise of one of the three magi come to worship Christ. Islamic figures are present in the works of Dürer, across a full gamut from negative representations of the persecutors of Christian martyrs to celebrations of Arabic learning and science. Tokens of China, in the form of blue and white porcelain bowls, can crop up in impeccably classical motifs such Giovanni Bellini and Titian's *Feast of the Gods* of 1514 (Figure 1.9). Van Eyck's *Arnolfini Wedding* is replete with tokens of the international trade in which its protagonist engaged. Holbein's *Ambassadors* of 1533 is also stocked with signifiers of the expanding trade, and the expanding knowledge, of Europe ranging from the Turkish carpet covering the table to the astronomical instruments on it, and both a celestial and a terrestrial globe (Figure 1.10). This terrestrial globe, in fact, is a particularly potent indicator of things to come. Probably made in Nuremburg, it shows in red the line running from north to south, determined by the Treaty of Tordesillas in 1494. The line divided the world between Spain and Portugal: it is

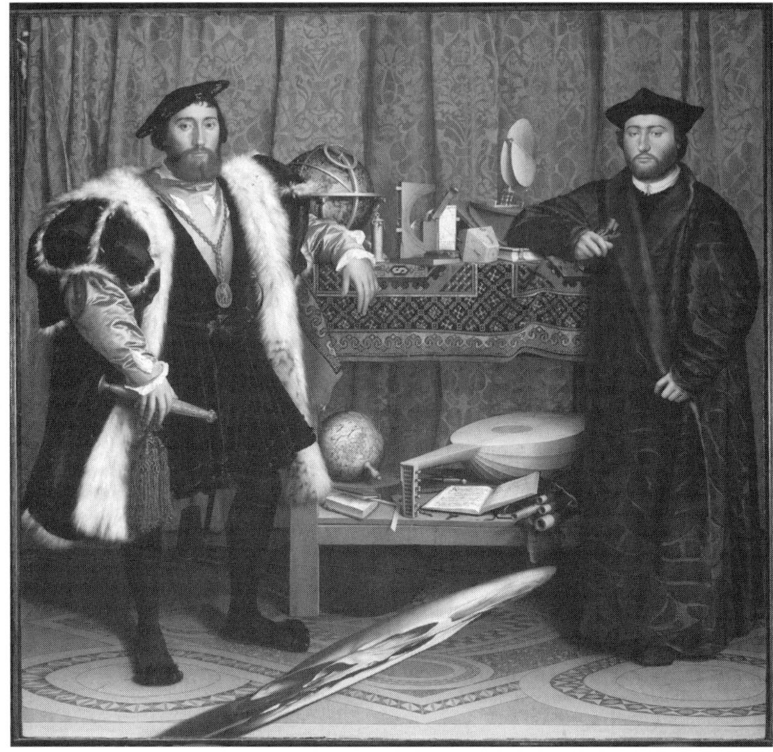

Figure 1.10 Hans Holbein, *The Ambassadors*, 1533, oil on oak, 207 × 209.5 cm. © 2013. Copyright The National Gallery, London / Scala, Florence.

visibly labelled *Linea divisionis Castellanoru et Portugallen*. These are only a few of the many tokens of worldedness that leak into the art of the European Renaissance, though there is nothing else as consistent and deep as the presence of the Islamic cast in Venetian art in the years around 1500.

For their part, the Ottomans suffered a decisive setback when their siege of Vienna failed in 1532. Although their pressure on Europe continued, and indeed the second and final failed siege of Vienna did not happen for a further 150 years, that reverse nonetheless marked the limit of their westward expansion. Gulru Necipoglu has argued that the Ottoman court's patronage of European artists began to come to an end at around the same time. The "halt of Ottoman military expansion" and the resulting "definition of geographical boundaries" began to impose more of "a barrier to the flow of ideas between East and West." The relative permeability of the earlier period was lost. She goes on, "The outcome of a heightened awareness of fixed frontiers was the accentuation of the 'otherness' of each realm."[69] This does not however mean that images of the Ottomans disappeared from the West, and it certainly does not mean that the stereotypes of a later "orientalism" became immediately fixed. In his *Orientalism*, Edward Said, as we have seen, had argued that from the eighteenth century onwards, European art

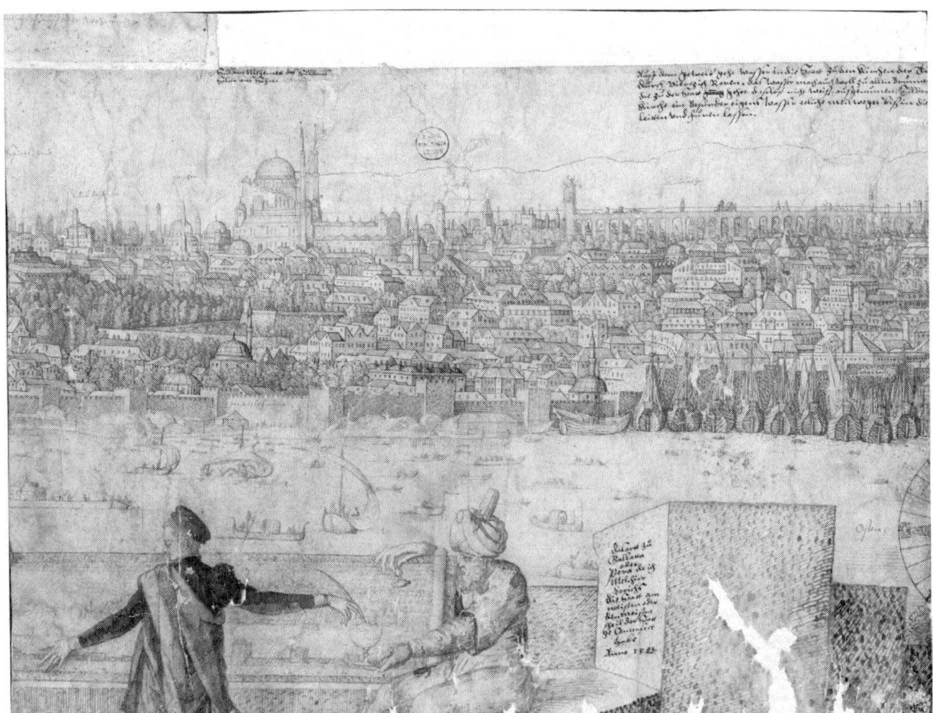

Figure 1.11 Melchior Lorck, *Prospect of Constantinople* (detail of central section), drawing, 1559. Leiden University Library, BPL 1758, sheet 11.

and scholarship constructed an image of the East as fundamentally inferior to the West. Several examples show that in the sixteenth century this was far from the case. As discussed above, in c.1530–1540, that is, around the time of the Turk's maximum perceived threat, Titian's studio produced an arresting painted image of Suleiman the Magnificent (Figure 1.4). Probably based on studies made by European envoys to the Turkish court, which were used to illustrate the many printed books on the threat of expansionist Islam, the portrait testifies to the presence of "the Grand Turk" in European consciousness. The same can be said of the engraving of a procession of Suleiman's nobles on horseback through Istanbul made by the Flemish artist Pieter Coecke van Aelst in 1533. Van Aelst's trip to Istanbul was undertaken on behalf of the Flemish van der Moyen tapestry company. Although it did not result in any tapestries being commissioned, it nevertheless produced an image which, like the Titian studio's portrait, testified to the power which all of Europe associated with the Ottoman Empire.

Later still, in 1559 the Danish-born artist Melchior Lorck produced an extraordinary panorama of Istanbul while accompanying a diplomatic mission from the Holy Roman Emperor to the Ottoman court (Figure 1.11). No less than eleven metres wide, it was subsequently displayed in the Library of the University of Leiden, one of the most advanced centers of European learning. After his return, Lorck worked up many of his sketches into printed illustrations for a variety of books published in western Europe, not least his own illustrated volume published in Antwerp in 1574.[70] Lorck's *Prospect of Constantinople* showed a view of the city across the waters of the Golden Horn, from a position not far from the earlier Genoese watchtower on the slopes of Galata. Lorck depicted himself in the center accompanied by a high-ranking Ottoman official. Behind them the water is full of traffic, and behind that rises the city with its mosques and the fourth century Aqueduct of Valens. Whatever else it is, this is not a Western imperialistic representation of a subordinate country. Although made by a European artist, the image of their capital city is in effect being authorized by the Ottomans for Western consumption. As Marina Warner has commented, "the visiting artist from Europe is able to record the city, its layout, its dwellings, its fortifications, its trade and shipping, but by permission, and that permission is granted because the Turkish empire has nothing to fear from being revealed to foreigners, so confident are its citizens in what they have achieved and what they are."[71] Echoing the argument we encountered earlier about the inappropriateness of Said's model of "orientalism" for the earlier Renaissance period, Warner writes of Lorck's image: "It isn't possible to read into this scene a vision of the Orient as a place of 'luxe, calme et volupté'... that tendency doesn't emerge until a good two hundred years later." Quite to the contrary, Lorck's image constitutes "an awed tribute to Ottoman wealth and efficiency."[72]

So, even towards the end of the period signified by the term "Renaissance," relations between western Europe and its eastern "other" were not what they were subsequently to become. The Renaissance was a period before the age of the modern empires, when the lineaments of West and East hardened into cultural and racial stereotypes that have only begun to be questioned in our own day. Nonetheless, the sense of those interactions between continental Asian civilizations and the increasingly dynamic western Eurasian peninsular was about to undergo truly epochal transformation. Since biblical times, indeed earlier, the eastern Mediterranean, spreading westwards into Europe and eastwards into Asia, had been the crossroads of the world. In 1488, however, the Portuguese navigator Bartholomeo Diaz rounded the southern tip of Africa; in 1498, Vasco da Gama reached India; before that, in 1492, the Genoese Christopher Columbus sailed west and stumbled across America. By 1522 a fleet under Ferdinand Magellan had sailed all the way round the globe. A new horizon was, with remarkable rapidity, being drawn around a new world.

Notes

1 *The Independent*, London, December 18, 2004.

2 Vasari 1965, pp. 50 and 88.

3 Burckhardt 1990, p. 98.

4 Elkins and Williams, eds, 2008, p. 43.

5 Burckhardt 1990, p. 19.
6 Elkins and Williams 2008, p. 251.
7 Elkins and Williams 2008, p. 255; Farago 1995.
8 See Greenblatt 1980.
9 Martin 1997, p. 1315.
10 See Nelson 1966. Nelson discusses the mixture of classificatory archaism and orientalizing prejudice which separated art-historical accounts of Byzantine art from contemporary Western medieval art.
11 See Howard 2000.
12 Wittkower 1989, p. 4.
13 Wittkower 1989, p. xxviii.
14 Schwab 1984, p. 16.
15 In fact Schwab's view of the fifteenth- and sixteenth-century Renaissance was quite orthodox: "a family matter inside a hermetic little Mediterranean room" (p. 16). If anything he overemphasizes the inward-looking nature of the earlier Renaissance as "wholly classical" in nature (p. 23) in order to dramatize the contrast with his "second Renaissance" and its openness to the East. Schwab's *Oriental Renaissance* is discussed in Chapter 3.
16 Schwab 1984, p. 6.
17 Schwab 1984, pp. 1, 2, and 6.
18 Jardine and Brotton 2000, p. 61.
19 Jardine and Brotton 2000, p. 12 and p. 61.
20 Said 2003, p. 3.
21 Said 2003, p. 7.
22 Said 2003, p. 3.
23 Said 2003, p. 7.
24 Jardine and Brotton 2000, p. 61.
25 Jardine and Brotton 2000, p. 184.
26 Jardine 1996, pp. 9 and 19.
27 Brotton 2002, p. 219.
28 Brotton 2002, p. 436.
29 For further discussion, see Paul Wood, "Art in fifteenth-century Venice: an aesthetic of diversity", in Richardson, ed., 2007, pp. 213–247.
30 De Commynes and Sansovino, as quoted in Martin and Romano, eds, 2000, pp. 20–21.
31 Howard 2000, p. 142.
32 Tafuri 1995. Tafuri contrasts the Venice that "preserved as a valuable heritage the institutions and mentality of the late middle ages" and the city that "partakes of the new mental universes under construction" (p. ix), i.e. the Renaissance.
33 As Howard has noted, this aspect of Venice was recognized in the nineteenth century by Ruskin, who wrote that "the Venetians deserve especial note as the only European people who appear to have sympathised to the full with the great instinct of the Eastern races" (quoted in Howard 1999, pp. 37–38).
34 See Martin and Romano, 2000, p. 19.
35 See Panofsky 1991.
36 Belting 2011, p. 135.
37 Belting 2011, p. 1.
38 Belting 2011, p. 90.

39 Bell 2012.
40 Belting 2011, p. 146.
41 Belting 2011, p. 162.
42 Belting 2011, p. 4.
43 Pedrocco, 2002, p. 56.
44 See Valensi 1990.
45 Jacopo de Promontorio, a Genose merchant, quoted in Babinger, 1978, p. 431.
46 Nicolo Sagundino; see Raby 1980, p. 242.
47 Kritovoulos of Imbros, writing in 1467, quoted in Brotton 2002, p. 196. See also Raby 1982a.
48 da Bisticci 1963, p. 99.
49 Roper 1962, p. 202. The connection between representations of Henry VIII and Italian princes is made by Greenblatt 1980, p. 261, n.18.
50 In this connection, it is interesting to note that among the gifts taken to Mehmet by Gentile Bellini was Gentile's copy of a pioneering album of perspective drawings that he had inherited from his father, the artist Jacopo Bellini.
51 Venetian reports, cited in Valensi 1990, pp. 181 and 182.
52 The oft-cited Islamic prohibition on images does not appear in the Koran but in the Hadith, a subsidiary text. In the fifteenth century it was a patchily enforced custom rather than a universally applied religious edict. See Bloom and Blair 1997: "It is often said that figures were banned in Islam from the start, but this is untrue. The Koran itself has little to say on the subject … Since the Koran has little in the way of narrative, there was little reason to present stories in religious art, and in time this absence of opportunity hardened into law" (p. 30).
53 Baxandall 1972, p. 3.
54 The authorship of the figure studies of Ottoman people is disputed. The British Museum and the London National Gallery (in the 2005 catalog to the exhibition *Bellini and the East*, ed. Campbell and Chong) ascribe them to Bellini. Raby makes a case for their attribution to the little-known Costanzo (Raby 1991, p. 211), and he is followed in this by Jardine and Brotton 2000, p. 32. For good measure, even the name "Costanzo da Ferrara" is now in dispute, and in Campbell and Chong, the author of the portrait medal of Mehmet is given as "Costanzo di Moysis" (pp. 126–127).
55 See Vickers 1978.
56 Mack 2002, p. 149.
57 For the two interpretations see, respectively, Pixley 2003, p. 9 and Bagci 2004, p. 434.
58 See Necipoglu 1989, pp. 401–427.
59 Howard 2000, p. 36.
60 Fortini Brown 1988, p. 146.
61 Smith, R. 1979. Cf Kaplan 1986, p. 130: "The Venetians themselves, until well into the sixteenth century, did not especially prize black children, but adult Africans were frequently employed as gondoliers."
62 Venice was not alone. Other Italian city-states using slaves included Florence, Genoa and Rome. See also Mignolo 1995.
63 Smith, R. 1979, p. 50.
64 Fortini Brown 1988, pp. 87–97.
65 Raby 1982b, p. 17.

66 Fortini Brown 1988, p. 191, original Bellini document, p. 293.
67 See Howard 2000, pp. 67–74.
68 Wittkower 1989, p. 4.
69 Necipoglu 1989, p. 424.
70 MacLean, ed., 2005, p. 93.
71 Warner 2011, p. 173.
72 Warner 2010, pp. 15–17.

References

Babinger, F., 1978, *Mehmet the Conqueror and his Time*, trans. R. Mannheim, Princeton University Press, Princeton. First published as *Mahomet II, Le Conquerant et Son Temps*, 1954.

Bagci, S., 2004, in D.J. Roxburgh, ed., *Turks: A Journey of a Thousand Years, 600–1600*, catalog entry 226, Royal Academy of Arts, London.

Baxandall, Michael, 1972, *Painting and Experience in Fifteenth Century Italy*, Clarendon Press, Oxford.

Bell, Julian, 2012, "Don't look," review of Belting *Florence and Baghdad*, *London Review of Books*, October 25, pp. 13–14.

Belting, Hans, 2011 *Florence and Baghdad: Renaissance Art and Arab Science*, trans. Deborah Lucas Schneider, The Belknap Press of Harvard University Press, Cambridge, MA and London. First published as *Florenz und Bagdad: Eine westöstliche Geschichte des Blicks*, 2008.

Bloom, J. and S. Blair, 1997, *Islamic Art*, Phaidon, London.

Brotton, Jerry, 2002, *The Renaissance Bazaar: From the Silk Road to Michelangelo*, Oxford University Press, Oxford.

Burckhardt, Jacob, 1990 [1860], *The Civilization of the Renaissance in Italy*, ed. Peter Burke, Penguin Books Ltd., Harmondsworth.

Campbell, C. and A. Chong, eds, 2005, *Bellini and the East*, National Gallery Publications, London.

da Bisticci, Vespasiano, 1963, *Renaissance Princes, Popes and Prelates: The Vespasiano Memoirs*, Harper and Row, New York; original composed c.1480–1498.

Elkins, James and Robert Williams, eds, 2008, *Renaissance Theory*, Routledge, New York and London.

Farago, Claire, ed., 1995, *Reframing the Renaissance. Visual Culture in Europe and Latin America 1450–1650*, Yale University Press, New Haven and London.

Fortini Brown, Patricia, 1996, *Venice and Antiquity*, Yale University Press, New Haven and London.

Fortini Brown, Patricia, 1988, *Venetian Narrative Painting in the Age of Carpaccio*, Yale University Press, New Haven and London.

Greenblatt, Stephen, 1980, *Renaissance Self-Fashioning: From More to Shakespeare*, The Chicago University Press, Chicago.

Howard, Deborah, 1999, "Ruskin and the East," *Architectural Heritage* 10: 37–53.

Howard, Deborah, 2000, *Venice and the East*, Yale University Press, New Haven and London.

Jardine, Lisa, 1996, *Worldly Goods: A New History of the Renaissance*, Macmillan, London and Basingstoke.

Jardine, Lisa and Jerry Brotton, 2000, *Global Interests: Renaissance Art between East and West*, Cornell University Press, Ithaca, NY.

Kaplan, P.H., 1986, "Sicily, Venice and the East: Titian's Fabricius Salvaresius with a black page," in *Europa und die Kunst des Islam 15 bis 18 Jahrhundert*, Akten des XXV Internationalen Kongresses für Kunstgeschichte: Wien 4–10 September, 1983, Vol. 6, Böhlau, Vienna, pp. 127–136.

Mack, R.E., 2002, *Bazaar to Piazza: Islamic and Italian Art 1300–1600*, University of California Press, Berkeley and Los Angeles.

MacLean, Gerald, ed., 2005, with a foreword by William Dalrymple, *Re-Orienting the Renaissance: Cultural Exchanges with the East*, Palgrave Macmillan, Basingstoke and New York.

Martin, J., 1997, "Inventing sincerity, refashioning prudence: the discovery of the individual in Renaissance Europe," *American Historical Review*, 102 (5): 1309–1342.

Martin, J. and D. Romano, eds, 2000, *Venice Reconsidered*, Johns Hopkins University Press, Baltimore.

Mignolo, Walter D., 1995, *The Darker Side of the Renaissance*, University of Michigan Press, Ann Arbor.

Necipoglu, G., 1989, "Sulyeman the Magnificent and the representation of power in the context of Ottoman–Hapsburg–papal rivalry," *The Art Bulletin* 71 (3): 401–427.

Nelson, R.S., 1996, "Living on the Byzantine borders of Western art," *Gesta*, 35 (1): 3–11.

Panofsky, Erwin, 1991 [1927], *Perspective as Symbolic Form*, trans. Christopher S. Wood, Zone Books, New York, pp. 258–330. First published as "Die Perspektive als 'symbolische Form,'" in the *Vorträge der Bibliothek Warburg* 1924–1925, Leipzig and Berlin.

Pedrocco, F., 2002, *The Art of Venice: From its Origins to 1797*, Scala and Riverside, Florence and New York.

Pixley, M.L., 2003, "Islamic artefacts and cultural currents in the art of Carpaccio," *Apollo* 158 (November): 9–18.

Raby, J., 1980, "Cyriacus of Ancona and the Ottoman Sultan Mehmet II." *Journal of the Warburg and Courtauld Institutes* 43: 242–246.

Raby, J., 1982a, "A sultan of paradox: Mehmed the Conqueror as patron of the arts," *Oxford Art Journal* 5 (1): 3–8.

Raby, J., 1982b, *Venice, Dürer and the Oriental Mode*, Sotheby Islamic Art Publications, London.

Raby, J., 1991, "Portrait medal of Mehmet II, in circa 1492: art in the age of exploration," catalog entry 107, National Gallery of Art, Washington.

Richardson, Carol M., ed., 2007, *Locating Renaissance Art*, Yale University Press, New Haven and London.

Roper, William 1962 [c.1560], *The Life of Sir Thomas More*, in R.S. Sylvester and D.P. Harding, eds, *Two Early Tudor Lives*, Yale University Press, New Haven and London.

Said, Edward W., 2003, *Orientalism*, Penguin Books Ltd., London. First published 1978.

Schwab, Raymond, 1984, *The Oriental Renaissance: Europe's Rediscovery of India and the East 1680–1880*, Columbia University Press, New York. First published as *La Renaissance orientale* 1950.

Smith, R., 1979, "In search of Carpaccio's African Gondolier," *Italian Studies* 34: 45–59.

Tafuri, M., 1995, *Venice and the Renaissance*, MIT Press, Cambridge, MA and London. First published 1985.

Valensi, L., 1990, "The making of a political paradigm: the Ottoman State and Oriental despotism," in A. Grafton and A. Blair, eds, *The Transmission of Culture in Early Modern Europe*, University of Philadelphia Press, Philadelphia, pp. 173–204.

Vasari, Giorgio, 1965 [first, Latin edition, 1550; second, Italian edition 1568], *Lives of the Artists*, ed. George Bull, Penguin Books Ltd., Harmondsworth.

Vickers, M., 1978, "Some preparatory drawings for Pisanello's Medallion of John VIII Palaeologus," *The Art Bulletin* 60 (3): 417–424.

Warner, Marina, 2010, "A view of a view," *London Review of Books*, May 27, pp. 15–17.

Warner, Marina 2011, *Stranger Magic: Charmed States and the* Arabian Nights, Chatto and Windus, London.

Wittkower, Rudolf, 1989, *Selected Lectures of Rudolf Wittkower: The Impact of Non-European Civilizations on the Art of the West*, ed. and compiled by Donald Martin Reynolds, Cambridge University Press, Cambridge.

2

Enlightenment and New World

America

Both the classical antiquity of Greece and Rome, and its "renaissance" in fifteenth-century Italy happened in societies which were centered on the Mediterranean. As we have seen the Mediterranean continued to be the area of transitivity where those western European cultures met and traded with cultures further to the east. The so-called Silk Road brought goods out of central and eastern Asia which were then transported across the sea to Europe, and the Mediterranean kept southern Europe in touch with the Islamic Levant and the Maghreb stretching westwards to Morocco. As Wittkower wrote, "the Mediterranean always was an inland waterway that pulled peoples together rather than kept them apart."[1] The Mediterranean was a watery commons which kept the increasingly dynamic western peninsular of Eurasia in mutually productive contact with the richer continental heartlands to the east. But at the end of the fifteenth century the axis of history tilted, and a hitherto unsuspected "New World" was opened to European eyes.

The story of Columbus' accidental discovery of America as the by-product of a Spanish attempt to break the Portuguese monopoly on sea-based trade with the East, is too well-known to repeat here. It is, however, worth recollecting that Columbus carried letters of introduction from Ferdinand and Isabella, the Spanish monarchs, to the "Great Khan," held to be the ruler of China – though, being based on the reports of Marco Polo, this information was two hundred years out of date. It is also worth underlining the point that for the rest of his life, and despite increasing evidence to the contrary, Columbus persisted in thinking that he had found China, and that the island of Cuba was the island of Japan, Marco Polo's "Cipango." By the time of his third voyage, Columbus had come to the conclusion

Western Art and the Wider World, First Edition. Paul Wood.

that the world was not spherical, but pear-shaped, "round everywhere except at the stalk where it juts out a long way ... like a woman's nipple on a round ball." What this meant was that "this land stands highest on the world's surface, being nearest to the sky" which accounted for the "very mild climate." It also led Columbus to believe that he was in the vicinity of the earthly paradise, the location of which had hitherto been a matter of dispute. What turned out to be the mouth of the Orinoco, Columbus believed to be one of the great rivers flowing from paradise, which "lies at the summit of what I have described as the stalk of a pear."[2] Still believing himself to be off the east coast of Asia, Columbus noted that "the gateway is already opened to gold and pearls ... spices and countless other things," and he hoped to press on "to open up trade with Arabia Felix as far as Mecca."[3]

The point of this is not to imply that Columbus was going mad. Columbus' theory was undoubtedly eccentric, but the reason for repeating it is twofold. The first is to underline that even though the Renaissance is usually held to mark a break with the medieval and the beginning of the modern, nonetheless an earlier cosmology was still very much in play at the end of the fifteenth century. The second is to emphasize just how utterly unexpected was the discovery of the "new world" and the extreme lengths to which European Renaissance explorers and intellectuals would go in order to try and make the discoveries conform to their existing frame of reference.

For anyone who is about to travel nowadays, especially to somewhere new, one of the first things to do is to pack a camera. The desire for a visual record is paramount, certainly stronger than the desire to write about it. This was not always so. There are no visual records of the journeys of early European travelers across Asia such as Marco Polo and William of Rubruck, and none, either, of the first Portuguese encounters with Africa or the Spanish discovery of America. In his discussion of the bizarre and seemingly contradictory legalistic rituals with which Columbus took possession of the lands he found, Stephen Greenblatt notes that they took place in the presence of a "recorder." That is, a kind of notary whose job it was to observe and record that everything involved in claiming territory for the Spanish crown was being done properly according to protocol. As Greenblatt points out, this had more to do with establishing priority over any possible future claims by competing European powers than with the rights of the indigenous population. But it was the literary record that was deemed sufficient. No artists traveled on these voyages, and no visual record was kept. Greenblatt observes that the encounter with the New World unleashed "a flood of textual representation." But that same encounter, which we can hardly even conceptualize without summoning up some composite mental image derived from later paintings and films, resulted in only "a much smaller production of visual images."[4] In fact the very earliest encounters resulted in none.

There is no single, simple, explanation of why this should be. Partly it is to do with a lack of the requisite skills. As we have seen in the Introduction, William of

Rubruck actually lamented the inadequacy of verbal description to convey some of the things he was seeing, but he lacked the ability to make a convincing visual representation. One of the acknowledged features of the Renaissance was the way it transformed the status of visual art from a mere craft skill to a scholarly accomplishment. But in the late fifteenth and early sixteenth centuries this conception had not traveled beyond Italy, and neither did it affect the milieu from which Portuguese and Spanish, Dutch and English ship's crews were drawn: obviously not the common sailors (who were largely illiterate) but not the priests, the doctors or the "gentlemen" officers either. A partial exception, however, concerns Baldesar Castiglione's early sixteenth-century *Book of the Courtier*, which included a recommendation that drawing and painting skills, despite appearing "mechanical," could be useful to a gentleman and were something that "our courtier should certainly not neglect."[5] That book had an impact in Elizabethan England, where Italian culture was fashionable, and it functioned as something of a conduit for Renaissance ideas. Painting was not as developed in England as in Italy, either technically or socially, and "limning," essentially painting in watercolor on paper, an activity a gentleman might pursue, was distinguished from the painting of visual supports and decorations for court entertainments, which was still regarded as an artisanal craft skill. Nonetheless, there is evidence that in the circle around Walter Raleigh some of the gentleman courtiers had mastered the art of producing likenesses. One of these, John White, was to produce the most comprehensive set of visual representations of the inhabitants of North America at the moment of European contact. Even then, his drawings themselves were almost completely unknown until the twentieth century. They achieved their fame and their considerable impact from being translated into the new medium of printing.

Part of our modern sense of the ubiquity of visual images derives from our inheritance of the sheer explosion of imagery that begins with printing and culminates in the camera. Printing begins at around the same time as the voyages of exploration, but it was not until the late sixteenth century that it began to be used to circulate images of the New World. Curious as it may sound, and despite the development of perspective in the early fifteenth century which enabled the production of more emphatically lifelike visual images than ever before, it seems as though "art" just was not for that sort of thing, and that "sort of thing" in turn was not yet a fit subject for "art." In the mid-twentieth century, the modernist curator and historian Alfred H. Barr explained the development of abstract art by saying that by "a common and powerful impulse" artists in the European avant-garde "became bored with painting facts." There is a sense in which he could not have been farther from the truth. Whatever happened later on, the astonishingly mimetic art of the Renaissance was not in any serious sense about "painting facts."[6] Works of visual art were enormously complicated and laboriously achieved things, designed painstakingly to convey complex ideological propositions about power, both spiritual and temporal. Anthony Pagden has pointed out that in the Renaissance worldview "it was believed that the nature of the universe and of man could be known only through a body of authoritative texts," mostly the Bible, certain texts of antiquity, and commentaries upon them. By contrast, "empirical data was only of secondary importance and, by and large, had to be fitted into a framework already established by the texts."[7] Over the next two hundred and fifty years, as the European Renaissance evolved into the Enlightenment, as the scientific temper grew, a debate did develop about the relationship of art to naturalistic description. But in this earlier period, "art" is much more concerned with models of ideal beauty than it is with factual accuracy and attention to the particular. It is true that figures such as Leonardo da Vinci and Albrecht Dürer produced startlingly impressive representations of moving water, unusual animals, or even a tussock of grass, but they were the exceptions.

When it comes to curiosity about the "outer world," it does seem that Leonardo had dealings with the Turkish sultan over an engineering project, although no visual material has survived. And on his journey to the Netherlands in 1520–1521, Dürer, while in Antwerp, made a dignified and humanist portrait drawing of his host's black servant, *Katherina, aged 20*. Even more unusual for a famous European artist, on the same journey Dürer actually saw Aztec objects that had been sent back to the Spanish court by Cortez. They were in the baggage train of Charles V, en route to his coronation as Holy Roman Emperor, when Dürer saw them in Brussels on August 27, 1520. Dürer commented at some length in his journal on the various objects "from the new land of gold," including "a sun all of gold a whole fathom broad, and a moon all of silver of the same size," not to mention "very strange clothing" and "all kinds of wonderful objects of human use." Dürer concluded, "All the days of my life I have seen nothing that rejoiced my heart so much as these things, for I saw amongst them wonderful works of art, and I marvelled at the subtle *ingenia* of men in foreign lands."[8] Dürer would have been using the word "art" in its sense of "skilled accomplishment," though there is no doubting his openness to the new things he saw. But he did not use the occasion to make a visual record. This says something, perhaps, both about the complex relation of "art" in its elevated Renaissance sense to the world of objects, and also about the conceptual difficulty involved in representing things never before encountered. In fact, Dürer did subsequently make an unusually tentative sketch of some South American material which was incorporated into marginal designs for the Holy Roman Emperor's prayer book, but this is an exception which proves the rule. Even Dürer, with his non-Italian, northern European interest in the particularity of the visual world, did not produce an album, or a series of prints, or a painting, of American subjects.

There is a sense in which one only has to say that to realize how peculiar it would have been, at that early date. Despite the mastery of techniques allowing mimetic accuracy, art was not a form of illustration. With the partial exception of the brief vogue around the turn of the fifteenth and sixteenth centuries for a form of orientalism in Venetian art that had a great deal to do with contemporary power relations in the eastern Mediterranean, representations of examples of Islamic or Chinese visual culture (such as Turkish carpets, porcelain bowls, and so on) formed no more than a minor, albeit fascinating, sub-theme within European Renaissance art. When it came to America, which was immeasurably more unfamiliar than the East, it is the relative absence of visual images which stands out.

Interestingly, one of the very first artistic images of America to appear in European art came in around 1505 in a Portuguese painting of the Adoration of the Magi. In the biblical story, three wise men, magi, traveled from the east to worship Jesus. It became conventional to represent one or more of the kings as black, or as recognizably non-European, through their clothing or headdress. So it was only taking this a step further when the "Master of Viseu" equipped one of his magi with a Brazilian feather headdress. The point being, of course, that it was still at this point unclear where the new lands were. If they were indeed located at the eastern end of Asia, as Columbus himself thought, then such a king might well have traveled westwards all the way across Asia guided by the star to Bethlehem. Though rare, comparable images of Brazilian "Indians" commemorating more secular activities, can also be found at a relatively early date in three-dimensional form. These include a carved frieze in the Church of St Jacques in Dieppe dating to the 1520s which marks the activities of the merchant Jacques Ango and, in Burford Church in Oxfordshire, the 1569 memorial to Henry VIII's barber, Edmund Harman, who had business interests in Brazil.

Jan van Mostaert's *West Indian Landscape* of c.1540–1550, a picture which has been referred to as "the earliest known painting of a new world subject,"[9] underscores the complex crosscurrents at work. Among the things which are noteworthy about it are that it was painted in Europe on the basis of verbal reports of activities in the New World and that its representation of the naked "Indians" is entirely generic. Although Protestantism was in general more open to scientific inquiry than Counter-Reformation Roman Catholicism was, religious conflict shadowed much visual representation at this period. What motivates Mostaert's picture is not the desire to empirically record a hitherto unknown form of life in all its difference and particularity. It is, rather, a visual contribution to the Protestant "Black Legend" of Spanish cruelty, which was being experienced in the Spanish Netherlands as well as in the New World.

Both the paintings and the relief sculptures mentioned here are isolated examples of art containing reference to the New World, in however oblique and transposed a form, in the first decades after Columbus. Dürer made a small sketch of a few bits of Americana in 1515: a feathered headdress and a skirt-like garment, as well as what may be a ceremonial wand or scepter. But when he came to imagine a composition for them, he fitted them onto a completely Europeanized body. When they emerge on the page of the Emperor Maximilian's prayer book, they seem almost to share more with the marginalia of an illuminated medieval manuscript than a lifelike Renaissance artwork. The first naturalistic representations of South Americans did not emerge until the late 1520s; and again they were made in Europe.

One of the most disquieting features of European encounters with other worlds in the early modern period is the readiness with which the explorers transported various native people, either voluntarily or most often not, back to Europe. This was a practice which predated Columbus and continued after him, through the eighteenth century, and on into the twentieth, for the display of "native villages" at World Fairs and the like. Before him, Africans had gone back with the Portuguese to Lisbon, partly for the purpose of securing military alliance against their enemies, partly on religious grounds to receive instruction in Christianity. In his nineteenth-century study of the Renaissance in Italy, Burckhardt notes a kind of human menagerie kept by Cardinal Ippolito Medici, described as "a troop of barbarians ... all of them perfect specimens of their races" and including "North African Moors, Tartar bowmen, Negro wrestlers, Indian divers and Turks."[10]

Hernán Cortés came upon the Aztec Empire in Mexico in 1519. Within a very short space of time, through a peculiarly repulsive mixture of greed, treachery, superior weapons, and disease, the Spanish had obliterated Aztec culture. It is no overstatement to say that the Spaniards of the Renaissance had no interest in cultural difference as we understand it today. In the inseparably intertwined spheres of commerce and religion, they were more interested in melting down the gold they found into easily transportable bars than admiring its workmanship. For most of them (Father Bartolomé de las Casas being the most notable exception), the "Indians" they encountered were either probably not human at all or at best benighted heathens to be saved for Christianity by fair means or foul, rather than investigated for their customs and artifacts.

In 1528 Cortés sent a group of Mexicans to Europe, where they were paraded to the Spanish court then sent to Rome for the pope's entertainment and from there on to the Spanish Netherlands. They included jugglers and ball players, and when they were in Toledo some of their activities were captured by Christoph Weiditz. Weiditz, a draughtsman from Augsburg (whose presence in Spain testifies to the Habsburg connection), is relatively little known as an artist in his own right, but in 1528–1529 he traveled through the Spanish Netherlands, on to Spain itself, and then back to Augsburg via France and northern Italy. His aim appears to have been to obtain a license allowing him to produce medals, and indeed he did produce a medal of Cortés. But while on the journey he made an album of ink drawings, colored in for greater accuracy, of people engaged in the pastimes of daily life, itself quite an unusual thing to be doing at the time. When he was in Toledo he encountered the Mexicans, and the result was what the London Royal Academy catalog to its *Aztecs* exhibition of 2003 called "the earliest known realistic representations by a European of the inhabitants of the new world."[11] He showed two single figures, one wearing a feathered cape, another holding a parrot, and also depicted two people playing a game involving counters, and two more playing with a ball. Most extraordinary of all, in a series of three related images showing successive movements sequentially (rather like a modern strip cartoon), he pictured a juggler lying on his back on a geometrically decorated mat, twirling a wooden log in the air with his feet (Figure 2.1).

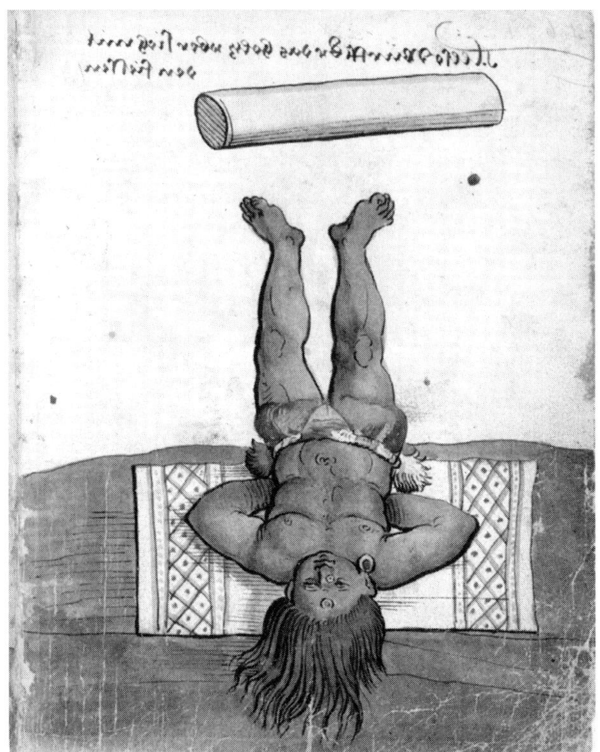

Figure 2.1 Christoph Weiditz: *Tractenbuch*, 1529–1530 (Aztec juggler), Codex, 154 folios, paper, 99 × 14 cm (twentieth-century binding). Germanisches Nationalmuseum, Nuremburg, Hs 22474, f. 9r. Photo: Germanisches Nationalmuseum, Nuremburg.

White and De Bry

Remarkable as they are, Weiditz's images are effectively decontextualized. No representation of ways of life in the new hemisphere was made until later in the century, and both of these were outside the Spanish sphere of influence, in North America. Jacques Le Moyne de Morgues and John White produced drawings of, respectively, the French Huguenot colony in Florida in the 1560s and the British in "Virginia" (modern North Carolina) in the mid-1580s. Neither of these visual records became widely known until they were printed by Theodor de Bry in Frankfurt from 1590 onwards. It is no coincidence that all three men were Protestants.

Theodor de Bry's *America* was one of the grandest publishing projects of his or any other age, yet it was only part of a larger work completed after his death by his sons. The fourteen-volume *America* (or "Great voyages"), published in German and Latin and begun in 1590, was not completed until 1630. The thirteen-volume "Small voyages," also in German and Latin versions, which was begun in 1597 and completed in 1628, concerned voyages to the East Indies and Africa. The first volume of *America*, which consisted of Thomas Harriot's "Briefe and True Report" on the "new found land" of "Virginia" and included printed versions of John White's drawings, was also published in English and French versions. When the art historian Hugh Honour compiled an exhibition and accompanying book of representations of America in the build-up to the bicentennial of the United States, he was stating what had by then become an accepted truth when he wrote that White's pictures were "the first and by far the fullest visual account of America."[12] It is therefore sobering to realize both that these images were first published to a wide audience a century after Columbus' arrival in America, and secondly, to realize how few they are. De Bry's version of Harriot's "Briefe and True Report" included twenty-one printed images of the Algonquian inhabitants and their surroundings. The catalog of the 2007 British Museum exhibition of John White's work contains sixteen of his original drawings of the Algonquians.[13] (The imbalance was either the result of drawings having been lost or the engraver improvising in order to improve and amplify existing drawings.)

All of Le Moyne's images of the Huguenot settlement in Florida were destroyed or lost after printing, not deemed worthy of preservation. The closest we have to them are two copies of Le Moyne's drawings of a Timucuan chief and his wife made by White, probably in the late 1580s when both men were in London, before Le Moyne's death in 1588. It was at this time that de Bry, also in London, conceived his idea for the *America* project. White's original drawings were little known (the first English printing of Herriot's report having been made without illustrations). It is probable that he made copies of them himself for de Bry which were then used in the printing and also subsequently discarded. Nothing is then known of White's original drawings until an album of them turned up in 1788, another two hundred years on. This album then remained in a private library in Dublin until being sent for sale at Sotheby's in London in 1865, whereupon they were almost destroyed by fire, and, in a damaged state, entered the collection of the British Museum. It was not until the early twentieth century that they became more widely known and comparisons became possible between White's original drawings and de Bry's printed versions.

This relationship introduces a key point of tension into the question of the veracity of European representations of the rest of the world. The question will be discussed in more detail in relation to eighteenth-century images of the Pacific, but here, too, at the turn of the sixteenth and seventeenth centuries, the question of the "truth" of visual representations cannot be avoided. The basic point, and it is a far-reaching one, is that visual images tend to be conventional. There is an enormous literature on both the mechanics and the philosophy of visual perception which it is quite beyond our present scope to engage. But Bernard Smith makes the point clearly in his discussion of eighteenth-century encounters between European artists and people and landscapes that were new to them. Smith invoked "a cognitive theory of perception: that seeing is conditioned by knowing."[14] The argument here is that "seeing" involves "seeing-as"; that is, that perception involves elements of interpretation, of striving to reconcile perceptual information with conceptual frameworks. In the postmodernist period this position has sometimes been taken to an extreme to underwrite claims for a radical incommensurability between different worldviews or different cultural formations: the idea that language constructs the world, and that "reality" is an effect of language. Once again it would be out of place to go too far into this debate here. There is undoubtedly a premium on translation between different languages, and, given the foregoing, translation between different cultural perspectives, but I would want to follow Smith in agreeing that subscribing to a cognitive theory of perception does not of necessity precipitate one into a form of extreme cultural relativism.

Whatever the finer points of theoretical dispute, Smith is surely right to assume that in the case of eighteenth-century representations of the people and culture of the South Pacific – and by extension, of sixteenth- and seventeenth-century representations of America – it is possible to distinguish between relatively "accurate and faithful descriptions" and "distortions and errors"; and it is also possible to read "silences" – the cases where some things may be omitted not necessarily to mislead or falsify in a mendacious fashion but because they may not conform to a complex and multifaceted sense of what is at stake. As we have seen, the encounter with new worlds gave rise to a flood of verbal descriptions and arguments. The point about arguments is that they proceed from different assumptions about the world. It would be naïve to think that a visual description is either simpler than a verbal description or somehow insulated from the clash of points of view on the basis of which all representation seems to proceed. The way a complex visual representation is constructed out of an interplay of lights and darks, lines and colors is both different from and similar to the way a verbal representation is based on the systematic relationships of conventional signs in language. This is not to say that pictures are like sentences, because they are not. But neither is it the case that something called "resemblance" or mimetic accuracy supervenes over all choice in the construction of a visual representation. Drawings, paintings, sculptures, etc. are not photographs; indeed, as we have learned, even photographs include elements of choice in their constructions of meaning. Most of the time, what counts as a visual truth, as a relationship of "resemblance" between some marks on a flat surface and a three-dimensional thing in the world is no simpler or less convention-bound than the relation between words and things.

One only has to look at White's depictions of the plants, birds, and animals of the new world to see that he was capable of an extraordinary degree of fidelity to visual appearance. If White's lizards and parrots, seashells, flies, and flamingos do not convey visual "truths," then nothing does. Of course, everyone is familiar with the fact that even as great an artist as Dürer, while capable of representing a hare with breathtaking fidelity, made something like an engine of war out of a rhinoceros when working from a verbal description. But although even he has occasional lapses – his alligator leaves something to be desired – for the most part White's flora and fauna (none of which were included in de Bry's printed version of Harriot's Report) are scrupulously observed and recorded.[15] It is with the representation of human beings and their complex relationships that gaps begin to open up, gaps which can only increase when the multilayered and above all public process of printing comes into play.

Let us take two examples, a figure group and a landscape. White made his visual records as a complement to Thomas Harriot's textual account of the new colony of "Virginia." As such it was intended to persuade others, back in England, of the benefits of following. The result has been that it is widely accepted that, for all their accuracy and documentary value, White's pictures offer a positively inflected and somewhat sanitized image of the area's indigenous inhabitants. There are no scenes of conflict between the settlers and the Indians, no representation of practices such as cannibalism and human sacrifice, no indication that the native inhabitants quickly began to die of European diseases. There is also no sense that the area was undergoing a drought which had caused crops to fail, as a consequence of which the inhabitants scarcely had enough food for themselves, let alone to support additional incomers. Instead, the image of indigenous life is of harmony both among themselves and with the Europeans in a land of plenty. Twenty-first-century postcolonialists, no less than sixteenth-century would-be colonists, need to see what White does not show.

White made two pictures of "towns," including the settlement of Secoton (Figure 2.2). As well as showing houses and crops this picture included scenes of

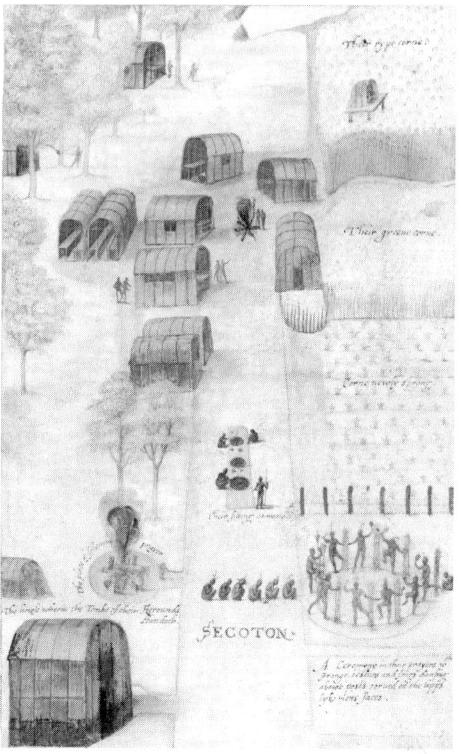

Figure 2.2 John White, *The Town of Secoton*, 1585, watercolor over black lead heightened with bodycolor, inscribed in brown ink with notes, 32 × 20 cm. British Museum, 1906, 0509.1.7. The Art Archive / British Museum / Eileen Tweedy.

the inhabitants eating and engaged in social rituals involving their religion, a circular dance, and praying around a fire. The intention was to demonstrate a level of social organization – to show that the Indians were not mere savages – and the presence of a form of organized religious belief, the implication of which was that they would be capable of being converted to Christianity. White emphasized the fecundity of the land by showing corn crops in three stages, "newly sprung," "green," and "ripe," something which was not actually the case. When the scene was engraved for publication in the first volume of de Bry's *America* these aspects were emphasized further. The three-stage corn crop was supplemented by fertile plots of pumpkins, sunflowers, and tobacco, and the layout of the village as a whole was neatened up and formalized, to suggest, in the words of the British Museum catalog "pathways and gardens rivalling those of an English country house."[16]

The difference between drawings made on the spot and prints produced in a workshop for wider circulation marks a feature of European images of encounters with the wider world which continued to be of great significance. The difference is frequently most pronounced in the representation of human figures. In White's original drawing of the wife of a "chief of Pomeiooc" and her daughter (Figure 2.3), the two figures are placed relatively close together as well as being set on the blank white of the page. The two figures are not located in any wider spatial environment but only in relation to each other. In de Bry's engraving, however, the entire orientation of the image is shifted from "portrait" to "landscape" format (Figure 2.4). The figures' relationship to each other is extended laterally, and they are also set against a quite detailed, spatially recessive landscape background in which indigenous people are involved in a variety of practices of hunting and fishing. The most noticeable thing is the way that in the print, as compared with the drawing, the main figures are Europeanized. Their skin color is lightened and the woman's tattoos are minimized; curiously she is given some on her legs where none exist in the drawing, but those on her arms are lightened and those on her face almost disappear. The facial features of both mother and daughter are made significantly more European. In terms of pose, the girl is made to lean forward at a much more pronounced angle as if actively demanding her mother's attention, while the mother looks down at her as if responding. The girl is also taller and physically more robust and shapely than in the drawing. The mother herself, standing with both feet on the ground in the drawing, is translated in the print into a Renaissance contrapposto pose with her weight on one foot, meant to introduce a sense of movement and dynamic tension. In both the drawing and the print the girl is holding a European doll, but in the print, as well as being more precisely delineated, the doll is turned round, and the girl is also given a European rattle which is not there at all in the drawing. It has been claimed that the doll was of an unusually expensive kind, perhaps given because of the high social status of the mother and daughter.

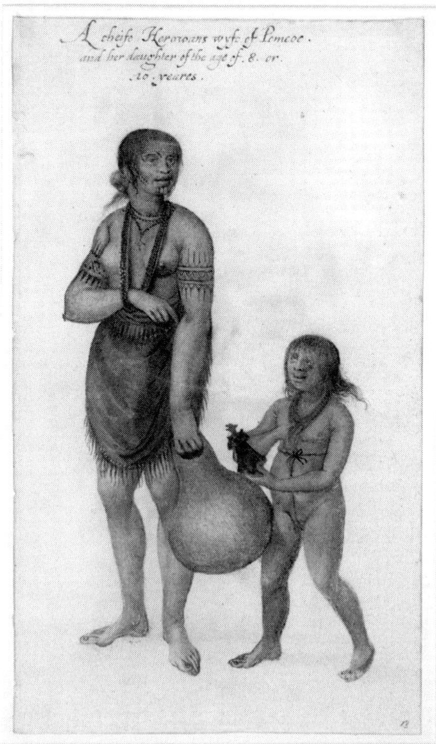

Figure 2.3 John White, *A wife of an Indian werowance or chief of Pomeiooc, and her daughter*, 1585, watercolor over black lead, heightened with bodycolor, white, and gold, inscribed in brown ink, 26 × 15 cm. British Museum, 1906, 09.1.13. © The Trustees of the British Museum.

The overall effect seems to be to bring the pair within the recognizable orbit of a European family ambience. It minimizes some of the difference evident in the drawing, such that a viewer of the print might be more inclined to think that the people of Pomeiooc are "more like us" than the original drawing might have suggested – which given that the purpose of Harriot's brochure was to encourage colonists, is no small part of the point of the exercise. The sense of "scientific," or at this date at least of relatively objective, looking has to be balanced against the propagandistic, commercial nature of the enterprise. This is a very delicate area, however, and speculating about what sense the sixteenth-century viewer of de Bry's print may have made of it must remain in large part just that: speculative. The author of the relevant passage in the modern British Museum catalog, though, presses her reading further. For her, White's original drawing "depicts a self-content, proud and vigilant woman." Whereas, in de Bry's print, the group "lacks all contentedness, confidence and harmony which, as a result, leaves the onlooker with a strong feeling of cultural superiority."[17] I find it hard not to see this reading

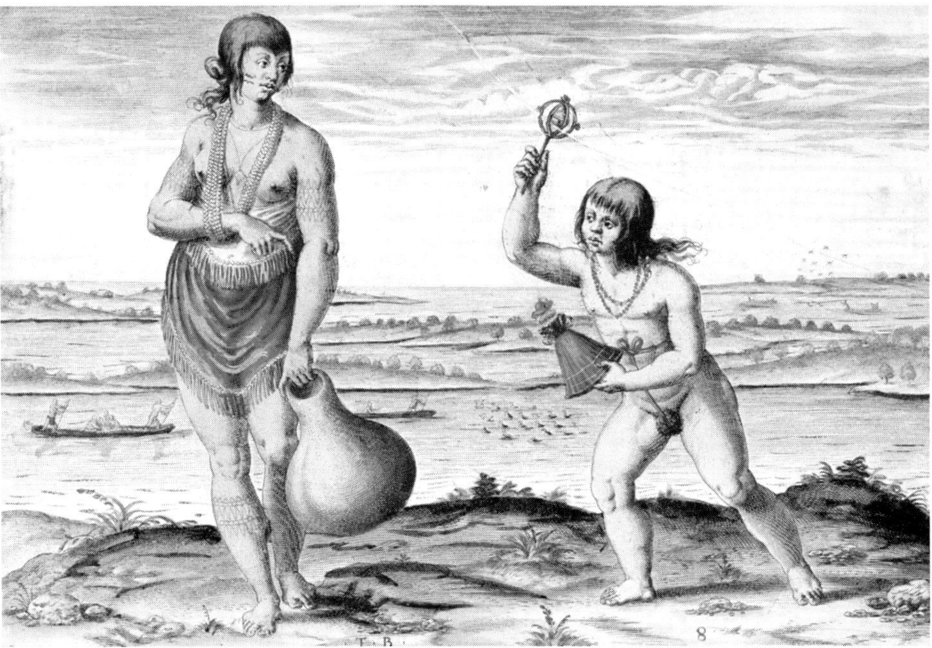

Figure 2.4 Theodor de Bry after John White, *A Chief Lady of Pomeiooc*, color engraving from *America*, 1590, plate 8. Service Historique de la Marine, Vincennes, France / Giraudon / The Bridgeman Art Library.

as a product of a late-twentieth- / early-twenty-first-century cultural politics. The sense in which the conventions of European art were employed in the early modern period to frame for public consumption images of people from elsewhere in the world is now readily seen as a touchstone for a kind of already implicit racism, forming a continuum with the explicit racism of the later imperialist period of the nineteenth century. Certainly these images are by no means "neutral," always loaded, never less than complex. But simply to press them into a congenial template of our own day seems, paradoxically, to share more with the original operation of forcing the images into a Eurocentric mold than would leaving the matter of their meanings open and less readily decideable.

For all their remarkable fidelity at one level, then, White's watercolors of the native peoples of America occupy an unstable semantic terrain. They both are and are not "truthful" in their own right, in the implied selection of what to represent and what not to represent. And when translated into the medium of print they become even more susceptible to a recoding into the conventional categories of European representation, involving both the protocols of "art" and evolving and contested ideas about humankind itself.

The pictures of Le Moyne and White as they became widely available through de Bry's prints came to form a kind of lexicon or repertoire, a basis for images of the American Other in European representation on into the eighteenth century. In this they share something with the Venetian images of Ottomans, Mamluks, and "orientals" generally, produced around the turn of the fifteenth and sixteenth centuries, relatively few in number in themselves but providing an anchorage for numerous subsequent depictions long into the future. It is a significant point that such images were more influential in helping to construct and inflect a European picture of the world than were any artifacts of the native peoples themselves which found their way into Europe.

North American objects of wood or bone or leather had a comparable reception to similar things brought back from the Pacific two hundred years later. What is perhaps more surprising from a modern perspective is the fate of objects from the developed civilizations of the Aztecs and Incas. Despite the recorded appreciation of an artist such as Dürer, or indeed the "wonder" felt by sundry monarchs to whom they were presented, almost all the metal objects imported to Europe were melted down. An important category emerges here. For the things that were preserved and studied were retained not as "art,'" but as "curiosities."

European Responses

As long ago as 1975, Hugh Honour noted of the Aztec objects brought to Europe in the early sixteenth century, that "they appear to have had no influence whatsoever on the arts of Europe."[18]

Honour went on to contrast the way in which earlier European artists in the fourteenth century had incorporated devices from Chinese and Islamic objects as decorative elements in Gothic ornament. In contrast, "by the early sixteenth century, Europeans had become much too obsessed with their classical past to respond to the products of cultures as different from their own as the Maya, Aztec and Inca." Interestingly, he adds the observation that "such objects seemed to them still more barbarous than those in the Gothic style from which they had just shaken themselves free."

This returns us to a group of ideas discussed earlier. Although modern scholarship has been interested to reemphasize connections between the Renaissance period and the medieval period, as well as between Italy and other places from Antwerp to Prague, there remains a sense in which to those involved at the time, the arguments of Vasari and others reinforced a sense of their own distinction, both from what had gone before – that is historically – and from what took place elsewhere – that is, geographically. It subsequently became a cliché of Western thinking that its mimetic art indicated not only a technical advance over, but also a civilizational superiority over, other cultures. This sixteenth-century response, whereby European Renaissance art sailed serenely on, untouched by any implications of cultural or artistic relativism that might have been derived from the encounter with such radical Others, suggests something of that attitude. It also implies something slightly different: that for all its status as a cornerstone of the subsequent Western canon of art, the development of perspective in the Renaissance, and its accompanying quality of lifelikeness, served to *reduce* the openness of European artists to the products of other cultures. Even as European artists were extending their capacity to encompass images of the people and products of other cultures within the terms of their own representational codes, that very ability helped insulate Europeans from engaging with the beliefs and practices of the Other as equals.

This development in the sphere of art fits with another evolving circumstance. As we have seen, when artifacts from overseas were retained they were kept as "curiosities" rather than as works of "art," which was a quite separate category reserved for a particular range of European cultural products. However, the construction of princely and scholarly "cabinets of curiosities" had other implications. The range of human artifacts seemingly had little or no impact on the making of "Fine Art" within the force field of the European academies between the Renaissance and the Enlightenment. However, the second order of "curiosities," namely "natural curiosities," most certainly did have an influence on the emerging practice of science. Strange birds and plants, new foodstuffs – including the pineapple as well as the potato – fishes and tobacco and other exotic luxuries, all had a profound impact on the European mind, stimulating the desire to analyze, describe, classify, and explain, as well as consume.

There is thus something of an asymmetry between the responses of European art and science to the New World. But there is also something which is shared. In the way they create a distance between the observer and the observed, between subject and object, both perspective and the burgeoning scientific attitude form a powerful combination separating European culture and society from the various Others it encountered. In the late medieval and early Renaissance periods, encounters took place on a much more equal footing. By the time of the "high" Renaissance an imbalance was beginning which formed the framing condition for subsequent encounters and relations in later periods. Perspective in art, or rather, the coherent fictive space it enabled, dovetailed well with the emerging scientific temper and the kind of representation it required.

This is an issue with potentially far-reaching implications. We have already encountered the question of the development of perspective and Belting's claim that it depended on Islamic science. This argument for the significance of cultural interaction is well taken, but there can be no question that whatever the hybridity of its derivation, perspective became the hallmark of the Western tradition of visual art after the Renaissance. Panofsky, building on Cassirer, has called it a "symbolic form": in Julian Bell's gloss, "a cohesive set of symbols" with which to "give shape to the world."[19] The implication here is that a mode of representation to some significant degree sets the terms for the way in which the thing represented is understood. It is a short step to saying then that the world comes to the West in the terms of its dominant representational modality, that perspectival representation as it were delivers up the world to the West. It is this kind of claim, and not merely the fact that mimetic accuracy in drawing was taught in art schools throughout the British and French empires, that underwrites the postcolonial argument that perspectival art was complicit in the operation of imperialism. It is easy to overinflate the rhetoric of such a claim and make it sound ridiculous. On the other hand, however, there is no doubting that the development of a systematic grid of latitude and longitude was crucial to the European ability to navigate the oceans and ultimately establish empires. The objectivization of real space through accurate measurement of latitude and longitude is a sort of counterpart for the objectivization of virtual space through the grid of perspective representation. The emerging scientific outlook of the modern European worldview enabled both. And once one comes to regard representation as not merely reflecting but in important respects constituting or constructing reality, the more it is possible to draw connections between Western art and other operations of Western power. It would be ridiculous to claim that perspective causes imperialism, just as it is in my view ridiculous to argue that the thought of the European Enlightenment is inseparable from imperialism. But by the same token it would be no less ridiculous to maintain that there is no connection at all.

Something of the temper bred up by perspectival representation, the fundamental technique for the production of lifelikeness, and its elaborate codification through the academic system with its "Parts" of art and its hierarchy of genres, can be glimpsed from debates within the nascent Académie Royale in Paris. As part of the late seventeenth-century debate as to the relative merits of the Ancients and Moderns, Charles Perrault emphatically defended the achievements of the artists of the Renaissance over those of antiquity because of their use of perspective. In a brief aside he also let slip a sense of the way in which attitudes to the past history of art also carried over into geography. For Perrault, the achievements of Raphael, Titian, Veronese, and subsequently Poussin, set the standard of art. He then remarks that "some years before Raphael and Titian, there were paintings made – they still survive – the principal beauty of which lies in the fineness of line; you can count every hair in the beard and on the head of each figure." This does not sound like a description of ancient painting, or indeed of Giotto, but it might be a reference to fifteenth-century work, possibly from northern Europe. It is this against which the High Renaissance development is measured. However, in a telling aside, Perrault observes that "though Chinese art is very ancient, they have remained at this stage." That is, previous European art, as well as the most sophisticated example of non-European art that he can think of, is on a lower stage of development than modern Renaissance, and post-Renaissance work. He goes on, "They will, perhaps, soon learn to draw properly, to place their figures in noble attitudes, and attain exact expression of all the passions. But it will be a long time before they attain a perfect understanding of chiaroscuro, the degradation of light, the secrets of perspective and the judicious organisation of a large composition."[20]

For Perrault and his fellow academicians, perspective and the related techniques by which three-dimensional objects and space were mimetically rendered on a two-dimensional surface were not a culturally relative mode of representation distinguishing European art from, say, the Chinese or indeed the ancient Egyptian. They marked an absolute advance, one which any other culture would have to emulate in exactly the same way they would have to emulate European science and technology – and by implication the social forms which subtended those developments – if they were not to remain on some lower plane of development; and thus they were susceptible to being consigned to a subordinate position in the rapidly progressing modern world. With benefit of hindsight, it is almost too easy for us to see this against a backdrop of imperialism and slavery. To seventeenth-century European intellectuals, such a thought would simply be beyond the horizon of meaning. To the extent that meaning did attach to the cultural and social hierarchy implicit in Perrault's comparisons, they would be validated by ideas of civilization and barbarism. Moreover, such ideas were not short-lived. In fact they became the entrenched commonsense of European cultural comparison.

Science

However, academic art was far from being entirely in step with developing science. Indeed, the question of the relationship between art and science began to bear upon an increasing tension which was developing within the sphere of art itself. An important historical example of this occurs, somewhat paradoxically, at almost exactly the moment when "art" buttressed its status within European culture with the establishment of the French Royal Academy in 1648. Within the Catholic absolute monarchies, France particularly, art took on a public role within the functioning of the state that was not substantially challenged until the changed conditions of nineteenth-century modernity. However, as we have already seen in the case of John White, the Protestant temper seems to have left more room for a form of analytical visual inquiry. One should perhaps not make too much of this, for the Spanish had attempted a synoptic study of Mexico in the 1570s. But the results were not published until the middle of the seventeenth century. Moreover, both the visual records and decorations in the royal palace that had been based on them were destroyed by fire in 1671. The Dutch attraction to what has been called "an art of describing," however, did come into play as the merchant-capitalist Netherlands began to reach out into the world.[21] When the Dutch states separated from Spain in the early seventeenth century, their main efforts were put into the spice trade with the East Indies, present-day Indonesia. But another consequence was a short-lived Dutch colony in South America that existed between 1630 and 1654. The well-known Dutch East India Company was joined by a West India Company which set up a colony in the northeastern corner of Brazil. For a brief

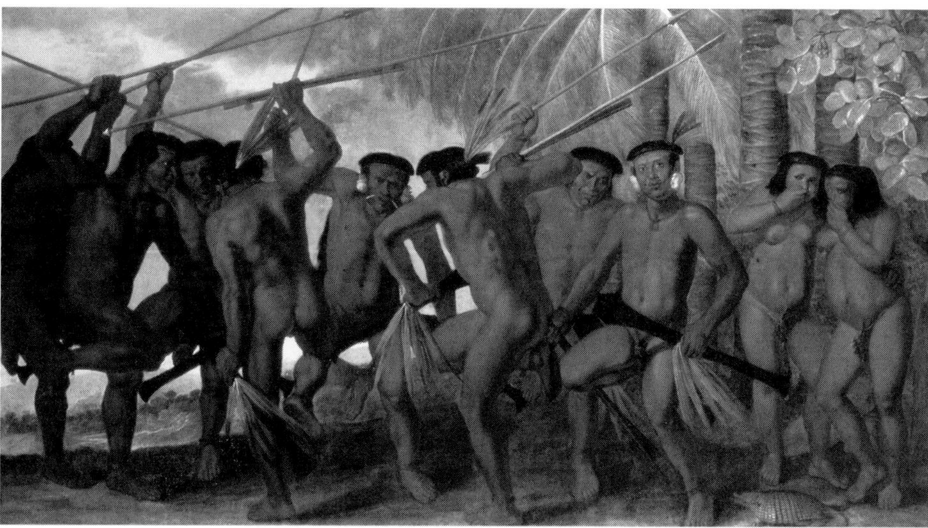

Figure 2.5 Albert Eckhout, *Tapuya Dance*, c.1645, oil on canvas, 168 × 294 cm, National Museum of Denmark, Copenhagen. Photo: akg-images.

period in the late 1630s and 1640s the governor of the colony was Maurits van Nassau-Siegen, who used his time to launch an ambitious scientific program (regarded not as divorced from but as complementary to the commercial aims of the organization) to document the flora and fauna, both animal and human, of the area. The resulting publication, the *Historiae naturalis Brasiliae*, remained definitive until the work of Humboldt in the nineteenth century.

As part of his team of researchers, Prince Maurits took scientists who investigated tropical medicine as well as mapping and documenting the colony; a task in which they were supported by two artists, Frans Post and Albert Eckhout. Post was a landscape painter who made drawings of plants and animals as well as the land, both wild and cultivated. On his return to the Netherlands he produced many composite paintings of Brazilian landscapes based on studies made *in situ*. Eckhout also made vividly detailed studies of South American fruits and vegetables of a presence that almost deserves the name "portraits." But he was also involved in documenting the human inhabitants. Both in his on-the-spot drawings and in subsequent worked-up large-scale figure paintings, Eckhout retained a degree of naturalism rare in European art before the nineteenth century. Many of his studies were of posed single figures. But one in particular documented on a grand scale (almost three meters wide) a multifigure scene of eight male members of the Tapuya tribe engaged in a ceremonial dance, with two female figures looking on (Figure 2.5). There was nothing comparable to this until William Hodges went to the Pacific with Captain Cook in the 1770s and on his return composed large-scale oil paintings of Tahiti based on his studies made from life during the voyage.

Allegory

But normative art in the baroque period remained relatively untouched by science. The principal way in which increasing knowledge of the world impacted on European art was through the use of allegory. The use of allegorical figures to represent the continents first appeared in the late sixteenth century and began to gather pace in the early seventeenth, perhaps stimulated by the publication of Cesare Ripa's *Iconologia* in 1604. Rubens, who had himself purchased several volumes of de Bry's *America*, produced an allegorical representation of the continents using male figures as river gods in 1615. In Rome, Bernini likewise employed the motif of river gods, accompanied by appropriate local fauna, to personify the continents in his 1651 fountain in the Piazza Navona: the Danube for Europe, Nile for Africa, Ganges for Asia, and the River Plate for America, whose representative figure was an armadillo. In the late 1670s, Louis XIV's artistic director, Charles Le Brun, decorated a staircase in Versailles used for the reception of foreign ambassadors with representations of the continents as if paying homage to the king. Again male figures were featured; for example, a classically proportioned nude "Indian" for America. This provided a model for similar schemes in England, as, for instance, in Louis Laguerre's murals at Blenheim Palace. Here, exotic figures, including Chinese, look down from an illusionistic balcony on real-life celebrations of the Duke of Marlborough's victories. But the predominant imagery for allegory soon settled into the use of female figures. Europe tended to be represented by a noble, fully draped, often armed figure, dispensing the benefits of civilization to her exotic, more lightly clad sisters surrounded by images of nature's fecundity. Such imagery became ubiquitous in two and three dimensions: in country houses throughout Britain, for example, as often as not funded by investments in the East India Company or in various West Indian plantation schemes. The culmination of this tradition is, however, to be found in Germany, in the Residenz of the paradoxically landlocked principality of Würzburg (Figure 2.6). Here, in 1753, one of the greatest artists of the age, Giambattista Tiepolo, composed a vast decorative scheme representing the continents around the four sides and ceiling of the grand staircase of the Prince-Bishop's palace.

During the long period of the dominance of the academic ideal in European art it happened more than once that vitality migrated to the margins of art. Thus in the nineteenth century the technical innovations which began to challenge the conventions of academic "finish" began in the relatively lowly genre of landscape. In the eighteenth century, as Smith noted, some of the pressure exerted on European culture by the discovery of a much wider, more multifarious world than could be accommodated within rehearsals of classical antiquity was released in the decorative arts. One of the key features of the modern system of the arts which began to crystallize in the eighteenth century was the categorical distinction between the "fine" arts, with its hierarchy of genres at the apex of which stood history painting, and the so-called lesser arts of decoration and craft. Thus a range of activities from tapestry

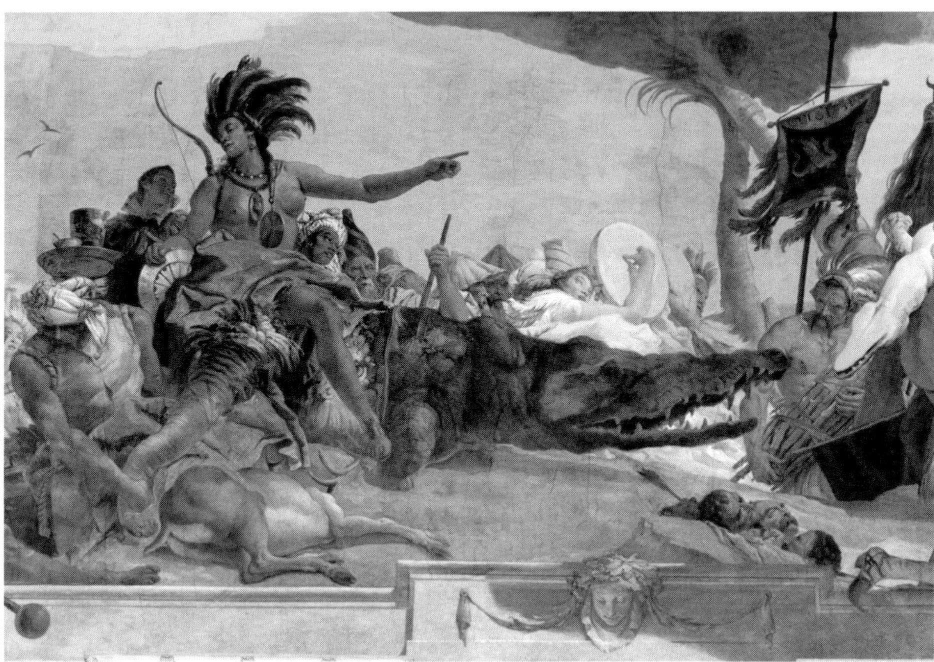

Figure 2.6 Giambattista Tiepolo, *The Continent of America*, detail from *Apollo and the Continents*, ceiling fresco, staircase, Würzburg, Residenz, Episcopal Palace, 1750–1753. Photo: akg-images.

to goldsmithing, interior decoration to print, many of which had been of equal if not higher status than painting, became downgraded. The French monarchy had been in receipt of gifts from Prince Maurits of Nassau, along with several other European royal houses, and though these did not issue in large-scale projects of history painting, the exotic imagery did eventually find an outlet in tapestry. Beginning in 1687, the royal tapestry factory of Gobelins produced *Les Indes*, a major series involving eight different scenes (followed in the mid-eighteenth century by an equally extensive second series). In similar fashion, Tiepolo's large-scale decorative scheme spreads round the walls and ceiling of the Würzburg Treppenhaus (staircase) without regard for single point perspective and the carefully staged dramatic climax of the typical academic history painting.[22] Instead the products and activities of the wider world spilled laterally across the walls, affording continually different views and points of interest to a mobile spectator. These include the masts and spars of trading ships, bales of stuff, exotic animals, traders – in one case, Europeans bargaining for pearls – and a profusion of strange costumes, all cohered, if indeed they are cohered, by the allegorical female figures around whom the activity is arranged. Europa is surrounded by the arts, painting, music, and architecture as well as symbols of the Christian religion. The other three continents effectively pay tribute to Europe, ranged around the walls facing Europe, who is the last to appear to the view of a spectator ascending the marble staircase. Asia fully clothed, rides sidesaddle on an elephant amid scenes of thriving commerce. Africa and America, both bare-breasted, the latter with a bow and arrow and a mighty feathered headdress, seated astride a gigantic alligator (an image of America since Ripa), preside over teeming images of the fruitfulness of their continents. In a comic note, a European artist appears to be clambering over the parapet, presumably anxious to capture the parade.

Enlightenment and Empire

By the middle of the eighteenth century, however, European attitudes were changing. Allegory was beginning to seem dated. Religion, which throughout the Renaissance and the seventeenth century had formed the backdrop against which all emancipatory discourse, political and scientific alike, was tested, was on the retreat. The Church, though it remained powerful, was no longer so dominant everywhere, the horizons of secular knowledge were expanding, and commerce, industry, and technology were gathering force. Under the impact of the Copernican revolution, which had disturbed the sense of an inviolable, divinely ordained universe, as well as the vastly expanded knowledge of the terrestrial globe, the intellectual horizon of educated Europeans was changing from that of their predecessors. The wonder is that art was so static. Whereas everything from agriculture to navigation had progressed by leaps and bounds, art still looked to the sixteenth century as a period of unsurpassed achievement. It is arguably a category mistake to regard art as susceptible to description in terms of "progress," and as we have seen, doing so was precisely one of the factors that aligned European art with a wider imperialism. Nonetheless, the sense of art continually looking to the past for its models during a period of dynamic historical change could and did lead to academic art coming to seem in important respects out of step with the modern world. The full force of burgeoning modernity would not be felt in the arts until the mid-nineteenth century. Indeed, its delayed reception is perhaps one reason for the sheer force of modernism's impact when it came, both symptom and cause of a profound split within the culture which echoed down to the second half of the twentieth century.

But that is to anticipate. Notwithstanding the tardiness of art, the world of the Enlightenment was already much larger and more complex than that of the Renaissance. However, despite the settlement of America by Europeans and the establishment of routine commerce between Europe and the "Spice Islands" of the East Indies, the world was not even fully mapped, let alone fully comprehended. The business of European expansion, whether we mean that literally in terms of political and economic power, or metaphorically in terms of expanding the frontiers of knowledge, was still at an early stage. It is unwise to project nineteenth-century images of race and empire unproblematically back onto the eighteenth century. The wider world was still a long way from being the property of the West.

At this time in the mid-eighteenth century, the earlier imperial power of Portugal and Spain had declined, and after a period of prominence in the seventeenth century, so too had that of the Netherlands. France and England were engaged in a struggle for global supremacy, to the point that there are grounds for considering the Seven Years War, fought out between them from 1756 to 1763, as the de facto first world war. It ended with the defeat of the French in North America and the beginning of a long period of British power in India (albeit initially not through the offices of the British state as such but through the activities of the East India Company). Although the British quickly lost control of North America they maintained a stake in its economic development, and there was little immediate threat from the French. Nonetheless, global power was still in the balance, as was to be proved in the next generation by the forces arising from the French revolution and the wars that followed. But meantime, the "revolutionary empire" of Great Britain (to use Angus Calder's phrase) turned its attention to the south and east to secure its global dominance.

Pacific

The British naval officer James Cook had already demonstrated unusual navigational and management skills during the conflict with the French in North America, which made him a prime candidate when the Admiralty began to look for someone to fulfill the daunting task of surveying the Pacific. Not that Cook was the first European to sail the Pacific. Spanish, Portuguese, and Dutch ships had staggered across it since Ferdinand Magellan's first circumnavigation in the 1520s.[23]

Since antiquity there had persisted the myth of a great southern continent, *Terra Australis*. Earlier voyages kept fuelling the fires with sightings of coastlines that were then never found again. By the 1760s, William Dalrymple, a prominent figure of the Scottish Enlightenment, influential also in London, had collated all available information, and the Admiralty was becoming interested in forestalling the French in the final discovery of the conjectured landmass. Tahiti had been stumbled across by Captain Samuel Wallis in 1766. Very quickly, stories of Wallis' encounter and the report of the French navigator Louis Antoine de Bougainville's visit in 1768 lit the touchpaper of the European imagination. For Bougainville, the island was "*une nouvelle Cythère*," the legendary island of Venus, a paradise on earth, an exotically sensuous realization of one of Boucher's arcadian pastorals. Added to that, the Royal Society, with the active support of George III, was petitioning for a voyage into the "South Seas" to further scientific knowledge: specifically, to calculate Earth's distance from the sun. This involved measuring the "transit of Venus" across the sun in 1769 from a base in Tahiti. These factors combined to prompt the Admiralty to organize Cook's three Pacific voyages between 1768 and 1780. The Cook voyages were thus at one level an expression of the

Enlightenment quest for knowledge. They were also a product of the workings of power – the contest for world supremacy between England and France.

Cook left England on his first Pacific voyage in the ship *Endeavour* in August 1768 and returned after three years in July 1771. On it he was accompanied by Joseph Banks, an independently wealthy landowner and botanist, who was influential within the Royal Society. He was subsequently to become its president for forty years, and as such, one of the central figures of the British Enlightenment. Because of its overtly scientific aspect, the first Cook voyage included two visual artists under the command of Banks: Alexander Buchan and Sydney Parkinson. Parkinson was a trained draughtsman whose task was to produce descriptive illustrations of natural phenomena such as plants, animals, and fishes and, importantly for the Admiralty, coastal profiles. Buchan's job was different. For Banks, the voyage offered an opportunity to undertake the Grand Tour to end all Grand Tours. As he responded to those who urged him to travel to Italy: "Every block head does that, my Grand Tour shall be one round the whole globe."[24] Buchan was to use his skills as a figure painter to provide the visual record of his master's encounters with the native inhabitants.

Buchan died en route, however, and left little behind except for a study of "Indians" on Tierra del Fuego. The result was that Parkinson had to shoulder the whole burden, something he did with considerable success, compiling a then unparalleled record of both natural and human novelty. The latter included Polynesian ceremonies and buildings and, not least, the widespread practice of tattooing. One of Parkinson's records of a Maori with facial tattoos has been accounted the most frequently reproduced image from the whole spectrum of Pacific exploration (Figure 2.7). Its combination of a relatively objective rendering of the patterns of the tattoo design on the subject's face and the obviously Europeanized head of its ostensibly Maori subject raises again the question encountered with John White's pictures of the inhabitants of North America. At issue in the Pacific, no less so than across the Atlantic, are the terms which European artists found to represent their Oceanic "Others": the question of their supposed distortion of reality because of their conditioning by the classical heritage of European art.

Having found and mapped the east coast of Australia on his first voyage, Cook was sent on a second voyage in July 1772, this time in the *Resolution*, with a second ship the *Adventure*. Again there was a contingent of civilian scientists and an artist. The naturalists were Johann Reinhold Forster and his son George, both of whom subsequently published accounts of the voyage. The artist was the young landscape painter William Hodges. Although Hodges did not make the greatest number of drawings and paintings of the Cook voyage artists he does have some claim to have produced the most ambitious works, in the form of oil paintings exhibited at the Royal Academy. These were worked up in London from drawings, sketches, and oil studies made on the voyage. The *Resolution* returned in 1775 after three huge sweeps of the southern ocean which effectively disproved the ancient myth of an unknown and rich *Terra Australis*.

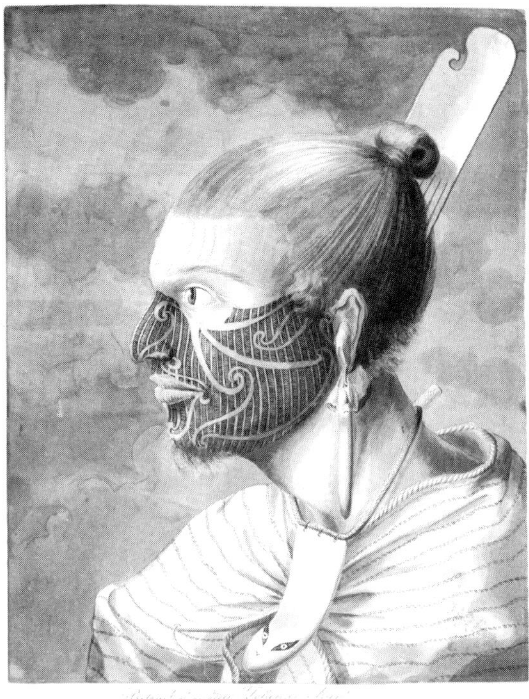

Figure 2.7 Sydney Parkinson, *Portrait of a New Zealand Man*, 1769, pen and ink wash, 40 × 30 cm. From "A Collection of Drawings," British Library Ms. Add. 23920, fol.54. Photo: akg-images / British Library.

Art and Visual Truth

Because of conflicts between Cook and the Admiralty on one side and the irascible Forster senior about the official publication of the second voyage, no civilian scientists were taken on the third voyage, which took place between 1776 and 1780 (and which was marked by Cook's death in Hawaii in 1779). However, an artist was taken, who now worked directly with Cook. The English-Swiss John Webber produced the largest number of studies, mostly in pencil and watercolor, of any of the three voyages. Webber was a skilled portrait painter as well as a landscape artist. But, like Parkinson on the first voyage, he was employed first and foremost as a draughtsman, committed to rendering subject matter, in his case sometimes with an element of picturesque narrative. Just as Parkinson's and Hodges' pictures cannot be "seen" without addressing the effects of classicism on European art, so Webber's pictures from the third voyage raise another aspect of the issue of the Europeans' "vision" of what it was they were experiencing. Webber's images repeatedly show scenes of harmony between the Europeans and the Polynesians. It is likely that, in a conscious attempt to distinguish themselves from the perceived cruelty of the Spaniards in South America, the English sought to offer an "enlightened" gloss on what were, in fact, often fraught and difficult encounters. Even a scene of human sacrifice in Tahiti lacks any of the conventional eighteenth-century devices to suggest powerful emotion. The probability is that Cook was molding an image, both visual and verbal, of the British civilizing mission to be conveyed in the subsequent official publication of the voyage.

With the benefit of our postcolonial hindsight, it is all too easy, therefore, to write off these complex mixtures of verbal and visual representation as the propaganda of imperialism. There is, however, a case, equally strong though not quite so simple, for trying instead to understand the participants' decisions within their own historical horizons, of distinguishing between different agendas which, in the Pacific at least did not, at this early date, extend to an overtly colonialist project. Post-voyage publications were themselves important aspects of the enterprise. In particular, the official account of the second voyage was a complicated and expensive printing job, the text complemented by an array of maps and pictures which required many hands to prepare. Such publications were partly contributions to knowledge, records of discoveries by Europeans of new people and places. But they were also in part self-consciously epic narratives, on a scale far surpassing those epics of antiquity, the *Odyssey* and the *Aeneid*. The account of the first voyage had been handed over to the professional writer John Hawkesworth and was compiled from several sources, such as journals kept by those on board, including Cook. However, Hawkesworth had not only produced a coherent narrative out of his disparate sources but had also deliberately embroidered the account of Polynesian social customs, especially in relation to sexuality, in order to generate a bestseller. He succeeded only too well, precipitating a scandal in England about the propriety of government involvement as well as deeply offending Cook himself. Those involved in producing the account of the second voyage knew that history was being made and that it was important to get the visual record, as well as the textual, right.

The point, of course, is what counted as artistically "right" in late eighteenth-century England. The paradigm was set by the *Discourses* of Sir Joshua Reynolds, President of the Royal Academy, in which he articulated a classically grounded "grand style" of careful modulation, harmony, and, perhaps above all, a sense of elevation, of art's mission to communicate an ideal. Such an ideal was to be found in the High Renaissance art of Raphael and, after the Renaissance, in the both the history painting of Poussin and the arcadian landscapes of Claude Lorrain with their harmonious coloring and soft atmospheric effects. The engravings for the voyage publications, mostly based on sketches and painted studies made on the spot, were undertaken by a group of London-based artists and craftsmen in the Italianate circle around Reynolds and the Academy. Prominent among them were Giovanni Battista Cipriani and Francesco Bartolozzi.

Visual Truth and Fiction

One of the results of their work can be seen in *A View of the Indians of Tierra del Fuego in their hut*, which appeared in the account of the first voyage. The unfortunate Buchan, while on board the *Endeavour*, made a gouache painting based on sketches he had made on the spot in Tierra del Fuego (Figure 2.8). Cipriani then worked up a drawing from Buchan's painting which formed the basis for an engraving by Bartolozzi (Figure 2.9), which appeared in the book of the voyage. The published image was therefore several steps removed from observation of the original scene.The basic information conveyed by the image is the same throughout: a family of Ona "Indians" sitting round a fire in a shelter made of branches. But the foreground figures in the published image, none of whom exist in Buchan's original study, have all been imported from a repertoire of classical poses: the nude child at the left, the two young fishermen returning with their catch at the right, and, most notably, the nubile girl in the center directing the fisherman to the fire. Bernard Smith argues that "Cipriani's task was to evoke the philosophizing sentiment while conveying the basic ethnographic information. He proceeded to transform Buchan's rather squalid hut-dwellers into comely youths and maidens and wise old men enjoying the delights of nature's simple plan."[25] However, this is not a case of simple falsification. As we have already noted, the relation between sense perception and the operation of the mind is a complex one. Conceptual frameworks and sensory data are not cleanly distinguished. Human beings tend to see something *as* something, rather than just to *see*. We can never know what Buchan, Parkinson, and the others "saw" in the South Seas. The varied translation of their images into an antique register, sometimes obvious, sometimes scarcely present, sometimes by their own hand, sometimes in the chain of processes leading to mass reproduction and publication, is not just evidence of an inability to see except through a classicizing framework. It is bound up with conventions of art, and also with changing views of humankind.

After the second voyage, William Hodges produced a series of "Landing" paintings depicting four "first encounters" between Europeans and Pacific islanders. It is significant that Hodges was not present on those occasions. Presumably the "first encounters" were too fraught with uncertainty and even danger to take an artist along in one of the boats. Accordingly, the images were retrospective constructions based on *verbal* accounts of what happened.

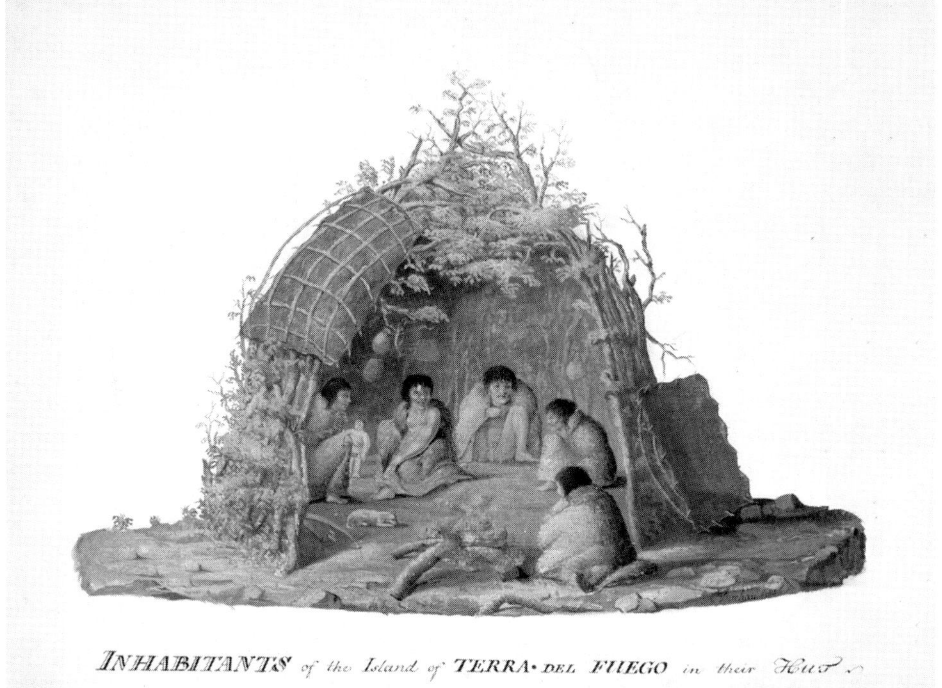

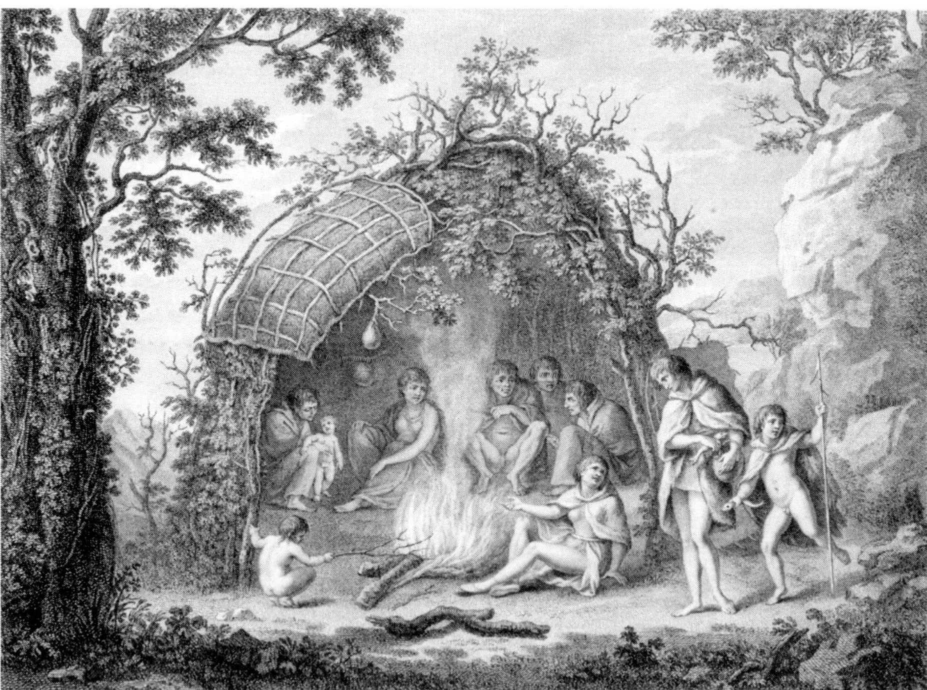

Figure 2.8 and 2.9 Above: Alexander Buchan watercolor. Below: Francesco Bartolozzi after Giovanni Batista Cipriani, *A View of the Indians of Tierra del Fuego in their Hut*, engraving from *A Collection of Drawings Made in the Countries Visited by Captain Cook in his First Voyage* 1768–1771, British Library, London, BL Add. 23920, f. 14. © The British Library Board / Robana.

The engraving of *The Landing at Middleburgh, one of the Friendly Islands* by J.K. Sherwin, which appeared in the official publication, even at the time ran into criticism from one of Hodges' own colleagues on the *Resolution*, the naturalist George Forster. Waspishly accusing Hodges of having mislaid his sketches and of making up for the deficiency "from his own elegant ideas," he remarks that "the connoisseur will find Greek contours and features in this picture, which have never existed in the South Sea," notably "elegant flowing robes" and "the figure of a divine old man with a long white beard."[26]

Yet, once again, what is going on here is not a simple falsification, as if Hodges was incapable of "seeing" the inhabitants of the Pacific in their own right. Rather, this was an official record of an encounter between cultures which had to represent it in a positive light according to the conventions of the day. Those conventions were both ethical and artistic. They conformed to an Enlightenment disposition to seek evidence of the universal perfectibility of people under the tutelage of a classically inspired European civilization. It would be simplistic to call this racism. Certainly it is possible to trace connections between eighteenth-century theories of successive stages of human development and nineteenth- and twentieth-century ideas of immutable racial characteristics – just as it is valid to draw connections between institutionalized knowledge and the operation of power. But to collapse later ideas into earlier ones and to reduce all knowledge to instrumentalism in the service of empire is less of a contribution to understanding than a closure upon it. We have to be circumspect, to be sure; but there is a difference between skeptical criticism and moral rectitude. For an eighteenth-century European artist the classical tradition was the horizon one worked within, even as tensions were emerging between that tradition and a cluster of more modern ideas concerning everything from subjective identity to empirical observation.

Hodges had two principal sources for his artistic repertoire. He had undergone training as a landscape painter during an apprenticeship in the studio of Richard Wilson. Wilson in turn had studied in Italy. There, he mastered the soft, classically inspired manner of landscape painting associated with Claude, which he subsequently applied to British landscapes. In addition, Hodges drew on a modernized form of history painting, the template for which had been set by the success of Benjamin West's *Death of General Wolfe* in 1771, with its mix of classical poses and modern dress. Hodges' painting is thus not the transparent depiction of a naturalistic "truth" but neither is it a kind of visual lie. Like all works of art, it is a complex representation. All such representations need to be set in the context of a tension between the classicizing, ennobling tenets of "Art" in the period of the early ascendancy of the Royal Academy and the growing scientific temper of the Enlightenment that demanded accurate, naturalistic reporting. The work which Hodges and the others did on the spot, and which *is* relatively descriptive and true to nature, has to be carefully distinguished from subsequent, worked-up representations, especially when these were produced for highly public contexts such as the official Admiralty-sponsored publications or exhibition at the Royal Academy.

Ideas of Human Development

The previously dominant European understanding of human variety was anchored in the Bible. When God created humankind he created one thing. However, after the Flood, the sons of Noah spread out into different parts of the world. Over time, according to the explanation derived from this account, the further humans were dispersed from the center of God's creation, that is, the Holy Land, the more degeneration set in, and different "races" emerged. It is important to recognize, however, that this conception of "race" is not the same as the supposedly "scientific" conception of race which began to emerge at the end of the eighteenth century. Subsequently, in the nineteenth century this became codified into a system of allegedly fundamental cognitive and moral differences signified by skin color – and modern racism was born. Some perception of difference and of the inferiority of "others" seems endemic to human society; certainly, Greeks, Egyptians, and Chinese, have all had their "barbarians." Arguably, though, this is not "racism" in its modern, pseudoscientific sense. Prior to the eighteenth century, and indeed for much of that century, humanity was deemed to be of one root (and even the misguided heathen was capable of salvation by being drawn back into the bosom of the Christian Church). The Christian explanation of human variety was collapsing, but it had not yet been replaced by the essentialist conceptions of "race" which had such a dolorous impact throughout the imperialist period, lingering on into the postcolonial present.

Having said that, though, it would be hard not to regard Hume as racist when he writes in 1742 of being "apt to suspect the negroes and in general all the other species of men (for there are four or five different kinds) to be naturally inferior to the whites,"[27] nor to impute the same to Kant when he explicitly agrees with Hume, asserting that the difference between black and white "appears to be as great in regards to mental capacities as in colour," in fact to be "fundamental."[28] This language of "species," "kinds," "inferiority," and "fundamental" difference is so close to modern racism that it would be splitting hairs to pretend otherwise. Likewise, as Stephen J. Gould has emphasized, Linnaeus, in his *Systema naturae* of 1758, the "first formal definition of human races in modern taxonomic terms," was all too willing to mix "character with anatomy" in an attempt to differentiate between African and European human beings.[29] Nonetheless the fact remains that at that date in the late eighteenth century there was as yet no "scientific" – or pseudoscientific – theory attempting to account for essential, biological racial distinction. These instances all, without doubt, reflect serious flaws in the philosophy of central figures of the European Enlightenment. The difficult question is whether they are aberrations or symptoms, whether their own philosophy of liberty is violated by these beliefs, or whether they are integral – a sort of Derridean "frame" telling the truth of the whole. Postcolonial theory tends to opt for the latter; I retain the hope that there is sufficient evidence in the works of Paine, Blake, and many European campaigners for the abolition of slavery to support the former case. Nonetheless, there can be little doubt that proto-racist elements in European Enlightenment philosophy must have helped pave the way for later scientific, institutionalized racism. All one can say is that such views did not go unchallenged, that difference and distinction existed within European thought as much as it exists anywhere else, and that radical supporters of universal human liberation continued to contest the closures perpetrated by more reactionary figures.

Rather than having a "scientific" answer to the question, the proto-anthropologists, proto-sociologists, and philosophers of eighteenth-century Europe were not certain how and why civilizations developed in some places and apparently declined in others. It was also unclear to them why some places appeared not to have developed civilization at all – where "civilization" was defined for them by factors such as complex social structures, legal codes, architecture, and writing. This was a key area, and one of the elements which had featured in earlier sixteenth-century Spanish arguments about the humanity or otherwise of the "Indians" of America. It is significant that even then, there was disagreement among European thinkers. Despite the orthodoxy of the Inquisition, there was Las Casas.[30] It was never an open and shut case commanding universal assent. Montaigne is the most prominent sixteenth-century European thinker to have contested claims that the "Indians" of Brazil were subhuman. In his essay "On Cannibals," he famously rejected the view that the actions of the Indians were any less human than actions committed in the recent French wars of religion: "I find, from what has been told me, that there is nothing savage or barbarous about those peoples, but that every man calls barbarous anything he is not accustomed to"; that there is "more barbarity" in contemporary tortures practiced on all sides "in the name of duty and religion" than in fighting a man and "roasting and eating him after his death."[31]

This is not, however, to say that Montaigne was a modern cultural relativist *avant la lettre*. His point, rather, is that there is a moral code and that good and evil exist in civilized societies as well as primitive ones. For Montaigne's argument was not, as a modern relativist's would be, that the Indians of South America had a developed culture. His position is closer to the modern theorists of "primtivism" who held that native peoples were purer and more authentic than decadent modern Europeans because of their proximity to nature. For Montaigne, the Indians "have hardly been fashioned by the mind of man, still remaining close neighbours to their original state of nature," a state "so simple and pure" as to have been unimaginable to Europeans.[32] Moreover, the values of the Indians most appealing to Montaigne, their courage and readiness to accept death before dishonor, remained for him classical virtues: his comparison of the Indians is to the Spartans at Thermopylae.

There is no question that, historically, it was the discovery of America that had really forced the issue of having to think through human difference. For once it was accepted that America was not the east coast of Asia it became apparent that

America was unknown to the Bible and could not be accounted for in terms of the diffusion of the sons of Noah. If anything, it was the other way round. In a famous statement in his *Two Treatises of Government*, written at the end of the seventeenth century, the English philosopher John Locke remarked that "in the beginning, all the world was America."[33] Writing in the 1690s, Locke preceded the new paradigm of historical thinking which began to emerge during the eighteenth century, but nonetheless this statement anticipates the growing belief that human development had gone through various stages, the earliest of which was exemplified by the aboriginal inhabitants of America. One of the consequences of this line of thought was that spatial remoteness became associated with temporal distance too. The idea grew that earlier, "barbarian" states of society (the "German" or Gaulish tribes relative to Roman civilization, for example), had now been discovered, surviving into the present, in places like America.

The first attempt to theorize a developing process of human history from a solitary situation akin to "wild beasts" through various increasingly sophisticated but still "barbarian" conditions until the full emergence of literate Christian civilization has been attributed to the Spanish Jesuit Jose de Acosta. His "history" of the "Indies" of 1590 was, by the early years of the seventeenth century, translated into all the main European languages. It is a short step from a belief in the coexistence in the present of different "stages" of human social development to the initiation of a discussion of the relative merits of the different phases of society. In particular, it was a belief that allowed some radical thinkers to entertain the idea that the progress of civilization had not been uniformly for the best, that much of the artificiality and even decadence which attended the growth of "polite" society might represent the loss of a kind of freedom, a kind of naturalness, which obtained in the original "state of nature."

The idea of a "state of nature" became something of a commonplace in seventeenth- and eighteenth-century sociopolitical debate. At the risk of oversimplification, conservatively inclined thinkers tended to regard it as a negative condition which had been improved upon by the development of complex social distinctions, legal frameworks, and the like; whereas more radical figures, with a stake in criticism of the status quo, tended to regard it as a time of greater equality and freedom before the imposition of class society. Thus, during the English revolution, the vice-chancellor of Oxford University can be found writing of "the bottomless lust and corruption of natural man," whereas the Hermetic thinker Robert Fludd expressed the hope that, on achieving the resurrection of Christ within, "man will recover his primitive state of innocence and perfection."[34]

The first use to have been traced of the actual phrase "noble savage" occurs in Dryden's play *The Conquest of Granada* of 1672, in which his character Almanzor declares, "I am as free as Nature first made man / 'Ere the base Laws of Servitude began / When wild in woods the noble Savage ran."[35] But the idea became pervasive during the eighteenth century, not least as a stick with which to beat the artificiality and lack of freedom of contemporary Europe. The concept is closely associated with Jean-Jacques Rousseau, though Rousseau himself never used the phrase. Nonetheless, the *locus classicus* for the idea is Rousseau's *Discourse on the Origins of Inequality*, which argued that the supposed progress out of the "state of nature" marked in fact a decline, a loss of the freedom and innocence which was humanity's birthright.[36]

It needs to be remembered that however widespread were misgivings about the state of contemporary society, Rousseau's idea that society in all its forms marked a decline from a pristine state of nature remained an oppositional perception. The widespread hankering for an imagined arcadian past for the most part functioned within a conventional wisdom that contemporary European society marked the greatest advance of human development. The "four stages" theory of human social progress articulated by thinkers of the Scottish Enlightenment, including John Millar and Adam Smith, postulated not a "descent," but an ascent from the "state of nature": progress from the stage of Hunting and Fishing through Pastoralism (the taming and herding of animals) to Agriculture and finally to Commercial society.[37] There were various grey areas here, not least the fact that agriculture seemed to achieve its ultimate development within and not before the development of commerce. But the basic armature of a theory of human social progress from "barbarism" to "civilization" is clear enough. It formed, in effect, the common sense of the period. For Samuel Johnson, there could be "nothing more false" than a belief in the superiority of the "savage life": "The savages have no bodily advantages beyond those of civilised men. They have not better health; and as to care or mental uneasiness, they are not above it, but below it, like bears." As far as Johnson was concerned, "one set of Savages is like another."[38]

Complicated Paradise

It was within the terms of this view of human progress that the discovery of the peoples of the Pacific came as a considerable shock. Bougainville, as we have seen, on the basis of a very short visit, thought Tahiti a veritable Garden of Eden. But the Cook voyages quickly brought evidence of a much greater social variety.[39] To the eighteenth-century mind, the "Indians" of North America exemplified the "state of nature." For them this was matched in the south by the "Indians" of Tierra del Fuego and the Australian Aborigines. But in Polynesia, societies which were completely different from Europe seemed nonetheless to range from conditions akin to such "barbarism" to societies with agriculture and a disposition to commercial activity, not to mention social stratification involving slavery, workers, and something resembling an aristocracy.

In 1776, after his return from Cook's second voyage to the Pacific, as part of his contract with the Admiralty, Hodges painted a scene in Matavai Bay, Tahiti (Figure 2.10). The overall effect is of a hazy morning light as the sun begins to rise in

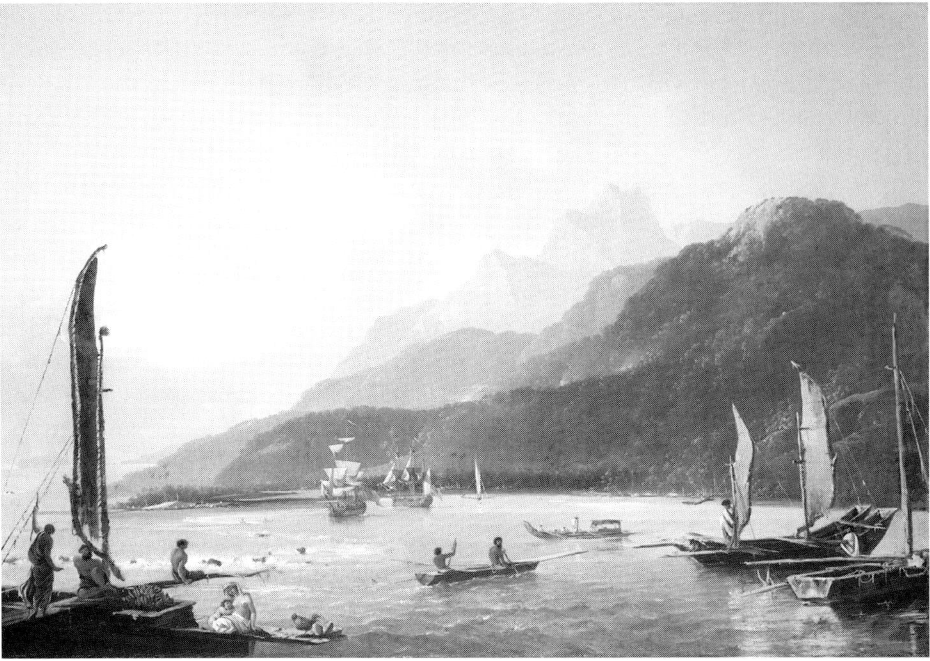

Figure 2.10 William Hodges, *A View of Maitavie* [Matavai] *Bay in the Island of Otaheite* [Tahiti], 1776, oil on canvas, 137 × 193 cm. © National Maritime Museum, Greenwich, London, BHC1932.

the sky, touching the ridges of the mountains yet leaving the wooded area coming down towards the water still in shade. This sense of atmosphere is almost palpable, and clearly derived from the European tradition of idyllic landscape, most closely identified in England with the Italianate paintings of the seventeenth-century artist Claude Lorrain; a tradition which Hodges would have imbibed from his teacher Richard Wilson. Yet the scene which this atmosphere envelops is not an arcadian idyll of repose and leisure in an undisturbed state of nature, nor even one of youthful shepherds and their flocks. It is a bustling scene of commercial activity. Two brown-skinned men are paddling an outrigger canoe across the water; others are apparently hoisting a sail on another double-hulled canoe. As well as people, the foreground group at the left includes a pile of fruit and vegetables and a chicken. In the middle ground, two European ships are moored. In the detail, canoes can be seen drawn up alongside, sailors line the decks, and trading between the two groups is taking place.[40]

Whatever it is, this is not, therefore, an image of timelessness, of a people outside history living in a state of nature. These events happened in August–September 1773. The ships are the *Resolution* and the *Adventure*. The sandy spit of land on which a large tent has been erected is "Point Venus," so named because that was the site from which the astronomical observations had been made during the first voyage. The tent itself was a combined workshop and hospital. This suggests a need to reflect further on the question of a Europeanizing vision. Hodges has undoubtedly adapted a typically Claudean atmospheric effect to represent a tropical sunrise. In itself this is hardly obtrusive, though the atmosphere is brighter than a misty view in the Roman campagna or the Mediterranean, and the land is less tamed than one would expect in a "classical landscape" intended to evoke an all-encompassing harmony. But in the left foreground two figures in particular introduce other elements from European tradition. The standing figure at the far left is in a pose associated with a philosopher of antiquity, and the full-breasted nursing mother with the suspiciously white skin strikes notes of fruitfulness and harmony rooted in the dual Christian–classical iconography mentioned earlier as central to the Western canon of art. Despite the particularity of what is being represented, this is less a snapshot of Tahitian reality in 1773 than a self-conscious, perhaps even a self-serving, representation of a cross-cultural encounter: "all is well and the benefits are mutual." For Smith, as well as his technical success in representing a tropical atmosphere for the first time in European art, Hodges has also represented a complex thesis (designed to satisfy the Admiralty) about the mutual benefits of commerce to societies of different types: the peaceful interaction of European civilization with natives who are at a sufficiently advanced stage to set aside their warlike tendencies, to trade, and to derive benefit from the contact.[41]

Some of the complexity of such representations begins to emerge when we set the picture in a wider context. For this was not the first painting of Matavai Bay that Hodges had attempted. The first, which was also developed on the basis of sketches and oil studies made on the voyage, as well as compositional "drafts" made in London, was made not for the Admiralty but for exhibition at the Royal Academy earlier in the summer of 1776. In the first version, there is no nursing mother in the foreground, no marquee, and above all, there are no European ships. Instead, the distant part of the bay is filled by two large war canoes. Another of these is more clearly visible in the middle ground, its fighting platform occupied by a warrior in a tapa-cloth robe and wearing an enormously tall headdress surrounded by feathers with an effect somewhat like a halo. This is an image of activity of a more self-contained kind, a sort of visual eavesdropping on a world precisely not interfered with. The European viewpoint, that is to say the viewpoint from which the scene is actually being *seen*, is not represented in the picture. The painting was one of a pendant pair. Hodges contrasts the masculine world of maritime activity at Matavai Bay with a different aspect of Tahitian life located on the south side of the island at Otaheite Peha (Figure 2.11). In this image Hodges gives full force to the idyll of the *nouvelle Cythère*, the arcadian bliss of voluptuous young women in a luxuriant landscape. The pair of pictures offers a different sort of meditation on Oceanic society. Here there are no Europeans with their floating fortresses and their commerce but instead a consciously gendered representation of two contrasting sides of a complex society, a man's world of work and possibly war, and a sexualized vision of guilt-free pleasure. Yet the Europe that is absent from the depiction is present as a value "framing" the pair: a sense that here is a world remote from everything European, but which for all that possesses a kind of truth which Europe in its over-refinement may have lost. It is an early statement of the romantic primitivism which continued to resonate in European art into the twentieth century.

The bather sitting on the bank to the right, however, strikes a different note. First there is her curious and unexplained gesture, almost as if hiding herself in the cloak-like white sheet. And emphasizing this note of surprise or unease, she is overlooked by the looming figure of a Polynesian carving, a *ti'i* figure. This figure has been increased in scale by Hodges to emphasize its presence in the scene. The father and son naturalists on the voyage, the Forsters, brought back two such figures, which they gave to Oxford University and which were described as "rude figures of a man or woman, seldom exceeding eighteen inches in height."[42] These figures relate to Polynesian cosmology and the potentially destructive powers of the divine realm. More telling still, in the distance at the extreme right-hand edge, there can be seen a spindly wooden construction with a horizontal form at the top. This is a shrouded corpse on a *tupapau* platform, several images of which were sketched by voyage artists. The palpable sexuality of the scene, wherein the almost formless bather melts into the luxuriant landscape beyond, is set off against reminders of the underworld and mortality.

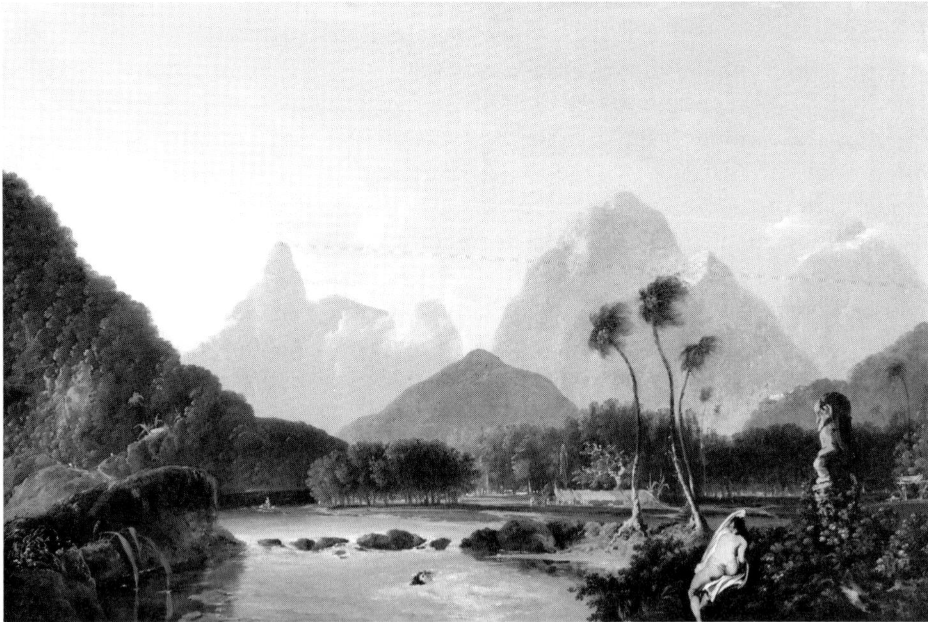

Figure 2.11 William Hodges, *View taken in the Bay of Otaheite Peha* (Vaitepiha), 1776, oil on canvas, 91 × 137 cm. Anglesey Abbey, Cambridgeshire, UK / The Fairhaven Collection / National Trust Photographic Library / John Hammond / The Bridgeman Art Library.

The meanings put into circulation by the two pairs of paintings are thus significantly different. In one, Hodges does seem to be striving to give form to a vision of arcadia, as if the Enlightenment voyagers had stumbled across something from Virgil. In the second version of *Maitavie Bay*, however, Hodges "updated" his meditation on life and death to include the Europeans in the picture, as it were to modernize arcadia, and thus to address a specifically contemporary interest in the Pacific rather than the myth of a timeless Eden.

Picturing the "Noble Savage"

Joshua Reynolds exhibited his *Portrait of Omai* at the annual Royal Academy exhibition of 1776 (Figure 2.12). Omai (whose name was Mai; the eighteenth-century English added the prefix "O," as they also did to Tahiti, which they called "Otaheite") was a Ra'iatean islander who traveled back to England on the second

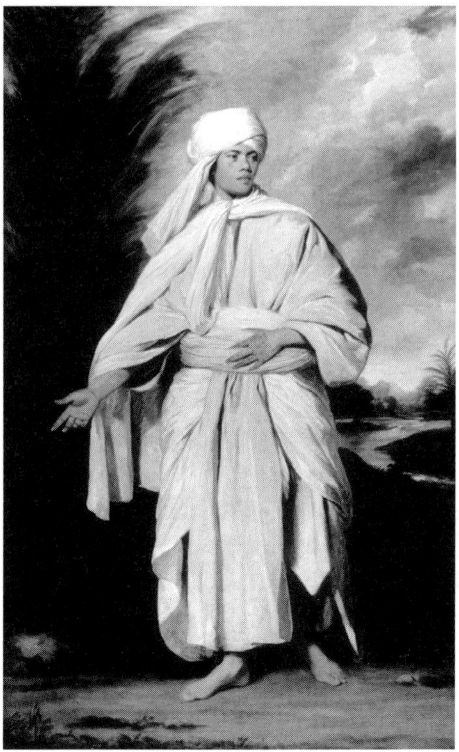

Figure 2.12 Joshua Reynolds, *Portrait of Omai*, 1775–1776, oil on canvas, 236 × 145 cm., National Gallery of Dublin, Ireland / Private collection. Photo Courtesy of the Cecil Beaton Studio Archive at Sotheby's.

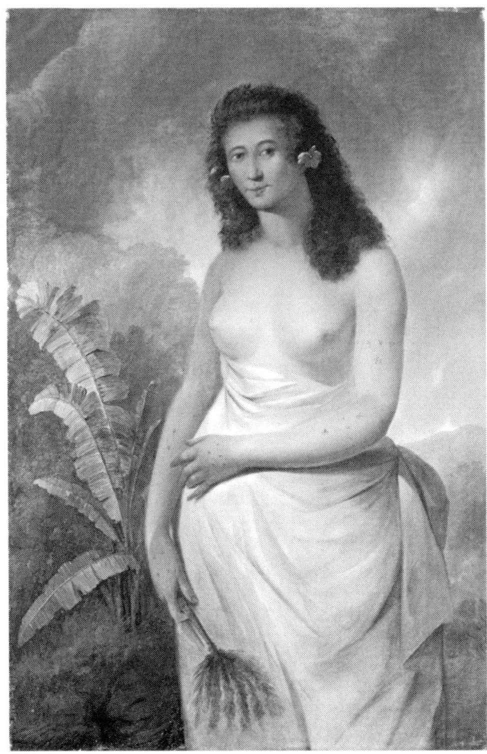

Figure 2.13 John Webber, *Poedua*, 1777–1785, oil on canvas, 145 × 96 cm. Private Collection / Photo © Christie's Images / The Bridgeman Art Library.

voyage and became something of a sensation in London society. He is shown full-length, a format normally reserved for high-status subjects, wearing a flowing white robe. It is loosely tied round his waist and he has another piece of material round his neck like an elegantly tied scarf. On his head is a white turban with a trailing side piece. Mai's feet are bare, the expression on his face is self-composed, not to say haughty, his right hand is open in a gesture whose significance is hard to pin down, but if more of the landscape in which he is standing were visible it would probably be seen to indicate those lands, as if they were his. The landscape is dark but seems fertile, with a river leading in to distant high mountains. Palm trees can be seen both in the distance and immediately behind him. The spectator's viewpoint is low, in effect looking up at the princely Mai. The image is the very type of the "noble savage."

Mai's female equivalent can be seen in the portrait of *Poedua* painted by John Webber on the third voyage (Figure 2.13). The portrait exists today in several different versions painted in oils in London from a lost study, or studies, made by Webber in Cook's cabin aboard the *Resolution* moored at Ra'iatea in November 1777. One of the factors complicating this ostensibly natural image of unspoilt beauty is that it was made while Poedua was actually a hostage. The word "hostage" is a particularly loaded one in the early twenty-first century, so a word of caution is in order. In Polynesia in 1777 Cook espoused the values of Enlightenment humanism, not the religious fundamentalism now routinely associated with hostage-taking. Nonetheless, from his point of view, in the last resort order had to be maintained on his expedition. When, as the ships prepared to leave the "paradise" of Tahiti for the last time, two of his sailors deserted to live with their adopted Polynesian "wives," Cook took the decision to hold three prominent Ra'iateans until the sailors were returned. These were the chief's son and daughter, and her husband. It was during this captivity of four days that Webber portrayed his "Polynesian Venus," as the picture became known.

The story is a salutary reminder not to take images at face value. Terms such as "charm," "beauty," "allure," all of which could be applied to the portrait, are being applied to a highly constructed representation. Poedua may well have been beautiful, indeed contemporary accounts testify to that – she was, after all, an aristocrat, well-fed, well-clothed, and well-leisured; but her beauty was translated by Webber into European terms, or rather into terms that could be relied on to appeal to Europeans. Again the low viewpoint plays a part, as with the portrait of Mai, but here the spectator is placed closer to the subject, almost one might say in touching distance, and what he sees (very much "he") is a carefully calculated image of a "natural" Venus; none of the artificial accoutrements of contemporary European beauty are present, but the image presented is one of a sensual broad-hipped body, naked breasts revealed to the viewer, thick black ringlets down to her shoulders, a half smile, flowers in her hair, and, of course, dusky though significantly lightened skin. The regal bearing of both Poedua and Mai, their dark-but-light skin, the two gazes – commanding in his case, inviting in hers – play off against the understated, but unmistakable, markers of their exoticism: the landscapes in which they are posed, and, crucially, their tattoos. Mai's are on the back of his left hand and his right wrist; Poedua's vary according to the version of Webber's painting in question, but in the present image are most obvious along her left arm, a series of cross- or star-like shapes in clusters on her bicep, her forearm and the back of her hand. The "dusky maiden" and the "noble savage," as realized in these two pictures – these two fictions, that is the point – made a powerful pairing in the European imaginary of its "other."[43]

Art and "Curiosity"

Many examples of Oceanic material culture were taken back to Europe. These included cloaks, baskets, canoe paddles, carved wooden boards, and figures either made from feathers or carved in stone such as the small, intricately carved Maori *tiki*. These things were usually either gifts or were exchanged for European goods like mirrors, iron nails, and implements. This is not to say, however, that the Europeans understood what they had been given, either in terms of an alien cosmology, or – of course – as "art." To the eighteenth-century voyagers, these things were classified as "artificial curiosities." Nonetheless, they did value them. When Joseph Banks had his portrait painted by Benjamin West he had himself depicted surrounded by various Oceanic objects and actually wearing one of the Maori cloaks which he subsequently gave to Oxford University. Cook himself presented one of the greenstone Maori *tikis* to King George III. But they had no idea of the socio-spiritual significance of these things in Tahitian or Maori culture. They could not, because they barely grasped that the people of Polynesia *had* a culture.

In the European conceptual framework of the eighteenth century, one of the key attributes of the civilized mind, in the view of the relatively small, educated elite whose opinions formed that framework, was the ability to generalize: to compare, to contrast, to judge, and to come to a balanced overview. By contrast, and from the same point of view, the hallmark of the "savage" was to exist in a world of particulars; precisely not to have a vantage point from which to be able to reflect and generalize (which is, of course, the claim postcolonial studies aim to rebut). In the philosophical overview of human social achievement of a European intellectual, one of the main differences between the cultural advancement of his own world and the savagery of newly encountered "Indians" was that the latter had no knowledge of a world outside their own – a universe composed, so to speak, of sticks and stones and animals and plants, and not of overarching schemes such as civilization and barbarism, of progress and degeneration, of Law and Religion, or indeed, of Art.

Just as the empirically based theory of knowledge held that the child's mind was a *tabula rasa*, a blank slate on which experience wrote, by a form of sociological extrapolation, "Indians" were held to be devoid of culture, religion, and similar traces of social complexity. It took some time for Europeans to be able to "read" the societies they encountered. American "Indians," and subsequently Aboriginal Australians, were seen as lacking society, as existing in an asocial state of nature (which is what allowed the British to designate Australia as *terra nullius*, "no man's land," when it clearly did have inhabitants). The situation with Polynesian societies was more complex, and hence more puzzling. People in the Polynesian islands clearly did live in societies: there were instances of agriculture as well as hunting and gathering, there were observable social ranks as well as customs and complex rituals. But the meanings of these remained opaque, even incomprehensible. The Europeans had little or no grasp of the wider cosmology in which they were embedded, and that could have made them so.

An important factor in play here is the very notion of "curiosity" itself. The cultural anthropologist Nicholas Thomas has argued that the term was used to identify both a disposition (in some human subject) and a category of objects: both "a subjective attitude" and "an attribute of things noticed."[44] These latter were subdivided into "natural" and "artificial" curiosities. That is, things like new fish, plants, and shells on the one hand, and things made by newly encountered human beings on the other. The "artificial curiosities" could range from objects such as decorated lintels to carved figures, as well as more functional items like clothes, utensils, and baskets. Today, when the concept of art has opened up to include a vast range of objects and activities, it is deceptively easy for us to visit exhibitions of "Maori art" or "Polynesian art." To regard once exotic products as "art" has become a kind of norm under a widely accepted rubric of cultural diversity. In the late eighteenth century it was not so. There was absolutely no question that any of the "artificial curiosities" encountered were "art." In the language of the day, they may have been more or less "curiously wrought," more or less "skillful," more or less "nice" or "neat" or "singular," but "art" was on a different plane entirely. Art was an index of civilization, and on the prevailing theory the places that were being encountered were not civilized but were savage or barbarous, or at most on a relatively low level of social development.

Thomas argues that "at this time there was no established anthropological discourse which actually linked propositions about artifacts to ethnological theory or political description in a systematic way."[45] It is as if the governing Enlightenment conception of different evolutionary stages of society, ranking peoples into different stages of relative savagery and civilization, did not map onto an equivalent theory about their material culture; there was an oscillation between seeing objects as evidence of barbarism and as evidence of certain levels of skill, which presupposed some sense of civilization. To make a visual analogy it is as if the eighteenth-century artists, explorers, and scientists lacked a system of perspective: they could see and be interested in "things" but they could not systematically link these things in relation to each other or to a wider social continuum. For Thomas, the idea that the array of things with which they were confronted could constitute a material culture with an aesthetic dimension, "a sort of physical counterpart to the totality of their manners and customs or social institutions" simply did not exist; such a notion was "the product of subsequent theory."[46]

One noticeable feature of the responses elicited by the objects that were collected is that the explorers' relatively positive expressions of "curiosity" tended to be reserved for abstract designs, whereas when they were confronted with recognizable representations of human bodies and faces these were mostly regarded as "grotesque": a divided response which can be traced to the distinction then becoming entrenched in Europe between the "fine arts," including painting and sculpture, and the "lesser arts" or crafts. Thus, George Forster wrote of a geometrically patterned basket collected in Tonga that "the taste and the workmanship of these baskets were elegant in the highest degree"[47]; and of clubs encountered in the Cook Islands, that they were "as highly polished as if our best workmen had made them with the best instruments."[48] Whereas, faced by a *tiki*, he could only see it as "an amulet with a rude carving of a human figure"[49]; and confronted by the large stone statues of Easter Island, his view was that "the eyes, nose and mouth were scarcely marked on a lumpish ill-shaped head; and the ears, which were excessively long … were better executed than any other part, though a European artist would have been ashamed of them."[50] The European standard of verisimilitude disqualified such things from being categorized as "art."

Thomas has argued that it is as if, for those involved in the first voyages and seeing everything within a European conceptual framework, the people they encountered did not have a recognizably different culture but lacked anything that was recognizably a culture at all, in eighteenth-century terms. This is not entirely surprising when we realize that "culture" then was not the expansive category that it has become today. On the contrary, it was restricted; it was the characteristic of "polite" society, and those outside of polite society, whether they were the lower orders at home or the newly discovered peoples over the oceans, did not have it. In eighteenth-century accounts, there was little sense of Polynesians having a *different* culture; rather, they were regarded as existing without culture.

Eurocentrism

It goes without saying that this is a wholly Eurocentric position. It is easy enough to say that now, yet it is a view which has only been challenged in art historical and anthropological literature relatively recently. However much that perspective might have been resisted on the ground, so to speak, in Polynesia itself, in academic art history other readings have been conspicuous by their absence. The Polynesian point of view has largely been occluded. It is not difficult to see why. The sense we have made of the European side of the encounter has been entirely determined by the visual and written records left behind by the voyagers, and by the secondary literature which has grown up around them. But there are no visual and written records of what the eighteenth-century Tahitians and Maoris thought was happening. There is certainly a secondary literature in the contemporary discipline of the anthropology of art, but it is based on the reinterpretation by modern scholars of the meaning of various surviving artifacts and also on oral tradition. Oral tradition is notoriously unreliable as a guide to the past because of the way it changes to suit the priorities of speakers in their present. Nonetheless, a substantially different picture has emerged through a conjoining of the counter-narratives of Oceanic oral tradition on the one hand and, on the other, a revised understanding of European sources. This latter has involved, firstly, attempts to reposition surviving Oceanic artifacts in terms not of Enlightenment categories of social development but of the cosmology within which they were produced. Secondly, it has involved a kind of reading-against-the-grain of European written accounts of Pacific encounters, alert to the traces in them of what have been called "indigenous countersigns."[51]

In the conventional perspective, Europeans acted upon the people they encountered, made their judgments and interpretations and effectively controlled the situation because of what was assumed to be their superior power – in every sense of the word – superior knowledge *and* superior weapons. Now, as a result of the shifts outlined above, anthropologists are more able to recognize indigenous agency. It is now widely accepted that the various peoples of Oceania played a much more equal part in the various transactions, commercial and social, that took place. They have become active rather than passive participants in a relationship over which they had considerable control. After all, the Europeans were a long way from home with absolutely no support systems outside of their own restricted capacities. They needed supplies; they needed repairs; they needed some place on land to rest and recuperate. In effect, they needed the people of the Pacific more than the Pacific islanders needed them.

Obviously, this relationship subsequently changed. European navigation and ships improved, trade increased, actual colonization began to happen. Above all, the imposition of European cultural norms through the work of Christian missionaries ensured that by the mid-nineteenth century the flow of power ran very much in one direction and indigenous Polynesian culture was suppressed. So-called idols were collected and burned, practices like tattooing were banned. The situation in the late eighteenth century had been significantly different. There was less of an attempt to intervene in and change the societies encountered than there was an attempt to observe and record them as they were. This may have opened the door for subsequent colonization and exploitation of resources; and to the extent that it does, it underscores the uncomfortable relation of knowledge and power. But it was not itself part of the voyagers' work. Indeed, George Forster famously wondered as early as 1777 whether "if the knowledge of a few individuals can only be acquired at such a price as the happiness of nations, it were better for the discoverers and the discovered that the South Sea had still remained unknown to Europe and its restless inhabitants."[52]

Tupaia

One of the few ways we can even come close to achieving some sense of what a Polynesian point of view might have been is suggested by a puzzling series of drawings of scenes of Polynesian life that survive from the first Cook voyage. Amongst other things, these show a *marae*, or temple ground, some canoes and fruit trees, a dancing girl, and a gift exchange between Maori and a European. Another pictures the elaborate costume of a figure known as the "chief mourner," who performed in a funeral at Tahiti in which Joseph Banks took part (Figure 2.14). It is a striking image, which led to all these pictures being designated as by "The Artist of the Chief Mourner," after the fashion in which anonymous medieval or Renaissance artists were described. Banks described the costume as "most Fantastical," and the violent performance of its wearer was formidable. Banks

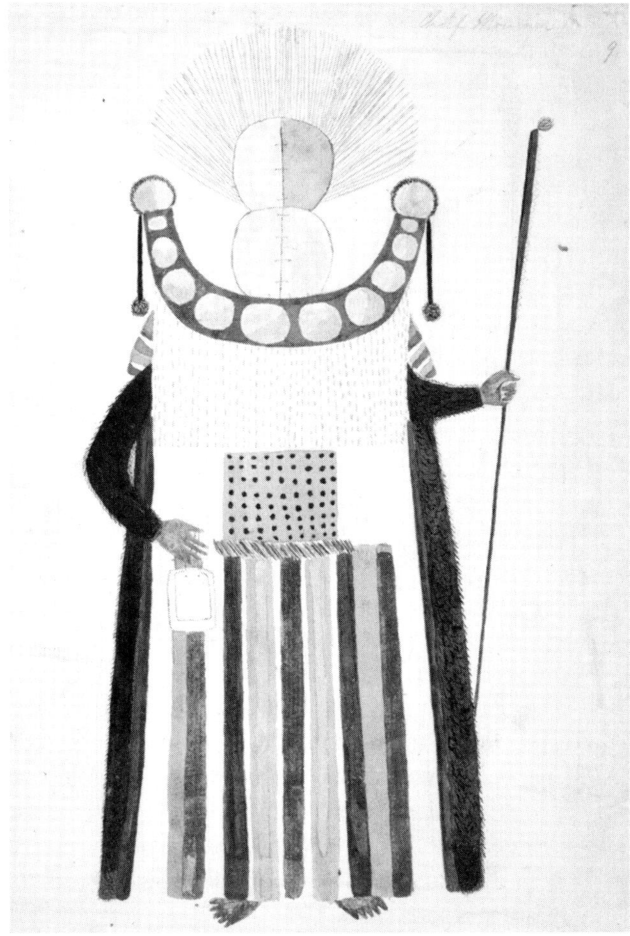

Figure 2.14 Tupaia, *The Costume of the Chief Mourner,* 1769, pencil and watercolor, 28 × 39 cm. British Library, London, BL Add. 15508, f. 9. © The British Library Board / Robana.

failed in his attempt to purchase it for his collection, though similar ones were obtained on later voyages and now survive in various stages of completeness in European museums. The drawing of the costume, though powerful, is clearly not by a trained hand such as that of Sydney Parkinson, the voyage artist. Bernard Smith believed the set of drawings to be by Banks himself, pointing out that no one else had access to "the precious store of pigment"[53] which was only to be used for the scientific project of capturing the hues of tropical specimens before they faded. However difficult it was to attribute the drawings, no one ever questioned that the author had to be one of the ship's European company. Not for over two hundred years did it dawn on anyone that the artist could have been Polynesian. Only in 1997 was a letter from Banks discovered which referred to the Polynesian *aroi* priest Tupaia having "learnd to draw in a way not quite unintelligible" and as displaying "the genius for Caricature which all wild people possess" in a drawing of Banks himself exchanging a lobster with a Maori in 1769.[54]

Banks was an aristocrat, and so, in his own terms, was the Ra'iatean Tupaia, often referred to as a "navigator-priest," but more adequately described by Nicholas Thomas as "a priest, a political strategist, less the stereotypic tribal elder steeped in tradition, than an indigenous intellectual with experimental inclinations.[55] Tupaia drew on his knowledge to assist Cook in navigating to New Zealand, and he had apparently hoped to travel all the way back to England in order to try and discover more about the source of the Europeans' skills and strengths. Banks described him as "certainly a most proper man, well born, chief *Tahowa* or priest of this Island."[56] The assumption now is that Tupaia saw European drawings being made and, in conversation with Banks as he traveled around with the *Endeavour*, expressed a desire to try it for himself. This is not the only time such a thing has happened. In the 1930s, the Arrernte man Albert Namatjira was assisting Rex Battarbee, an artist from Warrnambool in Victoria who was working on landscapes of the Australian central desert. Namatjira, who had already made many decorated boomerangs for the emerging tourist market, tried his hand at the watercolor painting technique and went on to become the first internationally celebrated Aboriginal artist.

Care is required in the interpretation of Tupaia's drawings. The image of the *Chief Mourner* is hieratic and as such quite powerful, but the image of the gift exchange looks naïve. The fatal mistake would be to reinforce the cultural stereotype of Pacific islanders, indeed any non-Western people, as naïve or childlike because they "cannot draw properly." This is a large and complex subject, as we have already seen, but the employment by Europeans of perspectival *mimesis* as an absolute yardstick by which to measure the competence of other cultures has been one of the most persistent stumbling blocks in the way of an acceptance of cultural relativism and diversity. Western illusionism is a spectator-based representational system. Other representational systems, including not only those employed by children and untrained adults but also those used by other cultures as diverse as the Indian, Chinese, and ancient Egyptian, exploit more or less object-based systems. In these, things are represented according to their conceptual significance rather than perceptual accuracy. The latter is regarded as contingent and ephemeral whereas the former confers on things their proper status. This scale of values is quite different from one which valorizes mimetic accuracy as seen from one artificially arrested viewpoint; as does the Western system based on perspective.

The key point is that we have here two *different* representational systems, not one true to perception and one false, and thus one superior and one inferior. Polynesian culture does not lack iconic representation, figures can be read in tattoos, wood carvings, rock engravings, and, of course, *tiki*. But such images are not mimetically descriptive. Tupaia is reaching beyond the conventions of his own culture, trying to represent what he believes to be significant, in an alien visual language. In the drawing of the Chief Mourner, Tupaia highlights the important aspects of the costume, not the accidents attendant on where the performer of the ritual is in the world, as an academically trained European artist would. Likewise with the image of a gift exchange between Tupaia himself and Banks. Whether Tupaia could have situated his figures in a coherent spatial continuum or not (and one assumes that, not having undergone an academic training, he couldn't), is beside the point. If he is doing nothing else here, Tupaia is implicitly asserting the equality of the Maori with the European, or the cosmic power of the Chief Mourner. The drawings are the product of the same individual who conversed as an equal with Banks, even seems to have irritated Cook by his "proud and obstinate" attitude,[57] and to have assumed leadership of the entire vessel when encountering new islands – to the extent that the Maori believed the ship *Endeavour* to be his. In the way they picture the world, Tupaia's drawings may appear childlike to a viewer habituated to Western convention, but they are not – any more than an apparently stylized ancient Egyptian picture of a funeral would be – the product of a childish mind.

Notes

1 Wittkower 1989, p. 19.
2 Columbus 1969, pp. 218–221.
3 Columbus 1969, p. 275.
4 Greenblatt 1991, p. 145.
5 Castiglione 1967, p. 96.
6 Barr 1974, p. 11.
7 Pagden in the introduction to Las Casas, 1992, p. xxxiv.
8 Dürer 1958, pp. 101–102.
9 Smith 1992, p. 11.
10 Burckhardt, 1990, p. 191.
11 Slenczka 2002, p. 495.
12 Honour 1975, p. 68.
13 Sloan 2007.
14 Smith 1985, p. vii.
15 Harriot 1972.
16 Sloan 2007, p. 110.
17 Kuhlemann 2007, pp. 86–87.
18 Honour 1975, p. 30.
19 Bell 2012, p. 13.
20 Charles Perrault, Preface and "Second Dialogue on the Three Visual Arts" from *Parallel of the Ancients and Moderns* in Harrison, Wood, and Gaiger 2000, p. 57.
21 Alpers 1983.
22 Alpers and Baxandall 1994.
23 For further discussion, see Paul Wood, "The other side of the world," in Barker, ed. 2012, pp. 261–297.

24 Banks, quoted in Smith 1985, p. 14.
25 Joppien and Smith 1985a, p. 16.
26 Forster, *A Voyage round the World*, London 1777, quoted by Joppien and Smith 1985b, vol. 2, p. 73.
27 Hume, "Of National Characters," in *Essays, Moral and Political*, 2nd edn, 1742; reprinted in Kramnick 1995, p. 629.
28 Kant 1960, p. 111.
29 Gould 1984, p. 35.
30 Las Casas 1992.
31 Montaigne 1991, pp. 231 and 236.
32 Montaigne 1991, p. 232.
33 Locke 1988, p. 319.
34 Hill 1979, pp. 292 and 300.
35 Dryden 1978, p. 30.
36 Rousseau 1984.
37 Meek 1976.
38 Boswell 1980, pp. 405 and 1304.
39 *James Cook and the Exploration of the Pacific*, exhibitions in Bonn, Vienna, and Berne, 2009–2011; Kaeppler, ed., 2009.
40 Quilley and Bonehill, eds, 2004, p. 91.
41 Smith 1985.
42 Johann Reinhold Forster, *Observations Made during a Voyage round the World* (1778, p. 522), quoted in Kaeppler, 2009, p. 147.
43 A searching analysis of the psychoanalytic implications of tattoos in eighteenth-century paintings of the Pacific region, especially in the work of William Hodges, can be found in Guest 2007, especially chapter 1, "The Great Distinction," which is a development of her earlier essay "The Great Distinction: Figures Of The Exotic In The Work Of William Hodges," *Oxford Art Journal* 12 (2) (1989): 36–58.
44 Thomas 1991, p. 127. A further, wide-ranging discussion of the concept of 'curiosity', with particular reference to travel-writing, can be found in Leask 2002.
45 Thomas 1991, pp. 130–131.
46 Thomas 1991, p. 131.
47 Forster 2000, p. 236.
48 Forster 2000, p. 238.
49 Forster quoted in Kaeppler, 2009, p. 173.
50 Forster 2000, p. 306.
51 Douglas 1999, pp. 65–99 (see especially the sub-sections "Indigenous countersigns – actions," pp. 70–73, and "Indigenous countersigns – actions, desires, agency" pp. 73–83).
52 Forster 2000, p. 306.
53 Joppien and Smith 1985a, p. 60.
54 Carter 1998, pp. 133–134.
55 Thomas 2003, p. 21.
56 Banks, quoted in Thomas 2003, p. 80.
57 Cook, *Journal*, in Beaglehole 1968, p. 442.

References

Alpers, Svetlana, 1983, *The Art of Describing: Dutch Art in the Seventeenth Century*, The University of Chicago Press, Chicago.

Alpers, Svetlana and Michael Baxandall, 1994, *Tiepolo and the Pictorial Intelligence*, Yale University Press, New Haven and London.

Barker, Emma, ed., 2012, *Art and Visual Culture 1600–1850: Academy to Avant-Garde*, Tate Publishing.

Barr, Alfred H., 1974 [1936], *Cubism and Abstract Art*, The Museum of Modern Art, New York.

Beaglehole, J.C., 1968, *The Journals of Captain Cook on his Voyages of Discovery*, Vol. 1 *The Voyage of the* Endeavour *1768–1771*, reprinted with addenda and corrigenda Cambridge University Press, Cambridge for the Hakluyt Society, 3 vols. First published 1955.

Bell, Julian, 2012, "Don't look," review of Belting *Florence and Baghdad*, London Review of Books, October 25, pp. 13–14.

Boswell, James, 1980 [1791], *Life of Johnson*, World's Classics, ed. R.W. Chapman, revised by J.D. Fleeman, with a new introduction by Pat Rogers, Oxford University Press, Oxford.

Burckhardt, Jacob, 1990 [1860], *The Civilization of the Renaissance in Italy*, ed. Peter Burke, Penguin Books Ltd., Harmondsworth.

Carter, Harold B., 1998, "Note on the drawings by an unknown artist from the voyage of HMS *Endeavour*" in Margarette Lincoln, ed., *Science and Exploration in the Pacific: European Voyages to the Southern Oceans in the Eighteenth Century*, The Boydell Press in association with the National Maritime Museum, pp. 133–134.

Castiglione, Baldesar, 1967 [1528], *The Book of the Courtier*, ed. George Bull, Penguin Books Ltd., Harmondsworth.

Columbus, Christopher, 1969 [1492–1504], *The Four Voyages*, ed. and trans. J. M. Cohen, Penguin Books, Hardmondsworth.

Douglas, Bronwen, 1999, "Art as ethno-historical text: science, representation and indigenous presence in eighteenth and nineteenth century Oceanic voyage literature," in Thomas and Losche, eds, *Double Vision: Art Histories and Colonial Histories in the Pacific*, Cambridge University Press, Cambridge, pp. 73–83.

Dryden, John, 1978 [1672], *The Conquest of Granada by the Spaniards* in *Works*, Vol. 11, ed. John Loftis and David Stuart Rhodes, University of California Press, Berkeley and London.

Dürer, Albrecht, 1958, *The Writings of Albrecht Dürer*, ed. William Martin Conway, Peter Owen Ltd., London.

Forster, George, 2000 [1777], *A Voyage Round the World*, ed. Nicholas Thomas and Oliver Berghof, assisted by Jennifer Newell, University of Hawai'i Press, Honolulu.

Gould, Stephen Jay, 1984, *The Mismeasure of Man*, Penguin, London. First published 1981.

Greenblatt, Stephen, 1991, *Marvellous Possessions: The Wonder of the New World*, The University of Chicago Press, Chicago.

Guest, Harriet, 2007, *Empire, Barbarism and Civilisation: Captain Cook, William Hodges and the Return to the Pacific*, Cambridge University Press, Cambridge.

Harriott, Thomas, 1972, *A Briefe and True Report of the New Found Land of Virginia. The complete 1590 Theodor de Bry edition*, with a new intro by Paul Hulton, Dover Publications inc., New York.

Harrison, Charles, Paul Wood, and Jason Gaiger, 2000, *Art in Theory 1648–1815: An Anthology of Changing Ideas*, Blackwell, Oxford.

Hill, Christopher, 1979, *Milton and the English Revolution*, Faber and Faber, London and Boston. First published 1977.

Honour, Hugh, 1975, *The New Golden Land: Images of America from the Discoveries to the Present Time*, London.

Joppien, Rüdiger and Bernard Smith, 1985a, *The Art of Captain Cook's Voyages,* Vol. 1, *The Voyage of the* Endeavour *1768–1771*, Yale University Press, New Haven and London.

Joppien, Rüdiger and Bernard Smith, 1985b, *The Art of Captain Cook's Voyages,* Vol. 2, *The Voyage of the* Resolution *and* Adventure *1772–1775*, Yale University Press, New Haven and London.

Kaeppler, A., ed., 2009, *James Cook and the Exploration of the Pacific*, exhibition catalog, Thames and Hudson, London.

Kant, Immanuel, 1960 [1764], *Observations on the Feeling of the Beautiful and Sublime*, trans. John T. Goldthwait, University of California Press, Berkeley, Los Angeles, London.

Kramnick, Isaac, 1995, *The Portable Enlightenment Reader*, Penguin, Harmondsworth.

Kuhlemann, Ute, 2007, "Between reproduction, invention and propaganda: Theodor de Bry's engravings after John White's watercolours" in Sloan, *A New World: England's First View of America*.

Las Casas, Bartolmé de, 1992 [1552], *A Short Account of the Destruction of the Indes*, ed. and trans. Nigel Griffen with an introduction by Anthony Pagden, Penguin Books, London.

Leask, Nigel, 2002, *Curiosity and the Aesthetics of Travel Writing 1770–1840*, Oxford University Press, Oxford.

Locke, John, 1988 [1698], *Two Treatises of Government*, ed. Peter Lazlett, Cambridge University Press, Cambridge, 2nd edn with amendments. First published 1960.

Meek, R.L., 1976, *Social Science and the Ignoble Savage*, Cambridge University Press, Cambridge.

Montaigne, Michel de, 1991 [1580], *The Complete Essays*, trans. M.A. Screech, Penguin Books Ltd, London. This translation first published 1987.

Quilley, Geoff and John Bonehill, eds, 2004, *William Hodges 1744–1797: The Art of Exploration*, National Maritime Museum, London, Yale University Press, New Haven and London.

Rousseau, Jean-Jacques, 1984 [1775], *A Discourse on Inequality*, trans. with an introduction Maurice Cranston Penguin Books Ltd, London.

Slenczka, Eberhard, 2002, *Aztecs*, Royal Academy of Arts, London, catalog entry 359.

Sloan, Kim, 2007, *A New World: England's First View of America*, The British Museum Press, London.

Smith, Bernard, 1985, *European Vision and the South Pacific*, Yale University Press, New Haven and London, 2nd edn. First published 1959.

Smith, Bernard, 1992, *Imagining the Pacific: In the Wake of the Cook Voyages*, Melbourne University Press.

Thomas, Nicholas, 1991, *Entangled Objects: Exchange, Material Culture and Colonialism in the Pacific*, Harvard University Press, Cambridge MA and London.

Thomas, Nicholas, 2003, *Discoveries: The Voyages of Captain Cook*, Allen Lane-Penguin, London.

Wittkower, Rudolf, 1989, *Selected Lectures of Rudolf Wittkower: The Impact of Non-European Civilizations on the Art of the West*, compiled and edited by Donald Martin Reynolds, Cambridge University Press, Cambridge.

3

Modernism and Modern World

Introduction

The story of modernism has been told many times and from many different points of view. It has been told as a story of triumph and of freedom. It has been told as a story of incorporation by the powers that be and of subsequent renewal, ever more radical renewal. It has been extended, revised, and fought over with an intensity that can seem perplexing to those who come to it with an innocent curiosity about "art." For there has always been more at stake than just "art" in the stories of modernism. There have been values at stake, judgments about what is important not just in art but in the modern world itself, of which art has been a kind of barometer. The volatility of modernity, its sheer magnitude, the bloodiness and also – though it is unfashionable to say so – the heroism of the wider modern condition, all of these have fed into descriptions of its art. The key point being that, from the perspective of its practitioners, including both its makers and its commentators, art has not been a sideshow to the real business of shifting money or otherwise making the world go round. It has not been something for the farmers and the businessmen, the politicians and the rich to relax and show off with. From the inside, it has meant more than all of that contingency, all that mere history. For some it has been a substitute religion in a largely secular age, its consummated experience a moment of grace won back from the flux of time. Even for those with their feet more firmly planted in material life, convinced that "the world is all that is the case," what art has had to say about the modern world has seemed to matter greatly, even as that world itself seemed often not to care. From planning and modeling the future to representing the "furthest nerve-ending" of the self-consciousness of the world as it is, the very

Western Art and the Wider World, First Edition. Paul Wood.

triviality of modern art in the great scheme of feeding and reproducing was its paradoxical strength.

It may, ironically, have lost some of that strength as it has moved from the margins to a position of increased prominence in the culture at large since the late 1980s. There still seems to be something wrong with saying that modern, or rather "postmodern" art has evolved into a new academy; but for all the qualifications you might feel the need to enter, it has done – or has done something very like that. All the billions of dollars spent on it, all the trillions of words written about it, surely testify to art's place in the world, whether that place be as participant in the spectacle or licensed jester. No longer a threat to the status quo, if indeed it ever was, the contemporary marriage of art to culture is a symptom of the evolution of both. The grandchildren of the avant-garde now manage the culture industry (in which we may as well include the education industry). So the question that has to be asked, the story that has to be told, becomes one about the identity of this culture we all inhabit, its history, and art's position in that history.

Over the second half of the twentieth century, the telling of art's story ceased to be the province of its enthusiasts. Once upon a time, stories of modern art had a heroic tinge, as pioneering artists fought themselves free from a stultifying dominant culture and helped create a kind of alternative vision of society which, if it did not quite succeed in overthrowing the regnant powers, at least enabled the willing, the sensitive, and the perceptive to create a world within a world. This changed with the advent of what was once called "the new art history," and the tenor of the accounts took on a negative cast – tracing not art's freedom from the academy and the world of conventional taste but its deeper complicities with the background of wealth and power. For much of that time, as the explanations of the formalists and spiritualists ceased to compel conviction, an array of Marxists, feminists, psychoanalysts, semioticians, and deconstructionists have all told stories of the modern movement according to their various lights. Most have been motivated by varieties of emancipatory impulse – emancipation both from the thrall of the dominant society as such (whether that was construed as bourgeois, patriarchal, or imperialist), as well as emancipation from previous narratives of art itself. For most of that time, only one thing united them: geography. Until very recently indeed practically all stories of modern art have been told by Europeans and Americans about Europe and America. Modernism has been a Western creation, indeed modernity itself has been seen as a singularly Western condition.

All of that is now emphatically over. The end of the Cold War and the full force of globalization (however that condition be perceived) have moved the goalposts on the field of art history. This altered state has impacted not just on our perceptions of the art of the present time (which is the business of Chapter 5) but the way we have to read the past of modernity (which is the business of Chapters 3 and 4). That said, we cannot change our spots overnight, and it will be a long time before a revised history of modern art in a modern world can be told in all its plenitude. For now we have to begin with what we have got, and see where the story leads.

In the Beginning ...

To seek the origin of modernism is to hunt the snark. Each narrative constructs its own beginning. Accounts stressing the autonomy of art and the expressive qualities of form tended to begin with Cézanne in the late nineteenth century. A more catholic sense of the modern movement perceived the beginning a few decades earlier with the Salon des Refusés in 1863, flagging the start of the avant-garde's break with the Salon, embodied in the *Déjeuner sur l'herbe* of Edouard Manet. The social history of art, seeking to embed art in the movement of class and capital, pushed that back to the revolutionary year of 1848 and regarded Gustave Courbet as the key figure and his *Burial at Ornans* as a key work. Subsequently, as interest grew in the wider origins of the modern condition in general, the furthest reaches of the modern in art were located in the late eighteenth century. T.J. Clark, with a provocative particularity that was probably never meant to be taken entirely seriously, nominated 1793 and Jacques-Louis David's *Death of Marat* as the moment when that sense of historical contingency which has marked modernity (rather than the dubious comfort of a divinely ordered Fate) entered definitively into art.[1] Michael Fried arrived at the first half of the 1760s as the point which marked a distinction between "different worlds," worlds represented in art by the difference between Chardin and Greuze, and in the wider culture by the inception of that condition which others have called alienation.[2] And so it goes on. In literature, T.S. Eliot discovered the "disassociation of sensibility" in the seventeenth century. Eliot had initially seen this in relation to Milton (and Dryden) and his response to the English revolution. But Eliot subsequently qualified this, and his qualification is worth quoting as a warning to those who risk being over hasty in their attempts to relate changes in art to changes in anything else.

> All we can say is, that something like this [i.e. a disassociation of sensibility] did happen; that it had something to do with the Civil War; that it would even be unwise to say it was caused by the Civil War; but that it is a consequence of the same causes which brought about the Civil War; that we must seek the causes in Europe, not in England alone; and for what these causes were, we may dig and dig until we get to a depth at which words and concepts fail us.[3]

I shall settle here for the argument of Paul Oskar Kristeller, made as long ago as the early 1950s, that the "modern system of the arts" has its beginnings in the eighteenth century. Kristeller was talking about all the arts, including music and poetry. But in the field of the visual arts, what he was indicating was the emergence of painting, sculpture, and architecture as "major" arts, and their consequent separation from practices such as tapestry, gardening, and others increasingly regarded as "minor" or principally decorative arts. Of course, this hierarchy is precisely one of the things that is being questioned in the recent period, broadly since the 1960s but with gathering force in the period of globalization, as the concept of "Art" has been opened up to include objects and practices that would have fallen outside earlier, essentially European, definitions. (Equally, it is no accident that Kristeller's thesis has been opened to debate in the field of philosophical aesthetics at the same time.) As Kristeller put it: "this system of the five major arts, which underlies all modern aesthetics and is so familiar to us all, is of comparatively recent origin, and did not assume definite shape before the eighteenth century, although it has many ingredients going back to classical, medieval and Renaissance thought." Kristeller's concern was not with developments in the individual arts as such but with the emergence of the system as a whole, that is, "their relations to each other, and their place in the general framework of Western culture."[4] Kristeller's was very much an historical vision; he commented at the end of his paper that "the various arts are certainly as old as human civilisation"; that it was our accustomed grouping of them that had a modern origin; and, prophetically as it turned out, that "the branches of the arts all have their rise and decline," that even the "distinction between the 'major' arts and their subdivisions is arbitrary and subject to change," and that already, "the traditional system of the fine arts begins to show signs of disintegration."[5]

Given that Kristeller was writing not long after the end of the Second World War, at a point when the "system" he was describing had been solidly in place for two centuries and in the modern visual arts had arguably yet to reach its apogee, this was prescient indeed. Anyone can see now that globalization is completing the undoing of the modern system of the arts that was definitively inaugurated by conceptual art in the 1960s (and was anticipated by certain manifestations of the avant-garde in the earlier twentieth century), but few had the historical perspective to moot that possibility then. More to the point for our present purposes, is to recognize, first, that the modern system of the arts had a beginning; and second, that it was European.

We have already seen something of how European artists and intellectuals struggled to find terms with which to deal with the societies and cultures they encountered in the Pacific in the late eighteenth century. That situation exhibited both similarities with and differences from the sense they were able to make of places with which they had a longer, albeit uneven, acquaintance: the other developed civilizations of Eurasia – the Islamic societies of the Middle East and Persia, India, and the more remote worlds of China and Japan. Clearly no short account can do justice to this breadth of experience, and here we shall have to be selective. Some general points are useful to establish, however. Perhaps the most important concerns present-day attitudes to these encounters. It has been a paradoxically shared feature of both earlier imperialist accounts and some contemporary postcolonial reassessments that they tend to over-emphasize the scale and extent of European domination. The sense of an inexorable, continually rising tide of European power has served both to underwrite an exaggerated rejection of all things European, good and bad alike and to reduce European culture to a reflex of imperialism.

The reasons for this are multifarious and complex and constitute a subject for debate in themselves, once again extending far beyond the present compass. One, however, concerns the key text of modern thinking on these subjects, Edward Said's *Orientalism*, originally published in 1978. *Orientalism* has had such an impact on the field of art history and cultural studies that it would be misplaced to debate its status here. That is not to say, of course, that in the many years since its appearance, it has not been subjected to criticism, some of it foundational. This debate is simultaneously a relatively specialized affair within the parameters of academic "orientalism" (construed as the multifaceted historical, cultural, political, and linguistic study of non-European societies from within the European academy) and a matter of pressing concern in the contemporary global polity – where questions of Western power are a daily matter for millions. The only point I want to highlight here comes early in Said's statement of his position. This is the famous argument that orientalism does not merely describe – or distort – its object but constructs it. It goes almost without saying that Said's position here is not original or peculiar to him but is part of a wider current of thought emerging in the mid-twentieth century and subsequently achieving dominance throughout the radical academy. Said himself cites Foucault. But the position is much broader, running not only through the spectrum of French post-structuralism but also standpoints as dissimilar as Gramsci's earlier radical Marxism and T.S. Kuhn's arguments about the nature of scientific progress. Were the term not out of fashion, it would almost be worth calling constructivism a *zeitgeist*. The varieties of constructivism, meaning the perception that the terms of thought go a long way, if not the whole way, to determining the objects of thought, have come to constitute the warp and weft of critical theory across the broad spectrum of cultural studies and social science since at least the second half of the twentieth century. Nothing is going to change that; and arguably, nor should it. Insofar as liberalism, both in its classical manner and its more recent, more conservative "neoliberal" guise, has constituted the voice of the status quo – call it "bourgeois society," "contemporary capitalism," or what you will – the manifold expressions of social constructivism have constituted the voice of opposition.

The Achilles' heel of this view is its tendency to disparage facts. If what is to count as a "fact" is believed to be a function of the categories in terms of which the world is being classified and described, then facts lose their status as an external check on argument. At the extreme, they are reduced to the status of internal counters within the game being played. As Foucault, and before him, Nietzsche, would agree, knowledge becomes a function of power. Knowledge clearly is not separate from power; if history tells us anything, it tells us that. But the point where the world disappears into the framework, the point where representation, or representability, is suspended and repositioned within narrative, is dangerous as well as liberating. It may be that the moment at which the promise of the latter outweighed the risk of the former is past. It shows how far we have traveled when it becomes a risky thing to say that attention to facts and to the criteria of rational argument are values with merit and not merely the subterfuges of conservative (read: bourgeois, patriarchal, imperialist) ideology.

History and Empire

In a recent comprehensive survey of empire from the beginning of the fifteenth century to the present John Darwin made a strong case for two complementary theses. The first of these concerns a position which he attributed to three of the preeminent analysts of the European social formation between the Enlightenment and the modern period: Smith, Marx, and Weber; thinkers who otherwise are characterized more usually for their differences rather than their similarities. This is the view that modern European capitalism "energised a stationary world." For Darwin, to the contrary, far from Europeans "discovering" Asia and galvanizing static societies, "Europeans were latecomers in a huge maritime commerce, pioneered by Asians, linking China, Japan, South East Asia, India, the Persian Gulf, the Red Sea and East Africa. Far from awaiting the Promethean touch of merchants from Europe, a 'global' economy already existed." In short, the widely shared supposition, widely shared that is among conservatives, liberals, and radicals alike, of a European galvanization of the East is "a travesty of the facts."[6]

This is a thesis which may expect to command ready assent from most contemporary critics of a "postmodernist" or "postcolonialist" cast. Its corollary, however, is less likely to find agreement. For, as Darwin also argues, this situation means that the history of the last half millennium is "far more contested, confused and chance-ridden"[7] than the assumption of an inexorable rise to Western supremacy would suggest. For long periods a broad "parity" held between the three main power centers of the Eurasian landmass, the Christian nations of the west, the Islamic powers in the central regions (including, from the early sixteenth century, India), and China in the Far East. Darwin argues that in the fifteenth century a "rough equality"[8] was maintained across all these regions, and moreover each of them experienced expansion. At this point Cairo was larger than any city in western Europe. Neither was this condition short-lived. The seventeenth century and even the early eighteenth century were a period of "early modern equilibrium." Western global dominance was for long periods barely on the agenda: "Three centuries after Columbus had made landfall, most of the North American mainland remained unoccupied and virtually unexplored by Europeans. It took nearly three hundred years for the corner of India where Vasco da Gama had landed to fall under European rule."[9] For much of this period, Darwin speculates, the idea that Europeans "occupying a niche in the maritime fringes of the Asian world might be harbingers of later Occidental domination would surely have struck most Asian rulers as risibly improbable."[10]

When the change came, it came quickly. In an extraordinary period of expansion, between approximately 1750 and 1830, Europe achieved the beginnings of a global dominance that for the next century and more carried all before it. But even within that domination there was negotiation, opposition, contestation. Even at its height, Western power was seldom absolute. Moreover, on the greater historical timescale it did not last all that long. By the middle of the twentieth century, political imperial rule was being ceded to a less direct economic domination. By the end of the century, that too was undergoing significant qualification with the rise to power of India and China. Darwin does not say this, but it begins to look as if another period of parity, albeit a potentially dangerous and unstable one, may be emerging.

The upshot of these arguments is that the period in which the West really achieved global domination is considerably shorter than it is often reckoned to be – reckoned to be, that is, both by the self-serving estimate of Western imperialists and their intellectual confederates on the one hand, and on the other by those now seeking to redress the balance. The fact and extent of Western power should not be minimized. It has been the backdrop to virtually everything in the modern period, and it has been scandalously absent from a great deal of even supposedly radical art history until quite recently. But by the same token it should not either be exaggerated, turned into something like a force of nature in an equal and opposite movement to that in which its "other" – the "Orient" – is transmuted into an intellectual fiction. They are two sides of the same coin, the real, empirical, dirty, *historical* coin, made in equal measure of meanings and guns, of bread and images. The high period of Western power was coincident with modernity, a period of about two hundred and fifty years, and it is already over, or beginning to be. It is not the five hundred years since the Portuguese staggered round the Cape of Good Hope and Columbus bumped into America. And it is most certainly not an ascending curve traceable back without interruption to Marco Polo in the late 1200s.

Marco Polo's journey has sometimes been doubted, though the balance of probability is that he did go to China. That he could do so was down to the *pax mongolica* of Genghis Khan and his descendants. But that did not last long. Within a century, East Asia was effectively closed again to Europeans. It was not until 1498 that the Portuguese found a sea route to India, and by the early years of the sixteenth century they had established trading posts as far away as China. In terms of cultural interchange, however, there was relatively little (beyond the trade in luxury goods such as porcelain and silk that we have already noted) until Jesuit missionaries began arriving in the Far East in the late sixteenth century. From the other side, in the first quarter of the fifteenth century, the Chinese Admiral Cheng-ho is now known to have conducted no fewer than half a dozen voyages of exploration around the coasts of Southeast Asia, and southern India, sailing as far as the Red Sea and even East Africa. A final, seventh, voyage took place as late as 1431. But in stark contrast to the questing Europeans, always the rough edge of mercantile capitalism and sometimes little more than pirates, the nationalistic Ming dynasty had no need of foreign contact. The voyages were suspended, Chinese subjects were forbidden to travel, the Great Wall was built to secure its land border, and China settled into what has been called a condition of "high level equilibrium," more or less independent of the rest of the world. It may seem an insubstantial thing to say, but it betokens a real difference: the Europeans were interested in China, for a thousand and one reasons ranging from profit to wisdom.

The Chinese were not interested in Europe. Their own world was felt to be rich enough, wise enough, and stable enough not to need more.

European Effects

That said, in terms of art and culture, the walls between Europe and the eastern parts of Eurasia were not impermeable. We are familiar with the ways luxury goods, and sometimes ideas too, came west. Other goods, and other ideas, traveled east. The Jesuits went to convert, as they had earlier in South America. To do this they took Bibles and other books with them. And their books contained pictures; pictures constructed according to the new post-Renaissance mode of a coherent fictive spatial armature and realistic illusions of three-dimensional figures disposed in that space. We have seen how some of the Ottoman elite in the late fifteenth century were fascinated by the possibilities of the new "Frankish" art. Throughout India and the Far East, beginning in the sixteenth century and continuing into the eighteenth century and beyond, wherever diplomatic missions and theological debates happened, perspective made artists sit up and take notice. I shall confine myself here to the discussion of three symptomatic examples.

Mughal India

Mughal art is world famous for its images of courtly life. That character of Mughal art, along with much Ottoman and Persian painting, should be enough to give pause to an over-ready assumption of Islamic iconoclasm, which was far from absolute. The first Mughal emperor, Akbar, encouraged the visual arts and is reported to have said "I cannot tolerate those who make the slightest criticism of this art. It seems to me that a painter is better than most in gaining a knowledge of God."[11] Mughal art was circumscribed by strict representational conventions, especially regarding the depiction of higher social ranks. But in a parallel fashion to the way in which European academic art was less rigid lower down its hierarchy of genres – permitting, for example, some of the technical innovations in landscape that later opened the way for modernism – in Mughal painting, peripheral images of lower-class figures (dancers, musicians, servants and the like) sometimes embraced a realism absent from the hieratic image of the rulers. Some in the Mughal court, including the emperor, had an interest in European art which extended to collecting it. For that purpose, in the late 1570s Akbar sent a mission to the Portuguese in Goa ("Golden Goa," the jewel in the crown of Portuguese operations in the East). Flemish prints and paintings seem also to have been available, presumably from the Dutch, who were also active in south and southeast Asia.

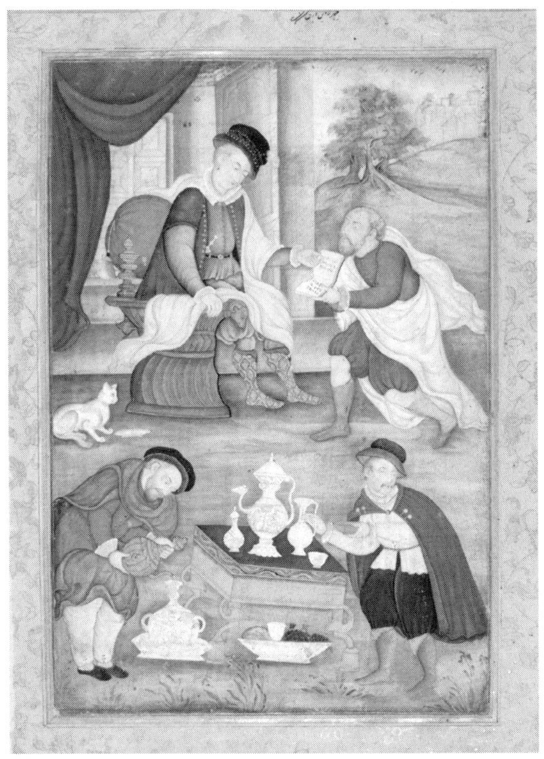

Figure 3.1 Mughal, attributed to Sanvala, *A Scene with European figures*, c.1600, opaque watercolor, image 26.4 × 17.5 cm (page 33.5 × 21.6 cm). British Library, London, Johnson Album 16, 6. © The British Library Board / Robana.

Mughal court artists were encouraged to copy illustrations from European books, including images of the Virgin and Child, of Jesus, and of saints. Occasionally this could extend to secular figures. One such instance, by the artist Sanvala, dates to c.1600 (Figure 3.1). It shows four Europeans. Two in the foreground are apparently drinking tea. Further back, another figure in European clothes sits in a chair, with a white cat on the floor next to him, and reads from a book being held for him by a fourth figure, who may be based on an image of St Paul (usually shown as balding). The table supporting the drinking utensils is depicted in a slightly off kilter perspective, while behind the seated figure there is a more convincingly rendered stone building with a column, a receding wall behind it and the kind of plush, draped red curtain familiar from many European Renaissance paintings. The overwhelming majority of Mughal art worked within its own conventions, but such early examples are testimony both to the fascination perspectival representation held for non-Western visual cultures as well as to the porosity that can be found in those "contact zones" where cultures meet and mix, and which is quite distinct from the aspiration to cultural purity more often identified with imperial heartlands. Much later, as European power grew in India in the late eighteenth and early nineteenth centuries, there emerged the so-called Company school of painting, a fully fledged hybrid form in which Indian artists drew on both native Indian and European representational traditions to serve the British imperium. The British Museum only completed its catalog of over 1,200 such works in 2011, showing how much remains to be done in the field of world art studies to recover such works from the margins to which Eurocentric history has consigned them.

Japan

At a later date than the cultural exchange taking place in Mughal India, something comparable happened in Japan. The late sixteenth century saw a policy of openness in Japan, with a considerable amount of foreign trade involving the Portuguese, Dutch, and British, as well as the arrival of Jesuit missionaries. But by the middle of the seventeenth century, like China, Japan turned to isolation. Despite this, however, or perhaps because of it, a new and remarkably "modern" form of social life emerged in the capital, Edo, which exhibited certain affinities with later Parisian *modernité*: the very form of life which did so much to stimulate the "painting of modern life" associated with Baudelaire and Manet. Just as features of the Dutch republic of the mid-seventeenth century can seem like a slice of modernity thrust back into the past, so the "floating world" of Edo in the same period serves to underline that while modernity itself was not something utterly unprecedented in the nineteenth century, neither was it wholly and solely European. In late seventeenth-century Edo, and with increasing force in the early eighteenth-century, a subcultural world of theaters and restaurants, places of social and sexual instability and encounter, of fashion and conspicuous consumption, gave rise to an art dedicated to capturing those fleeting evenings for those who enjoyed them. This was *ukiyo-e*, "pictures of the floating world."

Remarkably, whereas in nineteenth-century Paris, it was the manifestly different technical features of the Japanese *ukiyo-e* prints – their flat colors, their spatial dislocations – that stimulated avant-garde artists seeking a way beyond the confining protocols of the academy, in late-seventeenth century Edo a subgenre of these prints incorporated a stylistic feature adapted from European imagery: perspective. This appeared quite suddenly, around 1740, and it remains unclear quite how, or why. Timothy Clark notes that in 1720, as part of a reform package, in part stimulated by an interest in Western science and technology, the Shogun lifted a ban on the importation of European books, at least in Chinese translation. Clark comments, "It is tempting to suggest that this may have resulted in the appearance in Japan of European books on perspective."[12] Tempting, but as Clark scrupulously observes, unproven. There is no evidence of direct copying from European sources, and it is possible the Japanese perspective pictures derived from Chinese prints that had assimilated the European influence.

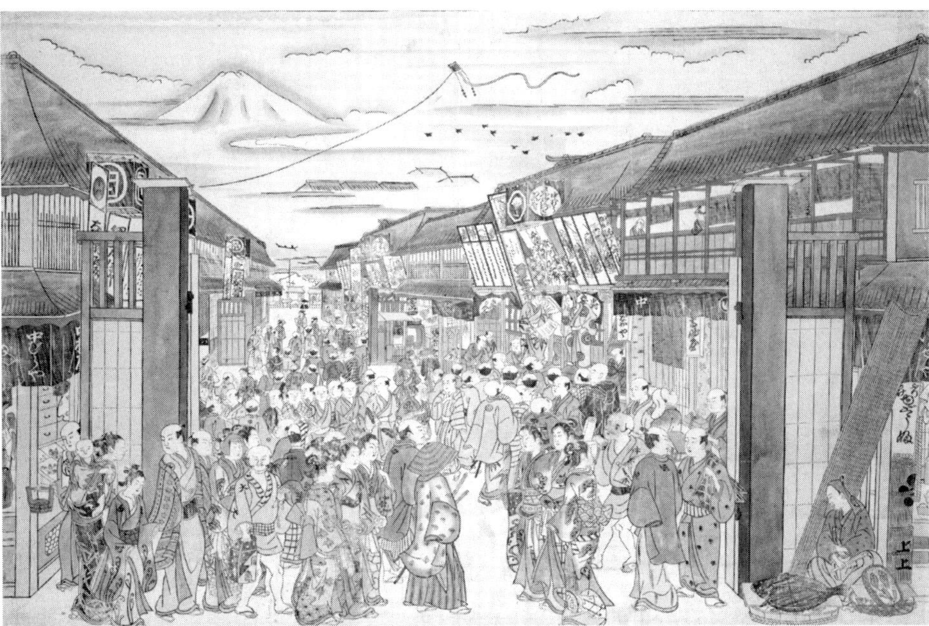

Figure 3.2 Okumura Masanobu, *Large Perspective Picture of the Kabuki Theater District in Sakai-chō and Fukiya-chō*, Edo Period, c.1745, woodblock print, ink on paper with hand-applied color. Museum of Fine Arts, Boston, William Sturgis Bigelow Collection 11.19687. Photograph © 2013 Museum of Fine Arts, Boston, all rights reserved / The Bridgeman Art Library.

An image such as Okumura Masanobu's *Large Perspective Picture of the Kabuki Theater District in Sakai-chō and Fukiya-chō* nonetheless shows the powerful effect such mixing could produce (Figure 3.2). A crowd throngs the street between rows of kabuki theaters, teahouses, brothels, and shops. Other large-scale prints (half a meter or more in width) show the interiors of theaters and shops and the various transactions taking place there. All are enlivened by subtle details of costume, fashion, internal textual descriptions on advertising posters and menus, as well as gestures and glances, the meanings of which would have been accessible to those enjoying the life and knowingly consuming representations of it but which now require expert decoding; again, not unlike the recovery of the more complex subtexts of the mid-nineteenth-century *peinture de la vie moderne*.[13] Certain of these views of the interiors of theaters were even recycled with just the area showing the action of the play on stage updated while the surround of the building and the audience remained unchanged.

A particularly notable feature of some of the outdoor views is the way in which the upper part of the image deliberately eschews the Western perspective representation and reverts to a more conventionally Japanese rendering of space: in the present case running together the kite flying over the foreground with the distant image of Mount Fuji. This appears to indicate a highly sophisticated grasp of the point that different conventions of visual representation are in play. There is no mistake here of the kind that would regard perspective as visual truth. In one of those endlessly intriguing recursions which the permeability of art invites as it moves through and beyond the borders imposed by the politics of nations, the multilayered images of the floating world not only "transform our vision" of that place and time, but as Clark also observes, "perspective prints were to exercise a profound long-term influence, informing the landscape vision of both Katsushika Hokusai and Utagawa Hiroshige."[14] They in their turn were to exert a no less profound influence on the European avant-garde, precisely as regards this question of representational convention.

China

Equally complex, hybridized representations were also being produced in China in the late eighteenth century, sometimes with the active involvement of European artists. In China too, this period, lasting from the middle of the seventeenth to the end of the eighteenth century and involving connections not only with a wide range of Asian countries but also with Europe, is seen as one of developing modernity. Restrictions on maritime trade had been lifted in 1684, and this ushered in a period of expansion. After the previous, more introverted and nationalistic period, this one involved an openness to Western ideas in the fields of science and mathematics as well as art. Indeed, perspectival representation was itself regarded as "scientific."

Whereas the traditional Chinese style associated with the *literati* retained a certain coded independence from the court, court art itself was intimately bound up with the practice of political power and represented a significant component of imperial authority. As well as portraits of leading figures, large-scale painting was used to record contemporary historical events of importance, including tours of inspection of the provinces and major diplomatic occasions. Jesuit scholars and artists had a considerable presence at the Qing court, involving a range of activities from diplomatic negotiations to map-making as well as painting. Several of these men became integrated into Chinese imperial culture, adopting Chinese names and receiving awards for service. Among the most prominent, Guiseppe Castiglione (Chinese name, Lang Shining) worked in China from 1715 to his death in 1766; Ignaz Sichelbarth (Chinese name, Ai Qimeng), originally from Bohemia, similarly worked there until his death in 1780. Such European painters, as well as undertaking work on their own, taught European techniques to Chinese artists, and Chinese and Europeans collaborated on major commissions.

One such collaboration, completed in 1755 and worked on by several hands including Castiglione and Sichelbarth, shows the *Imperial Banquet in the Garden of Ten Thousand Trees* (Figure 3.3). Over four meters wide and two meters high, it records the ceremony at which the Qianlong emperor accepted the submission of the

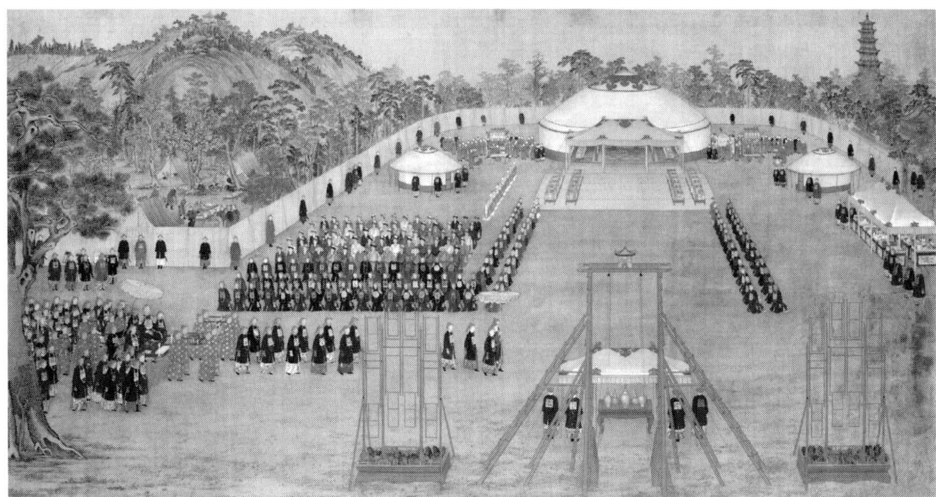

Figure 3.3 Attributed to Guiseppe Castiglione (Chinese name, Lang Shining), Jean-Denis Attiret (Chinese name, Wang Zhicheng), Ignaz Sichelbarth (Chinese name, Ai Qimeng), and Chinese court painters: *Imperial Banquet in the Garden of the Ten Thousand Trees*, 1755, horizontal wall-scroll, ink and color on silk, 221.5 × 419 cm, The Palace Museum, Beijing, GU6275. Photo provided by the Palace Museum / Hu Chui.

Torghut Mongols. Described as "a classic example of the hybrid Chinese-Western style,"[15] the landscape outside the enclosure is depicted in a relatively "Chinese" style, while within the enclosure in which the ceremony takes place perspectival depth is emphatically used to define the space. In single figure works, the European technique was less schematically employed and was used to bolster the realism, particularly of areas such as the face. In addition to such court art, in a manner comparable to the "Company painting" which emerged in late eighteenth- and nineteenth-century India, Chinese artists also produced hybrid works for export to Europe. One example of such is the series of five paintings which hangs in Claydon House in Buckinghamshire. Each of the paintings depicts people clad in "Chinese" clothes engaged in "Chinese" pursuits in "Chinese" landscape gardens, but all are represented in a distinctly Westernized style employing stable perspectival space and the modeling of figures.

East–West Crossings

What these examples show is that the thesis of Western dynamism contrasted to oriental stasis no more holds for art than it does for the wider socioeconomic situation. Outside of Europe, in limited but significant instances, cultural interaction took place. The evidence is there in the works. Certain Indian, Chinese, and

Japanese artists, a minority certainly (and here we must not forget, either, the example of Tupaia, discussed in Chapter 2), made efforts to come to terms with European art as it came to them through the miscellaneous activities of traders, missionaries, and diplomats. By the same token this implies the existence of an audience for such essays; again, small, but it was there. Without interest, there would have been no engagement; and there was considerable interest in Western achievements especially in science, technology, and organization. The domain of representation, art, would appear to have been included in this spectrum of interest.

In Europe itself at this period the situation is comparable. While the culture writ large remained inward-looking, fixed upon the classical–Christian heritage, there was interest, indeed increasing interest, in Eastern civilizations. However, there are telling differences between East and West. Moreover, it was the differences that were about to become pronounced. In the sphere of art itself, the obvious difference between Europe and the Eastern art forms it encountered was principally technical. But underlying this was something more philosophical. The technical distinction, as we have already seen, revolves around perspective and the way it was understood less as a representational convention than as the key to visual truth. The philosophical distinction involves the emergence during this same period of a systematic sense of Western superiority over other societies. As time went on, and the late eighteenth century turned into the nineteenth, this evolved into a scientific (or more properly, pseudoscientific) racism. This is the burden of Edward Said's *Orientalism* and much of the postmodernist, postcolonialist theory which succeeded it. No account of Western art's involvement with the wider world between the middle of the eighteenth and the middle of the twentieth centuries can avoid that.

Inception of "Orientalism"

The shift in attitude can be seen by juxtaposing two assessments of the Ottoman Empire. As we have seen, during the fifteenth and sixteenth centuries, a sense of awed admiration sometimes approaching fear was a recurrent theme in European responses to the rise of the Ottoman Turks, extending from well before the fall of Constantinople to the siege of Vienna and beyond. In an aside to an essay on a completely different topic, Montaigne, as if it were an entirely uncontroversial judgment, avers that "the mightiest, yea the best settled estate, that is now in the world, is that of the Turkes."[16] By the early eighteenth century, however, Montesquieu has the two fictional protagonists of his *Persian Letters* traveling through Turkey en route to Europe. The senior figure, Usbek, writes back to a friend in Isfahan, "I was astonished at the weakness of the Ottoman Empire." He deplores the political regime, the military, navigation, and the working of the land.

The Turks are deemed "incapable" of commerce, whereas the European merchants are "invariably industrious and enterprising."[17] What matters here is less the veracity of the assessment, let alone whether a Persian traveler would actually have felt that way, but the fact that the French author did. Neither was such a shift in attitude restricted to the case of the Ottomans. We have already noted the late medieval assessment of the power and riches of Cathay in Marco Polo's account, an estimate which, in the absence of further information carried right through to Columbus in the late fifteenth century. Yet describing mid-eighteenth century chinoiserie, Hugh Honour wrote unblushingly, in a book published in 1961, of "the spectacle of quaint little men and monkeys attired in richly embroidered silk robes."[18] The point being, of course, that Honour himself was writing at the end of the period wherein such assessments had become routine. Not for nothing did the Marxist historian Victor Kiernan title his critical history of European attitudes to the outside world in the imperial age *The Lords of Human Kind* – a phrase itself taken from the eighteenth-century writer Oliver Goldsmith.[19]

Starting in the last third of the twentieth century, or thereabouts, there has been such a profound transformation of values that it is now almost impossible imaginatively to reinhabit the ground of such an untroubled assumption of Western preeminence. Nor, of course, would one wish to. And it is extremely important to recognize that there were always oppositional voices, largely associated with the tradition of the Left. Yet under the impact of identity politics, even Kiernan's remarkable study, which concedes nothing to the "civilizational" pretense of Western imperialism, reads like a message from a lost world. It is quite clear that the prospect of a reconstituted historical–geographical materialism (which will be discussed in Chapter 5) must needs go through identity politics. It remains an unresolved and fiercely debated question how far the concept of racism should be read back in history. Pseudoscientific, racist essentialism is a product of the mid-nineteenth century. But there is no question that feelings of cultural, civilizational superiority came increasingly to mark European thought for a considerable period before that. The extent to which it is justified to call these feelings racist is not a matter which the present book can explore in depth – though neither can it be avoided. There is no question that European art is tainted by such attitudes, and a refusal to accept that would be blinkered to say the least, and probably racist itself in the here and now. This does not, in my view, mean that either art or philosophy is a mere reflex of imperialism or racism. It may well be that all manifestations of modern European culture, insofar as they address other cultures, are touched to some degree by shades of "orientalism" in the Saidean sense, and thus by shades of attitudes that some may retrospectively judge racist. Equally, others may refuse that retrospective judgment.

My point as it bears on the present discussion is more straightforward. It would, I believe, be unwarrantedly limiting, and heaven knows it has gone on long enough, to continue to produce introverted histories of Western art that remain ethically intact by avoiding difficult moral, historical, philosophical, and political problems.

Certainly, in addressing the historical "contact zones" one has to remain extraordinarily vigilant. But I do not feel that passing over them in silence is any longer an option; nor on the other hand, does every single picture, sculpture, or text have to be prefaced with a health warning to satisfy the contemporary thought police. A fine line has to be walked, and a reflex, almost ritualistic, condemnation of representations both visual and verbal from the period and the locale of European imperialism seems no more useful than keeping them in the art historical closet. We have Hegel *and* Marx, Gérôme *and* Manet, orientalism *and* the avant-garde; and furthermore, in my opinion, Marx, Manet, and the avant-garde continue to speak to our present multicultural, globalized situation. Critical histories which would have a hand in producing an as yet unrealized cultural formation more adequate to our own present and future have to be able to address all of our pasts, and not always from a position of assumed moral superiority.

Looking Out

From the late seventeenth century, and with gathering force during the eighteenth, objects and ideas from the rest of the world became a feature of the European worldview. This is the central argument of Schwab's *Oriental Renaissance*, mentioned in Chapter 1. Citing Edgar Quinet (from whom he took his title) Schwab argued that his "Oriental Renaisance" "marked the close of the neoclassical age, just as the Classical Renaissance had marked the close of the medieval age." Modern scholarship tends to fight shy of such confidently announced periodization. But there is much truth in Schwab's claim that the increased translation of texts from Oriental languages hitherto unknown in Europe, especially Sanskrit and Chinese, "produced an effect equal to that produced in the fifteenth century by the arrival of Greek manuscripts and Byzantine commentators after the fall of Constantinople."[20] To mention only a few key examples: the Jesuits had long been active in China, and in 1687 a translation of Confucius appeared in Paris. No less a figure than Leibniz responded with interest. At a less elevated, but perhaps more broadly influential end of the intellectual spectrum, the first translation of the *Arabian Nights*, by Antoine Galland, was also published in Paris in 1704.[21] In England, Sir William Temple published *The Gardens of Epicurus*, which included a more or less fantastical appreciation of Chinese gardens, as early as 1685. In a somewhat different register, *Robinson Crusoe* came out in 1719. As already noted, Montesquieu's *Persian Letters* appeared in 1722. William Chambers' *Designs of Chinese Buildings* was published in 1757. The first translations of ancient Zoroastrian and Indian texts appeared in the 1770s and 1780s, the *Zend Avesta* and the *Bhagavad Gita*. Voltaire, Diderot, and Rousseau all began to set Europe against what they knew of the whole world (including both the long known about, highly developed civilizations of East Asia and the newly encountered very different societies of the

Pacific). And so it goes on. Even Samuel Johnson produced an orientalist allegory in his *Rasselas, Prince of Abyssinia* of 1759.[22] European knowledge of the wider world was partial, and unmistakably framed by a growing sense of European superiority – even when other perspectives were used as a lever to criticize European decadence. Such knowledge was becoming part of the fabric of European modernity. Indeed, to put it a slightly different way, thought about modernity and its impact on art has for too long treated it as a wholly European phenomenon – political revolution, technological invention, the contradictions between industrial capital and finance capital, between city and country. Modernity, however, has a crucial, global dimension. The fact that this dimension has lately been exposed to witheringly negative interpretation, and culture rendered symptomatic of empire, should not obscure the scale and impact that the world had on Europe as well as the other way round.

Chinoiserie

Such "worlded" knowledge was also becoming part of the fabric of European modernity in a literal as well as a metaphorical sense. "Chinoiserie" is the name of the eighteenth-century fascination felt by cultivated Europeans for all things Chinese. Its key feature, as Hugh Honour pointed out long ago, is that for the most part it was a projection of European fantasies and desires rather than a true representation of China. Its other key feature is that its impact was overwhelmingly in what, by then, were becoming defined as the "lesser" arts. Honour's early study, half a century old now, is a catalog of pottery, textiles, tapestries, lacquerwork, costumes for masquerades and balls at court, and theatrical productions lower down the social scale; and, higher up the scale again, endless numbers of pavilions, bridges, and other architectural ephemera in aristocratic estates from England and France, Germany and Italy to Russia and Scandinavia. Moreover, of course, there were entire rooms of this type constructed within the real architecture, especially the country houses, of the upper classes.

At this time in Europe, little differentiation was made between different actual places in the "orient." China and Japan were effectively one, the latter often being believed to be geographically part of the former. Even India was not always differentiated. The decorated Chinese screens which adorned so many country houses were known as "Coromandel" because of the Indian coastal ports from which they were shipped to Europe. Yet the fact that at least some of the Europeans themselves were aware of the fantastical nature of their appropriation of the Orient is apparent from Oliver Goldsmith's humorous "Chinese Letters" from the early 1760s. As already briefly mentioned, there was a fashion for European authors to construct fictional Oriental observers, the better to lay bare the foibles of European philosophy and fashion. Montesquieu's *Persian Letters* was only the most eminent of many such; Goldsmith's work was a slightly later English equivalent. In one of them, Goldsmith's "Citizen of the World," Lien Chi Altangi, is called to the country house of a British lady. Expecting an assignation, he is instead presented with her collection of things "Chinese" to admire – things which he fails to recognize. The lady, who treats him like a specimen of exotic fauna, wants to see him eat beef with chopsticks and speak Chinese. She then shows him empty jars "of the right pea-green" (which in his view should have been usefully filled with tea) and tries to get him to praise "the beauties of that Chinese temple which you see at the end of the garden." But he cannot recognize it, and is equally unimpressed with the "several rooms all furnished, as she told me, in the Chinese manner; sprawling dragons, squatting pagods, and clumsy mandarins, stuck on every shelf." The upshot is that, since she has employed a designer, presumably at considerable expense, "and nobody disputes his pretensions to taste," it must be the Chinese philosopher himself who suffers from "want of taste" in chinoiserie![23]

The "fine" arts were affected less by the fashion for chinoiserie than were the decorative arts, and this is telling. It was all right to indulge in exotica in the spheres of decoration and entertainment. Higher up the cultural scale, the sphere of "Art" as such, at this historical juncture, had little or no truck with influences from beyond the classical–Christian core. Or rather, to sharpen the point, there *was* a burgeoning interest, but it remained very securely framed by the technical and philosophical protocols of the European canon. There is no sense in which European "Art" was about to be destabilized by its Other – yet. Representations of the Other were, so to speak, still no more than possible topics of conversation within an overarching European visual language.

Within this there were different inflections, ranging from realistic depiction to allegory. Joshua Reynolds' portrait of the Pacific islander "Omai" is the best known single example of the former. Another is to be found tucked away in Johan Zoffany's almost equally well-known group portrait of the members of the Royal Academy. In recent years this has achieved a certain notoriety among feminist art historians for the way it relegates the two female members of the Academy to the status of painted portraits hanging on the rear wall (which does little justice to Zoffany's sense of humor in smuggling them into a life-drawing class at all). Less often noticed is a figure in the crowd at the far left-hand side. As if to prove that not all "citizens of the world" were fictions, this is a likeness of the visiting Chinese artist Tan Chitqua, who went on to have some success as a modeler of portrait busts of society clients in London and Oxford. Similar depictions also occur in contemporary pictures involving the British in India, not least by Zoffany himself. Zoffany worked in India in the late eighteenth century, as did a range of other more or less well-known British and Irish portraitists and landscape painters (including William Hodges, who had earlier been round the world with Captain Cook). These kinds of pictures indicate a surprising amount of travel and cultural interaction between European artists and the East. But perhaps the commonest route by which the world found its way into European art was through allegory. The most pervasive of these, as we have noted, was the genre of allegorical representations of the continents, in both painting and sculpture. These usually involved female figures, more or less nude (except for Europe), adorned with some form of defining headdress – feathers or a turban – and accompanied by local flora and fauna: maize, palm trees, armadillos, alligators, camels, and the like.

In the field of eighteenth-century chinoiserie, a specific subgenre appeared in the work of the French *ancien régime* artists Jean-Antoine Watteau and François Boucher. In the comparatively frivolous atmosphere of the Regency, succeeding the death of Louis XIV, Watteau produced the mural decorations *Figures chinoises et tartars* around 1719 for the royal Château de la Muette. These are now lost, though engravings based on them convey an impression of what they were like: a mixture of the linear decorative forms of the antique "grotesque" and that "quaint" caricature of the Chinese person we have already encountered, all flowing moustaches and equally flowing robes. In Honour's estimation, these features of Watteau's imagery had an impact "throughout Europe."[24] The accompaniment of monkeys was given full rein in Christopher Huet's slightly later wall and ceiling decoration for the *grande singerie* in the Château de Chantilly. But here we are firmly back in the realm of decoration.

The artist François Boucher had been involved in the production of the engravings from Watteau's paintings in 1731, but he produced little else in the vein until the early 1740s, whereupon, his biographer, Georges Brunel, deems him then to have been "seized by a veritable Chinese mania."[25] As well as engravings and designs for a set of tapestries, he submitted eight paintings of Chinese subjects to the Salon of 1742. Several of these, including the *Chinese Marriage*, the *Festival of the Emperor of China* and the *Chinese Garden* and *Chinese Fishermen* (sometimes also known simply as *Chinoiserie*) are now in the museum at Besançon (Figure 3.4). All are relatively modest in scale and employ a similar cast of characters: willowy maidens; small and ephemeral pavilions; flowers, parasols, and exotic trees; and venerable sages. To the modern taste they are excruciating. Managing to be simultaneously sentimental and demeaning of their supposed subject, they are the exception that proves the rule when it comes to arguing that the "high" arts failed to deal in any significant way with the eighteenth-century interest in China.

Chinoiserie was an expression of the European desire for exotica, as much a symptom of tiredness with classicism as with any real reflection upon the implications of other ways of life. In an earlier age, when religion was all-encompassing, objects of desire or revulsion tended to be placed in heaven or hell (or off the edge of the map). By the eighteenth century, the figure of "China" seems to have served as a convenient hook from which to hang desires for a better life on this earth: better, that is, than the burgeoning hollowness and artificiality, the fashion-following and monetary greed that increasingly came to be seen as identifying modern European society. (A case could be made that in the nineteenth century the figure of "Africa" came to play the opposite role – the negative stalking horse, the "hell

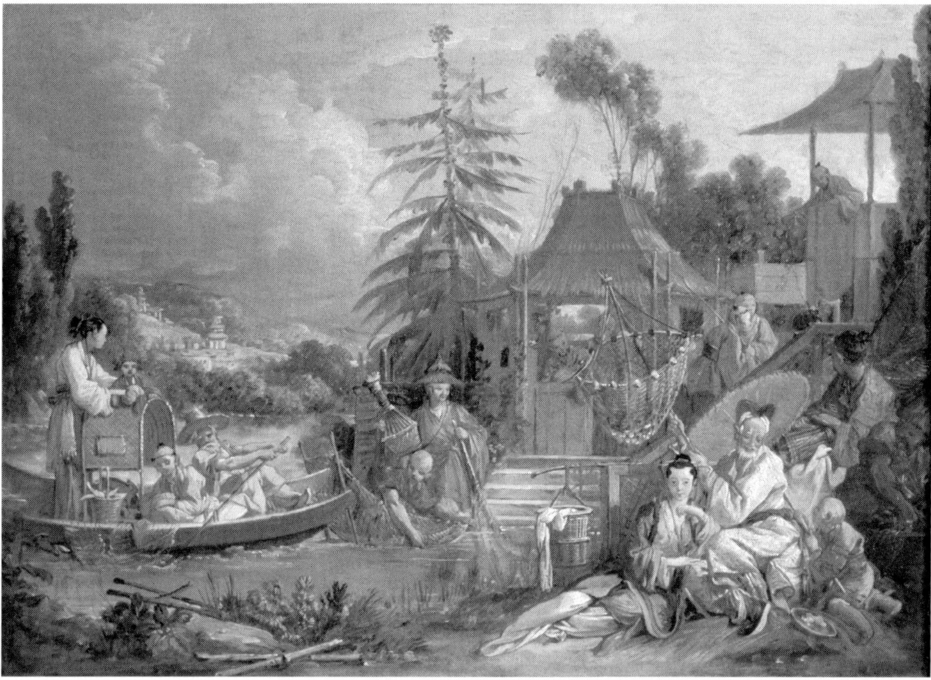

Figure 3.4 François Boucher, *The Chinese Fishermen*, c.1742, oil on canvas, Musée des Beaux-Arts, Besançon, France. © The Bridgeman Art Library Ltd. / Alamy.

on earth" motif, for those concerned to reinforce Europe's claim to civilization; again, this was a product of European fantasy rather than actual knowledge.) Chinoiserie was, so to speak, a manifestation of fashion rather than a reflection upon it.

Exclusivity

There is a case for thinking that perspective remained the stumbling block to a fuller engagement of Western art with the visual cultures of the wider world. In the visual arts, perspective was such a powerful device that it became invisible as a device. It became a figure not only for skill and accomplishment but for truth – visual truth. When it was combined with a sense of classicism as an objective standard that extended beyond painting into sculpture and architecture, the result was a combination that could, quite precisely, admit of no other. Montesquieu's late *Essay on Taste*, his last work, published in 1757, incorporates a wide-ranging rejection of all available alternatives to the Greek: Gothic, Egyptian, and Oriental.[26] For Montesquieu, the standard is set by Greek architecture. He concedes that this may at first glance seem uniform, but deeper reflection reveals that "Grecian architecture, whose divisions are few, but grand and noble, seems formed after the model of the great and the sublime. The mind perceives a certain majesty which reigns through all its productions." By contrast, "Gothic architecture appears extremely rich in point of variety, but its ornaments fatigue the eye by their confusion and minuteness." For Montesquieu, Gothic embodies "perplexity and confusion in its ideas." When he refers to "one foot placed precisely in the same position with the other, or any two of the corresponding parts of the body placed exactly in the same direction," "studied symmetry," and "sameness of attitude," it is hard (despite his invocation again of Gothic) not to see this as an early reference to Egyptian art. And given the eighteenth-century propensity to elide India and China, his rejection of "the stupid uniformity that is observable in the Indian Pagods" is surely a critique of the Orient *tout court*. Too much confusion and too much uniformity are two sides of the same coin, united by their distance from classical unity-in-diversity.

We have already encountered Perrault's earlier critique of Chinese painting. In similar vein, at the end of the seventeenth century, the Jesuit Père Louis Lecomte had written from Beijing that "the imperfect notion the Chinese have of all kinds of arts is betrayed by the unpardonable faults they are guilty of." He goes on to argue that in Chinese architecture "there wants that uniformity in which consists the beauty and convenience of our palaces. In a word there is, as it were, deformity in the whole, which renders it very unpleasing to foreigners, and must needs offend anyone that has the least notion of true architecture."[27] "True" here, of course means Greek. The philosopher Giambattista Vico, writing in 1744, also echoed Perrault's argument of the previous century when he observed in *The New Science* that the Chinese "do not yet know how to make shadows in painting, against which highlights can stand out; whence, since it has neither relief nor depth, their painting is most crude."[28] Finally, in his *Observations on the Feeling of the Beautiful and Sublime* of 1764, no less a figure than Immanuel Kant can be found routinely dismissing Indian religious sculpture as "monstrous" and Chinese painting as "grotesque."[29] In sum, during the eighteenth century, as previously, even though Europeans now had much increased contact with the rest of the world, and notwithstanding their growing interest in it, in terms of the visual arts they continued to perceive European classicism in general, and perspectival representation in particular, as an absolute standard against which all others were measured, not as legitimate variants but as deficient.

Somewhat paradoxically, given the tropes of freedom often associated with art, there were glimmerings of an emergent relativism in philosophy (as with the interest in Confucianism), to an extent even in religion (as the Enlightenment began to erode the hold of the church), but not, as yet, in art. When cultural identity, the high ground of civilization was at stake, "Art" was European, and it was also intimately connected to Christianity. Other visual cultures (unrecognizable as such, in modern terms, it might be added) were regarded as symptoms of lesser social orders, all the way through to barbarism: at best either "curiosities" or vehicles for decoration and ornament. Insofar as "Art" meant more than that, insofar as it was held to contain a moral and spiritual dimension that elevated it above the merely quotidian – or rather, insofar as it had a moral and spiritual dimension that was capable of representing the elevation of *human life* above the quotidian – then it was compacted within the European, Judeo-Christian imaginary.

Hegel

The greatest, or depending on your point of view, the most notorious articulation of this position is to be found in the G.W.F. Hegel's "Lectures on Fine Art," given in Berlin in the 1820s and delivered for the last time in 1828. The English text of these lectures, published as *Hegel's Aesthetics* (compiled later from Hegel's own notes and others taken by his students), runs to over 1,200 pages.[30] As such, a proper engagement with Hegel's argument is quite beyond my present scope. It is beyond me also in the sense that I am not a philosopher. The only reason I presume to address the matter at all here is that neither are so many of those others who, with gathering force in recent years, have repeatedly condemned Hegel as the root cause of all that is worst in the discipline of art history.

Hegel was such a protean figure in the European philosophical tradition that reactions against his work have tended to be extreme. Most notoriously, Karl Popper, writing during the Second World War, regarded Hegel as a precursor of twentieth-century totalitarianism.[31] To the English ordinary language philosophers of the earlier twentieth century (many of whom such as Bertrand Russell, G.E. Moore, and J.L. Austin had a profound impact on conceptual art and its critique of the pieties of institutional modernism) Hegel's work was largely nonsensical. To the French structuralists (who were also influential on the post-conceptual political avant-garde of the mid-century) the Hegelian tradition and its influence on Marxism was the epitome of what needed to be cast aside to revivify the radical tradition. To contemporary postcolonialists, likewise with a considerable impact on art practice, as well as to many of those with an investment in the notion of a "world art history," Hegel is the bête noire of Eurocentrism, to some indeed, an out and out racist. It is probably true to say that, if not in the field of professional academic philosophy then certainly across the broader front of putatively progressive cultural activity, Hegel's stock could not be lower. Merely to impute Hegelian tendencies to a position is tantamount to disposing of it.

Neither is this surprising. For the first time for several centuries, Western power is beginning to be balanced across the globe – but only beginning: the pressure for egalitarianism has to be maintained. Likewise, for the first time, a fully globalized culture is emerging. This again is on a knife-edge, and it is yet to be seen whether this is a recipe for a mass chloroforming, for historical amnesia on a scale that can only serve the status quo, or the germ of a more open situation. In this uncertain condition, it is no wonder that Hegel appears a reactionary dinosaur whose influence has been malign. Read in the context of the contemporary postcolonial condition, his Introduction to the *Philosophy of World History* can be a shock. On Native Americans: "Obviously unintelligent individuals with little capacity for education. Their inferiority in all respects, even in stature, can be seen in every particular."[32] On Africa: "It has no historical interest of its own, for we find its inhabitants living in barbarism and savagery in a land which has not furnished them with any integral ingredient of culture."[33] On Asia: "The whole Eastern part of Asia is remote from the current of world history and plays no part in it."[34] Hegel's apparent reduction of the rest of the world either to nullity, or at best to the status of a prologue to European preeminence is summed up in the dictum "World history travels from east to west; for Europe is the absolute end of history, just as Asia is the beginning."[35] These kinds of judgments are by no means isolated, and it is easy to see why, for many in the current climate, they are enough to vitiate Hegel's work *in toto*.[36]

For many working in the field of art history, as well as in the broader field of cultural studies, Hegel's impact has been deemed negative. Craig Clunas, the historian of art in China, laid Gombrich's influential but Eurocentric *Story of Art* at Hegel's door. Gombrich's treatment of Chinese art (and Gombrich here is very much a figure for a general sense of "conventional" art history) as "essentially unchanging" is traced above all to Hegel: "one of the first to articulate the absolute contrast between a dynamic forward-moving 'West' and a static, unchanging 'East.'"[37] Writers of color have, understandably, been fiercer in their condemnation. Kobena Mercer, in a discussion of representations of gender, race, and sexuality in the photographs of Robert Mapplethorpe extends his target beyond contemporary conservatives to the broader tradition: "In the discourse of Western aesthetics, as Kant and Hegel both emphasised, it was unthinkable that Africans could embody the aesthetic idea by which the narcissistic self-image of the West saw itself at the transcendental centre of world civilisation."[38] More recently, in an endorsement of Susan Buck-Morss' path-breaking study of Hegel's intellectual relationship to the Caribbean slave revolts of the late eighteenth century, Walter Mignolo asserts that "Hegel's spirit is tainted with the blood and suffering of enslaved Africans in the European colonies." In effect his thought is deemed part of the erasure of colonialism from Western philosophy, an exemplar of the European Enlightenment's complicity in imperialism.[39]

I am not going to attempt a rebuttal of these various criticisms of Hegel. I have neither the expertise in early nineteenth-century philosophy to do so nor the contemporary political disposition to want to. That is my point. Most of the time, such criticism does not proceed from a philosophical engagement with Hegel's argument. It gains its force from a generalized moral and political condemnation of beliefs which Hegel articulated, beliefs which were widespread in the European thought of his time, albeit not universal. The present study attempts to investigate the relationship between Western art and the wider world in the period since the Renaissance with a view to stimulating a broader understanding of artistic diversity (which tends too often to be a victim of academic specialization) and a greater openness in the teaching of the subject in the future. As far as the field of art history is concerned, then, the obvious vice of Hegel is that he systematically discriminates against the art of other cultures, that he offers a Eurocentric and progressivist account of art which has had repercussions down to the present. But, on the other hand, his virtue is that, more than anyone else up to the time when he was writing, he tried to situate the development of European art in a world context. Going far beyond Kant's unoriginal derogation of Indian and Chinese art, and combining empirical, historical detail with an overarching conceptual scheme, Hegel sought to account for how art works, how it has changed, and why it matters.

We cannot demand of Hegel, or anyone else, that they write outside of the terms of their own world. Two centuries earlier, Descartes had commented that although he did not doubt there were reasonable men in Persia and China, he was writing for those amongst whom he was destined to live. In his philosophy of art, Hegel did try to reach out to the world and to organize it within the terms of an historical consciousness that was then still new. Almost any text by someone writing in Europe in the late eighteenth/early nineteenth centuries will be marred by some form of more or less implicit racism, sexism, Eurocentrism, etc. We might not like some of the concomitants of this but, short of ending our engagement with European art and philosophy, there is nothing else to do but work through it, acknowledging the good and the useful as well as rejecting the negative. In a word, it is unproductive to practice anachronism, more important to situate Hegel within the horizon of his own intellectual world.

In some respects, Hegel stands between two worlds, between the past and the present. He is not, for example, in the position of the young Marx in the mid-1840s, working in Paris and being immersed in an extreme crucible of social modernity. He is working in a politically (and technologically) undeveloped situation in a Germany still divided into minor principalities, more or less unindustrialized yet heir to a highly developed intellectual and cultural tradition. Most importantly, Hegel is thinking within a newly emergent consciousness of history, something that simply has not existed before, and he is trying to knit together into a coherent historical explanation features of modern society as diverse as the state, the law, and art. Vico's cyclical philosophy of history, briefly mentioned above, is already more or less archaic by the time Hegel is writing. Furthermore, the different aspects of Hegel's wide-ranging work are not isomorphic. As Michael Podro wrote in his study *The Critical Historians of Art*, although the "main currents" of Hegel's general philosophy "make themselves felt" in his *Aesthetics*, this latter is "irreducible to his general philosophy of history."[40] Hegel's main purpose in the *Aesthetics*, in Podro's formulation, is to advance two lines of argument between which there is a tension. On the one hand there is a purely conceptual question concerning how art bears upon the achievement of human freedom. On the other, there is the more empirical, historical question of how art developed towards its (then) present position. This involves Hegel in thinking about the issue of what sense modern Europeans can make of the art of temporally and spatially different cultures; that is, both non-European art and the pagan antiquity of Europe itself.

Clearly these are both important and complex matters, and the intellectual tools Hegel brought to them are not those that would be used today. Two in particular are significant here. The first is the Enlightenment-derived sense of historical development and progress (encountered in Chapter 2 as the "stages" theory), which was seen as culminating in contemporary Europe. The second is that although this leads Hegel into criticizing non-European art, his argument concerns the moral and intellectual content of that art, as he saw it, and not merely its form, or the level of skill of its practitioners. Thus, it is not "foreshortening" as such in painting that marks the epochal advance, nor the achievement of lifelike modeling in sculpture; for Hegel it is what those formal and technical developments bespeak in terms of human self-consciousness that matters most.

It might be useful to offer a glimpse of what Hegel actually tries to say about art. In his Introduction he writes, "we must … recall again that the Idea as the beauty of art is not the Idea as such … but the Idea as shaped forward into reality"; going on: "There is here expressed the demand that the Idea and its configuration as a concrete reality shall be made completely adequate to one another."[41] In other words, the thought manifest materially in a work of art is not the abstract thought of a work of philosophy but somehow it must embody such a conceptual content just as adequately as the abstract thought does. This is not a conception of art as a vehicle of entertainment or decoration but a view that art can reflect back to human beings a sense of their identity comparable in its depth and complexity to that provided by philosophy and religion.

It is precisely this perspective that leads him on to criticism of non-European art.

> The defectiveness of a work of art is not always to be regarded as due, as may be supposed, to the artist's lack of skill; on the contrary, defectiveness of *form* results from defectiveness of *content*. So, for example, the Chinese, Indians and Egyptians, in their artistic shapes, images of gods, and idols, never get beyond formlessness or a bad and untrue definiteness of form. They could not master true beauty because their mythological ideas, the content and thought of their works of art, were still indeterminate, or determined badly, and so did not consist of the content which is absolute in itself.[42]

For Hegel, it is the deficient mythological ideas that, so to speak, drag down the form. By contrast, in his view "only in the highest art are the Idea and the presentation truly in conformity with one another, in the sense that the shape given to the Idea is in itself the absolutely true shape, because the content of the Idea which that shape expresses is itself the true and genuine content."[43] The technical characteristics, the forms of non-European art, which as we have seen, many before Hegel had disparaged (for qualities such as relative lack of lifelikeness, or monotony, or at the other extreme, unbridled caprice) are here related to the philosophical and religious worldviews whence they emerge. In the modern European terms of Hegel's outlook, articulated to Christianity – particularly Protestantism – positive values include individualism, equality under the law, *habeas corpus*, private property, and the existence of a public sphere; and negatives attach to their perceived absence elsewhere in the world.

Against this general background, Hegel regards art as having progressed through three stages: the Symbolic (by which he means a range of non-Western or "pre-Greek" arts); the Classical (the art of classical Greece and Rome); and Romantic (the Christian art of the modern period, i.e., the Renaissance and after). In the Symbolic phase, meaning is seen as being external to the form of the art, being linked to it by a kind of non-artistic stipulation or convention. In common with virtually all educated Europeans of his day, for Hegel, the definitive emergence of human consciousness into a condition of freedom had first occurred in classical Greece and had subsequently bonded with Christianity to produce a fully fledged modern consciousness. In the art of that culture, its meaning was held to be not external but bodied forth from within; content and form were, so to speak, fused rather than merely mixed.

Hegel may not have been blessed with the full panoply of deconstructive contemporary philosophy, but neither was he ignorant of cultural difference. On more than one occasion he acknowledges, for example, "How often do we hear it said that a European beauty would not please a Chinese, or a Hottentot either, since the Chinese has inherently a totally different conception of beauty from the negro's, and his again from a European's, and so on."[44] Or again: "It is said … that such a facial formation has occurred to the Greeks alone as the really beautiful one, while the Chinese, Jews, and Egyptians regarded other, indeed opposite formations as just as beautiful or more so, and that therefore, verdict against verdict, there is no proof that the Greek profile is the model of genuine beauty." But for Hegel, the difficulty, and the whole point, is that such relativism is "only superficial chatter."[45] Hegel writes as a modern European and also as a Christian. He has to go to considerable lengths to establish that there is one Beauty, which matches and is at one with a single World Spirit; and this, from our point of view, whatever the subtle difference involved, one might as well call God.

Other Ideas

One of the things that distinguishes Hegel's account of the development of art is the space he devotes not just to the European classical tradition but to Indian, Chinese, and Egyptian art. As we have seen, China had long been of fascination to

Europeans, and, especially with the expansion of the French and British empires in the eighteenth century, India was not far behind. Egypt was a rather different case. The mysterious and extinct civilization of ancient Egypt cast a long shadow through the European consciousness. In the classical world, Herodotus had already written about it in his *History*. In the medieval world, the pyramids featured in the Byzantine-inspired mosaics in the domes of San Marco in Venice, where they represented the granaries of Joseph, built during the Israelites' captivity. In the Renaissance, the rebuilding of Rome saw the city liberally dotted with ancient Egyptian obelisks. But surrounding all of this interest was the fact that nobody actually knew anything about Egypt. It was all fantasy, ever since the loss of the language in late antiquity.

What shifted European access to other cultures up a gear was the Napoleonic expedition at the very end of the eighteenth century. This was at one level a straightforwardly imperialist enterprise. In geopolitical terms, following the French loss of America to the British in the Seven Years War, Napoleon was interested in cutting Britain's supply lines to India in order to extend French influence in Asia. However, in a fashion comparable to the Cook voyages in the Pacific, imperial strategy was compacted with the Enlightenment project of building up knowledge of the world. Napoleon took an army of *savants* with him as well as soldiers. And though the army did not last long (cut off by Nelson's defeat of the French navy at Aboukir Bay and quickly abandoned by Napoleon himself), the intellectual project had a lasting impact. In a word, the geographical – and historical – Other was opened up to science. The massive publication *Description de l'Egypte*, appearing in ten volumes between 1809 and 1828, accompanied by no less than nine hundred engraved illustrations, lifted knowledge of Egypt onto another plane. The most significant event, however, which was bound up with all this mapping and describing, was the translation of the Egyptian hieroglyphic script by the French linguist Jean-François Champollion. After almost two thousand years of silence, Egypt could now begin to be understood. The translation was, of course, a process rather than a single event, and much work was undertaken also by English scholars – indeed the Rosetta Stone, which enabled the translation, ended up in the British Museum, *de facto* spoils of war. But Champollion's literally world-changing first lecture about his breakthrough, which had happened on September 14, 1822 was given to the French Academy thirteen days later on September 27.

After that, Egypt's presence in European culture ballooned. Indeed it has never stopped. Like chinoiserie, its major impact was in the practical and decorative arts. A century later, Hollywood films, not to mention the cinemas they were shown in, testified to the continuing fascination with Egypt. Buildings, jewelry, interior decor, all bear the imprint of Egypt. In art it became a cornerstone of "orientalism," not least, to the Victorians, because of the imbrication of Pharaonic Egypt with the Children of Israel and hence with the Bible. David Roberts' mid-nineteenth-century expeditions to Egypt and the Holy Land were only among the most successful of many artistic projects to bring the world of the ancient Middle East into a modern European consciousness. Hegel's philosophy may not be congenial to the modern multicultural temper, but he was nothing if not alert to the very latest scientific and intellectual developments of his time when he tried to fit the new knowledge of Egypt into the schema of his idealist philosophy.

Indeed, it is important to realize that Hegel was not working in a vacuum, either in terms of the contemporary development of science, or indeed philosophy itself. Within the worldview of late eighteenth- and early nineteenth-century German philosophy there had already emerged a kind of cultural relativism. In his 1777 essay on Winckelmann, Herder, as Michael Podro points out, had already "challenged the idea that Egyptian art should be judged by Greek standards," and "pointed to … the way in which the products of one society were conditioned by the purposes and ideas of that society, and that its purposes may not be ours." Such ideas were broadened and generalized in his *Ideas on the Philosophy of the History of Mankind* of 1784. A similar embrace of the ideas and literature of the Eastern world is also evident in the work of the brothers August Wilhelm and Friedrich Schlegel in the early years of the nineteenth century. Likewise, in the first edition of his *World as Will and Idea* of 1818, the philosopher Arthur Schopenhauer was open to Indian philosophy and incorporated its insights into his own version of German Idealism.[46]

The significant point, surely, is that German philosophical Idealism in the early Romantic period represents an evolving, multifaceted discourse at the forefront of the European encounter with the thought and cultures of the wider world. And that Hegel, preeminent figure though he was, represents one strand within that discourse. To be sure, his position is in many respects uncongenial to the pervasive relativism of our own culture, much less congenial than the Schlegels' or Herder's cultural openness, for example. It is curious and noteworthy that Hegel's attempt to locate visual art in a spectrum of historical and geographical development should have been so much less open than many of his contemporaries' attempts to address poetry, literature, and philosophy. The extent to which that marks a problem with Hegel's philosophy or a problem for the visual arts remains a matter for debate. But taken as a whole, German Idealism surely must needs be addressed in terms responsive to its own diversity. It is usually a recipe for a singularly rigid criticism to demand of historical actors that they overstep their own intellectual horizons or be condemned for failing to match ours.

Hegel's writing on the visual arts is a curious mixture of the descriptively vivid and the conceptually abstruse; and this conceptual difficulty is connected with the fact that Hegel writes within a tradition which is remote from the competences of all but the most specialized modern reader. Though he employs all too comprehensible, and to us even outrageous observations and judgments, to remainder the totality of the conceptual structure within which they are made risks getting things inside out. It is one thing to establish that European Enlightenment and Romantic thought falls far short in practice from its lofty rhetoric of human freedom; it is one thing to demystify early modern European thought by illustrating how its characteristic belief in its own preeminence aligns all too readily with other practices aimed at establishing that priority in trade, politics, and warfare. It is quite another to regard Hegel's theory of the state, or of history, let alone of art, as a mere apologetics for slavery or as a precursor of modern totalitarianism.

Orientalism

Hegel seems to have become, in some quarters, a kind of lightning conductor for a position that would reject historical European thought and historical European art *tout court* as mere symptoms of imperialism and worse. It is important, however, to distinguish such an extreme postcolonialist position from that which has become a kind of cultural dominant within the more or less radical, more or less critical, scholarly and artistic milieu since the middle of the last century: namely, the anti-formalist, anti-idealist drawing out of connections between knowledge (and art) and power. A good part of the vehemence of this countertradition can be traced to the entrenched nature of the orthodoxy it set out to combat: which is to say, the admixture of formalism and idealism that, particularly in the Anglo-American sphere after the end of the Second World War, had systematically excluded attention from such connections.

It was this mindset, and its complicity with the actual machinery of world domination, that Edward Said, following Foucault, sought to lay bare in *Orientalism*. Somewhat surprisingly, Hegel does not even appear in the index of *Orientalism*, despite mentions of Kant, Hume, Herder, Friedrich Schlegel, and a host of other thinkers; Said's principal focus was on literature. In common with much of the intellectual radicalism of that time, class analysis and feminism as well as nascent postcolonialism, Said's argument contained elements of overstatement and intransigence that have not weathered well. In retrospect these are a double-edged sword. At the time they functioned as a rallying cry and were a key part of the oppositional spectrum's appeal. It is hard now to recover a sense of the complacency and self-regard of the status quo, particularly in the fields of literature and art, the prohibitions on bringing "politics" into the debate, indeed on bringing anything into the debate that threatened the autonomy, the sanctity of canonized art and its normative history. On the other hand, the thirtieth anniversary of *Orientalism*'s publication reignited controversy in unproductive ways with neither camp able to see any virtue in the opposition. For the scholarly but defensive Robert Irwin, Said's was a "work of malignant charlatanry"[47] without a single saving grace. On the other side, among those concerned to defend Said, criticism was regarded as tantamount to a form of treason. Be that as it may, despite the negative aspects of much of what the Right now dubs "political correctness" (by which is meant the driving of artistic and intellectual inquiry by overt moral and political agendas), there can be little doubt how much the field of world art studies has opened up in recent years, nor of the extent to which *Orientalism* was a significant element in that process.

Some indication of the distance traveled can be derived from the catalog of the London Royal Academy exhibition of 1984, *The Orientalists*. The cover featured a particularly twee 1880 Renoir of a little (white) girl dressed up in a sort-of "Arab" costume which was praised in the text for its "compositional sophistication" and "technical brilliance." In the main essay, Said's thesis received scant attention, and that negative. The sentence "Some commentators have tried to view all Orientalist manifestations as an aspect of cultural imperialism" is indexed in a footnote to "E. Said" and disposed of in the next sentence: "Yet the evidence would suggest that this is too simplistic an interpretation …"[48] Arguably it is. But it says something of art history that six years after its publication, the defining contribution to the wider field of orientalist studies merited only such summary dismissal in a catalog supposedly devoted to the subject. The thinking involved finds expression elsewhere in the same essay where the "range" of ways of "exploring an encounter between two cultures"[49] is rendered as a kind of sliding scale beginning with "the strictly art historical issues" and moving through "the study of art within its cultural context" all the way out to "the analysis of art as an aspect of politics" in which "the encounter is seen as the domination of one culture by another."[50] This characteristically modernist assertion of a core of technical or aesthetic concerns around which cultural and political questions hover as a set of optional extras (an option seldom exercised by the status quo, moreover) has now itself receded into history. But it gives a good indication of what Said, as well as a wide range of feminist and Marxist historians, were up against, as well as accounting for a good deal of the vehemence of their critique. A genuine orthodoxy had to be blasted out of the way. The problem is that, thirty or forty years later, the descendants of that position have come to form a new orthodoxy within the academy. Alongside the genuine advances which have opened up the subject far beyond the constraints that were just normal within institutionalized modernism, this can itself begin to operate its own forms of closure. Foremost among these (both representing routinized overreactions to previous modernist autonomy claims), are a tendency to regard art as merely symptomatic of wider psychic and political forces and a concomitant neglect of the aesthetic dimension as if it were no more than the symptom of a now vanquished orthodoxy.

In *Orientalism* Said did not address the visual arts, a task that was taken up by Linda Nochlin in her now famous essay "The Imaginary Orient." This was first published in 1983, though it had its origins in a slightly earlier critique of an exhibition very similar to the one just discussed. This was an exhibition celebrating, in the words of its title, *Orientalism: The Near East in French Painting 1800–1880*. Nochlin took the curator of this exhibition to task for his deliberate avoidance of the political dimension and a failure to address the question of the complicity of orientalism in the visual arts with colonialism. At stake was the question of what counted as "normal" in art history, skepticism about its prevailing "celebratory mode," and an invitation to bring to bear "historical and political awareness and analytical sophistication" on what Nochlin termed the "obfuscated areas of our discipline"[51]; in essence the contradictions of class, gender, and race which subtend the production of art in modern history.

Although it could be argued that this is a battle that will not be over until peace and harmony reign in the world, in the more restricted compass of art history the enemy has almost everywhere been put to flight. Not that a lot of rubbish is not still talked and written about art, of course, especially in the mass media now that it has become fashionable. But the sheer restriction on the parameters of relevance (as well as the celebratory mode) that was once normative in art history, now no longer holds. The principal object of Nochlin's critique was the academic painter Jean-Léon Gérôme, a suitable target not least since one of his pictures was used for the cover of the paperback edition of Said's book. It has to be said that once one has evacuated the airless chamber of the academic modernist art history of several decades past, knocking over targets such as Gérôme is like shooting ducks in a row. Gérôme was an out-and-out conservative, in politics, including cultural politics, as well as in the practice of painting (Figure 3.5). More or less contemporary with the avant-garde, his work could not be further removed from its early essays in the acknowledgment of the materiality of representation, its prompting of self-consciousness on the part of the spectator, indeed from the whole critical register of what avant-gardism meant. (And which we have learned to read largely because of the work of pioneering historians of that generation: Nochlin herself, Clark, Pollock, Orton, and many others.)

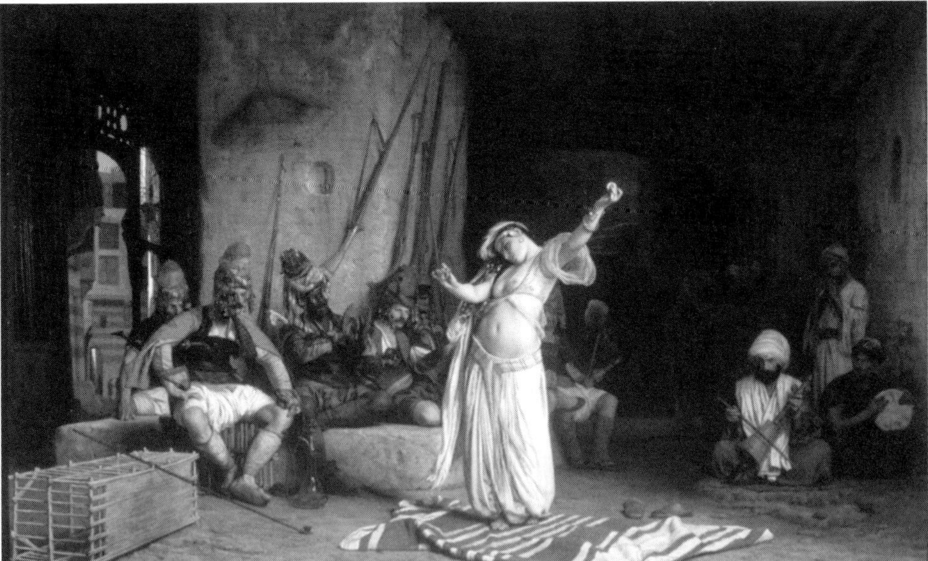

Figure 3.5 Jean-Léon Gérôme, *The Dance of the Almeh*, 1863, oil on panel, 50 × 81 cm. The Dayton Art Institute, Dayton, OH, USA / Gift of Mr Robert Badenhop / The Bridgeman Art Library.

Gérôme still feels like an open-and-shut case for the would-be critical art historian. The best one can say of him is that at least some of his orientalist subject matter is not as devoid of interest as the worn-out classicism of Bouguereau and kindred devotees of the academic nude. Aside from his subjects, the technique with which they are depicted is of interest mainly for what it goes to such lengths to conceal – the facticity of the representation and the presence of the (voyeuristic) spectator; both, of course, hallmarks of the pathologocial compulsion of the academy for maintaining business as usual, even as modernity was destroying the foundations of its dream factory. One feels differently about Delacroix. Delacroix is taken to task in a two-page detour for his *Death of Sardanapalus* of 1827–1828, painted some years before the artist's own trip to North Africa in 1832 and several decades before Gérôme's career. Presumably this picture was just too inviting a target to forgo for someone of Nochlin's commitments: a bevy of beautiful naked women being ritually slaughtered by muscular men under the all-consuming gaze of an indolent Oriental potentate was asking for it from a socialist, feminist, anticolonialist historian in the glory days of deconstructing the canon.

To be fair, Nochlin does admit that "it would be ridiculous to reduce Delacroix's complex painting to a mere pictorial projection of the artist's sadistic fantasies"; nonetheless, what she calls "Delacroix's psychosexuality," and which is read out of the painting (Sardanalpalus being regarded as "a surrogate self"), is clearly troubling to her.[52] In this regard, Nochlin accuses Delacroix of adding into his *Sardanapalus* features which were absent from the Byron poem which stimulated it, as if this were prompted by Delacroix's own psychosexual proclivities. Yet the mass slaughter of concubines was a perfectly standard trope in the construction of the discourse of oriental despotism. Its inclusion in Delacroix's Salon submission could just as readily be a product of his reading as of his sexual fantasies.[53] If indeed Delacroix did have sadistic fantasies, the possibility that he might have subsumed them in art (as perhaps Cézanne may have done later) does not receive any discussion. What seems to matter most is Nochlin's own feminist outrage at the subject of violence to women, rather oddly backed up by contemporary bourgeois criticism of the picture when it was originally shown. Delacroix had clearly touched a nerve in the bourgeois Salon-going audience of his day, but it isn't allowed by Nochlin to be the same nerve that Manet touched a quarter century later with *Olympia*. It seems to have been possible to concede to Manet's technique a critical dimension in face of academic protocols that is withheld from Delacroix. Yet Baudelaire, Manet's principal early supporter, placed him in the lineage of Delacroix, even regarding Delacroix as the preeminent modern painter.

Until this moment, as we have seen, European artists' encounters with the wider world took the form of illustrating it. The center held. The academic European frame absorbed the world into itself. Yet it is precisely this academic framework, finally wrenched out of kilter by the avant-garde of the 1860s and after, that is placed under stress by Delacroix. His brushwork and his color are the main vehicles of this, and by his own testimony, they were stimulated by – to an extent even perhaps produced by – his experience of the Orient. *Sardanapalus* pre-dates the trip to North Africa, but in its technique and its imaginative danger it offers something like the receptive seed which the sun of Africa could fall on and cause to germinate. It is not a routine academic treatment within which the East can be tamed. In both subject and manner it is excessive. There *is* something dangerous and nasty about the *Sardanapalus*, but the same can be said of a great deal of transgressive art and literature that we would be poorer without. Modernity seems to have required a form of risk-taking, even savagery, to get its measure. Modernism was, often at its best, an art of extremes, and Delacroix has his extremism. Would anyone argue that a critical modernism in literature would have profited had De Sade been silenced? This is where the dimension of the aesthetic has some power. One of Gérôme's voyeuristic slave markets or belly dancers is simply not on the same level as Delacroix aesthetically, that is, technically and in terms of the disturbing expressive effect generated. That counts for something. The point about a Gérôme nude is that it doesn't threaten anything, it doesn't offer up a sexual threat at all; quite the reverse, it provides a kind of cover under which a voyeuristic desire can exercise itself safely underneath the ideology of art. Delacroix rips and tears; he doesn't peep. This certainly isn't comfortable, but neither does it aspire to leave things as they are. A powerful imagination, neutered of its sexuality and shorn of its dark side, seems like a contradiction in terms. It certainly feels like an unconvincing vision of art, however much it might satisfy in social work.

Of course, none of this is to say that Delacroix is not a complex, even ambivalent, figure, socially conservative and aesthetically radical both. His writings on his North African experience are a case in point. It would be quite easy to argue that Delacroix commits one of the cardinal sins of orientalism by dehistoricizing the orient. There is no question that he does do this, having frequent recourse to two registers: antiquity and nature. He comments, "this people is wholly antique," observes "figures like Roman consuls," or again, "like Roman senators or Greeks at the Panathenean festival."[54] He sees people in Tangier as "closer to nature in a thousand ways" and as "simpler and more primitive" even than those he encountered in Algiers. But the reason he is doing this deserves reflection. First, he is speaking as an artist. He is using his experience of North Africa to disparage academic classicism, mentioning David by name, and the "over-praised beauty of fashionable paintings." For Delacroix, the whole academic routine of the Grand Tour and the Prix de Rome is worn out. Indeed, "Rome is no longer to be found in Rome." That is to say, academic classicism has become a form of kitsch, and genuine beauty – one might say timeless beauty – is to be found elsewhere. "Elsewhere" here means outside the reach of modernity. His own "more advanced civilization," with its "restlessness ... which urges us on to novelties" is by comparison deficient: "in our corsets, our tight shoes, our ridiculous pinching clothes, we are pitiful."

When he does edge explicitly into the realm of politics, the same kinds of theme recur. While extolling the beauty of the place, he comments that "economists and

Saint-Simonians might find much to criticise as regards human rights and equality before the law." Yet at the same time he purports to find "something democratic" in ordinary behavior, a "natural truth and nobility" which is in stark contrast to what he dreads returning to in France: "your newspapers, your cholera, your politics." This all represents a complex mix of values, part of the Romantic primitivism which has its roots in notions of the "noble savage" and the way in which eighteenth-century figures as diverse as Montesquieu and Rousseau were deeply critical of the artificiality and decadence of emergent modernity. It also looks ahead to the equally Romantic primitivism of the later nineteenth and early twentieth centuries which was such a central part of the avant-garde. This is contradictory and ambivalent territory. On the one hand there are strains which lead to irrationalism in philosophy and to fascism in politics. But on the other hand there is a distrust of mere materialism, a sense of the spirit and of beauty transcending the mundane, a profound sense of the inadequacy of the actual and a striving for utopia that if one were to extirpate it altogether would lead to the loss of a good part of art as such and the greater part of the modernist avant-garde.

Nochlin, not surprisingly, cites the passage about Saint-Simonians, rights, and equality in a discussion of the picturesque in relation to orientalism. She argues that Delacroix made a clear distinction between the "visual beauty" of Morocco on the one hand and, on the other, "its moral quality, which he deplored."[55] I am not so sure that this is right. Delacroix seems to compact ethics and aesthetics rather than to separate them. The picturesque, which certainly was a feature of representations of the East in art, was usually deployed in order to make the exotic palatable to bourgeois taste back in the metropolitan centers. But we have already seen that Delacroix does not do this; in fact, he is capable of offending conventional taste by his extremism. Whereas Gérôme and other artists of academic orientalism, such as Henri Regnault, do create, through their "objective" technique a form of voyeurism which gives the bourgeois spectator room and distance to survey what he desires but simultaneously deplores, Delacroix's powerfully subjective technique pulls the viewer into the risky space rather than leaving him comfortably outside it. In that respect he seems closer to Manet and the avant-garde rather than to academic orientalism.

As we have already said, none of this is clear-cut and it is certainly not easily approvable from within what has become the normative ethical position of the new academy. Delacroix was not a Saint-Simonian socialist, but his aristocratic hauteur allowed him a critique of bourgeois aesthetics *and* morality that chimes well with the future avant-garde. The position of the non-Western in this is ambiguous and contradictory. Nochlin cites another passage from Delacroix's *Journal* in which he is critical of some Persian miniatures he saw in 1850, singling out their lack of perspective and what he sees as a kind of awkward motionlessness.[56] He does seem to see this as symptomatic of a culture in which "women are degraded" and in which "there is no society" (meaning presumably the institutions of civil society not merely "society" in the sense of salons and parties). For

Delacroix, Persian art reflects this: it is "stationary." We are back with the sense of a dehistoricized Other. Delacroix is deeply critical of academic European art and of modern market- and fashion-driven life, and can see virtues in more "organic" forms of life that he encountered outside the Western orbit. Yet he cannot countenance those own societies' self-representations because they lack something that European art does have and which he calls, ambiguously, "a certain illusion of projection" – which I take to mean an ability to reach out and engage the individual. Individualism is itself, therefore, contradictory. Negatively construed, it leads to fashion-following, materialism, "turbulence," and the loss of a harmonious form of life; positively, it opens possibilities of subjective and emotional engagement that is itself the hallmark of a genuinely modern art, and which is paradoxically absent from the art of those societies more rigorously circumscribed by tradition. If anything, it is this tension in Delacroix's own art that at least partially redeems it from the strictures that so readily apply to the majority of artistic orientalism.

Orientalism and Naturalism

Not everything in orientalist art is as obviously client to the dominant mix of sexualized prurience and imperialist superiority as Gérôme's slave markets and harem scenes. Indeed, even Gérôme himself was capable of producing images which offer a more "objective," less sensationalized sense of oriental society, ranging from commercial transactions, to mosque scenes, to landscapes. Not much thought was given in the early "orientalist" critiques of Gérôme's pictures to his contemporary reception. Or rather, the assumption seems to have been that their influence can only have been wholly negative and corrupting, reinforcing sexist and imperialist stereotypes in the worldview of the European bourgeoisie. Amelia Edwards was certainly a representative of the European bourgeoisie, albeit a far from conventional one. In 1874 she undertook a journey "a thousand miles up the Nile," as a result of which she became one of the leading figures in late nineteenth-century Egyptology. Thereafter she dedicated her life and her fortune to the preservation of the relics of the civilization of ancient Egypt and the expansion of knowledge about it. Subsequently she founded the Egypt Exploration Society and endowed the first Chair of Egyptology at University College London. She was equally certainly an "orientalist" in the sense that she was wont to contrast the "magnificence" of the ancient ruins with the "sordid routine of Arab life": "mud hovels, mud pigeon-towers, mud yards and a mud mosque."[57] It would be a curious perspective that allowed this bias – when all is done and said, an understandable bias in an educated middle-class European lady of the late nineteenth century – to outweigh a sense of the value of her contribution to knowledge of an ancient North African society. And Amelia Edwards, far from despising Gérôme's pictures, seems to have regarded them, some of them at least, as compatible with her own project. Towards the end of her book, she writes:

> I shall not soon forget an Abyssinian caravan which we met one day coming out from Mahatta. It consisted of seventy camels laden with elephant tusks. … Beside each shambling beast strode a bare-footed Nubian. Following these, on the back of a gigantic camel, came a hunting leopard in a wooden cage and a wild cat in a basket. Last of all marched a coal-black Abyssinian nearly seven feet in height, magnificently shawled and turbaned, with a huge scimitar dangling by his side. … Anything more picturesque than this procession, with the dust driving before it in clouds, and children following it out of the village, it would be difficult to conceive. One longed for Gérôme to paint it on the spot.[58]

This account may not be especially "correct" to a modern sensibility, but the thing is, she *saw* it; and she saw it *as* a representation by Gérôme. It would surely be futile to reject this connection between Gérôme's project and the project of producing scientific knowledge of a lost society; worse still to use Gérôme's failings to dismiss the knowledge itself.

Gérôme's output has in fact been recently reopened to more wide-ranging analysis, the subject of a Getty Institute research publication and a survey exhibition at the Musée d'Orsay, complete with scholarly catalog. His work has been reread, as it were from different directions: on the one hand for the complexity and self-consciousness of its construction of orientalist fantasy; on the other, less in terms of its academic orientalism than for its commitment to ethnographic realism. From Nochlin's original Saidean perspective, this made little difference. Gérôme's putatively objective technique was precisely one of the main objects of her criticism, wherein it is seen as dedicated to concealing the reality of representation in the name of a transparent or immediate access to reality itself. From that point of view, a striving for pictorial accuracy itself lay at the root of the problem. One way of putting it might be to say that Gérôme was found guilty of combining a semantic falsification with a syntactic one: he was using a flawed pictorial grammar to circulate flawed meanings. In Nochlin's own words, "strategies of 'realist' … mystification go hand in hand with those of Orientalist mystification."[59]

The intervening years have tended to moderate the deployment of modernist strictures against pictorialism. Already, pre-modernist pictures had been scrutinized for the subtle and multifarious ways in which they had acknowledged their own status as representations.[60] Within the modern period, social realist strategies are now more likely to be debated within their own horizons rather than for failing to be adequately modernist, and here again a wide range of practice has been revealed. The time around the historical emergence of modernism in the nineteenth century has been one of the last to be revisited. Yet in the recent rereadings, some of the subtlety of Gérôme's practice has been opened up. This includes his use of photography, the way in which a minutely researched naturalism of detail was combined to produce a fictive whole. In the words of Dominique de Font-Réaulx, Gérôme's "guise of accuracy and verisimilitude" was constructed out of "juxtaposition, invention, artifice and collage, all efficiently staged through a fully controlled composition."[61] Surprisingly, Gérôme's ostensibly transparent naturalism turns out to be as self-consciously and artfully put together as a cubist collage. What remains at issue, of course, is the purpose of the construct. Far from the imputation that Gérôme's images involved a kind of incompetence below their detailed surfaces (as when it was claimed his representations of Islamic script were indecipherable), something more interesting is shown to be in play, involving the manipulation of empirical detail to serve the preconceptions of his metropolitan audience. It comes close to a kind of inverted deployment of science in the interests of collective fantasy. This is indeed the terrain of Said's claim about orientalism as such, and even revisionist historians tread carefully around images involving the representation of gender difference in ethnographically sensitive contexts.

Some of the same concerns apply in literature. For Said, Flaubert was one of the main perpetrators of a demeaning orientalist vision of Eastern societies – not least because of his account of his journey to Egypt with Maxime du Camp, and the sexual encounters they enjoyed. Yet Flaubert's painstakingly observed naturalism and sensitivity to the fleeting moment cannot be dismissed without something of considerable value being lost. No less than Delacroix, he commits the sin of regarding the Orient as timeless: "The dances that we have performed for us are of too hieratic a character not to have come from the dances of the old Orient which is always young because nothing changes. Here the Bible is a picture of life today." Indeed the image comes up so often in European encounters with the East that one does wonder whether they can all have been so completely mistaken; was there not something of permanence that survived in the way of life, despite the modernizing tendencies of Muhammed Ali's regime? Moreover, Flaubert is intensely aware of the clichés of academic writing about the East, and that is *not* what his writing is about: "So here we are in Egypt, 'land of the Pharaohs, land of the Ptolemies, land of Cleopatra' (as sublime stylists put it)." What matters for Flaubert is more evanescent, something no academic would have perceived.

> We rise at dawn; drawn up on the beach are four slave-traders' boats. The slaves come ashore and walk in groups of fifteen to twenty, each led by two men. When I am on my camel, Hadji-Ismael runs up to give me a handshake. The man on the ground raising his arm to shake the hand of a man mounted on his camel, or to give him something, is one of the most beautiful gestures of the Orient; especially at the moment of departure there is something solemn and sad about it.

Flaubert is renowned for finding the heart of the matter in an apparently insignificant detail; something not far removed from Baudelaire's prescription for the *modern* artist. Here it is the raised arm at a moment of departure which somehow crystallizes both the teeming medley of sensations on the one hand and the stasis and melancholy on the other which make up Flaubert's imaginative sense of the Orient. It may not represent the whole of the nineteenth-century Orient, but it would seem mistaken to claim that there was no such element. It would be idiotic to claim that Flaubert was not a man of his time. But who else in 1851, having struggled to the top of the Great Pyramid to watch the sunrise, would have bothered to note the encroachment of Western commercialism:

> There are two things: the dry desert behind us, and before us an immense, delightful expanse of green, furrowed by endless canals, dotted here and there with tufts of palms; then, in the background, a little to the left, the minarets of Cairo ... On the side of the pyramid lit by the rising sun I see a business card: *'Humbert. Frotteur'* fastened to the stone.[62]

Said's discussion of Flaubert is long, complex, and, in the face of the protocols of then-orthodox literary criticism (just as Nochlin's analysis in the face of then-orthodox art history), necessary. But it shouldn't put anyone off reading Flaubert. There is much that is recoverable.

Flaubert is a far cry from Gérôme, at least some of whose orientalism arguably has more to answer for. Nonetheless, recent discussion has also looked into the possibility of rereading some of Gérôme's work as having moved away from a classicizing orientalist fantasy onto the terrain of a more scientifically driven ethnographic naturalism. This in its turn was a deeply problematic practice because of the way in which ethnography developed connections to nineteenth-century pseudoscientific racism and the development of racial typologies. Peter Benson Miller has acknowledged how this "later gave rise to the construction of racial inequality," but qualifies this by pointing out that "in mid-nineteenth century France it seemed to offer a means for artists to represent human types more accurately."[63] To be sure, this is a long way from the modernist drive to establish a form of artistic autonomy. But one of the central paradoxes of the avant-garde is the way in which that strategy departed from the earlier Saint-Simonian notion of the avant-garde as leading society forwards in step with progressive science.

It has long been accepted that early modernism was a result of French artists, notably Manet and his generation, trying to come to grips with contemporary Parisian modernity, specifically the effects of the modernization of Paris under Baron Haussmann. Yet Paris was not the only city to undergo drastic modernization in the late nineteenth century. Viennese modernity produced an equally complex cultural formation, albeit less emphatically in the visual arts than in music and the work of Freud on human consciousness itself. Modernization gave rise to the "secession" movements in the late nineteenth century, but just as in France, a different sort of art also flourished: an outgrowth of the academy inflected towards naturalism. In France, Fernand Cormon employed similar naturalistic techniques to those found in the work of Gérôme, not to depict the spatial, geographical Other, but in order to arrive at a scientifically credible representation of the temporally remote. The ostensibly biblical subject of Cormon's *Cain*, now in the Musée d'Orsay, cannot disguise the fact that its real subject is prehistoric man. As a result of such work, at the very end of the century, Cormon provided decorations for the Museum of Natural History in Paris offering a visual representation of human evolution.

Similarly, the Naturhistorisches Museum in Vienna (which forms a pairing with the adjacent Kunsthistorisches Museum, and which was part of the city's version of Haussmannization) incorporates a hugely ambitious artistic project designed to complement the advance of science rather than to carve out its own aesthetic sphere. Dating from the period 1882–1889, there were originally 110 paintings, involving the labors of twenty-seven artists, mostly associated with the Vienna Academy. The purpose of the art was not merely decorative; it was intended to complement and amplify the displays of the human and natural sciences. All the pictures were made in three specified sizes, a small rectangle, a square, and a larger rectangle: 1.90 m × 0.95 m, 1.90 m × 1.90 m, and 1.90 m × 3.80 m. All had a standardized frame with a gold plaque at the top indicating the subject as well as the artist. To produce them, the artists were sent out on research trips to sketch in the actual locations, or where that was not feasible, photographs were made by scientists working on the spot and the paintings were based on those. For historical subjects, the latest archaeological data was used. Subjects ranged from the mineral deposits of the Austro-Hungarian Empire, including mining projects, through to scenes of geological interest elsewhere in the world including imaginary reconstructions of landscapes of the Late Cretaceous period and images of human evolution, including cave dwellers, Stonehenge, and indeed the civilization of ancient Egypt. The cycle also included naturalistically accurate representations of sites of archaeological interest from around the world, including the Taj Mahal, Mexican temples, the statues of Easter Island, and the ruins of Angkor Wat (Figure 3.6).

The point is that these are works of modern art. They are certainly not works of modern*ist* art, but simply to dismiss them under the catch-all rubric of "academic" is to lose sight of something quite interesting: to lose something of the complexity of the modern. The relationship of a mode of representation to the thing represented has been one of the hinges of the modern movement. The fact that naturalism suppresses its own status as representation under an ideological rubric of visual truth does not make it merely a conservative symptom of the past illicitly lingering into the present. Rather, what is at stake here is a different view of the role of art in modern society, a different view of the relation Western art might have to knowledge of the wider world. Ironically it is closer to the view held by the early nineteenth-century utopian socialists who first formulated the concept of the avant-garde than it is to what the avant-garde subsequently became. This is difficult terrain, as indeed is the whole question of the relationship – contradictory or complementary – between modernism and realism.[64] But the important point for the present discussion is that the work of such artists, including Gérôme and other "orientalists," is itself more nuanced than has often

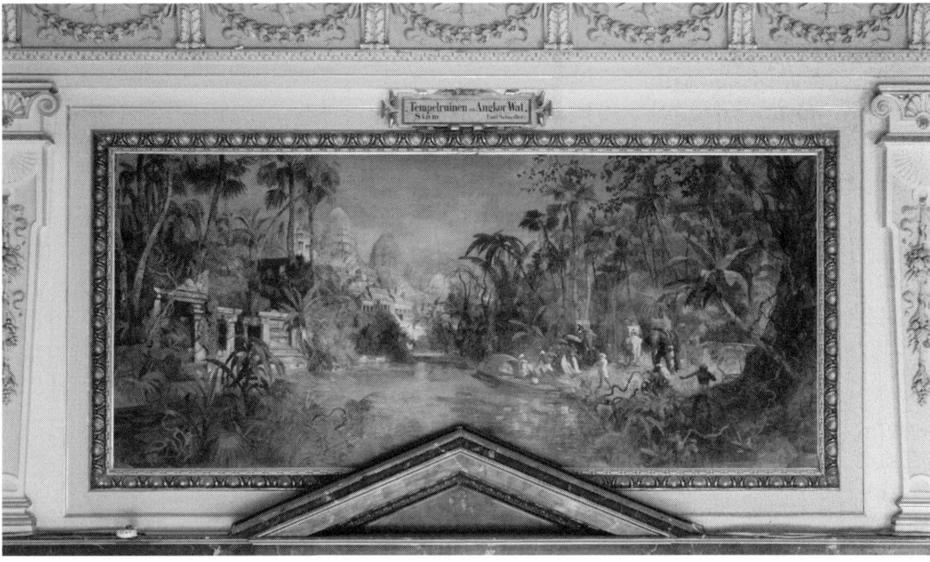

Figure 3.6 Emil Jakob Schindler, *Temple Ruins of Angkor Wat, Siam*, c.1882–1889, oil on canvas, 190 × 380 cm. Natural History Museum, Vienna.

been realized. To an extent it may be regarded as involved in a search for modern forms of realism as an "alternative to, not a continuation of, the faltering classical tradition."[65]

Orientalism Revisited

The overall situation has been well summed up by Mary Roberts in a consideration of Gérôme's work in Istanbul, including commissions by some members of the Ottoman elite. Acknowledging Said's and Nochlin's critique of the way in which Gérôme's apparent naturalism actually served to "dissimulate" the complicated and tensioned modernity of the nineteenth-century Ottoman Empire and to produce instead a "picturesque, eroticised diversion for the delectation of the European viewer," she nonetheless refrains from the normative condemnation. Instead she advocates "an approach that embraces a more contested and geographically encompassing production and reception" in order to "augment and nuance our understanding." What is required is a loosening of the historian's grip on the moral high ground in favor of "further cross-cultural interpretive work."[66]

Other nineteenth-century orientalist artists, many of them British, are also beginning to be the subjects of reappraisal. The Scottish painter David Roberts was cited in "The Imaginary Orient" for verbal comments accompanying his volumes of lithographs of *Egypt and Nubia* and *The Holy Land*, as well as for a

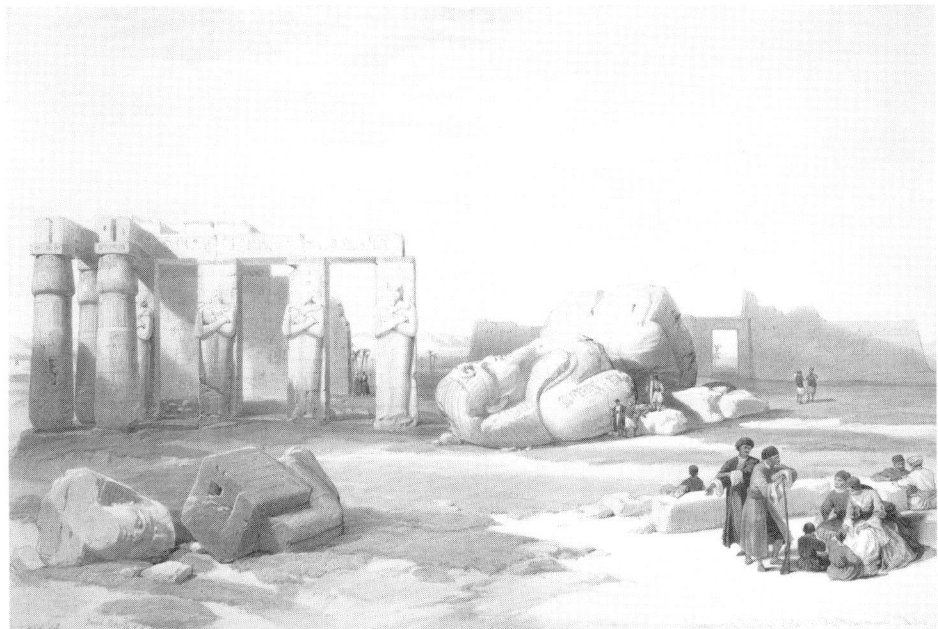

Figure 3.7 David Roberts, *Fragment of the Great Colossus at the Memnonium, Thebes* (also known as *The Colossus of Rameses II in the Ramesseum*), lithograph from Roberts *Egypt and Nubia*, 1844–1849, Vol. 2, pl. 48. Photo: akg-images / De Agostini Picture Library.

characteristic range of pictorial devices. The former go to claims about a decayed social and physical fabric in the Eastern world, and what to Roberts and many other Europeans seemed an oriental trait of "idleness"; the latter relate to representations of architectural decay. One might add Roberts' recurrent device of placing contemporary Egyptians as small figures disposed among the ruins of ancient grandeur (Figure 3.7). There would be no point in trying to exonerate Roberts and his peers from a range of mid-nineteenth-century beliefs extending from patronizing remarks about the value of Nubians as honest servants to an overweening sense of the superiority of things European. These are explicit. Thus, in the Introduction to Roberts' volume of views of *Egypt and Nubia*, written by William Brockendon, "Fellow of the Royal Society," the nations of Europe are deemed to be "in the highest state of enlightenment yet attained by any community of the human family," in contrast to which Egypt is held to have fallen from historical eminence to an "ignorant and degraded condition in the present day."[67] From Brockendon's Victorian Christian perspective, Islamic culture represented a degenerated barbarism and the history of modern Egypt was of "little interest"; indeed, contemporary Egypt as a whole signified only for its geographical location: its strategic importance en route to "our vast possessions" in India.[68] There is no getting away from this aspect of the nineteenth-century European outlook, even though it tends to be more baldly stated in the prose than in the pictures. The more

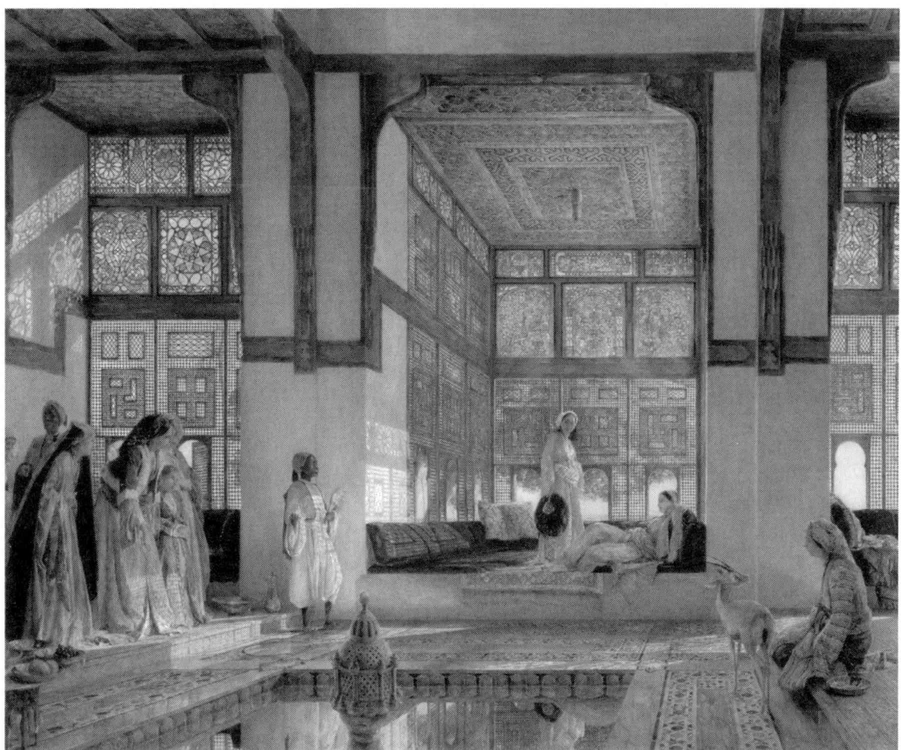

Figure 3.8 John Frederick Lewis, *A Lady Receiving Visitors (The Reception)*, 1873, oil on wood, 63 × 76 cm, Yale Center for British Art, Paul Mellon Collection.

interesting point now seems to be not just to write off Roberts out of hand but to see how much more his visual representations contribute than the imperialist rhetoric surrounding them. A kind of three-cornered contest is played out between modern Europe, the modern Orient, and ancient Egypt. Many, possibly the majority, of Roberts' images evoke a pervasive melancholy concerning the decay wrought by time, and the inevitable fall of imperial grandeur. They are also in themselves a record of a now lost condition in which the relics of ancient Egypt could be encountered. Roberts, just as much as Flaubert, was damningly critical of the encroachment of Western tourism and the effect it was having on the ruins.

A further sense of beginning to go beyond the rather one-dimensional censoriousness of earlier treatments of European orientalism can also be found in the 2008 exhibition of British orientalist painting which, crucially, was not just shown in London but also traveled to Istanbul and Sharjah. This clearly evinces a development beyond *both* the historically disingenuous formalism of earlier treatments of orientalist art, *and* its politically driven denunciation in the wake of Said's critical reading in terms of complicity with imperialism. Thus Emily Weekes prefaced an historically informed and interpretively flexible reading of the nineteenth-century work of John Frederick Lewis (see Figure 3.8) with a set of acute observations on the comparative failure of contemporary art history (relative to other disciplines) "to work through the faults" of Said's critique and "develop more nuanced lenses through which to view" orientalist paintings. This third stage of address to those works which, for all of their being marked by many of the conventions and suppositions of their time – artistic and sociopolitical alike – in multifarious ways also reworked them, seems to offer a great deal: pushing art history beyond its canonical comfort zones while yet pressing beyond that species of moral rectitude that weakened so much earlier critical work. Weekes writes that "despite the polemical and political interpretations that many Orientalist works have attracted in recent decades … these paintings have in fact much left to tell." She goes on to argue that implicit and hitherto unnoticed criticism of the metropolitan "home" culture, as well as the variety of particular responses which have been overlooked in the drive to link artworks with grander imperial projects, all need further examination; and "perhaps most importantly, genuine moments of cross-cultural understanding, respect and commemoration have yet to be restored to the historical record." In a more nuanced fashion than Nochlin's earlier critique of naturalism would have permitted, Weekes' reading of Lewis opens up a different vista. Whereas "our received wisdom concerning Orientalism would compel us to believe that Lewis used his technical prowess to celebrate Britain's convictions of cultural superiority in the nineteenth century, a new reading might suggest that he used it to question the beliefs of his subjects – and, more importantly, those who viewed them."[69] Such comments as these by Emily Weekes, Mary Roberts, and others seem to point to an emerging third phase in the art historical study of modern European representations of the wider world: one which is finally capable of moving beyond both the once orthodox formalism that relegated such work to the margins of the Eurocentric canon, and the reactive mode that focused on "orientalism" only to denounce European representation of its various Others as *a priori* client to imperialism.

Modernity

An apprehension that the modern condition demanded new forms of representation had begun to emerge in the early nineteenth century with Romanticism.[70] In his review of the Salon of 1824, the novelist Stendhal inveighed against huge academic pictures, full of nude figures copied from classical bas-reliefs, arguing that "the time has come for good painters to try and be modern," to represent "people as they are today."[71] The most resonant theoretical attempt to articulate just what it was that made people "as they are today" different from their forebears, and thus to define the modern condition, did not appear until Baudelaire's review of the Salon of 1846. Addressing himself explicitly to the new bourgeoisie, as the majority force in French society, he proceeded to delineate the "heroism of modern life." For Baudelaire in 1846, all beauty contained "an element of the eternal and an element of the transitory"[72]; it was this latter that characterized the modern condition, that was overlooked in the continuing adherence to academic classicism, and that artists should recognize. It is one thing, however, to recognize a need, quite another to be able to fulfill it.

No visual artist responded to Baudelaire's call in the 1840s, the final years of the July monarchy in France, which were largely a period of eclecticism in the arts. Even by the late 1850s, when Baudelaire composed his fullest account of the situation which "The Painter of Modern Life" should aspire to represent, no artist had yet appeared who seemed able to capture the fleeting and transitory aspects of urban modernity that for Baudelaire defined the new situation.[73] Baudelaire's essay was in fact centered on the popular illustrator Constantin Guys, and it was in this field, rather than "fine art" as such, that representations of fashion and leisure first appeared. Such illustrators also played a prominent role in the negotiation of modernity in England. Examples might be furnished from prints of the urban entertainments of the Vauxhall pleasure gardens in London or Paul Sandby's watercolors of sites such as Ascot and Windsor from the mid-eighteenth century onwards.[74] But, as with prevailing representations of the geographically distant, first in chinoiserie and then in fully fledged "orientalism," so it was with nascent representations of urban modernity and popular culture: the frame remained in place. England was the most dynamic new capitalist state. But after the end of the French revolutionary wars, and even more so after the Reform Bill of 1832, the relatively stable condition of capitalism in England meant that the field of artistic representation remained mostly within the orbit of the academy. The painstaking literary naturalism of the Pre-Raphaelite Brotherhood marked the limit of English artistic radicalism. But the more disruptive situation in France created the conditions for the emergence of a genuinely dissident subculture in the arts. London did of course experience social stress and conflict, and it produced its own distinctive culture of modernity. But conflict remained contained and negotiated. Not so in Paris, which displayed unparalleled volatility both politically and culturally, making the new conditions sharply visible to intellectuals and artists. It was the emergence there in the 1860s of an artistic avant-garde deeply opposed to the conventions of the academy that created the possibility of both something more lasting than illustration *and* something more vivid, more modern in itself, than the artistically conventional images of modern life that were appearing in England.

It was the art of Manet and his followers, the impressionists, that definitively established the connection between modern subjects and modern techniques. One of the main things that made Paris new in the Second Empire was its physical modernization under the program of Baron Haussmann. Nothing could have been further from Haussmann's mind than the creation of a new art. His modernization of the city was a response to contemporary capitalist crisis – in David Harvey's words, its purpose was "to absorb the surpluses of capital and labour power" that were blocking productivity.[75] Nonetheless, the new boulevards, with their attendant buildings from the Stock Exchange to the Opera, from railway stations to department stores and covered arcades, really precipitated that modern life that Baudelaire had first glimpsed the decade before. It was this constellation of features, especially the new forms of commodified leisure in music halls, cafés, and bars, that stimulated the new art. Traversed by all kinds of fissures of class and gender, freedom and power, these were the places and the experiences that both demanded and received a Baudelairean modern art. Fashion, the crowd, the dandy, the prostitute, carriages, cosmetics, and of course, cafés and shops, were the visible features of the new life: the extraordinary cocktail of modernity that was Haussmann's Paris. The sexual, the social, the power relations of the modern world were being worked out there. The undoubted strangeness and extremism of art like Manet's was the result of an effort to represent that equally extreme new condition; and, importantly, to represent the underlying forces which were shaping it, not just to illustrate what it looked like. The conservative Delacroix felt that "this new world, good or bad, which is trying to reach the light across our ruins, is like a volcano under our feet."[76]

Manet and "Japonisme"

"Modernity" as a subject in art historical literature has been discussed almost exclusively in terms of temporality. The notion of a modern art, of a modern condition, is, after all, principally defined against a sense of the past. Academic art is one aspect of this "pastness," with its roots in an amalgam of memory and the fiction of an even deeper past, the past of classical antiquity mediated through the Italian Renaissance. This temporal vector is the fundamental measure of something's being considered modern. But the European modernity that began to emerge in the late eighteenth century, and that was established at least in the leading metropolitan centers by the middle of the nineteenth century, also had a significant spatial dimension. Modernity was measured not just against a European past but also against a non-European present.

As we have seen, since the late eighteenth century, non-Western subjects had begun to be introduced into the academic repertoire within the subgenres of chinoiserie and orientalism. But in the visual arts, the key thing is that such "exotic" subjects, even when at their most challenging in terms of their violence or their sexuality, were subsumed within long-established technical conventions of representation. We have encountered a spectrum of responses. Even when he had recourse to photography, an artist like Gérôme continued to employ a stable framework to depict his exotic subjects. Whereas, a Romantic like Delacroix stretched his technique, and was therefore of more interest to the new avant-garde. But at bottom, illusionism – or *mimesis* – the technical keystone of the European

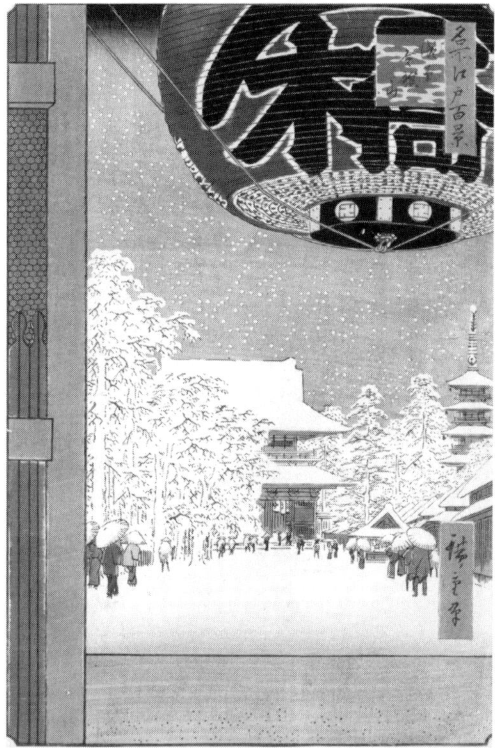

Figure 3.9 Utagawa Hiroshige, *Kinryuzan Temple at Asakusa*, c.1856, from the series *One Hundred Views of Famous Places in Edo*, color woodblock print. Private Collection / Photo © Christie's Images / The Bridgeman Art Library.

post-Renaissance academic canon, held. European representational decorum continued to frame its depicted subjects, however modern, however exotic.

With the advent of the avant-garde, that changed substantially. It has become a commonplace to say that the impressionists were *influenced by Japanese prints*. But what does this mean? It was actually modernist art history that established this connection. Modernist explanations of modern art emphasized formal and technical matters. The Japanese woodblock prints which appeared in Paris around 1860 were radically unlike European art (see Figure 3.9). Most obviously, they lacked halftones that modulated shading from light to dark, which, because of the way they enabled the depiction of three-dimensional objects in virtual space, formed the technical basis of illusionistic representation. In a word, the Japanese prints seemed flatter, employing large, unmodulated areas of color. Other features of the Japanese prints, such as the way figures were allowed to be cropped by the framing edge, as well as visually startling juxtapositions of foreground and background, rapidly made an impression on the nascent avant-garde.

As we have seen in the case of Baudelaire, it is one thing to sense the need for a new pictorial language, quite another to deliver it. It is important to see that it was specifically the dominant academic tradition with its often elevated subject matter and its strict standards of "finish" that seemed unable to meet the representational challenge of modernity. Yet a new visual language cannot just be wished into existence. As a result, Manet and others were trying to look beyond the core Franco-Italianate academic tradition for hints as to how to deal technically with the representation of modernity. Of particular interest to them were Spanish and Dutch art, both for their relatively freer application of paint, as in the work of Velazquez and Goya, Rembrandt, and Hals and also for the evident interest in daily life which had been the hallmark of the Dutch seventeenth century (and which had been subjected to criticism by the academic proponents of the "grand style"). Lying even further off-limits from the moribund academic canon, and hence also of interest to the avant-garde, were visual manifestations of popular culture, such as the cheap colored prints from Epinal. It was into this mix of different representational possibilities that the Japanese prints fell, when they turned up, almost accidentally, in mid-century Paris.

There is no doubt about their impact. It has long been known and the evidence from the time, both in the form of written testimony and the pictures themselves, is unequivocal. None other than Baudelaire wrote to his friend Arsène Houssaye in 1861,

> I have had a packet of *japonneries* in my possession for a long time now. I share them with my friends, and I have kept three of them for you. They are not bad at all (the Japanese equivalents of Epinal prints, two sous apiece in Edo). On rag paper and in bamboo or Chinese red lacquer frames, they are highly effective.[77]

Later, in 1878, Theodore Duret wrote that "it took the arrival of the Japanese prints among us for someone to dare to sit down on the bank of a river, to juxtapose on one canvas a boldly red roof, a high white wall, a green poplar, a yellow road and some blue water. Before the example of the Japanese, it was impossible."[78] For Duret, it was the sight of Japanese prints that made avant-garde painters finally understand "that there were new methods for reproducing certain effects of nature which till then were considered impossible to render."[79] Clear evidence of the technical interest in Japanese composition can be seen in Manet's own prints. In painting, both in its composition and its subject matter, Manet's large, complex portrait of his defender, Émile Zola, attests to an interest in japonisme in the avant-garde milieu. On the shelf, alongside a print, or possibly a photograph, of his own *Olympia* can be seen a Japanese print of a famous wrestler; and behind Zola is a painted screen which belonged to Manet himself. Edgar Degas' use of Japanese-derived techniques such as radical foreshortening, strong diagonals and abruptly cut-off figures is even clearer than that of Manet. Degas himself had an extensive collection of prints. Slightly later, Vincent van Gogh similarly collected Japanese prints, copied them, and incorporated the lessons in his own compositions. Mary Cassatt adapted Japanese composition in her innovative images of female domesticity. Examples could easily be multiplied. The technical impact of Japanese prints, and the more widespread fascination with Japanese culture, both within the avant-garde and beyond it in the world of interior decoration and fashion, is not in doubt.

My main concern here is with the radical effect of that technical impact, in terms of the way it enabled far-reaching change in art. At the same time it should be recognized that, just as with chinoiserie before it in the eighteenth century, japonisme in the nineteenth, both in Paris and in London, was a *fashion* among the cultivated bourgeoisie. It is this aspect that Proust catches in his description of the courtesan Odette de Crécy's apartment, no less eclectic in its orientalism than Goldsmith's English country house of a hundred years earlier: its "dark painted walls hung with Oriental draperies, strings of Turkish beads, and a huge Japanese lantern suspended by a silken cord (which last, however, so that her visitors should not be deprived of the latest comforts of Western civilisation, was lighted by a gas-jet inside)." Odette's "large chrysanthemums," "enormous palms growing out of pots of Chinese porcelain," her "pink silk dressing gown" and the "great cushions of Japanese silk which she pummelled and buffeted as though to prove she was prodigal in these riches, regardless of their value," were the trappings of an essentially pretentious lifestyle.[80]

In the struggle to broaden art history from a restricted "modernist" interest in the technical concerns of an autonomously conceived art (which had featured the technical impact of Japanese prints) and to relate it instead to a wider social condition of modernity, some of the implications of this Japanese "influence" have become occluded. The hallmark advance of the "new art history" of the 1970s and 1980s was to reposition the art of the avant-garde in relation to contemporary nineteenth-century modernity, rather than to view it retrospectively, and to an extent anachronistically, through the lens of subsequent twentieth-century modernism. But some of the radical implications of the avant-garde's interest in japonisme tended to be lost in the identification of modernity exclusively with Paris: the effects of Haussmannization, the commodification, the alienation, and the spectacle of modernity. For art history, "modernity" came to mean "Paris." But "Paris" does not mean just "Haussmannization," nor, later, the Eiffel Tower. Or rather, Haussmannization and the Eiffel Tower both signified that Paris was a world city. The "universal exhibitions" brought the world to Paris, just as to London. For good or ill, nineteenth-century European modernity was world-facing. *Round the World in 80 Days* is, after all, a nineteenth-century text, conceived while Jules Verne read a newspaper in a Paris café. More than that, the French construction and engineering industry of the Second Empire did not just build the boulevards, the Opera, and the new department stores. In 1869 it completed the Suez Canal. The French Empire may have been second to the British, but it was equally global. Even after the disastrous Franco-Prussian war of 1870 and the trauma of the Paris Commune the year after, French capitalism survived, and the French Empire did too.

There is no doubt that the majority of early French avant-garde art seeks to represent new forms of life in the modern metropolis. But sometimes the worldedness of that modernity leaks through. The Japanese print phenomenon is the most important aspect of this. But its implications are not solely technical. In a recent study of the impact of japonisme on French literature, Jan Walsh Hokensen has drawn attention to earlier attempts to assess the true cultural–historical significance of Japanese prints for the visual arts. Thus, the German historian Klaus Berger argued that the encounter marked nothing less than a "Copernican" moment in art.[81] As long ago as the 1970s the literary historian Gabriel Josipovici had assessed the deep impact of such a different mode of representation as being primarily conceptual rather than just technical. For him its key effect was the way it enabled European artists to realize that Renaissance-academic single-point perspective was not a "datum of experience," that is, a "natural" way of representing the world, but the product of convention. "This is not simply a widening of the cultural horizons; it is the discovery of the relativity of artistic norms." Such representational conventions were, moreover, rooted in wider "metaphysical assumptions" of European Renaissance civilization, including those of a stable, unified viewing subject, a clear distinction of that subject from the object of his gaze, and the very possibility of the rational ordering of space.[82] It is this range of concerns that makes japonisme a matter of much more profound significance for Western art than the earlier fashions for chinoiserie and orientalism. These latter remained contained by the European perspectival armature. Japonisme, by contrast, was a key element in the constellation of conditions which ruptured the coherent space of academic representation and thus opened the way for the radically different art of the modern and contemporary periods – and ultimately, therefore, for the possibility of a revision of the relation of Western art to the wider world.

It is as if it was only the force of the struggle to represent modernity, which had bred avant-garde skepticism about academic convention, that made the different representational mode of the Japanese prints visible as art. Before Japan had been "opened" to Western eyes and to Western markets by forcible American intervention in 1854, after two centuries of seclusion, various examples of Japanese visual and material culture had made their way to the West. A museum of it had existed in the Netherlands since 1828, along with scholarly studies. But the crucial point is that this had no impact in artistic terms. Indeed, after the "opening" of Japan by the Americans, the first exhibition of Japanese culture had taken place in London. But it had little effect on art in England, its main impact being in the fields of interior design and craftwork – an echo of the situation we encountered with chinoiserie in the eighteenth century. It took the avant-garde aspiration to a counter-academic representation of modernity to create the connection with art, to be able to see the Japanese print *as* a demonstration of the "relativity of artistic norms." As the brothers Edmond and Jules de Goncourt noted in their *Journal* of January 1862, "Art is not one, or rather there is no single art. Japanese art is as great as Greek art."[83] The sudden emergence of such cultural relativism is indeed testimony to a kind of Copernican revolution in art.

There are indications that in terms of subject matter as well as formal devices, nineteenth-century proto-globalization is not entirely absent from avant-garde art. Manet, who surely is one of the most *intelligent* artists, seems to have been aware of the implications more than most. In a series of works in the late 1860s, in the final years of the Second Empire, and then again towards the end of his life, he made several paintings which seem to indicate an awareness of the spatial, geographical aspect of modernity. The first and last of these were two "seascapes" painted in 1864 and 1880. Both incorporate "Japanese" formal elements: the high horizon, the sea as a relatively flat wall of water seen as if from an elevated viewpoint, the displacement of elements to the edges of the picture. Both are a long way from a conventional history painting in the academic tradition. Yet that is precisely the ground on which they aspire to stand. The 1880 *Escape of Rochefort*, of which Manet painted two versions, represented the escape of the exiled Communard Henri Rochefort from the French penal colony on New Caledonia in the South Pacific (to where he had been transported with others, including Louise Michel).[84] The 1864 picture represents an engagement from the contemporary American Civil War in which a smaller Confederate vessel was engaged and sunk by a Union corvette off the coast of Cherbourg after having initially sought refuge in the French port (Figure 3.10). Spectators watched from the shore. It would have been relatively easy to make a melodrama out of this, as indeed contemporary popular prints did. But eschewing conventional heroics and sentimentalism alike, Manet used unequivocally modern means to offer a curiously distanced representation of a foreign war suddenly getting close to home.

The same "distant" quality, a kind of Brechtian alienation-effect *avant la lettre*, is evident in his next attempt at history painting. In 1867 he embarked on what was probably his single most ambitious project: to represent the *Execution of Maximilian*. Only historians know about Maximilian now, but in 1867 the circumstances surrounding his death bespoke scandal. The scion of Austrian Habsburgs, installed on the Mexican throne, depended on French military support. The withdrawal of that support, under American pressure, revealed the limits of real French power, despite imperial rhetoric. Maximilian's execution by Mexican nationalist forces, added to newspaper reports of his personal bravery, made the case a flashpoint for Republican opposition to the Second Empire. To this end, Manet generated no less than three large-scale oil paintings and a related print in his attempt to arrive at a truthful representation of the consequences of imperial hypocrisy. This he achieved through a combination of assiduous research in the contemporary periodical press,[85] and a studied reworking of Goya's *Executions of the 3rd May 1808*. Commonly acknowledged as a universal condemnation of man's inhumanity to man, Goya's image also happened to relate to an earlier episode of French imperialism gone wrong, the first Napoleon's Peninsular War in Spain. Manet did not waste all that effort on something that didn't matter. The execution of Maximilian was a subject that, though it happened thousands of miles from Paris, got to the heart of a darker aspect of Second Empire modernity than is normally associated with the "painting of modern life."

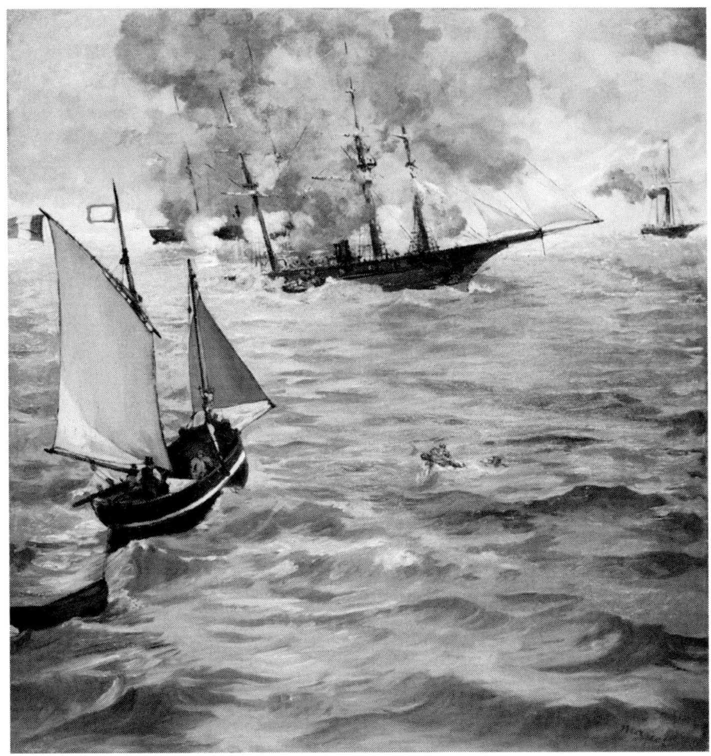

Figure 3.10 Edouard Manet, *The Battle of the Kearsarge and the Alabama*, oil on canvas, 1864, 134 × 127 cm. Philadelphia Museum of Art, John G. Johnson Collection. Inv. No. 1027. Photo: akg-images.

Manet was able to bring this mordant quality to bear on another aspect of Parisian social life that is very much associated with Baudelarean modernity: prostitution. His most remarkable treatment of this is, of course, *Olympia*. But he also ventured onto the terrain wherein orientalism met the demi-monde in costume. Manet's *Sultane* of 1871 does nothing if not serve to underline that the avant-garde's technical radicalism meant little if it was not accompanied by a critical intelligence. Surely Renoir's orientalist fantasies, such as *Parisian Women in Algerian Dress* (also known as *Harem Scene in Montmartre*), ironically painted in the very next year, are closer to something one would expect from Gérôme. The type of reflection Manet was able to bring to bear on this overdetermined point where sexuality, commodification, and empire all join hands in the night, is of a different critical order. Stripped of its glamour, the model's pose, somewhere between dejected and resilient, carries much more critical force than Renoir's costumed cocottes; and her facial expression has much of that same inscrutability performed by the girl behind the *Bar at the Folies-Bergère* – which T.J. Clark made into a figure for the whole experience of modernity at the point where sex and class meet; the difference being that, with the *Sultane*, the orient is in there too.

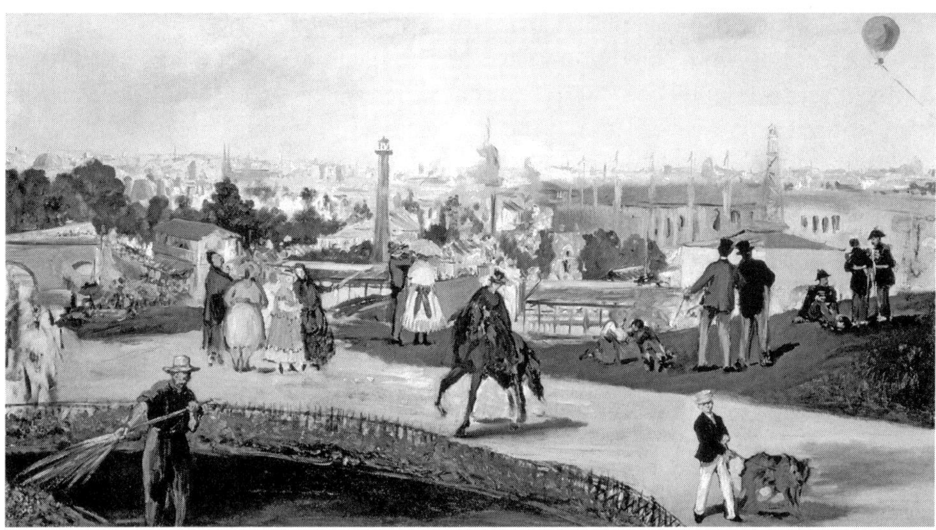

Figure 3.11 Edouard Manet, *View of the Universal Exhibition*, 1867, oil on canvas, 107 × 197 cm. Nasjonalgalleriet, Oslo, Norway / The Bridgeman Art Library.

The more overtly public face of nascent globalization had also caught Manet's attention, and again it is the emptiness of it all on which Manet is able to fasten. His tactic seems to be to emphasize dislocation. The *View of the Universal Exhibition* of 1867 is one of the strangest works of his entire career (Figure 3.11). Nothing seems to fit together. The figures are out of scale, the middle ground is missing, the showground itself looks like a cardboard castle. Even the position from which it was painted was artificial, the shape of the natural hill having been modified – by Haussmann – in order to provide a more pleasing vantage point. The hollowness of official spectacle has seldom been more convincingly demonstrated, by the apparently simple (but of course, actually complex) expedient of, as it were, allowing the joins to show. This was the second "universal exhibition" to be held in Paris, following the first, in 1855, which in turn had set out to emulate the "Great Exhibition" held in London in 1851. In all of these, the rest of the world, parceled and packaged and re-presented for consumption, was brought before the inhabitants of the imperial metropolis.

As it happened, the star attraction of the one that Manet painted in 1867 was the Japanese pavilion. After the success of a display of Japanese art in London in 1862, the Japanese government threw its weight behind the Paris display, intending to open a window to the West and stimulate mutually profitable trading relations. It is a small point, though an interesting one, that the display of woodblock prints added at the last minute came from the collection of the French avant-gardist Philippe Burty. In Japan itself such things were not valued at all, being regarded as modern and debased, not fit to officially represent the ancient heritage of Japanese culture: not the face one ruling class wanted to present to another on the sacred altar of business. As we have already seen, the principal subject of the Japanese printmakers was itself a kind of modernity. The "fleeting" or "floating world" they depicted was eminently comparable to that which the nineteenth-century Parisian avant-garde were striving to represent. The artists of the "green houses" of Yoshiwara, the nocturnal district of Edo, shared more than a little with those of Pigalle and the boulevards of Paris, both in terms of the techniques they employed and the subjects they used those techniques to represent.

Manet was many things. To modernists he was the point of departure. To radical art historians he was the quintessential artist of modernity, of urban modernity as exemplified in the salons, the nightlife, and the boulevards of Paris. He most certainly was that, but his Paris was worlded. The city itself and its bourgeoisie were made out of imperialism as well as capitalism, and Manet knew it.

Primitivism

For any account of Western art's relations with the rest of the world, there is no avoiding primitivism. For better or for worse (and the present-day consensus has it that it was for worse, if not the worst), "primitivism" is the sign under which the art of the modernist avant-garde treated the arts of the wider world. For the most part, however, it was not the whole of the world that was involved. During the long period we have been discussing, stretching from the middle of the fifteenth century to the middle of the nineteenth century, the principal exotic focus for European artists and intellectuals had been the cultures of highly developed Eastern civilizations, the worlds of Islam, India, and China, and then, in a crucially different register, Japan. There was curiosity about the different kinds of world, worlds that were characteristically thought of as "savage" or "barbaric" or "primitive," that had been revealed to European eyes in America and in the Pacific. But they were scarcely comprehended in any recognizably modern "sociological" sense and had no impact on art beyond the provision of subjects for the visual record, such as it was. For the artists of the modern movement in the late nineteenth and early twentieth centuries, the position was dramatically reversed. There was relatively little engagement with the great civilizations of the world. Important though they were to the individual artists themselves, the engagements of Henri Matisse with Islamic North Africa and of Gustave Moreau with India, are the exceptions that prove the rule. Overwhelmingly, modernist artists who looked beyond their own urbanized, industrialized, bourgeoisified, capitalized heartlands of Western Europe looked at two places: the Pacific, and most important of all, Africa.

That list of adjectives provides the clue. Industrialization, the city, the dominance of the middle class, the increasing commodification of everything, they were what "modernity" had become. It was not a congenial place for the radical artist, distanced from the core values of his host society. Employing a version of the ideology of the "noble savage" updated to fit the age of empire, modernists conjured a vision of the "primitive" as everything the modern wasn't – and that they wanted to be. Another range of adjectives came over the horizon: "free," "spontaneous," "direct," "expressive," "authentic." These were the elements of a modernist artistic persona that became the commonsense of art until the second half of the twentieth century. Every single one has been put to the sword by postmodernist, feminist, and postcolonial theory since then.[86]

Once again, as with the discussion of orientalism above, the situation has now evolved. Uncritical celebrations of expressionist modernism are a thing of the past. But by the same token, the revelation of modernist primitivism's complicity with colonialism is now also historical. It can still be useful to see from where the ideology of primitivism derived its strength, to recognize some of the contradictions into which it was forced even as it was embraced, and finally to set what modernism proposed against what the academy still practiced.

Full-blown modernist primitivism was a phenomenon of the early twentieth century, but its roots can be traced to the different situation of the closing decades of the nineteenth century in the symbolist milieu. The painting of modern life, otherwise often referred to by the style label "impressionism," is widely regarded as having entered a crisis in the 1880s. Indeed, the final impressionist group exhibition took place in 1886. There was more at stake than just individuals going their own ways, a deeper shift in the concerns of the avant-garde. As we have seen, the project of representing modern life was rooted in a strong sense of temporality, of the present making its demand on the artist, and a failure to heed that demand consigning the artist to conservatism. Yet from the late 1880s, for many in the avant-garde, present-day reality seems to have become an imaginative constraint rather than a means of liberation from a dead past. To some, at least, of a younger generation of the avant-garde, by definition displaced from the core cultural values of the middle class (if not always from its social and political values), contemporary bourgeois life represented closure, hypocrisy, and falsehood, rather than the route to a modern truth. For them, it had ceased to be the material out of which a critical art could be made. Impressionism was an amalgam of, on the one hand, naturalism, an objective, quasi-scientific commitment to scrupulous looking, and, on the other, a commitment to the integrity of the painting as an entity whose own internal relations were no less important than the relations between the representation and its motif. Keeping those two aspects in balance seems to lie at the heart of the impressionist enterprise. However, with the decline of naturalism, considered as an attempt to fix the look of the present, the constraints on what a painting could be made out of were significantly loosened.

Some of the ideas involved were articulated by the symbolist writer Albert Aurier. Aurier, contended that "the objects in the painting have no meaning at all as objects, but are only signs." This amounts to a claim that the meaning of a painting is not to be identified with the things it depicts in the "real world" outside the painting. Instead, the "objects" in a painting have their life in relation to the other features of the work, that is, they relate to each other rather like words in a poem or notes in a piece of music. For Aurier, the goal of painting "can never be the direct representation of objects. Its aim is to express Ideas, by translating them into a special language." The result would be an art that eschewed the "banality of the photograph" and was instead "simple, spontaneous and primordial." Aurier is here sounding a note that would continue to echo through the avant-garde: that artistic authenticity is not to be found in appearances, not in the surface phenomena of a civilization become decadent, but that it should instead be sought in "simple" and "primordial" experiences. The most advanced art, for him "the true and absolute art," was in fact "fundamentally identical with primitive art."[87] Hitherto, symbolism had been a literary movement. Aurier's article was in effect its manifesto for the visual arts and took its cue from recent work being done not in Paris but in Brittany by the circle around Paul Gauguin.

In a work such as *Vision after the Sermon*, painted in the autumn of 1888, Gauguin had already abandoned naturalism, both in terms of the spatial relations within the painting and the colors of represented objects. It was evidently a modern painting, in the sense that it would have made no sense at all outside of the avant-garde. But it was in no sense a painting of modern life. Instead of observing life on the fashionable boulevards of Paris, Gauguin – a sometime stockbroker before he abandoned work on the Bourse for the life of a full-time artist – was now to be found striving to get in touch with the superstitious faith of the Breton peasants, and praising not Baudelaire's patent leather shoes but his own clogs as they "resound on the granite soil" of Brittany.[88] Skeptical historians have made much of the rhetorical nature of Gauguin's primitivism, pointing out that there was a flourishing colony of artists in Brittany who were not far from being part of an early tourist trade, and who certainly got there by train; pointing out also what a canny operator Gauguin was, never losing sight of a need to figure in the marketplace. Certainly, when Gauguin took his flight from civilization a stage further and emigrated to Polynesia, he traveled by steamship to what was by then a French colony. All of this is undoubtedly true, and primitivism was nothing if not internally contradictory. An ideology is, after all, supposed to be the imaginary resolution of a real contradiction. The real contradiction is that modernity was oppressive. The real *political* resolution of that contradiction, from one point of view at least, would be to work to change those oppressive conditions. But artistically, the resolution seems to have lain in a transformation of values. Not everyone agreed. The anarchist painter of modern life, Camille Pissarro, was shortly to criticize Gauguin for "pillaging the savages of Oceania,"[89] and in doing so having abandoned "our modern philosophy which is absolutely social, anti-authoritarian and anti-mystical." But to turn the values upside down, to devalue the modern and to value the primitive struck a chord in the avant-garde, even to the point of displacing the painting of modern life from the center ground of avant-garde activity. It is an open question what this says about the social role of art; but short of a complete social transformation, primitivism with all its contradictions did afford a kind of critical leverage against industrialized modernity and its mass culture. And in Gauguin's own case there was a certain paradoxical realism to the project. Once he had given up the stock exchange and committed himself to art, his only station in life, precarious as it was, was the Parisian avant-garde, and primitivism provided his productive point within it. It may not be the whole truth, but it was certainly a partial truth, that European modernity and European art had well and truly lost any heroism they might once have had. On the eve of his departure for Tahiti, Gauguin wrote, "Terrible times are in store for the next generation: gold will be king!! Everything is rotten, men and the arts alike."[90]

For two years, from 1891 to 1893, and then again for the eight years from 1895 until his death in 1903, Gauguin lived and worked first in Tahiti and finally in the Marquesas islands, about as far from "civilization" as it was possible to get. Back in Paris in the mid-1890s, between his two sojourns in the Pacific, Gauguin wrote a fictionalized, self-mythologizing account of his life there under the title *Noa Noa*. The phrase means "perfume," or "scent," and is associated in Gauguin's mind with the sensuality and the freedom he thought he had found in the people of Polynesia and which was so singularly lacking in the "rottenness" he had left behind. In *Noa Noa*, Gauguin recounts a parable. He tells the story of going off into the forest with a young Tahitian to collect wood for a sculpture. Gauguin's writing is a mix of plain and portentous, and it is not always easy to tell exactly what he means; mystery and suggestion tends to win out over clarity. But in the story, Gauguin, the middle-aged white man, seems to be sexually tempted by the sight of his androgynous companion. Overcoming this temptation (something he conspicuously failed to achieve with the young women of the islands), Gauguin experiences a rebirth:

> Yes, wholly destroyed, finished, dead, is from now on the old civilisation within me. I was reborn; or rather, another man, purer and stronger came to life within me. This cruel assault was the supreme farewell to civilisation, to evil. … Avidly I inhaled the splendid purity of the light. I was indeed a new man; from now on I was a true savage, a real Maori.[91]

The figure Gauguin cuts here may be ridiculous, sinister, or tragic, depending on your point of view. Alienated white men going downhill in the tropics were becoming a staple of Conrad's fiction at around the same time. Most of Gauguin's Tahitian works represent an imaginary arcadia from which all trace of modernity has been excluded. For historical materialists, as well as postmodernist critics, this makes them falsifications of colonial reality. From a different point of view they can be seen as meditations on matters transcending the merely historical. It is not a cut and dried issue, sociologists and spiritualists both have their supporters. What perhaps can be said is that both representations of modernity reduced to a positivistic recording of phenomena and representations of a make-believe arcadia untroubled by the contradictions of modernity are alike somewhat one-dimensional.

Sometimes, however, Gauguin's primitivism could achieve a greater complexity. It was, after all, itself a modern construct, a kind of improvisation by a modern intellectual. Despite the aspiration to a kind of primordial purity ("new man," "true savage," "real Maori"), it was itself a synthesis, almost stuck together from a repertoire of

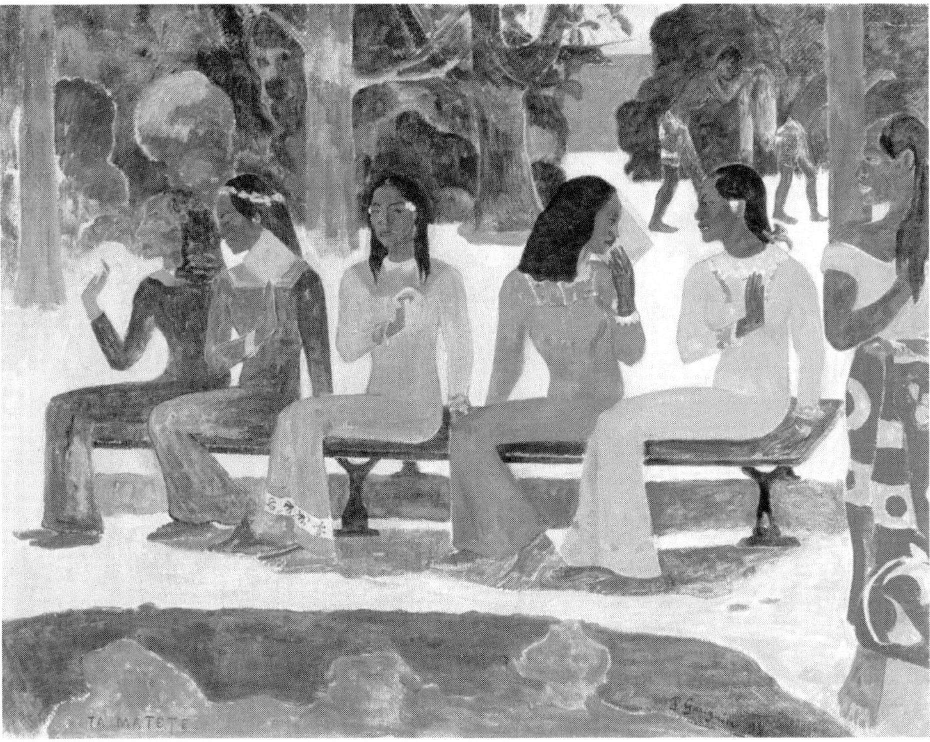

Figure 3.12 Paul Gauguin: *Ta Matete (We Shall Not Go to Market Today)*, 1892, oil on canvas, 73 × 92 cm. Basel, Kunstmuseum. Photo: akg-images / De Agostini Picture Library.

motifs ranging from Christian symbolism to pagan Tahitian myths to old master art to modern photographs of ancient temples and tombs. Occasionally, "modern life" could make an appearance, albeit oblique and displaced. At least once Gauguin seemed to represent the snake in arcadia, despite himself. *Ta Matete*, painted in 1892, shows a group of Tahitian women sitting on a bench, with what looks like a municipal flower bed in front, and behind them a glimpse of the sea through some trees (Figure 3.12). Mostly, Gauguin excluded signifiers of modernity from his painting, concentrating instead on Tahitian myth or metaphysical doubts, as in *Where do we come from? Who are we? Where are we going?* – one of his well-known late works dating from 1897. At first, however, before moving into rural areas, Gauguin had been struck by the gap between the myth he had created for himself and the reality of Papete, the French colonial capital of Tahiti. In June 1891 he had written to his wife that "the Tahitian soil is becoming completely French and little by little the old order will disappear. Our missionaries had already introduced a good deal of protestant hypocrisy and wiped out some of the poetry, not to mention the pox which has attacked the whole race."[92] It is this which forms at least part of the content of *Ta Matete*.

I have already mentioned the flowerbed; the bench is also unmistakably European, with its little green painted iron legs. The women are not wearing

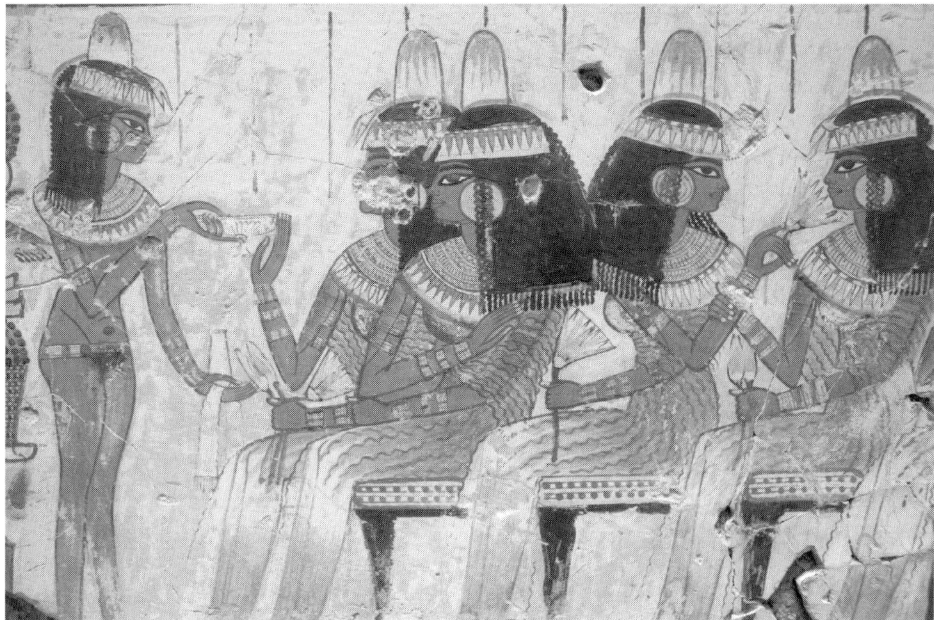

Figure 3.13 Fragment of Nebamun tomb painting of female guests at a banquet, thirteenth century BCE. London, British Museum. Photo © Steve Vidler / Alamy.

Tahitian clothes, but neither do they seem to be wearing the shapeless coverings that Christian missionaries had induced the native women to wear. Gauguin was perfectly well aware of these. In fact in a work painted in Brittany in 1894, between his two periods in the Pacific, he produced the unusual hybrid *Young Christian Girl*. The vertical composition is dominated by a three-quarter-length figure. The background of a Breton landscape, complete with cottages and chimney pots, and visible to either side of the large central figure, is painted in the flattened, chromatically high-keyed style developed in Polynesia. But still stranger is the fact that the young girl, eyes downcast, hands clasped in prayer, is clad not in the characteristic Breton peasant costume of black dress and starched white hat but in one of the brightly colored, loose-fitting smocks dispensed by missionaries to women in the Pacific to cover up the nakedness which the Christians found so troubling.

This is not the type of clothing being worn by the young women in *Ta Matete*. On the contrary, they are wearing elegant, fashionable dresses. Disposed along the bench, parallel to the picture plane, they look like figures on a frieze. And so they are. A clue is given by the hand gesture of the woman at the far left. Gauguin had taken with him a large array of source material in the form of prints, drawings, and photographs. Among these were photographs of ancient Egyptian wall paintings from the tomb of Nebamun, grain-accountant in the temple at Karnak, which Gauguin had seen in the British Museum.[93] Some of these fragments showed a banquet attended by well-dressed men and women (Figure 3.13). Exceptionally for ancient Egypt, these paintings displayed a vivacity, even a kind of impressionist spontaneity, which must have caught Gauguin's eye. His fashionably dressed Tahitians are disposed after the manner of Nebamun's guests. The clue to what they are doing there is given partly by the title, and partly by a detail which is absolutely key, but easy to overlook. The title has been translated as "We Shall Not Go to Market Today," and refers to the market square in Papete which, as Belinda Thompson puts it, was "the nearest Tahitian equivalent to the night-life district of Pigalle."[94] Tahitian sexuality, and its radical disjunction from European custom, had been the fuel that fired the myth of a paradise on the other side of the world since the first encounters of European sailors with the islanders in the late eighteenth century. These women however were Europeanized prostitutes waiting for the sailors. Their ship is what can be seen, out to sea, in the gap between the bushes. It has been suggested that the rectangular cards two of the women are holding are official certificates declaring their freedom from venereal disease. This conjunction of the new decorative art of symbolism marked by flat planes of increasingly non-naturalistic color, with an ancient source and a modern subject represents an unstable complexity rare in Gauguin. Normally, the past wins out over the present, myth over history. Here, for once, primitivism becomes complicated and made strange by an admixture of modernity.

The Question of Origins

Nakedness. Sexuality. Paganism. Human sacrifice. Cannibalism. These are the kinds of things that jumped into the minds of nineteenth-century Europeans when they thought of Africa. They found them disgusting and frightening. Conversely, for younger figures in the avant-garde, rebelling against suffocating dress codes, hypocritical bourgeois morality, and the repressions of the established church, the first three at least seemed quite attractive. The avant-garde did not reject the normative nineteenth-century European view of Africa, or the Pacific, as places lacking civilization and historical development; they inverted the values attached to that assessment.

Artifacts and utensils from other parts of the world had been accumulating in European museums for some time. The Spanish and Portuguese of the Renaissance had had little interest in the material culture they encountered. For them, the religious rituals they encountered were the work of the devil and the objects used in them likewise. Only the stones and precious metals they were made of had value. By the time of the Enlightenment encounter with the Pacific these views had moderated somewhat, albeit not entirely. Curiosity meant that objects were brought back to Europe in increasing numbers from the late eighteenth century. That said, later missionaries to the Pacific continued to destroy what they saw as "idols" and did all they could to root out indigenous religions as well as other social practices such as tattooing. In the case of Africa, the unavoidable fact was mass slavery involving the transportation of millions across the Atlantic. On the whole, art had shamefully little to say of this, the Wedgwood abolitionist medallion, verses by Blake and Wordsworth, and Turner's *Slave Ship* being honorable exceptions. In the 1805 version of *The Prelude*, Wordsworth called slavery "this most rotten branch of human shame."[95] But slavery as an institution itself did much to color the European view of Africa, not least through the pseudoscience of race theory. Charles Darwin himself abhorred slavery, and while he employed the distinction, entirely conventional in his day, between "civilized" and "savage," his theory of evolution postulated the common descent of humankind.[96] But out of his hands, not least through the slogan (which was not Darwin's) "survival of the fittest," evolutionary theory was bolted on to earlier essentialist theories of racial distinction such as that of the Comte de Gobineau to produce a potent ideology sustaining European beliefs about the civilizing mission of Empire.

The development of social science as well as natural science during the nineteenth century meant that for a multiplicity of reasons, more and more physical manifestations of radically different forms of life found their way into the collections of European ethnographic museums. It is often said that avant-garde artists encountered African and Pacific carvings and other objects in these museums; and it is true they did. But the image conjures up a sense of active, questing artists stumbling into fusty back rooms and transmuting ethnographic dust into aesthetic gold. No less a figure than Picasso himself, discussing the genesis of the *Demoiselles d'Avignon*, invoked the specter of his 1907 encounter with "dusty manikins" in the Trocadero, "all alone in that awful museum."[97] Yet since the mid-nineteenth century, ethnographic museums had been sites of cutting-edge scientific debate about human social development and the question of the origins of art.

The standard view, essentially evolutionist in character, had been developed most notably by Gottfried Semper. In the wake of the Great Exhibition in 1851, Semper worked in England and was active in the circle around Henry Cole in establishing the South Kensington museums. In essence his view was that decoration and ornament had their origin in "fundamental forms"[98] such as the crisscross pattern produced when materials such as rushes or grasses were plaited together to make screens for protection against weather. Such weaving or plaiting then gave rise to ornament on pottery, perhaps where a textile pattern had become impressed in the wet clay. What ensued was a long evolutionary process towards imitation: "a formal development beginning with geometric abstraction and culminating in naturalism."[99] However, in the late nineteenth century an alternative view developed postulating more or less the opposite process: that "art was originally representational, in the service of religion or magic, and degenerated into mere geometric pattern-making, as the meaningful motif was copied and miscopied."[100] Relevant factors here include the first, highly controversial, discoveries of Paleolithic cave paintings, and the evident difference between their vivid naturalism and the relative stylization of artifacts or decorated utensils prevalent in the ethnographic museums.[101] The revisionist account was also partially indebted to the publication in 1892 of Max Nordau's much-contested book, translated into English as *Degeneration* in 1895.[102] This view subsequently exerted a baleful influence on twentieth-century art when it came to underpin the Nazi attack on the avant-garde in the 1930s. In the 1890s it was a response to fears for the continued progress of European civilization prompted by what Nordau called "the *fin-de-siècle* state of mind," which he associated with pessimism and negativity. The thesis was adapted by anthropologists to try and account for the various forms of geometric ornament which were so prevalent among the artifacts being brought to Europe from places like Africa and the Pacific, places which were in their view "uncivilized."

Primitivism and Expressionism

Where this bears upon our present concerns is that it was precisely the "distorted," that is to say, non-mimetic forms of such artifacts that appealed to avant-garde artists trying to find a language to express their own dissatisfaction and alienation from the industrialized, commercialized modern societies in which they found themselves; *and* from the normative forms of self-representation of those societies. To the scientists and social theorists the artifacts in the ethnographic collections were symptoms of ways of life which subsisted on a lower rung of the evolutionary ladder, and thus stood in need of civilizing influence. For the avant-garde artist they offered the possibility that by translating such forms into their own art, their critique of the hypocrisy of bourgeois society and their attempt to produce a new and more honest art would gain greater force and power. From our present point of view, it goes almost without saying that both perspectives now appear almost equally mistaken. Certainly the expressionist avant-garde has lately been subjected to just as much criticism as has its colonialist doppelganger. In my view, however, it remains important to recognize the difference between the two positions as well as the unstated similarities they share.

For a long time the standard assumption in accounts of the Western avant-garde was that whereas it was legitimate and invigorating for European artists to have increased the expressive power of their work by drawing on African models, if the situation was reversed, a modern African work drawing on Western examples would be rendered compromised and inauthentic. That sort of assumption has long been a thing of the past. But it has been replaced by another position which risks being just as misleading. A wall label may seem a flimsy and ephemeral thing, almost beneath the level of proper academic attention. But such things have a way of condensing normative views. Thus, a note attached to a display of modern African art in the Brunei galleries at the School of Oriental and African Studies in London states: "From Cubism on, African artefacts have inspired developments in modern art, yet modern African artists have had to come to terms with Western orthodoxies imported along with Western political domination."[103] Some complex claims are condensed here. The first is that African objects inspired European modernism, notably cubism. A second is that Western orthodoxies (which could mean anything from academic perspective to norms associated with the modern movement) were imposed on African artists. A third is that this was a function of Western domination of Africa, in effect that art was complicit in imperialism. There are those who would argue that such claims are outrageous and untrue. I am not one of them. In my view there is considerable justification for all of them. But also, in my opinion, it is the qualifications that matter; the claims are partly, rather than entirely, justified. If they are taken to mean that Western modern art was somehow stolen from Africa, or that the avant-garde is at one with "Western political domination," then they shade into falsehoods. The qualifications and the grey areas matter.

Picasso acknowledged a connection between the *Demoiselles d'Avignon* (Figure 3.14) and the artifacts he encountered in the Trocadero. But he was careful

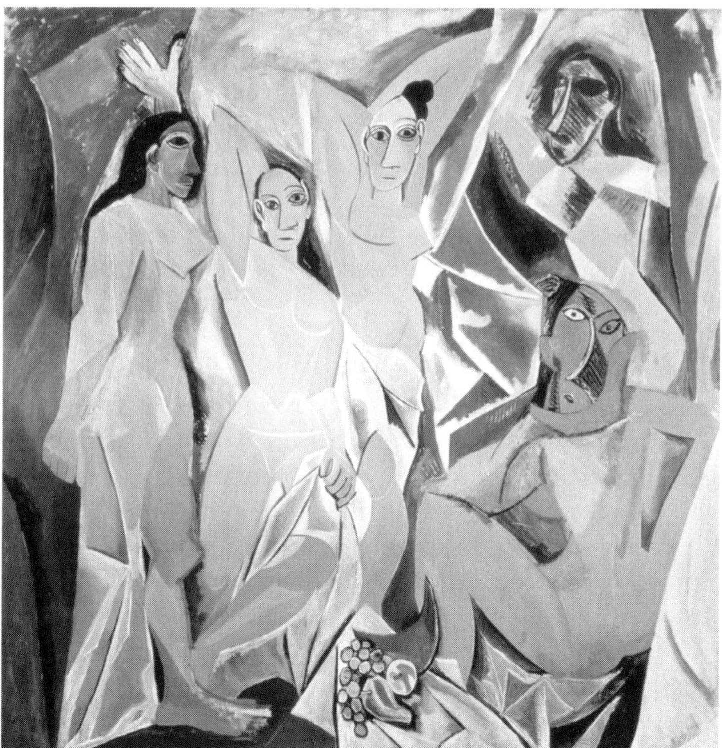

Figure 3.14 Pablo Picasso, *Les Demoiselles d'Avignon*, 1907, oil on canvas, 244 × 238 cm. Museum of Modern Art, New York / Giraudon / Bridgeman Art Library. © Succession Picasso / DACS, London 2013.

to claim that their impact was psychological rather than formal. Faced by evident similarities between some of the features of figures in the painting and the characteristics of African masks, it is hard not to see this as disingenuous. But it is also equally possible that by the time he made his retrospective comments, Picasso was being defensive about precisely the kinds of claims that cubism had been rooted in African sculpture. At least three of the faces in the *Demoiselles* are clearly mask-like, and in particular the one at top right seems to bear a strong resemblance to an Etoumbi mask from the Congo, especially in the long curved nose, but also the stripes on the cheek and the black holes of the eyes and mouth. Alfred H. Barr, in the catalog to his *Cubism and Abstract Art* exhibition of 1936, did much to establish such connections. Barr designated Picasso's work of around 1907, the crucial transitional period before the inception of cubism, as his "Negro period." By a series of visual comparisons Barr made the case for a connection between African source material, various smaller studies, and the *Demoiselles* itself, which he deemed symptomatic of "the Negro period at its most barbaric."[104] In a later study Barr explicitly described the features of the demoiselle's head, "a flat-ridged nose, a sharp chin, a small oval mouth and deleted ears" as being "characteristic of certain African Negro masks of the French Congo."[105] He illustrated the "Itumba" mask to prove his point.

Barr was not only one of Picasso's greatest supporters in general, but almost single-handedly established the *Demoiselles* as the Genesis-work of twentieth century modernism through his purchase of it for the Museum of Modern Art. So when he makes such a connection, it counts for a lot. However, in the 1980s, in his now notorious *Primitivism* show, William Rubin demonstrated that none of the four masks that have been put forward by art historians as direct models for Picasso's *Demoiselles* could actually have been seen by him in 1907. In the case of the Etoumbi mask specifically, "none of the three masks of this type known to exist came out of Africa before 1929."[106] There is no question that Picasso saw, and was deeply affected by, African sculpture in the early twentieth century. There is equally no question that many European artists, including members of the Brücke group, *did* directly copy motifs from work they encountered in ethnographic museums. These included carved roof beams depicting sexual acts from a men's house on the island of Palau in the Pacific. What Rubin's argument does is to reinforce the need for care in mapping the relations between "primitive" and "modern" art. Even in instances where relatively direct transcription did take place, let alone in cases of more generalized influence such as the *Demoiselles*, it can be claimed with considerable justification that the transaction involved was a complex one. African carvings are an undeniable element in the constellation of factors out of which Picasso and others made their modern expressionist art; but they were not in any sense the simple cause of it. The "affinities" that certain artists felt to exist between the emotional responses to modernity that were driving their own formal experiments and the characteristics they observed in "primitive" carvings, required reading them against the grain of the dominant cultural responses of their day.

Academy and Empire

Avant-garde art was bound into imperial power relations between Europe and Africa. But it had a less straightforward relation to them than many other examples of more conservative art, prominent at the time but much less well-known today. The artist and traveler Herbert Ward is a relatively late exponent of the kind of nineteenth-century academic naturalism discussed above.[107] His work at the time was seen to sit within a discourse of quasi-scientific objectivity, though in hindsight it can be seen to play into the racist stereotypes of the age of empire. His *Idol Maker* of 1906 is a far cry from both the guild-trained artisan of the Benin bronzes or the awe-inspiring spell cast on Picasso in the Trocadero (Figure 3.15). Despite some realistic elements, such as the way an African artist might hold a piece of wood while carving it, it is hard to imagine the sculpture doing anything other than reinforce stereotypes of the primitive or the savage.

Other art was more explicitly tuned to an imperialist agenda. The bronze statues made by Arsène Matton between 1910 and 1922, today displayed in the rotunda of the Africa Museum at Tervuren outside Brussels, depict a range of classically robed

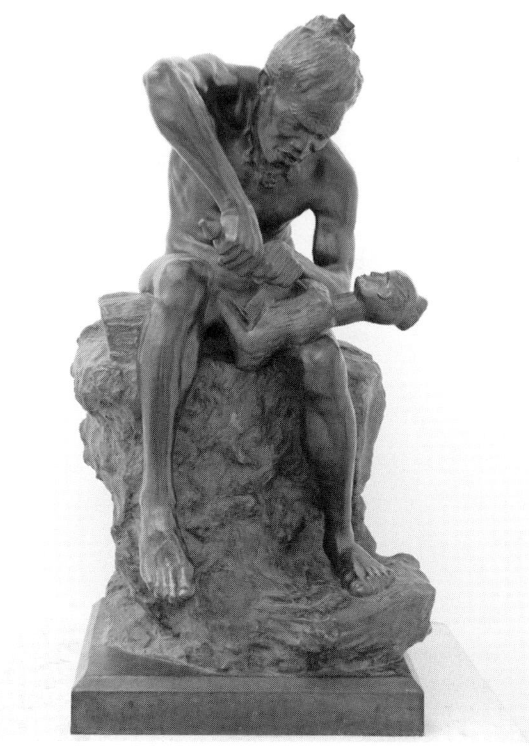

Figure 3.15 Herbert Ward, *The Idol Maker*, 1906, bronze. © National Museum of Wales, Cardiff.

European types standing tall and erect with native figures in a variety of supplicating poses clinging to their legs: respectively, *Belgium Brings Civilization to the Congo*, *Belgium Brings Security to the Congo*, and *Belgium Brings Welfare to the Congo*. The straightforward imperialist propaganda involved needs no further comment. The fourth in the series does, however. A variant on the others, this one keeps the cringing native figure, this time a voluptuous naked female, yet the standing figure is not a European but a turbaned Arab. The title, *Slavery*, gives the game away: Arab slavers persecuting the native population as justification for European intervention. This theme is further echoed in the complex scheme of the monumental tribute *Pioneers of the Belgian Congo* by Thomas-Jules Vincotte, which is located in the Parc du Cinquantenaire, also in Brussels (Figure 3.16). The multifigure composition consists of a long semicircular freize decorated in shallow relief, flanked at either end by figures in the round of two Belgian soldiers. In front of this, in the bowl of the fountain, a reclining black youth is an allegorical figure of the Congo River; atop the whole thing another allegorical figure, this time female, represents Belgium as a young woman receiving the black race into her care. The relief itself shows a procession of native figures moving from right to left representing the advance of Africa towards civilization, denoted by seated Belgian officers and watched over in their journey by a missionary with a cross. The right-hand figure shows a Belgian soldier heroically sacrificing himself for his wounded captain, while the left-hand figure, on close inspection, can be seen to be standing on the

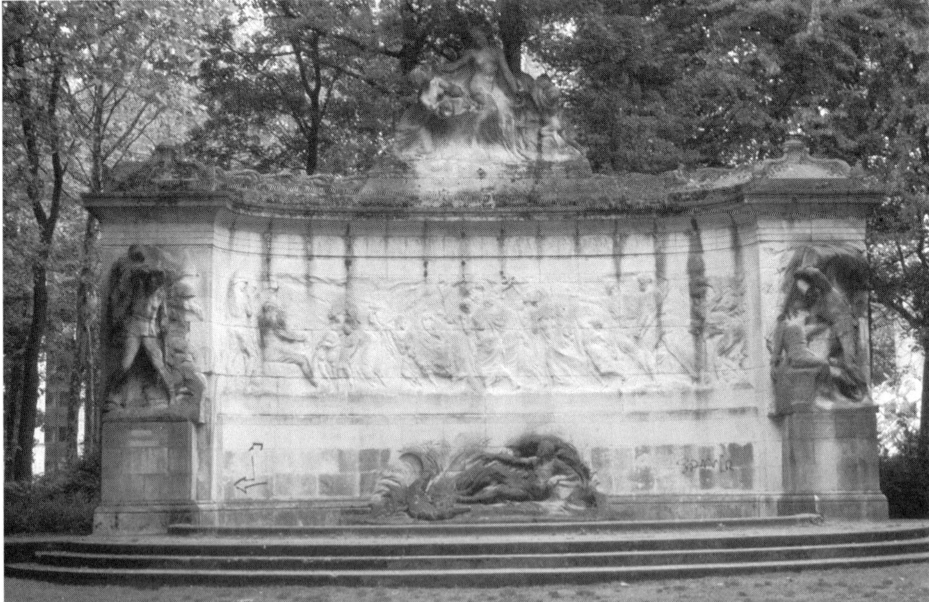

Figure 3.16 Thomas Jules Vincotte, *Pioneers of the Belgian Congo*, 1921, stone monument in the Parc du Cinquantenaire, Brussels, Belgium. Photo: Paul Wood.

head of a mean-looking Arab, who is being trodden into the ground. Once again, Arab enslavement of Congo natives is used as justification for the civilizing mission of Belgium. The millions who suffered mutilation and death in Leopold's private fiefdom in the pursuit of rubber, ivory, and other precious commodities, remain unrepresented.

It is against such a background that the work of Picasso and other modernists needs to be considered. The work of early twentieth-century avant-gardists may not stand up well to scrutiny from the moral high ground of a century later. But if we regard them within the boundary of their own cultural and political horizons, the significance of their transvaluation of those normative values may emerge in a better light. Certainly the two should not be assimilated in the catch-all category of "European art." Respect for difference is as essential in that case as it is anywhere else.

Benin

There is one case in particular in which the two discourses of science and art, anthropology and aesthetics, intersect with interesting consequences. This is the case of the Benin bronzes.[108] In February 1897, while burning and looting Benin city as part of the process of extending their imperial writ across West Africa, the British happened upon a cache of bronze and ivory artworks in the king's palace. The ivories were carved elephant tusks. The bronzes were a mixture of free-standing three-dimensional sculptures and more "pictorial" plaques decorated with figures in relief. The British army collected up the artworks and sold them on the open market to defray the costs of the so-called Punitive Expedition and assist the dependents of soldiers wounded or killed in the fighting. They were bought by a mixture of private collectors and public museums, including the British Museum in London and the Ethnographic Museum in Berlin. The bronze sculptures in particular were without precedent and threw the racist stereotype of Africa as a place devoid of culture populated by almost sub-human savages into disarray. They demonstrated high levels of technological and craft skill in the difficult technique of lost wax metal casting and implied the prior existence of a hitherto unsuspected civilization of considerable social complexity. The sculptures were several hundred years old and, most astonishing of all to Europeans convinced of the superiority of their own mimetic art, the cast metal heads of the kings and queens were powerfully lifelike.

At least one of the many interesting things about the Benin bronzes is that the artistic avant-garde was as uncertain in its response to them as were the ethnographic scientists. In the Western tradition, sculpture, broadly speaking, had been of two types: carvings, in wood or stone and casts in materials such as bronze. Bronze casting had been known in ancient China and Egypt, but the earliest bronze sculptures in the Western canon came from ancient Greece and later, Rome. This was then resumed in the Renaissance and continued in the post-Renaissance academic tradition. Carving, by contrast, as in the case of saints on the façade of a medieval cathedral, came to be regarded as an archaic method. In fact, medieval carving was probably one of the things intended by Aurier when he extolled the virtues of the "primitive." In this context, then, the Benin bronzes were in a peculiar situation. They came from what was perceived to be a "primitive" society, yet they themselves were anything but primitive. In terms of their material, and the sophisticated manufacturing process involved, they actually shared more with academic sculpture than with the values of the modernists. For two of the anthropologists who tried to account for them, they were seen as comparable in their technical mastery to the sculpture of the Italian Renaissance, that cornerstone of Western civilization itself. C.H. Read and O.M. Dalton wrote that the lost wax process had been "that by which many of the finest Italian bronzes of the best period were produced," commenting in some perplexity that: "we thus find the Benin savages using with familiarity and success a complicated method which satisfied the fastidious eye of the best artists of the Italian renaissance."[109]

Coming from the other side, avant-garde artists in the early twentieth century had begun to investigate once more the expressive possibilities of direct carving into their chosen material. Significant figures included Constantin Brancusi, Henri Gaudier-Brzeska, and, later, Henry Moore. All of these artists were impelled by the power of a sense of direct contact with the material, and, needless to say, by the relation of that idea to the notion of a "primitive" and hence an "authentic" expression. From among the German expressionist group, the Brücke, at least two examples exist of artists trying to come to terms with the Benin sculptures. In 1911 Ernst Ludwig Kirchner made a drawing based on a plaque in the Dresden ethnographic museum, while in 1912 Max Pechstein produced a colored wood block print (Figure 3.17) related to another plaque in the ethnographic museum in Berlin (Figure 3.18). In both cases the forms were significantly changed in order to bring the relatively rounded modeling of the bronze plaques into conformity with the more distorted, and hence authentically "primitive" forms encountered in directly carved wooden masks and "idols." In Pechstein's case, the male figure was unclothed, relative to his original model on the plaque, and accompanied by two fully nude "primitive" females.[110] The same disposition is evident in expressionist theoretical writing, as well as their actual artistic practice. In an essay in the *Blaue Reiter Almanac* of 1912, Ernst Macke composed a striking evocation of the register of responses joining modern "popular" culture with archaic "primitive" culture as a way of responding to "our complicated and confused era." Thus, "in the vaudeville theatre the butterfly-coloured dancer enchants the most amorous couples as intensely as the solemn sound of the organ in a Gothic cathedral," just as "the fire dance enthrals the African or the mysterious drumming of the fakirs enthrals the Indian." Macke then simply assimilates the Benin bronzes into his list of authentically primitive art, effectively sidelining any considerations about their process of manufacture, let alone their

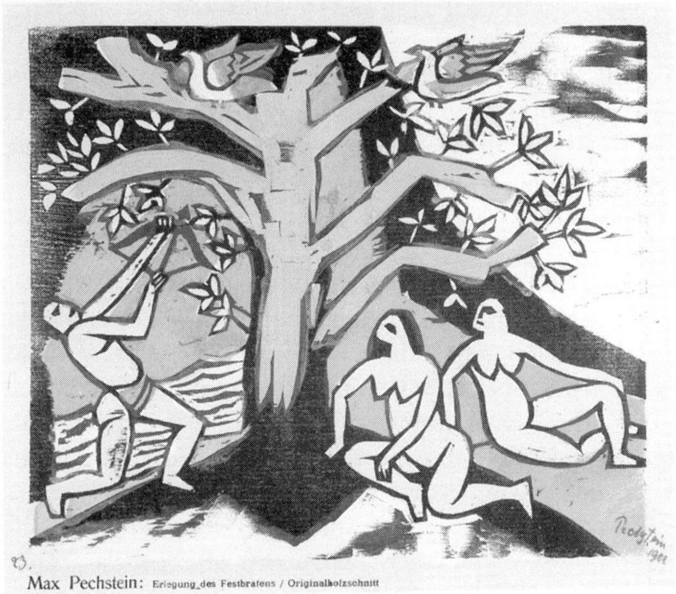

Figure 3.17 Max Pechstein, *Bird Hunters* (*Erlegung des Festbratens*), 1912, colored woodblock print, 22.5 × 26 cm. Collection Hermann Gerlinger in the Museum Moritzburg, Halle. © Pechstein Hamburg/Toekendorf / DACS, 2013.

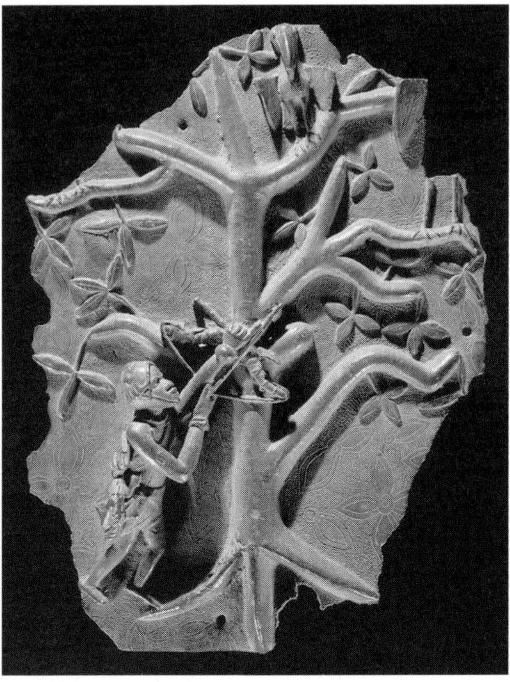

Figure 3.18 Benin brass plaque, *Master of the Leopard Hunt*, relief plaque showing a bird hunt, 45 × 34 × 5 cm. Ethnologisches Museum, Staatliche Museen zu Berlin. © 2013. Photo Scala, Florence / BPK, Bildagentur für Kunst, Kultur und Geschichte, Berlin.

status as a sophisticated court art: "The cast bronzes of the Negroes from Benin in West Africa, the idols from the Easter Islands in the remotest Pacific, the cape of a chieftain from Alaska, and the wooden masks from New Caledonia speak the same powerful language" as medieval European carvings.[111]

In essence, Macke has to misrepresent the Benin bronzes to make them conform to the "primitivist" paradigm. The same point is made from precisely the opposite direction by the German critic Carl Einstein's refusal to make that assimilation. A theoretically sophisticated defender of cubism, Einstein asserted the link between the revolutionary new art and African carving, writing in his *Afrikanische Plastik* of 1921, "With the fledgling Cubism, we examined the African works of art and came upon perfect examples"; perfect, that is, from the point of view of fracturing the conventions of academic representation. But then he had this to say about the bronzes: "while maintaining this point of view" (i.e., of the mutual fruitfulness of "structural," non-pictorial African carving and cubism), "despite their technical sophistication, the highly esteemed arts of Yorubaland and Benin seem to us of no decisive significance."[112] That is to say, to acknowledge the specificity of the cast bronzes as a sophisticated court art organized at least in part around idealized imitation was to render them technically – and hence also emotionally and conceptually – uninteresting to the avant-garde project.

Fry and Primitivism

Einstein was active in the circles of the interwar revolutionary avant-garde, and will be mentioned again in Chapter 4. Roger Fry, a critic more often identified with canonical modernism, also had something interesting to say about primitivism; for those inclined to treat Fry as a gentrified precursor of later American formalism, it is a complex claim with significant implications for the normative conception of modernism itself. Fry was not alone in this, but was part of what might be called a discourse of early modernism. It drew on elements from both French and German thought. The former, as already noted, emerged from a symbolist milieu in the writings of Aurier and others and was given a further, more classicist inflection by Maurice Denis. Denis' essay on Cézanne was translated into English by Fry, whose introductory note contained the key statement that the new art aimed at the "direct expression" of what he called "imagined states of consciousness"[113]; that is to say, not through the imitation of appearance but through the kind of emotive suggestion that had previously been regarded as the province of music (and of poetry, in a specific, symbolist-inflected musical sense of what a poem was).[114] The second major element looked back to the tradition of German idealist thought, both Kant and Hegel, notably, but also Schopenhauer. As early as 1906, in his doctoral thesis subsequently published in 1908, Wilhelm Worringer, explicitly citing Schopenhauer, had developed an overarching thesis linking the modern condition, and by extension contemporary art, to the primitive condition. In so doing he differentiated the modern from the Renaissance and its antecedent in classical antiquity. Under the opposed rubrics of "empathy" and "abstraction," Worringer drew up a contrasting list of art styles: "style" being what he called the "outward fruit" of the "psychic state" in which "mankind found itself in relation to the cosmos" at different historical moments. The "empathetic" style, which he regarded as the artistic manifestation of "a happy pantheistic relationship of confidence between man and the phenomena of the external world" was identified with antiquity and the Renaissance. But this condition was far from universal. For Worringer, the art of many other cultures, distinct from that classical culture in both time and space, exhibited an altogether different psychic relation to the world, one of "great inner unrest," and even "spiritual dread." These included "savage peoples," and in a separate category, "all primitive epochs of art," in which he seems to include both Byzantine and Egyptian art ("the lifeless form of a pyramid"), as well as the art of "certain culturally developed Oriental peoples." All of these manifested an "abstract" principle, "an impulse directly opposed to the empathy impulse."[115] As can be seen, this type of schema replicates a common division within Eurocentric thought of the preceding several centuries but inverts its values (as we have already observed in the case of the notion of primitivism itself). Although Worringer himself was ambivalent about the connection, he was widely taken also to be commenting on the modern condition and the form taken by modern expressionist art movements – for example, the German Brücke group with their "primitivist," distorted forms.

In 1908 Fry wrote an extensive paper on an exhibition of the art of the South African "bushmen" (now known as the San people) in which he made an important distinction between "aboriginal" Paleolithic art, and what he called "primitive" art. Drawing on the anthropological debates about the origins of art mentioned above, Fry regarded Paleolithic art such as that found in the caves of Altamira (and in which he included the art of both the South African San and Australian Aboriginal people) as essentially realistic, that is, as exhibiting the "power of transcribing pure visual images."[116] For Fry this was to be distinguished from what he called "the primitive drawing of our own race."[117] This was Neolithic, and, like the art of children, was principally concerned not with transferring a "visual sensation" onto a flat surface but with expressing a "mental image which is coloured by his conceptual habits." This distinction between Paleolithic and Neolithic art, between "perceptual" and "conceptual" modes of representation, is one which is often overlooked in criticisms of modernist primitivism. But it was crucial for Fry in his account of modernist art, and its break with the conventions of academic art, indeed its break *through* to a kind of visual (in the case of painting) or plastic (in the case of sculpture) truth.

In his later 1920 paper on "Negro Sculpture" Fry was thus led to a far-reaching conclusion. For Fry, it goes without saying, art was of no small moment, not at all a leisure activity, some form of recreational relief from productive economic activity. In Fry's view, true art (as distinct from merely conventional cultural forms such as academic nineteenth-century art), that is to say, "the power to create expressive plastic form" was nothing less than "one of the greatest of human achievements." Fry was led to the paradoxical conclusion that people whom he called "certain nameless savages" have possessed this power, "not only in a higher degree than we at this moment, but than we as a nation have ever possessed it." For Fry this was the culmination of a sixty-year process. The inception of the French avant-garde in the 1860s had seen the previous "right little, tight little round little world" in which Greek art, some "Roman copies" and "some Renaissance repetitions" were considered "the only indisputable art," begin to be overthrown. Again, it goes without saying that few if any competent observers would assent to such a belief now, but it is crucial to Fry's modernist perspective that the formal innovations of early modernism, particularly those of Cézanne, amounted not to the replacement of one set of artistic conventions by another but a break *through* the relativity and artificiality of academic convention to some universal underlying truth about human perception and cognition: one through which the moderns were enabled to reestablish contact with the most authentic regions of human experience. With a sense of awe, Fry recognized that "knowledge and perception have poured upon us so fast that the whole well-ordered system has been blown away." The African sculptures Fry encountered at the Chelsea Book Club (which says something in itself) were for him manifestations of "complete plastic freedom," and it was on them which an adequately modern art had to build, not the shibboleths of a tradition that was now in all essentials moribund.

This is the power that the discourse of the "primitive" had in early modernism. But, of course, what is really historically significant about it is what primitivism fails to do; and this is a double-edged blade because ultimately it strikes at the heart of modernism itself. Fry concluded his essay with the thought that "it is curious that a people who produced such great artists did not produce also a culture in our sense of the word." The crucial points underlying this are twofold. One is, of course, its obvious underlying racism. The second concerns the idea of art involved. For me it is both of these in conjunction that deserve attention. Fry describes what he sees as "the creative aesthetic impulse" and its close cognates, "sensibility" and "taste." The philosophical psychology involved is that these are instinctive, and have, as it were, to be won back from cultural convention. This is easy, almost too easy, to disparage from a postmodernist position, but it has strengths as well as weaknesses. The valorization it implies for intuition, impulse, going out on a limb, risk-taking, and so forth are surely prerequisites for innovation, for breaking through convention. That is the whole point: creativity is not planned, and its fruits, as often as not, are uncongenial to those who remain committed to the framework that has been broken.

As far as it goes, this seems a reasonably accurate assessment of the situation of the early modern movement. But in the end, what the separation of art from mind, art from language, creativity from criticism does is to disarm art in the face of the next wave of cultural assimilation. Which is precisely what happened. Abstraction, once it had become the official art of a remade modern culture, became the stuff of corporate décor. This is the real force of Lucy Lippard's barb about late modernist all-over abstraction of the late 1960s, that it had become "visual muzak." This does not just mean that it was boring, with all peaks and troughs smoothed out. It means that it had become a corporate cover for something else – either lulling the viewer of art into a belief that all was well with the world (that the corporation had its benign aesthetic), or of a different but related kind of anesthetic, smoothing the path of consumption (that the corporation's material provision is equally benign). That was, of course, a long way beyond the horizon for Fry's generation. But the fatal weakness in the embedded conception of art is an essential complement to the racism of the cultural thesis. For when Fry remarks that "two factors are necessary" to make a culture: on the one hand, "the creative artist," but on the other, "the power of conscious critical appreciation and comparison," he is claiming that Africa lacks people like himself: a cultural intelligentsia. To claim that Africa lacks "a conscious critical sense and the intellectual powers of comparison and classification" is quite precisely to consign Africa to a dehistoricized condition, in effect to reduce culture to nature.[118] And with that we are straight back to the imperialist stereotype. Modernist primitivism gives with one hand and takes away with the other. We have grown accustomed to the accusation of the second of these. But one has to be reminded of the first to see why it matters.

As one might expect from the greatest cataclysm to hit European civilization, the First World War had a profound impact on art. Not that one would necessarily have divined this from modernist art history, which tended to present a picture of artistic development as insulated from material and historical factors, or at least to be essentially uncontaminated by them in its aesthetic effects. Expressionism as a movement, with its characteristic overvaluation of subjectivity, was effectively derailed by the war. A range of more objectivist, "constructive" impulses held sway in the European avant-garde; the musical composer as model for the abstract artist was replaced by the engineer or the architect. This does not, of course, mean that primitivism entirely lost its capacity to stimulate. In relatively provincial artistic cultures, such as England, for example, a figure like Henry Moore was able to derive inspiration in the late 1920s from sojourns in the British Museum much as Picasso had done in the Trocadero a quarter of a century earlier. But for all their dubious philosophical idealism, for all the reactionary political implications of some of their claims, figures like Worringer and Fry had a point. Modernism was a response not so much to a Baudelairean sense of the heroism of modern life but to the dream having turned into a nightmare.

Later Modernist Primitivism

In the eighteenth century, the figure of the noble savage derived its force from contrast with the early perception that progress had its downside. At the turn from the nineteenth into the twentieth century, the perception by some critics and artists that modernity was in the grip of an industrialized Moloch was not exactly falsified by the advent of world war, however one-sided and backward looking some elements of their critique might have been. It should not be entirely surprising, therefore, to find that primitivism had one last, belated efflorescence in the face of what, to many, looked like the final wreck of the Western dream of material progress. When the twentieth-century version of the Thirty Years War – begun in 1914, ended in 1945 – had run its course, Europe was materially and spiritually devastated. The sheer exhaustion was perhaps best captured by Samuel Beckett. However, other forces were also at work. In a story by now over-rehearsed to the point of cliché, some of the vitality of European culture in the visual arts migrated to America.

As early as 1943, that is, before the existence of the Nazi extermination camps had become widely known, before the advent of nuclear weapons, but for all that faced by "total war" on an unprecedented, global scale, certain innovative artists in America had explicitly embraced "myth" as the bedrock of their art. The solecisms of interwar would-be ameliorative art – American scene painting, rural regionalism, even (or especially) left-wing social realism – all seem to have been "blown away" (to use Fry's figure again) by the storm of modernity devouring itself. Adolph Gottlieb, Mark Rothko, and Barnett Newman sought to cut through present ideologies with the assertion that "art is timeless." Modernist technical features, such as large shapes, acknowledgement of the picture plane, and flat forms were for them not symptoms of "art for art's sake." ("That is the essence of academicism.") Quite to the contrary, "they destroy illusion and reveal truth." For them, not only was the subject "crucial" but the only subject-matter that was valid was "tragic and timeless." Once again, modern artists professed "spiritual kinship with primitive and archaic art."[119] (Figure 3.19)

These American artists were living in the most technologically developed, materially wealthy society the planet had ever seen. Yet time and again they evoked a kinship with the primitive. Jackson Pollock, as is well-known, spoke of his interest in both the techniques and the "plastic qualities" of Native American Indian art, and in an echo of Gottlieb, Rothko and Newman asserted "the basic universality of all real art."[120] Newman organized two exhibitions for the Betty Parsons Gallery in New York, the first of pre-Columbian stone sculpture in 1944, the second of Northwest Coast Indian painting in 1946. Also in 1946 he wrote a review of the major exhibition of the *Art of the South Seas* shown at the Museum of Modern Art early that year. Asserting the connection sketched by Worringer nearly forty years earlier, Newman argued that "the reason primitive art is so close to the modern mind is that we, living in times of the greatest terror the world has known, are in a position to appreciate the acute sensibility primitive man had for it."[121] The next year, in his essay "The Ideographic Picture," Newman made the connection explicit, observing that "there has arisen during the war years a new force in American painting," and that this work "is the modern counterpart of the primitive art impulse."[122]

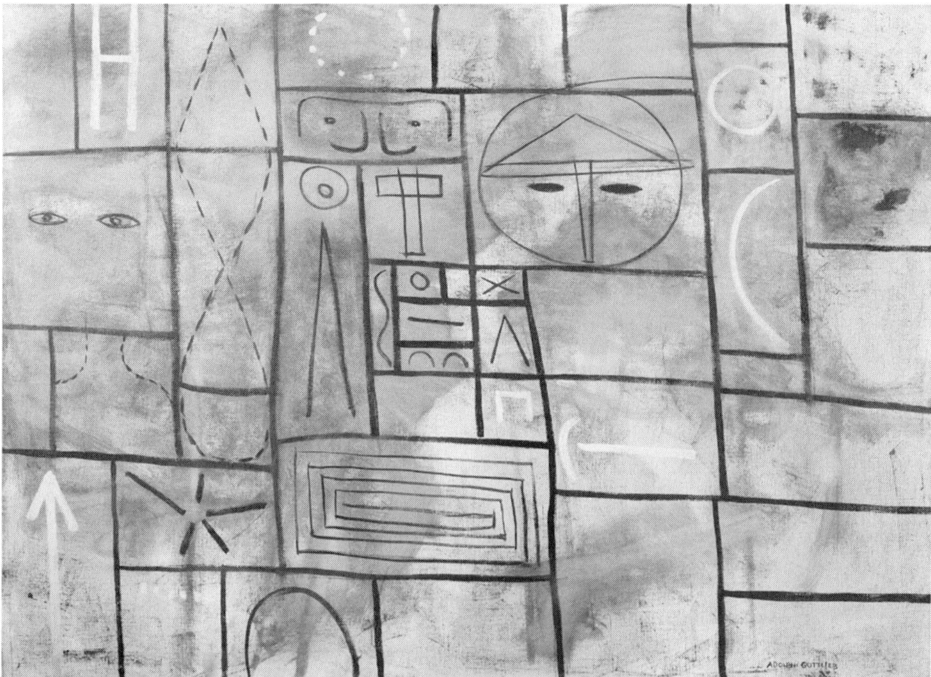

Figure 3.19 Adolph Gottlieb, *Labyrinth No. 2*, 1950, oil on canvas, 91.4 × 121.9 cm. © Adolph and Esther Gottlieb Foundation / VAGA, NY / DACS, London 2013.

Newman and the others were adamant that theirs was not a scientific interest but an aesthetic one. Thus the pre-Columbian stone sculpture was shown "freed from the distractions of the usual ethnological jumble of sculpture, pottery, textiles, and other artifacts, which, although of genuine interest to the student of archaeology and ethnology, is a source of confusion to those looking for an aesthetic experience." Once again it is important to grasp that, for those concerned, this decontextualization was not intended as aestheticization in the sense of connoisseurship or a kind of delectation, but as a way of cutting through the inessential and transient features of culture and history to reach the pure plastic embodiment of "the elemental mystery of life."[123] As Rothko put it in 1947, this was "the fact of mortality" and the consequent "appetite for ubiquitous experience in the face of this fact."[124]

From the first articulations of the idea of the noble savage in the eighteenth century, constructed as a point of critical leverage against the decadence of contemporary European society, gathering force as a form of resistance to the annihilating force of industry and empire, going all the way through to this short-circuiting of the distance between archaic and modern in the wake of Auschwitz and Hiroshima, the figure of the "primitive" other carried enormous weight in Western art. Mostly, the artists took what was to hand, and generalized from it. The European artists of the late nineteenth and early twentieth centuries drew on the forms revealed by their parent empires, especially in Africa and the Pacific. Russian artists drew on the Asian societies encountered by their own expanding imperialism along its long land frontiers. Arshile Gorky, Armenian refugee in America, represents a kind of transplanted example of this. With his references to his Armenian childhood in works such as *Garden in Sochi*, however, Gorky was an exception. For the most part, the mid-century American modernists looked to America itself for their primitivism. Once they had, as it were, dug down through Mediterranean myth, Newman, Gottlieb, and others drew their principal stimulus from pre-Columbian cultures ranged across South and North America.

Those artists were not aestheticizing primitive art as a way of extending the remit of Western culture over ever-wider areas of the world. In their own view, they were, if anything, attempting to resist the spread of that culture in its broadest sense – its fetishization of scientific rationalism, positivism, its reduction of all questions to materialism and consumption. But they themselves, of course, were caught up in that very culture whose excesses they sought to resist. Pollock pronounced a greater truth than perhaps he was aware of when he said "an American is an American and his painting would naturally be qualified by that fact, whether he wills it or not."[125] After 1945 America was the most powerful nation on earth, and New York was, in effect, the capital of a new empire. Modernist internationalism was soon to become indistinguishable from American cultural imperialism.

But American nationalism was not the only nationalism abroad in the world in the postwar years. On the brink of the dissolution of the old European empires – the British, the French, the Belgian, the Dutch – many subaltern, resistant nationalisms began to emerge. It was more than anything this political development that really killed off the cultural ideology of primitivism. On the wall of Chorlton on Medlock town hall in Manchester, England, a building coincidentally adjacent to the art college, there is a plaque commemorating the Fifth Pan African Conference held there in October 1945. Participants included Kwame Nkrumah, Jomo Kenyatta, Amy Garvey, and W.E.B. Du Bois. As the words on the plaque say, "Decisions taken at this conference led to the liberation of African countries." For in the end, Fry – and with him the entire construct of primitivism – was mistaken. The rest of the world, Africa included, did have a culture, did have a history. It was Fry's Eurocentric spectacles that prevented him from seeing it. In 1948 India gained independence from Britain. Ghana followed. In the 1950s Algeria and Vietnam began to free themselves from France. The epoch of European imperialism was not permanent, and it is mistaken to project it too far back in history. It lasted for around two hundred years. By the mid-twentieth century it was as good as over. To be sure, Western domination of the world did continue under American hegemony. But the Bandung Conference of 1955, which announced the concept of "non-alignment" and ushered in the idea of the "Third World," did nothing if not sound the death knell of primitivism. The myth of an extra-historical condition had been overtaken by history.

Notes

1 Clark 1999, ch. 1, "Painting in the Year 2."
2 Fried 1988, p. 61.
3 Eliot 1975, p. 266.
4 Kristeller 1990, p. 165 (from ch. 9, "The Modern System of the Arts," pp. 163–227; first published 1951–1952 in the *Journal of the History of Ideas*).
5 Kristeller 1990, p. 227.
6 Darwin 2007, pp. 11, 12, and 13.
7 Darwin 2007, p. x.
8 Darwin 2007, p. 50.
9 Darwin 2007, p. 17.
10 Darwin 2007, p. 56.
11 Losty and Roy 2012, p. 27.
12 Clark, "Image and Style in the Floating World," in Clark *et al.* 2001, p. 30.
13 Clark *et al.* 2001, catalog entry 66, pp. 176–177.
14 Clark *et al.* 2001, p. 30.
15 Chongzheng and McCausland in Rawski and Rawson 2005, catalog entry 76 pp. 407–408.
16 That wording appears in the third edition of the Jacobean translation by John Florio, published in 1632 (Book 1, p. 66). In the standard modern translation by M.A. Screech, the unmistakeable sense of Turkish puissance haunting the sixteenth-century version is less apparent. Here, Montaigne is more flatly made to state: "The strongest State to make an appearance in our time is that of the Turks" (Screech 1991, p. 162). The difference may be thought telling.
17 Montesquieu 2008, p. 26.
18 Honour 1961, p. 88.
19 "Pride in their port, defiance in their eye, / I see the lords of human kind pass by" Oliver Goldsmith, *The Traveller*, 1765, Kiernan 1969 frontispiece.
20 Schwab 1984, p. 11.
21 The publishing history of the *1001 Nights* is complex. Galland published the "Voyages of Sinbad" in 1701 though they seem not to have formed part of the original Arabic stories. The first two volumes of the "Arabian Nights" proper appeared in 1704, and the cycle went on until 1717. By this time Galland's version exceeded in length any collection of Arab tales, and it is assumed he made up some himself. There is a long history thereafter of pirated and more or less fraudulent editions. A "full" version, including later additions, appeared in the nineteenth century and is often referred to as the "Egyptian rescension" (see Mardrus 1959). The shorter "Syrian rescension" (Haddawy) more faithfully represents the medieval cycle. In his *The Arabian Nights: A Companion*, Robert Irwin (2004) recommends Husain Haddawy's translation (1990).
22 Johnson 2000.
23 Goldsmith 1837, Letter XIV, pp. 52–53.
24 Honour 1961, p. 90.
25 Brunel 1986, p. 166.

26 Montesquieu, *Essay on Taste* [1757], extracts in Harrison, Wood, and Gaiger 2000, pp. 526–531, quotations from pp. 528–530.
27 Lecomte, quoted in Honour 1961 from a French work of 1910 which I have been unable to check. One has to assume that here Lecomte is praising a quality of "unity" rather than "uniformity" as such, which, as Montesquieu recognizes, can produce boredom.
28 Vico 1968, Section 38, paragraph 99, p. 51.
29 Kant 1960, p. 110.
30 Hegel 1988.
31 Popper 1945.
32 Hegel 1980, p. 164.
33 Hegel 1980, p. 174.
34 Hegel 1980, p. 172.
35 Hegel 1980, p. 197.
36 Laurence Sterne had wittily dismantled this Eurocentric prejudice over half a century before Hegel got around to pronouncing it as a conclusive truth of history; thus showing, perhaps, that not all Europeans were quite so keen to be presented as the culmination of all human endeavor (a lesson that seems to be lost on the most fervid of Hegel's detractors). The passage is worth quoting in full. Tristram Shandy's father, Walter, is holding forth about philosophy. Uncle Toby keeps popping his balloons.

WALTER: *That we and our children were born to die, but neither of us born to be slaves* … *Eleazer* owns he had it from the philosophers of *India*; in all likelihood *Alexander* the Great, in his irruption into *India*, after he had over-run *Persia*, amongst the many things he stole, stole that sentiment also; by which means it was carried, if not all the way by himself (for we know he died at Babylon), at least by some of his maroders, into *Greece*, from *Greece* it got to *Rome*, from *Rome* to *France*, and from *France* to *England*: so things come round …

TOBY: By land carriage I can conceive no other way …

WALTER: By water the sentiment might easily have come down the *Ganges* into the *Sinus Gangeticus*, or *Bay of Bengal*, and so into the *Indian Sea*; and following the course of trade (the way from *India* by the *Cape of Good Hope* being then unknown) might be carried with other drugs and spices up the *Red Sea* to *Joddah*, the port of *Mekka*, or else to the *Tor* or *Sues*, towns at the bottom of the gulf; and from thence by karrawans to *Coptos*, but three days journey distant, so down the *Nile* directly to *Alexandria*, where the SENTIMENT would be landed at the very foot of the great staircase of the *Alexandrian* library, and from that store-house it would be fetched …

TOBY: Bless me! what a trade was driven by the learned in those days! … (Sterne 2003 [1759–1767] pp. 332–333)

37 Clunas, "What about Chinese Art?" in King, ed., 1999, p. 134.
38 Mercer 1991, p. 192. See also Mignolo 2011.
39 Somewhat strangely, Mignolo's comment ignores a distinction the book itself is concerned to draw. For Buck-Morss, Hegel, in his figure of the Master/Slave relationship

in the early *Phenomenology of Mind* of 1805–1807, is *responding* to the slave revolt in Haiti. Her contribution is precisely to uncover this connection, occluded by generations of Hegel scholarship. For Buck-Morss, the lectures on the *Philosophy of History* from the 1820s mark "a retreat" from Hegel's earlier position, which she characterizes as "the radical politics of *The Phenomenology of Mind*"(2009, p. 65). She further speculates that this retreat into a more reactionary position may itself also have been a response to the negative turn in the Haitian revolution, involving the massacre of white people there (Buck-Morss 2009, pp. 68–73).

40 Podro 1982, p. 17.

41 Hegel 1988, Vol. 1, pp. 73–74.

42 Hegel 1988, Vol. 1, p. 74.

43 Hegel 1988, Vol. 1, pp. 74–75.

44 Hegel 1988, Vol. 1, pp. 44.

45 Hegel 1988, Vol. 2, p. 730.

46 Podro 1982, pp. 1–2. This is not to imply that Hegel differed from his Romantic contemporaries by failing to address literature in his *Aesthetics*. To the contrary, literature occupies an important place in his discussion of both the symbolic and classical modes, and poetry was for him the characteristically modern, or Romantic, art.

47 Irwin 2007, p. 4.

48 Stevens, "Western Art and its Encounter with the Islamic World 1798–1914," in Stevens, ed., 1984, p. 19.

49 Stevens 1984, p. 15.

50 Stevens 1984, p. 23 n. 4.

51 Nochlin, "The Imaginary Orient" (*Art in America* 1983) in Nochlin 1989; quotations from pp. 56 and 57.

52 Nochlin 1989, respectively pp. 42, 58 n.11, and 43.

53 While Nochlin does acknowledge this possibility she slights it as the artist "evidently doing his homework." His visual and literary research is made to count for less than his alleged "sadistic fantasies" (Nochlin 1989, p. 42).

54 Delacroix, "Letters and Notes on his Journey to North Africa" (1832); all quotations from the extracts rptd in Harrison and Wood with Gaiger 1998, pp. 84–88.

55 Nochlin 1989, pp. 51–52.

56 Delacroix 1948, p. 215.

57 Edwards 1891, p. 141.

58 Edwards 1891, p. 205.

59 Nochlin 1989, p. 37.

60 Steinberg 1972, ch. 3 "Other Criteria."

61 de Font-Réaulx, "Gérôme and Photography: Accurate Depictions of an Imagined World" in Cars, de Font-Réaulx, and Papet, eds, 2010, p. 219.

62 All quotations from Steegmuller 1996, pp. 81, 79–80, 180–181, and 53.

63 Benson Miller in "Gérôme and Ethnographic Realism at the Salon of 1857" in Allan and Morton, eds, 2010, p. 115.

64 See Wood, "Realisms and Realities" in Fer, Batchelor, and Wood, eds, 1993 pp. 250–333. For further discussion of modern realisms see Moi 2006 and Potts 2013.

65 Benson Miller in Allan and Morton 2010, pp. 116–117.

66 M. Roberts, "Gérôme in Istanbul" in Allan and Morton 2010, pp. 119–134; quotations from pp. 119, 131.

67 Brockendon in Roberts 2000, p. 28.

68 Brockendon in Roberts 2000, p. 21.

69 Weeks, "Cultures Crossed: John Frederick Lewis and the Art of Orientalist Painting" in Tromans 2008; quotations from pp. 24–25, 23, and 32.

70 For further discussion, see Paul Wood, "Avant-garde and Modern World: Some Aspects of Art in Paris and Beyond c.1850–1914," in Edwards and Wood, eds 2012, pp. 17–51

71 Stendhal, from "Salon of 1824," extracts rptd in Harrison, Wood, and Gaiger 1998 pp. 30–37, quotations from pp. 37 and 31 respectively (December 22, 1824 and August 31, 1824).

72 Baudelaire, "Salon of 1846" extracts in Harrison, Wood, and Gaiger 1998, pp. 300–305.

73 Baudelaire, "The Painter of Modern Life" [1859/1863], extracts rptd in Harrison, Wood, and Gaiger 1998, pp. 493–506.

74 Oliver Goldsmith has his "Citizen of the World" visit the Vauxhall pleasure gardens (Goldsmith 1837, Letter LXXI).

75 Harvey 2003, p. 118.

76 Delacroix in Harrison, Wood, and Gaiger 1998, p. 331.

77 Baudelaire, letter to Arsène Houssaye, quoted in Berger 1992, p. 16.

78 Duret, quoted Hokensen 2004, p. 42, trans. p. 424 n. 8.

79 Duret, quoted in Smith 1995, p. 31.

80 Proust 1992, pp. 264–265.

81 Berger 1992, p. 1

82 Gabriel Josipovici, *The World and the Book*, Macmillan, London 1971, p. 194; cited by Hokensen 2004, p. 18.

83 Edmond and Jules de Goncourt, extracts from *The Goncourt Journal* rptd in Harrison, Wood, and Gaiger 1998, pp. 415–418, quotation from p. 417.

84 Stephen, "Exile in the Pacific," in Stephen, ed., 2001, pp. 32–55.

85 A comparable kind of diligence, ironically, to that for which Gérôme was admired in the preparation of his orientalist–naturalist tours de force. (Delacroix, it seems, was not alone among nineteenth-century artists in doing his "homework." Whether they were all sadomasochists is another matter.)

86 A short list would include: Carol Duncan's "Virility and Domination" (1973); Hal Foster's "The 'Primitive' Unconscious of Modern Art" (1985); James Clifford's "Histories of the Tribal and the Modern" (1988); the essays in Susan Hiller's *The Myth of Primitivism* (1991); Sally Price's *Primitive Art in Civilised Places* (1989); Shelly Errington's *The Death of Authentic Primitive Art and Other Tales of Progress* (1998) … The list is endless, and it does not even include the modernist theories they are criticizing, the most important of which were Robert Goldwater's *Primitivism in Modern Art* of 1938 and William Rubin's *Primitivism in 20th century Art: Affinity of the Tribal and the Modern* of 1984. Coming as it did almost half a century after Goldwater, Rubin's two-volume catalog, which accompanied an exhibition of the same name at the Museum of Modern Art in New York, appeared in an artistic and academic world that had already moved on. For all its undoubted scholarship, it came to be seen as the obituary notice of modernist primitivism and a not inconsiderable negative stimulus to its critics.

87 All quotations from Aurier, "Symbolism in Painting" in Harrison, Wood, and Gaiger 1998, pp. 1025–1029.

88 In a letter from Gauguin to Emile Schuffenecker in March 1888, quoted in Orton and Pollock p. 320.

89 Pissarro, "On Anarchy, Symbolism and Primitivism" in Harrison, Wood, and Gaiger 1998, pp. 1029–1034; quotations from pp. 1033 and 1031 respectively.

90 Gauguin, letter to J.F. Willumsen, summer 1890, rptd in Thompson, ed., 2004, p. 86.

91 Gauguin, *Noa Noa* 1994, p. 48.

92 Gauguin letter to Mette Gauguin, late June 1891, rptd in Thompson 2004, p. 111.

93 Parkinson 2008.

94 Thompson 1987, p. 152.

95 *The Prelude* Book 10 line 224 p. 183 (Wordsworth 1970).

96 Desmond and Moore 2009.

97 Picasso, speaking in 1937, quoted in Malraux 1994, p. 11.

98 Semper from *Science, Industry and Art*, in Harrison, Wood, and Gaiger 1998, p. 333.

99 Coombes 1994, p. 48.

100 Arscott 2008, p. 136.

101 Altamira was discovered, and the findings published, in 1879–1880, but they for long remained disputed. Other cave paintings were discovered in the 1880s and 1890s. Despite the accumulating evidence, the paleolithic paintings were not definitively accepted as genuine by the scientific establishment until the Montauban Congress of the French Association for the Advancement of Science in August 1902.

102 See Nordau 1993. Nordau's book, which represented a conservative fear of modernity indexed in large part to the non-classical forms of avant-garde art, was strongly attacked by radical critics. Notable among these was George Bernard Shaw, whose trenchant reply to Nordau did much to diminish the book's impact in the English-speaking world. See Harrison, Wood, and Gaiger 1998, pp. 806–812.

103 Gallery display label, observed *in situ* 2012.

104 Barr 1974, p. 30.

105 Barr 1980, p. 55.

106 Rubin, ed., 1984, Vol. 1, p. 262.

107 Marles 1996.

108 Wood 2012.

109 C.H. Read and O.M. Dalton, "Works of Art from Benin City," *Journal of the Anthropological Institute*, Vol. 27 (1898), p. 372; extract rptd in Richard Danson Brown, ed., *Cultural Encounters*, Book 3 of the Open University course "The Arts Past and Present," p. 84; as supplementary resource to "The Art of Benin: Changing Relations between Europe and Africa" by Kim Woods, Robin Mackie, Donna Loftus, and Paul Wood, pp. 1–87.

110 To add to the mix, and hence unwittingly to underline the synthetic nature of would-be authentic avant-garde primitivism, Pechstein's flat colors, if not his starkly angular shapes, seem to owe something to the example of Japanese wood block prints.

111 Macke, "Masks" in Kandinsky and Marc, eds, 2006 pp. 83–89, quotes from pp. 87–88 and 89.

112 C. Einstein, from *Afrikanische Plastik* (1921), translated and quoted by Kay Heymer, "The Art of Benin in German-speaking Countries: Notes on its Reception History in the Context of Avant-Garde Art', in Plankensteiner, ed., 2007 pp. 247–253, quotation from p. 250.

113 Fry in Harrison and Wood 2003, p. 40.

114 This claim about a "direct," that is essentially pre-linguistic, mode of expression subsequently became the prime target for postmodernist critics of canonical modernism

during the 1980s. For figures such as Hal Foster, the modernist expression-claim was a linguistic claim that denied its own status as language, an impossible assertion of unmediated meaning. This was part of a wider "linguistic turn" in the humanities during that period. A less dismissive attitude to the complexities of expression can be found in Richard Wollheim, *Painting as an Art* 1987, as well as some of the essays collected in *The Mind and its Depths*, 1993, notably "Correspondence, Projective Properties, and Expression in the Arts."

115 Worringer from *Abstraction and Empathy* in Harrison and Wood 2002, pp. 66–69; quotations from pp. 67, 68, 67, and 67.

116 Fry, "The Art of the Bushmen" (1910) in Fry 1981, pp. 60–69; quotation from p. 66.

117 Fry 1981, p. 60.

118 Fry, "Negro Sculpture" (1920) in Fry 1981, pp. 70–73; quotations from pp. 70, 71, 70, 70, 72, and 73 respectively.

119 Gottlieb, Rothko, and Newman "Statement" (1943) all quotations from Harrison and Wood 2003, pp. 568–569.

120 Pollock, "Answers to a Questionnaire" (1944) in Harrison and Wood 2003, p. 570

121 Newman "Art of the South Seas" (1946) in Newman 1990, pp. 98–103; quotation from p. 100.

122 Newman, "The Ideographic Picture" (1947) in Harrison and Wood 2003, p. 574.

123 Newman "Pre-Columbian Stone Sculpture" (1944) in Newman 1990, pp. 62–65; quotation from p. 64.

124 Rothko, "The Romantics were Prompted ..." (1947) in Harrison and Wood 2003, p. 573.

125 Pollock, "Answers to a Questionnaire" in Harrison and Wood 2003, pp. 571–573; quotation from p. 570.

References

Allan, Scott and Mary Morton, eds, 2010, *Reconsidering Gérôme*, The J. Paul Getty Museum, Los Angeles.

Arscott, Caroline, 2008, *William Morris and Edward Burne-Jones: Interlacings,* The Paul Mellon Centre for Studies in British Art, Yale University Press, New Haven and London.

Barr, Alfred H., 1974 [1936], *Cubism and Abstract Art*, The Museum of Modern Art, New York.

Barr, Alfred H., 1980 [1946], *Picasso: Fifty Years of his Art*, Arno Press New York for The Museum of Modern Art.

Berger, Klaus, 1992, *Japonisme in Western Painting from Whistler to Matisse*, trans David Britt, Cambridge University Press, Cambridge. First published 1980.

Brown, Richard Danson, ed., 2008, *Cultural Encounters*, Open University Press, Milton Keynes.

Brunel, Georges, 1986, *Boucher*, Trefoil Books, London.

Buck-Morss, Susan, 2009, *Hegel, Haiti and Universal History*, University of Pittsburgh Press, Pittsburgh PA.

Cars, Laurence des, Dominique de Font-Réaulx, and Édouard Papet, eds, 2010, *The Spectacular Art of Jean-Léon Gérôme (1824–1904)*, Skira.

Clark, T.J., 1999, *Farewell to an Idea: Episodes from a History of Modernism*, Yale University Press, New Haven and London.

Clark, Timothy, Anne Nishimura Morse, and Louise E. Virgin with Allen Hockley, 2001, *The Dawn of the Floating World 1650–1765: Early Ukiyo-e Treasures from the Museum of Fine Arts, Boston*, exhibition catalog, Royal Academy of Arts, London.

Clifford, James, 1988, "Histories of the tribal and the modern." First published 1985, rptd in Clifford, *The Predicament of Culture: Twentieth-Century Ethnography, Literature, and Art*, Harvard University Press, Cambridge MA and London. pp. 189–214.

Coombes, Annie E., 1994, *Reinventing Africa: Museums, Material Culture and Popular Imagination in Late Victorian and Edwardian England*, Yale University Press, New Haven and London.

Darwin, John, 2007, *After Tamerlane: The Global History of Empire since 1405*, Allen Lane, London.

Delacroix, Eugene, 1948 [1822–1863], *The Journal of Eugene Delacroix*, ed. and trans. Walter Pach, Crown Publishers, New York.

Description de l'Egypte, edited by E.F. Jomard and others, modern concise edition, Taschen 2007 [1809–1828].

Desmond, Adrian and James Moore, 2009, *Darwin's Sacred Cause*, Houghton Mifflin Harcourt / Penguin, Boston, New York, and London.

Duncan, Carol, 1973, "Virility and domination in early twentieth-century vanguard painting," rptd in Norma Broude and Mary D. Garrard, *Feminism and Art History: Questioning the Litany*, Harper and Row, New York 1982, pp. 292–313.

Edwards, Amelia B., 1891, *A Thousand Miles up the Nile*, George Routledge and Sons Limited, London, 2nd edn. First published 1877.

Edwards, Steve and Paul Wood, eds, 2012, *Art and Visual Culture 1850–2010: Modernity to Globalisation*, Tate Publishing.

Eliot, T.S. 1975, *Selected Prose of T.S. Eliot*, ed. with an introduction by Frank Kermode, Faber and Faber.

Errington, Shelley, 1998, *The Death of Authentic Primitive Art and Other Tales of Progress*, University of California Press, Berkeley, Los Angeles and London.

Fer, Briony, David Batchelor, and Paul Wood, eds, 1993, *Realism, Rationalism, Surrealism: Art between the Wars*, Yale University Press, New Haven and London in association with The Open University.

Foster, Hal, 1985 "The 'primitive' unconscious of modern art, or white skin black masks," rptd in Foster, *Recodings: Art, Spectacle, Cultural Politics*, Bay Press, Seattle, WA, pp. 181–208.

Fried, Michael, 1988, *Absorption and Theatricality: Painting and Beholder in the Age of Diderot*, The University of Chicago Press, Chicago and London. First published 1980.

Fry, Roger, 1981, ed. J.B. Bullen, *Vision and Design*, Oxford University Press, Oxford. First published 1920.

Gauguin, Paul, 1994 [1893, trans. 1919], *Noa Noa*, trans. O.F. Theis, Chronicle Books, San Francisco CA.

Goldsmith, Oliver, 1837, *The Miscellaneous Works of Oliver Goldsmith, M.B.*, Vol. 2, ed. Prior, James John Murray, London, 4 vols.

Goldwater, Robert, 1986, *Primitivism in Modern Art*, The Belknap Press of Harvard University Press, Cambridge MA and London. First published 1938.

Haddawy, Husain, trans., 1990, *The Arabian Nights*, W.W. Norton & Company, New York and London.

Harrison, Charles, Paul Wood, and Jason Gaiger, 1998, *Art in Theory 1815–1900: An Anthology of Changing Ideas*, Blackwell, Oxford.

Harrison, Charles, Paul Wood, and Jason Gaiger, 2000, *Art in Theory 1648–1815: An Anthology of Changing Ideas*, Blackwell, Oxford.

Harrison, Charles, and Paul Wood, 2003, *Art in Theory 1900–2000: An Anthology of Changing Ideas*, Blackwell, Oxford.

Harvey, David, 2003, *Paris, Capital of Modernity*, Routledge, London.

Hegel, G.W.F., 1988, *Aesthetics: Lectures on Fine Art*, trans. T.M. Knox, Oxford University Press, Oxford, 2 vols. This edition first published 1975.

Hegel, G.W.F., 1980, *Lectures on the Philosophy of World History: Introduction*, trans. H.B. Nisbet with an introduction by Duncan Forbes, Cambridge University Press, Cambridge. This edition first published 1975.

Hiller, Susan, ed., 1991, *The Myth of Primitivism: Perspectives on Art*, Routledge.

Hokensen, Jan Walsh, 2004, *Japan, France, and East–West Aesthetics: French Literature 1867–2000*, Fairleigh Dickinson University Press, Madison WI.

Honour, Hugh, 1961, *Chinoiserie: The Vision of Cathay*, John Murray, London.

Irwin, Robert, 2004, *The Arabian Nights: A Companion*, Tauris Parke Paperbacks.

Irwin, Robert, 2007, *For Lust of Knowing: The Orientalists and their Enemies*, Penguin Books Ltd., London.

Johnson, Samuel, 2000 [1759], *The History of Rasselas, Prince of Abyssinia*, Wordsworth Classics, Ware.

Kandinsky, Wassily and Franz Marc, eds, 2006 [1912], *The Blaue Reiter Almanac*, ed. with an introduction by Klaus Lankheit, Tate Publishing.

Kant, Immanuel, 1960 [1764], *Observations on the Feeling of the Beautiful and Sublime*, trans. John T. Goldthwait, University of California Press, Berkeley, Los Angeles, London.

Kiernan, Victor G., 1969, *The Lords of Human Kind: European Attitudes towards the Outside World in the Imperial Age*, Weidenfeld and Nicolson, London.

King, Catherine, ed., 1999, *Views of Difference: Different Views of Art*, Yale University Press in association with The Open University, New Haven and London.

Kristeller, Paul Oskar, 1990 [1951–1952]. "The modern system of the arts," in *Renaissance Thought and the Arts: Collected Essays*, Princeton University Press, Princeton, NJ.

Losty, J.P. and Malini Roy, 2012, *Mughal India: Art Culture and Empire*, The British Library, London.

Malraux, Andre, 1994, *Picasso's Mask*, Da Capo Press, New York. First published 1974.

Mardrus, J.C., 1959, *The Book of the Thousand Nights and One Night*, trans. Powys Mathers. French edition 1899–1904, English translation 1923, Routledge and Kegan Paul Ltd. The Folio Society, 4 vols.

Marles, Hugh, 1996, "Arrested development: race and evolution in the sculpture of Herbert Ward," *Oxford Art Journal* 19 (1): 16–28.

Mercer, Kobena, 1991, "Looking for trouble," *Transition* 51: 184–197.

Mignolo, Walter D., 2011, *The Darker Side of Western Modernity*, Duke University Press, Durham and London.

Moi, Toril, 2006, *Henrik Ibsen and the Birth of Modernism: Art, Theater, Philosophy*, Oxford University Press, Oxford.

Montaigne, Michel de, 1991 [1580], *The Complete Essays*, trans. M.A. Screech, Penguin Books Ltd, London. This translation first published 1987.

Montesquieu, Charles-Louis de Secondat, 2008 [1721], *Persian Letters*, trans. Margaret Maulden with an introduction and notes by Andrew Kahn, Oxford World Classics, Oxford University Press, Oxford and New York.

Newman, Barnett, 1990, *Selected Writings and Interviews*, ed. John P. O'Neill, text notes and commentary by Mollie McNickle, with an introduction by Richard Shiff, Alfred A. Knopf, New York.

Nochlin, Linda, 1989, *The Politics of Vision: Essays on Nineteenth-Century Art and Society*, Thames and Hudson.

Nordau, Max, 1993 [1892], *Degeneration*, intro. George L. Mosse, University of Nebraska Press, Lincoln and London. Trans. from the second German edition, 1895.

Orton, Fred and Griselda Pollock, 1980, "Les Données Bretonnantes," *Art History* 3 (3) (September): 314–344.

Parkinson, Richard, 2008, *The Painted Tomb-Chapel of Nebamun*, The British Museum Press, London.

Plankensteiner, Barbara, ed., 2007, *Benin: Kings and Rituals*, exhibition catalog, Völkerkunde Museum, Vienna.

Podro, Michael, 1982, *The Critical Historians of Art*, Yale University Press, New Haven and London.

Popper, Karl, 1945, *The Open Society and its Enemies. Volume II Hegel and Marx*, Routledge and Kegan Paul, London.

Potts, Alex, 2013, *Experiments in Modern Realism*, Yale University Press, New Haven and London.

Price, Sally, 1989, *Primitive Art in Civilised Places*, The University of Chicago Press.

Proust, Marcel, 1992, In *Search of Lost Time* Vol. 1, *Swann's Way*, trans. C.K. Scott Moncrieff and Terence Kilmartin, rev. D.J. Enright, Vintage Classics, Random House, London.

Rawski, Evelyn S. and Jessica Rawson, eds, 2005, *China: The Three Emperors 1662–1795*, exhibition catalog, Royal Academy of Arts, London.

Roberts, David, 2000 [1846–1868], *Egypt and Nubia*, White Star Publishers, Vercelli, Italy.

Rubin, William ed., 1984, *"Primitivism" in 20th Century Art: Affinity of the Tribal and the Modern*, 2 vols, The Museum of Modern Art, New York.

Said, Edward W., 2003, *Orientalism*, Penguin Books Ltd. First published 1978.

Schwab, Raymond, 1984, *The Oriental Renaissance: Europe's Rediscovery of India and the East 1680–1880*, Columbia University Press, New York. First published as *La Renaissance orientale*, 1950.

Smith, Paul, 1995, *Impressionism: Beneath the Surface*, Everyman Art Library, London.

Steinberg, Leo, 1972, *Other Criteria: Confrontations with Twentieth-Century Art*, Oxford University Press, Oxford.

Sterne, Laurence, 2003 [1759–1767], *The Life and Opinions of Tristram Shandy, Gentleman*, Penguin Classics, London.

Steegmuller, Frances, 1996, *Flaubert in Egypt: A Sensibility on Tour*, Penguin Books. First published 1972.

Stephen, Ann, ed., 2001, *Visions of a Republic: The Work of Lucien Henry*, Powerhouse Publishing, Sydney.

Stevens, MaryAnne, ed., 1984, *The Orientalists: Delacroix to Matisse; European Painters in North Africa and the Near East*, exhibition catalog, Royal Academy of Arts in association with Weidenfeld and Nicolson, London.

Thompson, Belinda, 1987, *Gauguin*, Thames and Hudson, London.

Thompson, Belinda, ed., 2004, *Gauguin by Himself*, Time Warner, London. First published 1993.

Tromans, Nicholas, ed., 2008, *The Lure of the East: British Orientalist Painting*, Tate Publishing.

Vico, Giambattista, 1968 [1744], *The New Science*, trans. Thomas Goddard Bergin and Max Harold Fisch, Cornell University Press, Ithaca, NY.

Wollheim, Richard, 1987, *Painting As an Art*, Thames and Hudson, London.

Wollheim, Richard, 1993, *The Mind and its Depths*, Harvard University Press, Cambridge, MA and London.

Wood, Paul, 2012 "Display, restitution and world art history," *Visual Culture in Britain* 13 (1) (March): 115–137.

Wordsworth, William, 1970, *The Prelude or Growth of a Poet's Mind*, ed. Ernest de Selincourt and revised by Stephen Gill, Oxford University Press, Oxford; 1805 text.

4

Avant-Garde, Contemporary, and Globalized World

To Mid-Century

"Modernist" and "Avant-garde"

The complexity of the individual case is a telling corrective to generalization. Nevertheless, even if one discards or modifies the model at a later stage, it can be helpful to consider the art of the twentieth century as informed by two distinct logics: on the one hand, a logic of purification and refinement, on the other, a logic of addition, layering, and juxtaposition. The former can be traced in the tradition often referred to as "modernism," the latter in the tradition of the avant-garde. It goes without saying that there are crossovers, exceptions to the rule, artists and works that straddle both camps, etc., etc. But for all that, the distinction can be useful. The former tends to valorize the autonomy of art, medium specificity, the achievement of originality through continuous technical innovation and to elevate the aesthetic response above all other ends of art. The latter, although assuming the practical independence of art from external determination, and certainly marked by relentless formal radicalism, nonetheless eschews medium-specificity and seeks to register the impact of wider social and cultural formations while in turn having an effect upon them. The first is conventionally identified with a formalist critical tradition extending from Denis and Fry to Greenberg and Fried and is usually regarded as having entered a terminal crisis by the late 1960s. Despite the hegemony of that tradition of "modernism" in the mid-century, especially in the Anglophone world, the avant-garde tradition was considerably more diverse in both its practice and its theory – diversity being, arguably, its hallmark. After the

Western Art and the Wider World, First Edition. Paul Wood.

crisis of modernism, it is, moreover, frequently seen as having mutated into an archipelago of heterogeneous practices that became globally dominant in the art world of the last third of the century. These were initially described as "postmodernist," but, especially after the end of the Cold War, are often regarded as having evolved into a distinct formation of "contemporary art."

Any such breakdown is going to be provisional, always and forever open to qualification, counterexample, and test-case. But for the present, its virtues outweigh its vices. We are in a workshop situation, where the rough and ready, the near-to-hand is required. Even at the risk of what has been called "cubocentrism," it does seem that both strands can be traced to cubism. To the extent that formalist modernism can be identified with abstraction, cubism provided a kind of technical springboard into a self-consciously "purified" abstraction which influenced two generations in Europe up to the Second World War as well as the foil from which a further phase of abstraction took off in America after the war. On the other hand, the equally unprecedented innovation of cubist collage, nothing if not a process of sticking bits and pieces of heterogeneous material together, enabled a kind of repeated transgression beyond the boundaries of medium-specificity, beyond the bounded, discrete work of art itself. The result was an engagement first with the surrounding real space, then with institutional parameters, and latterly a conceptual expansion beyond the conventional limits of the institution of art as such: the very antithesis of the medium-specificity and aesthetically grounded autonomy at the heart of modernism, the Long March through futurist soirée, and Dada cabaret, past the Readymade, the *Monument to the Third International*, and the *Merzbau*, through the *Theater Piece #1*, out of *The Store*, off the end of *Spiral Jetty*, and down – or is it up? – into the supposedly limitless aesthetic cosmos through which we presently float.

The great preoccupation of that long and complex tradition has been modernity. Most often it has been the modernity to hand, the Western modernity of urbanism, technology, commodity fetishism, and spectacle – and, of course, its underside of alienation and anomie. As we have seen, the conventional wisdom of that modernity was that the rest of the world lacked it. The discourse of primitivism might have embraced that putative lack, indeed turned it into its own currency, but a sense of Western exceptionalism was the default position until remarkably late in the day; certainly it remained unshaken until the post-Second World War period and frequently until much later, until after the 1960s. The widespread criticism attracted by the Museum of Modern Art's *Primitivism* show of 1984 testifies to the fact that by then it had become an anachronism, but it also speaks powerfully to the persistence of the idea and the fact that it still had to be fought against, if an openness more appropriate to the age was to be established in art – a domain which, after all, trades in the rhetoric of freedom more than any other.

In terms of the relationship of Western art to the wider world during the modern period, the key issue is imperialism. We have seen how Manet appears to have grasped that modernity had its global dimension in addition to the metropolitan issues which were his and other artists' primary concern. Primitivism registers empire in a *de facto* sense: the stuff on which it fed simply would not have been available to artistic regard without the imperial networks to bring it all back home. But primitivism doesn't *recognize* empire. That is the point. Its fundamental ideology of a pre-linguistic, prehistoric, pre-cultural human nature militates against a workable sense of the reality of history and the exercise of temporal power in the world. There are more things in heaven and earth than sociology, but repeated invocation of the spirit is nothing if not a recipe for political quietism.

In the early twentieth century the most robust rejection of political quietism, the most principled attempt to think through the contradictions of history, came from the revolutionary Left. In the spring of 1916 in Zurich, around the corner from the Cabaret Voltaire, Lenin composed *Imperialism, the Highest Stage of Capitalism*. The preface to its first publication bears the place and date of "Petrograd, April 26 1917" – that is, the critical, fluid period of dual power between the February and then the definitive October revolutions.[1]

At the same historical juncture, Trotsky sketched the theory of "combined and uneven development." Criticized now from postcolonialist positions (if it is acknowledged at all) for its roots in an Enlightenment "stages" theory of historical development, this theory nonetheless constructed a picture of capitalism as a world system.[2] Trotsky's political conclusions are unfashionable, but anyone who ignores the mutual determination of local, national, and global, *and* the equally critical mutual system of determinations at work between culture and economy within an overarching mode of production has little claim to understand let alone to represent the contemporary.[3] The fate of the Russian revolution (and by the end of the century, its virtual obliteration from collective consciousness as a force for emancipation) is a story for a different place. But the fact remains that from the outbreak of the First World War, and for a very long time afterwards, any artistic avant-garde worthy of the name was animated by a more or less leftist rejection of the status quo in general and by the force field of the Russian revolution in particular.[4] Moreover, at its most developed, this avant-garde rejection involved a critique of capitalist modernity *and* its imperialist dimension that went far beyond "primitivism" (not to mention the craze for things *nègre* that swept through fashionable Paris in the twenties).

Peter Bürger's theorization of the revolutionary avant-gardes was notoriously slippery about which avant-garde movements were to count, and the beginnings of a critical rereading are finally beginning to be broached.[5] For all that, despite not seeming to know what to do with individualistic tendencies like expressionism, not to mention politically rightist manifestations like futurism, the idea of a socially and politically as well as aesthetically transgressive avant-gardism remains fruitful. In his otherwise profoundly hostile poststructuralist critique of primitivism as manifest in Picasso's *Demoiselles d'Avignon*, Hal Foster recognized the existence of a less tarnished dimension of the avant-garde legacy. Referring to neglected aspects of surrealism, he briefly acknowledged the possibility of "a model of how the otherness of the primitive might be thought disruptively, not recuperated abstractly," and how some surrealists "politicised rather than aestheticised the primitivist–imperialist connection."[6] Surrealism, however, was not alone in its more complex, politicized understanding of the "primitive," there being in fact a significant tradition of this, flitting in and out of the more standard preoccupations of the avant-garde with the psychic and social aspects of European modernity.

Futurism

Futurism represents an excessively volatile point in the early twentieth-century avant-garde. Something of an exception which proves the rule, in one sense it operates as a kind of mirror image of primitivism, its rhetoric of the technological future counterposing the other's rhetoric of the primitive past. Gauguin's parable of being reborn in the South Pacific as a Maori warrior is matched by Marinetti's rebirth as a futurist machine–man out of the crash of his car in a factory ditch. Taken together, primitivism and futurism speak to the exhaustion and failure of the earlier avant-garde project of painting modern life. The focus on the present becomes deflected into fantasies of past and future as the present becomes imaginatively uninhabitable.[7] Yet there is also a strong element of the primitive compacted *into* Marinetti's futurism. This is particularly evident in his 1909 novel *Mafarka the Futurist*, set in a stylized hyper-violent North Africa that owes a certain amount to *Salammbo*, Flaubert's earlier orientalist vision of war in ancient Carthage.

Futurist visual art exhibits little of this primitivist dimension beyond the exotic fauna of the nightclub or cityscape, comparable to that which one finds in expressionism. But in Marinetti's fable it is unmistakable. Marinetti's characteristic mixture of violence and militarism, anti-feminism and racism produces the warrior Mafarka-el-Bar, "Commander-in-Chief" of a "great Arab army."[8] This Mafarka defeats the massed negro armies of Brafane-el-Kibir, "black hordes" that "converge upon us from every corner of Africa." He subsequently rapes and pillages his way to becoming "an almighty king who rules the whole of Africa," only to turn round and reject worldly preeminence as insufficient. In a Neitzschean turn he moves beyond his earlier adherence to Islam to found a "religion of externalised Will and daily Heroism" wherein he gives birth to his own son (thus rendering women unnecessary), the precondition of whose birth is Mafarka's own death. The son, a mixture of a primitive bird-idol and airplane, ultimately flies beyond the earth in an attempt to usurp the power of the sun, in the process destroying Earth itself. This dystopic vision is born of a hatred of the bureaucratic nightmare that Marinetti sees European modernity turning into: "this niggling yen for universal order and glum regularity." The same disdain for the contemporary bourgeois order earlier seen with Gauguin leaks into Marinetti's part-modern, part-medieval fantasy, his rejection of "the trading and economic meanness of men," the "greed of their mercantile eyes"; Africa figures as its polar opposite, which, rather than fearing, Marinetti positively relishes: an exaggerated caricature of imperialist fantasy, all violence, beauty, and barbarism. Thus Mafarka recognizes one of the negro generals "by the vermilion feathers flaming in his tousled hair, and by the countless strings of shells that clattered over his coal-black body, tattooed with blue moons." The women are just as dramatic: "Negresses dressed in crimson wool were dancing round the fires, sending up rapid, deafening yells." Unbridled sex and violence is everywhere. One can almost imagine some colonial officer in his compound dozing off to such dreams, though unable to express them half so vividly.

Marinetti, the happily married fascist who saw his alarming vision right through to an end in the Republic of Salo, represents something close to the nightmare of contemporary multiculturalist relativism. The point, however, seems less to blame avant-gardism per se than to recognise its power when it goes wrong. For Marinetti's politicization of the primitive, far from evoking liberation from empire, prefigures the Nazi dream of conquest: "My metallized brain sees clear angles everywhere, in rigid symmetrical systems. The days to come are there, before me, fixed, straight and parallel, like military routes plainly mapped out for the armies of my desires!" One of the things Marinetti's insanely reactionary version of avant-gardism does show is that "politicization" per se, or indeed the critique of humanism per se, are not to be mistaken for unequivocal goods. It all depends on the ends to which the politicization and the critique of bourgeois humanism – not to mention the use of the "primitive" – are put. In the politicization of aesthetics, the content of the politics matters.

Relativizing Representation

Dada's Australia

One of the earliest attempts at a radical avant-gardist inflection of the discourse of the primitive occurred at the Dada Cabaret Voltaire in Zurich. In 1916 and 1917 both Richard Huelsenbeck and Tristan Tzara recited what were called "Negro poems." Huelsenbeck's were made up, but Tzara drew on ethnographic research, including actual Aboriginal songs from central Australia. This source is not without interest. The songs were transcribed by the missionary-anthropologist Pastor Carl Strehlow who worked at Hermannsburg, the Lutheran mission where, twenty years later, Albert Namatjira first began to make his hybrid European–Aboriginal paintings of the central Australian landscape. Strehlow's translations were from the Aranda and Loritja languages into German, which made them accessible to the Zurich Dadaists. Published in a series beginning in 1907, they were the basis for Tzara's further translation into French. Strehlow produced two versions, one a word-by-word transliteration, the other a more accessible version developed from that. Tzara based his translation on the former. The result is comparable to the way the contemporaneous Russian avant-garde broke apart the Russian language in "trans-sense" poetry as well as in some of Malevich's paintings in order to destabilize bourgeois common sense. The sheer opacity to the normative protocols of European poetry is conveyed by an equivalent English transliteration of the Aranda "Song of the Snake":

> Snaking throwing ahead
> Twisting itself throwing ahead
> Snake skin lifting up
> At the sky lifting up
> Heart continuously beating
> Tail continuously beating
> Tail wants to die off
> Tail wants to trembling move.[9]

As Ann Stephen and Andrew McNamara point out, what the Dadaists were doing was using the Aboriginal songs as leverage against German high culture, in the hope of "exposing its complicity with the imperialism of the German Reich."[10]

Another important intervention in the "primitivism" discourse from within the Dada camp is found in the work of Hannah Höch (Figure 4.1). It amounts, in fact,

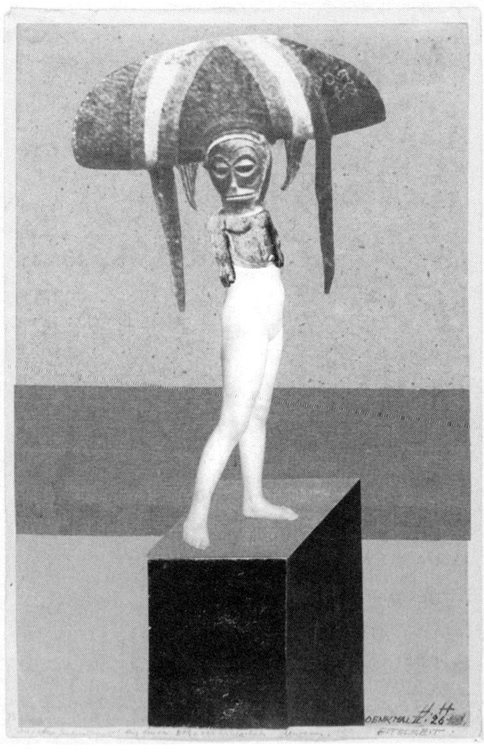

Figure 4.1 Hannah Höch, *Monument II: Vanity*, from the series *From an Ethnographic Museum*, 1926, collage, 26 × 17 cm. Germanisches Nationalmuseum, Nuremburg, HZ 6899. © DACS 2013. Photo: Germanisches Nationalmuseum, Nuremburg / DACS, London 2013.

to a calculated disruption of the assumptions of primitivism as exemplified in German expressionism. Whereas the expressionists typically employed signifiers of the "primitive" to suggest a "natural" freedom from bourgeois convention, Höch employed them differently. Far from indulging in a discourse of the "natural" she drew on "primitive" imagery to mount a critique of contemporary constructions of modern femininity by such institutions as the fashion industry. Furthermore, as Maud Lavin has pointed out, Höch was careful to use her primitive imagery not as if it were culled from some reservoir of exotically existing human nature but as something one encountered in the institution of the modern ethnographic museum.[11] By employing the technique of collage, she was able to juxtapose quite disparate elements, such as photographs of tribal masks or carvings, modern fashion plates, and geometric elements drawn from the language of constructivism to produce the kinds of visual collision that generated new meanings. The upshot was a series of relatively small, highly condensed works which yet mounted a multilayered critique of fashion and commodification, of the construction of "femininity," and of the institution of the museum (and by implication, of the "master" discourses of "civilization" and "barbarism"). For good measure, Höch's Dada collages also took their critical distance from normative modern art and its myths of "free expression."

Einstein's Africa

This use of the supposedly primitive to gain a point of critical purchase back upon the norms, the presuppositions, of European culture itself is also key to the work of Carl Einstein. We have already encountered Einstein's argument in an article of 1921 that from his perspective, that is from the viewpoint of the cubist-influenced avant-garde, the naturalistic Benin bronzes were of little interest. That text was a development of Einstein's principal work on the subject of African art, *Negerplastik*, of 1915, usually translated into English as *Negro Sculpture*.[12] This was amongst the very first texts to try and critically think through the implications of non-Western art from the position of avant-garde aesthetics.

Roger Fry, as we have seen, wrote on the pictorial art of the South African San people as early as 1910, but his own study, "Negro Sculpture," did not appear until 1920, and it is unlikely that he was aware of Einstein's text. Few were. Sebastian Zeidler has commented that, despite the more than one hundred images of African objects that accompanied the text of *Negerplastik* being almost immediately assimilated into the work of a wide range of European artists and designers, the text itself suffered a different fate: "few contemporaries read it closely, fewer understood it, and hardly anyone engaged with its argument more than superficially."[13] Moreover, Einstein's perspective was considerably more radical than that of Fry. In a general sense both were formalists. However, whereas Fry's formalism was part of the connoisseurial, Bloomsbury tradition that had its apotheosis in the anti-intellectual formation of post-Second World War Anglo-American modernism, Einstein's had more in common with the Saussure-derived Russian formalists of the second and third decades of the twentieth century, figures such as Jakobson, Shklovsky, and Volosinov who were themselves similarly occluded until the emergence of French structuralist semiotics in the work of Barthes and others in the 1950s and 1960s.

It has been made to seem too easy to dismiss the formalism of Fry and his contemporary Clive Bell, as that of Clement Greenberg later; both carry more force than the routine accusations of narrowness and elitism are able to admit. But there remains a sense in which these formations fit within a hierarchy of the Western academy that in the end seeks to refresh that academy rather than transform the foundations on which it is raised. Fry, and later in the 1930s Alfred Barr and others, tended to neuter the avant-garde of its political radicalism and substitute instead a notion of the "modern masters," on a par with the Old Masters, in carrying forward the torch of the Western canon. Einstein and kindred figures in the interwar avant-garde were cut from a different cloth: they were part of the revolutionary wave that saw bourgeois culture as responsible for, rather than a haven from, the repression and violence of industrial capitalism and its imperialist global system.

Zeidler has argued that Einstein's discussion was not a contribution to "properly academic knowledge of African art." It was not a history, it provided no contextual or sociological understanding, indeed in terms of its references to fetishism and religion it remained of a piece with contemporary ideology. But on the other side, Einstein's meditation on the formal qualities of African sculpture led him, in Zeidler's words, to a "theoretical exploration of sculpturality as a model of object experience in modernity";[14] and those reflections on the experience of objects in the modern world involved him in a parallel critique of conventional definitions of European subjectivity in relation to art.

As we saw in Chapter 1, the development during the Renaissance of perspective in pictorial art and equivalent conventions of naturalism in sculpture relied on a contemporary understanding of the spectator influenced by the new humanism, the perceiving subject, who, in effect, "completes" the work by perceiving it. The painting relies on the spectator standing in a specific position, determined by the principal vanishing point of the image, in order for it to work properly, in order, that is, to render it meaningful. Similarly, in sculpture the viewer completes the work by moving around it to reconstitute its totality through his perceptions. Central to this conception of the spectator are two factors, first the separation of the subject from his object, and second the integral nature of his perceiving consciousness. The European spectator is so to speak King and Creator of the world of representation, much as the European merchant was King and Creator of the world of commerce and trade – upon which world, it goes almost without saying, the world of representation, the world of *art*, was erected.

Einstein's post-cubist position, the structural connection he made between African sculpture and cubist representation worked in a different way, to different effect. For Einstein, African sculpture is not dependent on some "vague optical suggestion," that is, on completion by the spectator.[15] In his view, European sculptural tradition is weakened by its preoccupation with "the Pictorial."[16] By contrast, African sculpture is not nearly so dependent on the contingencies of perception and the movement around it of a spectator. It is altogether more objective, as he puts it, "unconditional, self-enclosed and autonomous."[17] The consequence of this is significant. As Zeidler puts it, it is not a question of the Western subject whose traditional "visual purview" with all its competences and assumptions is now "extended to include new 'primitive' objects" – in a way which paralleled the extension of European writ over the rest of the world through colonization and empire. Rather, the conventions of that optical naturalism are themselves "subjected to a primitiv*ization* by an alien perceptual modality."[18] For Einstein, it is not that there exists an integral Western subject whose consciousness can now embrace hitherto alien forms under the rubric of the "primitive" but that the primitive sculpture has the potential to critique the Western consciousness, to reveal its routines as conventions, not as nature. Rather than being a pliant function of the Western viewing consciousness, the African sculpture can, in effect, talk back to the viewing consciousness and demand *its* reformulation.

Einstein rejects "vague evolutionary hypotheses" and what he calls "a misguided concept of the primitive," that is to say, the conventional European view of African art. But he also rejects the conventional primitivist–modernist view: such "seductive and false phrases as 'people of an eternal prehistory' and so forth": the idea that African art held out the possibility of being able "to capture … a kind of origin." For him, African sculpture, as form, was more incisive, more powerful than anything in the Western post-Renaissance "pictorial" sculptural tradition. Einstein's essay was rigorously formalist, but it was his sense of African sculpture's intensity, its thoroughgoing exploration of fundamental sculptural problems, that is to say his formalism itself, that gave his thesis its critical force. For him this meant that, just like cubism, African sculpture was "realist" in a far more profound way than that offered by the contingent resemblances found in European academic art. It reversed the polarity, so to speak. "It became clear: the earlier verdict on the Negro and his art applied more to the judge than the judged."[19] Once one could see – and one needed to have grasped cubism in order to see – then, African sculpture turned the tables on the European tradition. It is this distinction, by no means hard and fast but fundamental nonetheless, between expanding the Western purview over the whole world, spatially and temporally, and subjecting the Western purview to critique *by* the rest of the world, that marks the line between "modernism," in the sense of an appreciation of the "modern masters" of a continuing art tradition, and the "avant-garde," in the sense of the striving for a transformation of that tradition, aesthetically and politically.

Schäfer's Egypt

Nothing could be further from an avant-garde consciousness than the work of Heinrich Schäfer. Einstein was a revolutionary who worked with the surrealists, fought on the Republican side in the Spanish civil war, and ultimately, like his German Jewish comrade Walter Benjamin, committed suicide when his attempt to evade the Nazis failed. Schäfer was a reactionary German nationalist who survived right through the Nazi period, whose modern translator felt it necessary to point out that "he was never apparently a Party member himself," while conceding how frequent references in his writings to "race" and "volk" make it likely that he "would probably have approved of some of the terminology of National Socialism as expressive of what was essentially German."[20] The two authors, that is, could not be further apart. But for all that, Schäfer's work on Egyptian art carried much of the same deconstructive force for canonical Western representation as did Einstein's on the conjunction of African art and cubism. In effect, Schäfer did for Egyptian visual art what Champollion did for the Egyptian language; that is, he decoded it.[21]

As we have seen, the normative Western system of representation has been perspectival. That is, it employs devices such as foreshortening, of "shading" from light to dark, and the elaboration of the spatial armature of "perspective." This is all done in order to present an "accurate" illusion of bodies disposed in three-dimensional space on a two-dimensional surface *when seen from the position of an individual spectator* (indeed, when seen by such a spectator *with one eye*). The camera, needless to say, mimics such monocular human perception (while introducing characteristics of its own in respect of various different types of lens, etc.). This system of representation was definitively realized in fifteenth-century Italy and elaborated in European academies of art over the next four hundred years. It found its antecedents in the classical civilizations of Greece and Rome from the fifth century BCE to approximately the fourth century CE. Ancient Egyptian art, and also the art of many other cultures both ancient and modern, does not do this. It proceeds from a different basis and produces different effects embodying different meanings. It was that "basis" that Schäfer set out to elucidate in his *Principles*.

There is no single, universally accepted term to describe the organizational principles Schäfer discovered. Some authors use the term "aspective," to contrast with "perspective," while others feel that this is potentially misleading (because of the partial sense it suggests of only dealing with "aspects" of representation). Schäfer himself coined the term *geradvorstellig*, which has been rendered into English as "based on frontal images." The basic distinction at work here is between perception and conception.

As Schäfer himself writes, "our eyes receive a picture of the world that is essentially different from the idea we have of the physical reality of things."[22] Thus – I glance across the desk to my cup of coffee and perceive the top of the cup as an ellipse. Yet I *know* the top of the cup is circular.

In perception, someone on the road a hundred yards away appears smaller than someone standing outside my window. But I *know* that they are both the same size. Schäfer's insight was that the art of ancient civilizations, as well as that of contemporary cultures uninfluenced by Western art, "does not follow the dictates of the eyes." Schäfer's follower and editor, the German Egyptologist Emma Brunner-Traut, puts it even more dramatically in her epilogue to the English edition of the *Principles*: "Egyptian pictures are ... to an extraordinary degree independent of the sense of sight"[23]

In terms of the reading of an Egyptian picture, this means that the representation of the figure we are looking at is not influenced by foreshortening. In fact, quite to the contrary, it is determined by an extreme avoidance of foreshortening. Each element is shown as if it were right in front of us. "Element" here does not mean "figure," in the sense of complete human figures. Rather, it means the elements out of which figures are composed – an arm, a foot, a torso, etc. Neither does it mean that the elements are actually only seen from the front. Feet, for example, are always represented as if seen from the side. What it means is that the elements are represented as if they are seen straight on. Or more to the point, they are depicted as if what is being represented is a mental image of the element in its entirety, not subject at all to the vagaries of perception – for example, to the spectator moving around the object, to moving one's head etc. That is to say, all accidental factors accruing to the perception of an object in real space and time are systematically excluded. The salient term to describe this state of affairs is that the Egyptian system of representation is not, like the post-Greek / post-Renaissance Western one, "observer centered." It is, rather, an "object-centered" system.

Schäfer admits that "it seems entirely obvious to most of us that we must render the perspective aspects of our visual impressions if we want to represent the outside world." He also says that for the most part we respond to people who do not do this – he cites "primitive" people, untutored adults, and children – "by feeling superior."[24] Yet it is perspectival representation, spectator-oriented representation, which has been the exception rather than the rule in human cultures. *Our* common sense is far from being universal common sense. Schäfer was at pains to point out that Egyptians did not literally "see" things differently from us. All human perception is, within certain norms, the same. As he says, no spear would ever have hit its target if the person who threw it did not have an ability to judge recession in space. The only alternative to the possibility that some people literally perceived objects in space differently is to accept that: "men have always been conscious of the phenomena of perspective at all periods, but for some reason they have not at all periods made use of this awareness in their drawings."[25] This "reason" at bottom, is that in the majority viewpoint, it is "appearance" that is regarded as "an illusion which distorts things"; that "the thing *is not* as it is shown in perspective drawing." What drives resistance to perspectival rendering is the experience of a "contradiction between perspective sense data and 'objective' reality."[26] And, importantly, it is the sense of "objective reality" that has been given priority.

In the spectator-oriented system of perspectival representation, the most fundamental move is to establish the spatial armature into which bodies can be placed. This is achieved through the device of the vanishing point with its accompanying orthogonals: that is, lines which appear on the flat surface as diagonals, but which represent surfaces or edges set at 90 degrees to the picture plane – for example, the roof line of a building disappearing into the distance. The next most important thing, however, is to establish the illusion of those bodies occupying the picture space themselves. This is achieved through "shading." Shading is the transition from light to dark which mimics in two dimensions the way light falls on an object in three dimensional space – for example, a ball. Establishing this illusion of three-dimensionality is a cornerstone of the perspectival system. It is completely absent from Egyptian painting. In this system, far from conveying "believability," shading would suggest the accidental, partial nature of the single viewpoint instead of what is actually being prioritized, namely an "objective" representation of the thing as it really is.

Almost a century after its first appearance, Schäfer's study remains controversial. Whitney Davis regards Schäfer's speculations about the relation between technical aspects of Egyptian painting and sculpture and a wider Egyptian "world view" as "idealist" and "essentialising." In general he regards the imputation of national-cultural worldviews as "highly undesirable";[27] unsurprisingly, given the politics whence they emerge in Schäfer's own worldview. Yet, at the other end of the spectrum, John Baines is more circumspect about the ideological aspects of Schäfer's thinking and regards his technical analysis as "the fundamental work on representation in Egyptian art," work which "solves with outstanding success" many of the problems of non-perspectival art.[28] Just as in the case of Hegel's opinions about other cultures discussed in Chapter 3, Schäfer's unpalatable politics does not mean that his work on object-based forms of representation has not made an important contribution to the critical relativization of what were once held by most Europeans to be universal principles of achievement and value in art. Looked at in that light, ancient Egyptian art, African sculpture, and cubism have much to say about the relation of Western art to the arts of the wider world.

Surrealism and Ethnography

The early twentieth-century Western avant-garde's most sustained attempt to forge a connection with the rest of the world premised on the revolutionary rejection of imperialism in all its forms, political and cultural alike, is to be found in surrealism. From its 1925 involvement with the Communist Party opposing French participation in the suppression of the Riff revolt in Morocco until long after it had ceased to be a driving force in radical culture, when in 1960 surrealists worked with Jean-Paul Sartre and Simone de Beauvoir to support the struggle for Algerian independence, the surrealist group matched its attack on conventional culture with a principled opposition to imperialism.

Perhaps the most clear-cut example of this was their work against the massive Exposition Coloniale held in Paris in 1931. This exhibition, which ran from May to December of that year, was explicitly designed to unite the French nation, attempting to recover from the capitalist crisis of 1929 under the notion of a "greater France." This encompassed not only the homeland of France itself but its worldwide empire in a combined economic and cultural project: prosperity would revive and the "civilizing mission" of France, long central in Europe, would extend throughout the world. According to the historian Jody Blake, 330 million francs were lavished on the project, and the resulting exhibition was seen by approximately 8 million people, about half of whom came from outside France itself.[29] As with previous international exhibitions dating back to the nineteenth century, the Exposition Coloniale involved not only displays of indigenous arts and crafts but also musical and theatrical performances as well as simulated "native villages" populated by people brought from the colonies to Paris to illustrate the diversity of life in the empire. For the surrealists, and for the wider revolutionary Left in general, the whole thing was a gigantic charade, organized to deflect attention from the real causes of the crisis and to conceal the actual barbarity of imperial practice which flew in the face of the ideology of the "civilizing mission."

The surrealists issued oppositional posters and texts, the first of which opened with the plain injunction "Don't Visit the Colonial Exhibition." It pointed out how the opening of the exhibition had been preceded by the arrest and deportation from Indo-China of a communist student who had been involved in a demonstration outside the Élysée Palace against the execution by French colonial authorities of forty activists in Vietnam. It drew connections between this case and the execution in the United States of the anarchists Sacco and Vanzetti, just as it also went on to draw connections between the church and the big capitalist companies Citroën and Renault: that the whole idea of a "Greater France" was actually about increasing the power of these corporations, and that the real purpose of the Colonial Exhibition itself was "to try to indoctrinate this fraudulent concept." It continued: "The citizens of the metropolis must be given the feeling that they are proprietors so that they can hear the echoes of faraway gunfire without flinching," and ended with a call for the "immediate evacuation of the colonies" and the bringing to trial of those responsible for the massacre in Indo-China.[30]

This is serious agitational politics, carrying a risk of legal challenge, and it points to the existence of a substantial potential opposition in France at that time, much as some of the inflammatory activities of the German Dadaists a decade earlier would not have been possible without a similar oppositional constituency. The point is that the surrealists' activities were part of a broader front of leftist political challenge to capitalism as a system, taking strength from the still recent example of the Russian Revolution, and further stimulated by the social crisis caused throughout the developed nations by the Wall Street Crash. At that historical juncture, capitalism not only was but *was seen to be* much less secure than is routinely claimed today. The surrealists were catching this political current and drawing out dimensions which the orthodox Left was prone to neglect, including both the role of imperialism and the role of culture and ideology in propping up the system.

Exhibition

Following their first intervention aimed at stopping people going to the Exposition Coloniale, or at least making them think twice about doing so, the surrealists most important initiative was the organization of a counter-exhibition, *The Truth About the Colonies*, which ran from September until after the official exhibition had ended (Figure 4.2). From the late 1920s there were tensions between the surrealists and the French Communist Party because the group led by André Breton increasingly sided with the continuing revolutionary tradition exemplified by Trotsky's Left Opposition against the emerging centrist bloc of the Stalinist bureaucracy. Nonetheless, the exhibition broadly fell within the remit of the Third International,

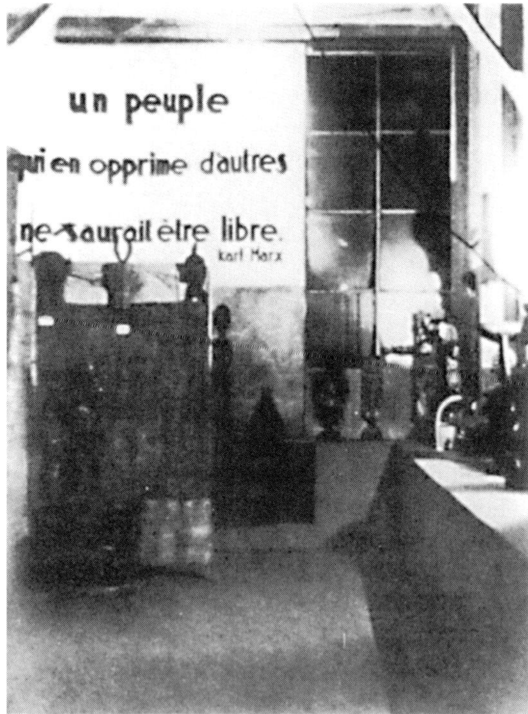

Figure 4.2 Installation view of exhibition *La Verité sur les Colonies*, Paris, 1931. Reproduced from *Le Surréalisme au service de la Révolution*, December 1931. Photo: ACRPP, France.

which, following Lenin, continued to regard imperialism as the "highest stage of capitalism," and thus to connect the anti-imperialist struggle with revolutionary activity in the developed capitalist nations. Increasingly, by contrast, the Stalinist position was to develop Socialism in One Country, that is Russia itself, and actually to deflect revolution elsewhere, the most serious example of this being the disastrous mishandling of the nascent Chinese revolution in the mid- to late 1920s. As a result of the continuing presence of the International in this relatively early phase of Stalinism, the surrealist exhibition *The Truth About the Colonies* was held in the Soviet pavilion originally designed by the architect Konstantin Melnikov for the Paris International Decorative Arts exhibition of 1925, which had been taken over as a "Palais des Soviets" for use by trade unions and other groups.

The mismatch was huge. According to figures provided by Blake, the surrealists' budget was a fraction of 1 percent of the official exhibition (less than 30,000 francs as against over 300 million), and the number of visitors it attracted (just four thousand) was similarly dwarfed by that of the eight million who flocked to the Exposition Coloniale itself. The salient fact, however, is that the exhibition existed at all. The Left as such, which in the 1930s was almost exclusively focused on political and trade union organization among the industrial proletariat, was forced to acknowledge that imperialism had a cultural dimension. And on the other side, the proponents of radical art were presented with the argument that a practical political element had to be fostered if all the utopian claims about radical new visions were to penetrate beyond the elevated social milieu in which they characteristically subsisted.

Most of the surrealist-organized exhibition consisted of visual information showing the harsher realities of empire, countering the rosy picture of prosperity drawn by the official exhibition and detailing the costs, human and material, of the military conquest involved and the economic exploitation which followed. These focused on such scandals, well-known at the time, as the high death rate among conscripted native workers in the colonies. On one such project, the building of a railway in French Equatorial Africa, even the government admitted fatalities ran at nearly 20 percent.[31] The exhibition, however, also included both performances of music and a display of visual art. The works shown were for the most part drawn from the collections of indigenous arts that had been made by the surrealists themselves. By the 1930s there was nothing intrinsically radical about this, indeed with the widespread fashion for "art nègre" it had become conventional.

The surrealists were severe about such double standards. Their revolutionary anticolonialism found its most explicit formulation a few years later in the tract "Murderous Humanitarianism," which was published in Nancy Cunard's enormous anthology, *Negro*, in 1934. In this text, as its title implies, they rounded not only on the "soldiers, priests and civil agents of imperialism" but also on "counterfeit liberalism." As the surrealists saw, this was often little more than a mask for real power: "The white man preaches, doses, vaccinates, assassinates and (from himself) receives absolution. With his psalms, his speeches, his guarantees of liberty, equality and fraternity, he seeks to drown the noise of his own machine guns."[32]

Already in 1931, works of "art nègre" had been on show in the official Colonial Exhibition. But what distinguished the surrealist display of similar material was the critical twist they added by exhibiting their works of indigenous art alongside a display of what were labeled "European fetishes." These included such things as devotional prints, sculptures of madonnas, and the like that were used by Christian missionaries in the colonies. The clear implication was that Christianity was no less "fetishistic" than the indigenous belief systems it sought to eradicate, and that the religious art associated with it was less powerful than the "primitive" art of the colonized. To drive the point home, the installation had as a backdrop a large poster with a quotation from Marx: "A people that oppresses another can never itself be free."

It is worth commenting, parenthetically, at this point, that Blake's laudable empirical study recovering the lost history of the surrealist anticolonial exhibition takes a curious turn with regard to this display. Driven by the political agenda of the contemporary American university, that is by the priorities of "today's scholars, working in the context of post-colonial studies," Blake begins to take a critical distance from the rather different priorities of Breton and his colleagues.[33] Rather than being distinguished from those whom they opposed they are assimilated to them. *The Truth About the Colonies*, it is now claimed, "like the government and the church, used art from the colonies to advance its own ideological programme." This is the world turned, if not upside down, then inside out. From the viewpoint of postcolonial studies, proponents of the revolutionary critique of empire are deemed to share more with empire than with those oppressed by it, *because* they are European.

The depoliticization of contemporary academe, particularly contemporary American academe, becomes alarmingly visible at this point; except that that is not quite correct. It is not depoliticization so much as the replacement of one sort of politics by another. In essence this involves the replacement of a revolutionary politics centered on class analysis, which maintained an insecure balance between economic and psychic determinants, by a politics that elevates "race" and ethnicity and cognate issues of identity above all others, and in so doing rejects arguments for radical change as illegitimately universalizing, if not incipiently totalitarian themselves. Throughout the discussion there is little evidence of an appreciation of conflicts within the interwar revolutionary Left. The surrealists are tagged as "Marxist-Leninists," and in their Second Manifesto of 1930, the group is deemed to have "reaffirmed its loyalty to Moscow." It is alarming how closely the language of postcolonialism can approximate the language of Cold War. In the contemporary political climate I find it worrying when the "quotation from Karl Marx" (namely that a people that oppresses others cannot itself be free) is held to be an attempt by the Left "to advance its own ideological programme" in consort with "diatribes against Christian missions." The fact that we appear to be living through a religious revival, and that both Christian and Islamic fundamentalisms play a prominent role in contemporary global politics seems to me a flimsy rationale for describing the critique of the role of religion in colonialism as a "diatribe" and the revolutionary critique of capitalism and imperialism as an "ideological programme" that shares more with the oppressors than it does with the oppressed. This is a politics that identifies the Left *tout court* with the Stalinist and post-Stalinist Soviet bureaucracy and rejects revolutionary politics from the standpoint of identity politics. If we are talking about who shares what with whom, it would seem to me that black revolutionaries of the 1930s and 1940s shared more with their contemporary white comrades than they do with a putatively "post-colonial" academy that uses identity politics as a justification for remaining within a de facto liberal political project. As Slavoj Žižek has repeatedly pointed out, it is the lack of a coherent revolutionary alternative to global capitalism that is doing most to guarantee its survival, even in the face of upsurges as profound as that of the Arab Spring of 2011 and its own deep economic crisis.

Mapping it Out

Significant though it was, the anticolonial exhibition was not the only manifestation of surrealist opposition to contemporary imperialism. A special issue of the Belgian journal *Variétés* published in June 1929 featured a map of *The World in the Time of the Surrealists* (Figure 4.3). Reworking the standard Mercator projection, the map operated a humorous but devastating series of reversals in order imaginatively to negate the contemporary power of capital and its culture. Centered on the Pacific, with the Atlantic marginalized in a direct inversion of the normative Eurocentric view, the map edited out the United States altogether, defined Europe not in terms of French but German influence, and made of England an

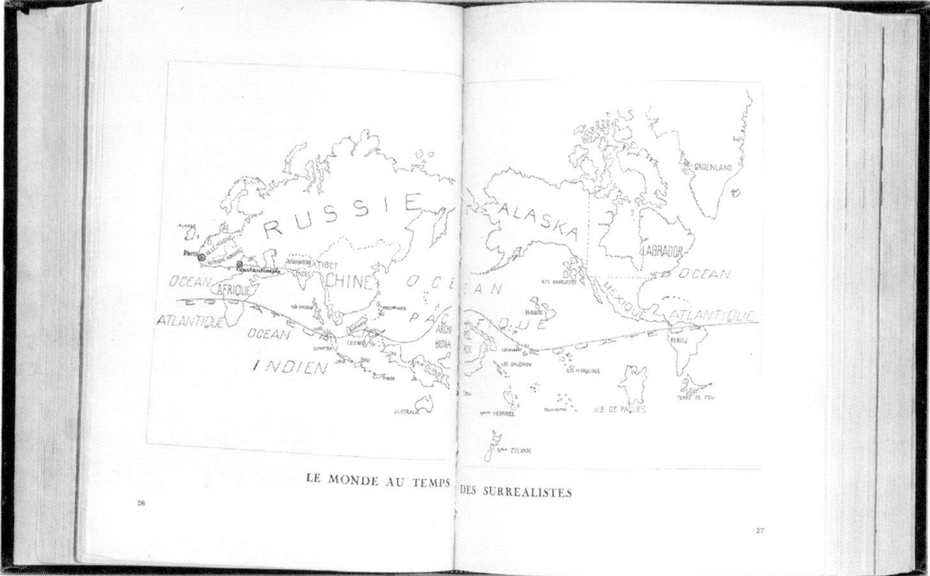

Figure 4.3 "The world in the time of the surrealists," 1929. New York, Museum of Modern Art (MoMA). © 2013. Digital image, The Museum of Modern Art, New York / Scala, Florence.

insignificant dot off the coast of Ireland. Interestingly, it did not particularly emphasize either South America, India, or Africa, which the surrealists had not at that point really begun to address. It conferred greatest importance on what were, so to speak, the two sides of the coin of surrealist radicalism: on the one hand the Soviet Union, birthplace and home of the international socialist revolution; on the other Alaska, Mexico, and the Pacific, especially New Guinea and Easter Island, the homes of that "primitive" art which posed a challenge, simultaneously formal and conceptual, to the continuing hegemony of the Western canon.

Clearly there is an ambiguity to the avant-gardist conception of the "primitive." On the one side it is susceptible, as we have seen, to the charge that the avant-garde was merely inverting the stereotype of imperialism by seeing "primitive" art as more authentic and natural than the decadent cultures of the over-civilized world. But on the other side, there is a more positive sense of its being used as a lever to dislodge the conventions of the latter. It is this aspect that is the really significant feature of the avant-gardist take on indigenous art: the potential it had to offer other models of social being, other models of cultural practice, than those enshrined within the Western canon of philosophy, literature, and art. As Michael Richardson has put it, there was an increasing tendency on the part of the surrealists, especially as their engagement with the Caribbean grew during the 1940s, to move away from the more standard sense of the "primitive" and "towards a sense of locating new values."[34] This use of non-Western forms and conceptions of art dovetailed with the interest in the unconscious to sustain a dual critique of Eurocentric cultural convention, both psychic and social.

As James Clifford has established, there was considerable mutual fertilization during the 1930s between the ongoing surrealist program of provocative contestation in the arts and practices of radical ethnography. Just as in the field of psychiatry Jacques Lacan was influenced by his early encounters with surrealist interest in the unconscious, so in the field of ethnography some of those associated with Marcel Mauss had productive relations with the dissident surrealist grouping around Georges Bataille. Surrealism in this sense was much more than an art movement. The short-lived journal *Documents*, edited by Bataille, enacted a kind of unstable collage method which functioned across the conventional boundaries of science and art to generate new insights about diverse and frequently overlooked forms of life. As well as the surrealists themselves, contributors included Marcel Mauss, Carl Einstein, and the ethnographer Marcel Griaule who in 1931–1933 led the Mission Dakar-Djibouti which contributed photographs, documents, and objects to the studies of the Musée de l'Homme. The account of this exhibition, compiled by its "archivist," the sometime-surrealist Michel Leiris, was published in *Minotaure*, the successor to *Documents*, in 1934. Some of the unstable diversity of *Documents* is captured in its own subtitle, printed on the cover of the fourth edition in 1929 as *Archéologie, Beaux-Arts, Ethnographie, Variétés*. "*Variétés*" indicates an interest in the realm of popular culture; "archaeology" an interest in ancient civilizations; and "ethnography" an interest in different cultures. These dimensions of spatial and temporal difference, ranging across geography and history, and allied to a transgression of the traditional boundaries of high and low, all point to an on-going challenge to, and reconstitution of, what art could be; or, as it may perhaps be better put, what a continuing, valid cultural practice might be, divested of the mystifications that had accumulated around the normative concept of "Art." In Clifford's words, the "fragmentation and juxtaposition of cultural values" involved in such a hybrid aesthetic–ethnographic practice opens the possibility for a "disenchanted viewpoint" wherein "stable orders of collective meaning appear to be constructed, artificial, and indeed often ideological or repressive."[35]

Caribbean

The non-Western place where surrealism enjoyed its most fruitful interaction was the Caribbean. Already, in the early 1930s, a group of Caribbean students at the Sorbonne, inspired by surrealist example, had published a journal entitled *Légitime défense*,[36] which included a stinging condemnation of "the abominable system of constraints and restrictions, the extermination of love and the confinement of dream, generally known under the name of Western civilisation."[37] This publication in its turn seems to have helped inspire another group of black students, including Léopold Senghor and Aimé Césaire to found their own short-lived journal. The discussions taking place in these circles are held to have been the starting point for the theory of "negritude" which went on to play a key role in the articulation of a specifically black consciousness, and as such to have a profound impact on independence movements in Africa and elsewhere in the mid-twentieth century. Senghor tended to conceive negritude in essentialist terms, as an underlying quality uniting all Africans. Paradoxically, it therefore shared something with modernist notions of an essential underlying form, through its vitalism and its emphasis on ideas of fundamental harmony and rhythm. In the hands of Césaire, however, with his background in Martinique, the theory of a specifically black consciousness took on more of the collage-like qualities associated with the mixing of cultures characteristic of the Caribbean; and, indeed, of the avant-garde.[38]

Such ideas found expression in his long poem *Notebook of a Return to my Native Land*, initially composed in 1938 before his return from France to Martinique, but long worked on thereafter. They also informed the journal *Tropiques*, which first appeared there in 1941, edited by Césaire, his wife Suzanne, and colleague René Ménil. Writing in *Tropiques* in 1943, against the accusation that surrealism was dead, Suzanne Césaire proclaimed it to be "living, intensely and magnificently," stating that "voices that would not be what they are without surrealism" could now be heard "in New York, in Brazil, in Mexico, in Argentina, in Cuba, in Canada, in Algiers."[39] Later postcolonial writers are apt to play down the extent of surrealist influence on Césaire on the grounds that to concede it would be to render Césaire's conception of "negritude" subservient to European models, and thus to reinforce the very colonial stereotype to which it was addressed. But this seems largely anachronistic, driven by the agenda of late twentieth-century identity politics rather than an acknowledgment of a historical situation in which black and European cultural radicals mutually influenced each other.

In *Return to my Native Land*, Césaire begins by drawing a contrast between existence dominated by European values and the feelings he has for that "native land." The first version of the poem was composed in Europe before Césaire returned to Martinique in 1939, and although the descriptions are of colonized life in Fort-de-France, they are surely informed by his experience of the European city. Césaire writes of "this flat town … inert, panting under the geometric burden of its forever renascent cross … burdened, clipped, diminished, alienated from its own flora and fauna," its people a "strange crowd … which doesn't know how to be a crowd … taking part in nothing which expresses, asserts, frees itself in the broad daylight of its own land." This arid alienation is then contrasted with another situation where "not only the mouths are singing, but the hands, but the feet, but the buttocks and the genitals, and the whole creature liquefying into sound, voice and rhythm," a place where "everyone lives as in a dream, genuinely," a land "where everything is free and fraternal, my land." The protagonist then celebrates the Caribbean, praising "Haiti where negritude stood up for the first time and said it believed in its humanity," and moving on to an angry denunciation of the European monopolization of claims to culture and civilization. He invokes an alternative composed in equal amounts of an assertion of Caribbean energy and surrealist *amour fou*: "Words? Oh yes, words! Reason … To me it is the whip's corolla. Beauty, I call you petition of stone. But ah! The raucous smuggling of my laughter … Because we hate you, you and your reason, we invoke dementia praecox flamboyant madness tenacious cannibalism." Césaire paints a picture of his dawning perception that "Europe has been stuffing us with lies and bloating us with pestilence for centuries." The stage is set for a revolution, not just of values, but in the normative order of things: "We do have to start. Start what? The only thing in the world worth starting: the End of the world, for Heaven's sake … Accommodate me. I am not accommodating you!"[40] These words, emanating from the midnight of the century, prefigure the assertion of independence, the rupture with the order of imperialism – and, of course, with its cultural excuse, primitivism – that began to be realized in historical practice after the war.

The First World War and the Russian Revolution had a catalytic effect on the early twentieth-century European avant-garde. The capitalist crisis of the 1930s, the concomitant rise of fascism and the slide towards the Second World War played an equally important role in the vitalization of radical art outside its normative metropolitan heartlands. Among those who escaped from occupied Europe along with other avant-gardists including André Breton and Marcel Duchamp was the Cuban painter Wifredo Lam, who had been in Europe since the 1920s. After arriving in Martinique, where Césaire was already active, Breton and others went on to New York, while Lam returned to his native Cuba. It was there, in 1943, that he painted *The Jungle* (Figure 4.4). This large, ambitious painting, over two meters

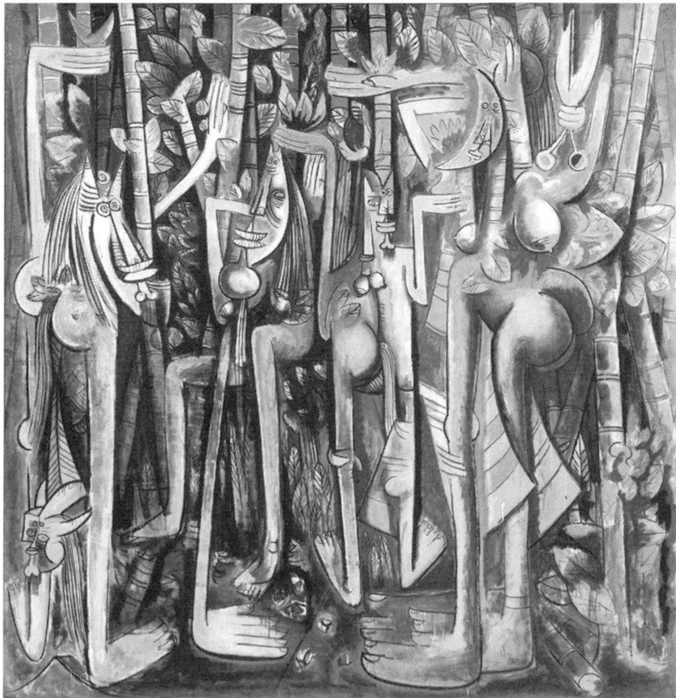

Figure 4.4 Wifredo Lam, *The Jungle*, 1943, gouache on paper mounted on canvas, 239 × 230 cm. Museum of Modern Art, New York, Inter-American Fund 1. © 2002 The Museum of Modern Art, New York / Scala, Florence. © ADAGP, Paris and DACS, London 2013.

square, has a claim to be one of the key moments when the avant-garde ceased to be solely European. For a long time, perhaps arguably since the craze for japonisme in the 1860s, 1870s, and 1880s, but definitely since the advent of fully fledged primitivism in the early twentieth century, the European avant-garde had drawn a significant part of its expressive resources from elsewhere. These resources were translated into the avant-garde mode; that is the point – the artists were not scientists, interested in excavating other ways of life in their own plenitude (even as some ethnographers became a little like artists in their method). This is well and good, it is the way the world works; picking something up and running with it is the way artistic change happens. Love and theft, as it has been said. But despite all that, the sense persists of the European avant-garde, notwithstanding its rhetoric of freedom, in effect plundering the colonies of their cultural capital in a way that paralleled the extraction of raw materials by empire proper. So long as the transaction was one-sided, it could hardly be otherwise. But in the work of figures such as Lam and Césaire, the current was reversed.

In the Anglophone world, something similar had also been happening in India in the interwar period, in the work of Rabindranath Tagore, Jamini Roy, and others. In an important historical development of reciprocal interchange, artists in a colonial situation were now seeking to take possession of the legacy of the European avant-garde – drawn itself, of course, in no small part from their heritage – and make it work for themselves.[41] Certainly, in works such as *The Jungle* by Lam, and Césaire's *Return to my Native Land*, there seems no question that a synthesis is being achieved between an expressive language drawn both from the European avant-garde, from Picasso, from surrealism, and from something else which is not European. Pierre Mabille, whose appreciation of Lam's work appeared in *Tropiques* in January 1945, suggests that as a boy in Cuba he imbibed not only the cultural influences of his Chinese father but more emphatically echoes of Africa. These came to him both personally, through his mother, herself the daughter of a slave brought from the Congo, and culturally through the persistence of Santería, the Afro-Cuban religion that emphasized the living relationship between people, nature, and the world of spirits, especially ancestors. In Mabille's imagination, the youthful Wifredo Lam heard "coming from the far reaches of the plain, the echoes of the ceremonies by which the blacks, his mother's blood brothers, asked the forces of the earth, through the power of the herbs, for beneficent support and the means to gratify their vengeance."[42] Lam subsequently travelled to Europe, eventually meeting Picasso and the Surrealists, among others, in Paris, and similarly absorbed the values of the avant-garde. After the exodus from Nazi-occupied Europe, Lam was forced to re-establish contact with the Tropics, a process which, on Mabille's account, was "not without serious difficulties."[43] It was out of this complex, forced re-engagement that *The Jungle* was made. Mabille compares *The Jungle* to Uccello's experiments in perspective.[44] What he seems to mean is that the work established a new paradigm. After a compelling, even disturbing, description of a Haitian voodoo ceremony – which he connects to André Breton's notion of "convulsive beauty" – Mabille makes the connection to Lam's work. In his view, for all its darker elements, which may well appear threatening to post-Enlightenment European regard, the ceremony is an acknowledgment of the power of the non-rational: that "in the life of the human organism, the individual's rhythm springs from the composition of the particular measures of its heart, its breath, its muscular movements, and other, deeper, unknown measures." For Mabille, this is fundamentally at odds with a European sensibility. He identifies such ceremony as breaking with a European model of center and periphery and instituting, instead, the sense of a "vast space, without gaps, all of whose parts act at the same time, all equally free and equally dependent on the totality, unaware of any external hierarchy and oriented toward their own destiny." For Mabille, this is the universe evoked by Lam's *Jungle*. And for him, the final point, the liberatory point, the point perhaps at which this vision intersects with revolutionary surrealism, is that this vision is in "total opposition" to "that other sinister jungle where a Führer, perched on a pedestal, awaits the departure, along the neo-classical colonnades of Berlin, of mechanised cohorts prepared, after destroying every living thing, for annihilation in their turn in the rigorous parallelism of endless cemeteries."[45]

The uncanny proximity of this nightmare to Marinetti's futurist dream seems to me to indicate not the need to evacuate avant-gardism as a kind of subspecies of "totalitarianism" but rather to sharpen its politics the better to be able to face a globalized capitalism that is presently far more deeply entrenched than it was in the early twentieth century. It is because of this that the attack on "reason" mounted by Césaire and the surrealists retains its power in an age when it might seem that corporate-sponsored irrationalism is the greatest threat to humanity. For theirs was less an attack on the mind as such than an attack on the stultification and restriction of the mind by the unchecked sway of instrumental reason. It is instrumental reason that works in tandem with engineered irrationalism to produce passivity, consumerism, and alienation – the very forces Césaire and Breton wrote so powerfully against. And by the same token it is an integrated sense of feeling and cognition, of the material and the psychic dimensions of reality, that continues to hold out the best prospect of resisting today's descendants of those the avant-garde opposed before. Identity politics helps nothing if it encourages historical amnesia.

Realisms

Having discussed both the mainstream modernism and the critical avant-gardes of the first half of the twentieth century in relation to the art of the wider world, I now want to consider a third aspect of Western art that is not often combined with them: realism. Despite increasingly sophisticated reflections on "modernist realism," there is a persistent tendency to regard more conventional forms of realism as conservative, and hence not really "modern" at all. But a full consideration of Western art's relations with the wider world must perforce address this widespread, though neglected tendency; the more so since it is little affected by the ideology of "primitivism," which so affects both modernism and the avant-garde.

An attenuated form of academic realism did of course persist in Europe even after the modern movement, in one manifestation or another, had become the normative art of the Western capitalist democracies. Even if the more radical tendencies of post-Cubist "modern art" were eschewed, some type of approach involving various kinds of departure from conventional illusionistic *mimesis* and intensified color – underpinned by a constellation of values involving self-expression, spontaneity, even decoration – was a major factor in conventional realism. The range runs from official portraiture to the kind of suburban domestic decoration found on sale in shopping malls and markets. It is not entirely without interest that one of the most popular of such works, for long the very synonym for kitsch, until it became a sort of curio in its own right, should have had an exotic subject: the many and varied forms taken by Tretchikoff's "green ladies": Chinese, Balinese, and the like (Figure 4.5). Along with tourist art, including, for example, various forms of "African" sculpture, such art has not been the subject of serious art historical discussion. It remains an open question as to whether it ought to be, or not.[46]

However, socially inflected realism was for long a significant force in Western modern art, exerting its own gravitational force back upon modernism and the avant-garde, not least at times of heightened political and social crisis. Especially in

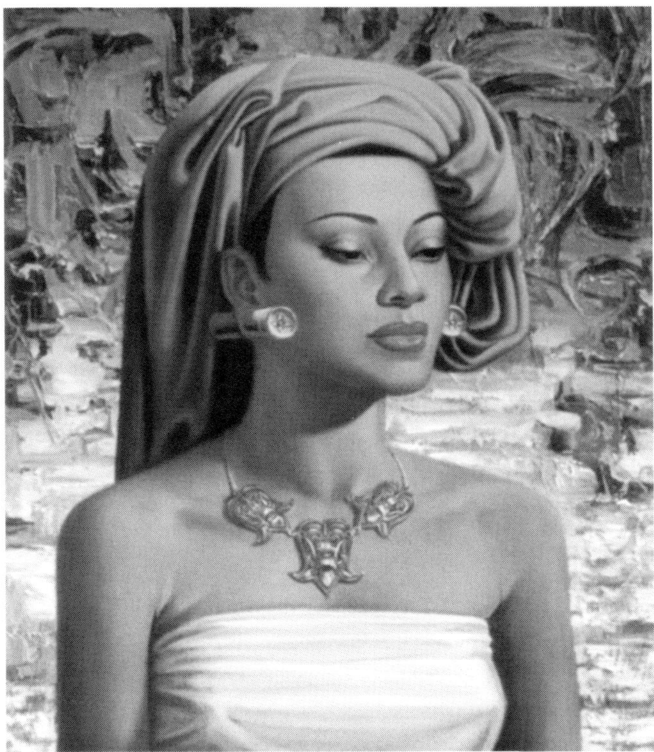

Figure 4.5 Vladimir Tretchikoff, *Balinese Girl*. Photo: www.vladimirtretchikoff.com.

its historically specific variant of socialist realism, that is as the official art form of the Soviet Union and its allies, such art and the values it embodies has carried considerable weight. It has still not, though, found its place in most accounts of modern art. Discussions tend to be self-contained, and often to treat the subject as a sort of dead end. Interwar social realism in the United States would be one such topic. So, too, a relatively short-lived interest in Soviet socialist realism that emerged after the end of the Cold War. As interesting as they may be in their own right, however, such histories have seldom, if ever, been integrated into a more complete picture of the arts of the world in the modern period.

Yet even in respect of the question being addressed here, such practices were by no means inconsequential. Given the sheer sway of the European empires, various forms of academic realism were pervasive in the colonial art schools which began to spring up throughout India, Africa, and the Caribbean. These practices certainly formed a foil for many of the attempts to forge innovative national schools in the wake of independence in the middle years of the century. Their history, however, like that of the popular and tourist art mentioned above, remains to be written.

There is also, though, a theoretical dimension to this omission. An exclusive focus on the modernism/avant-garde dyad and its "postmodernist" succession –

with the concomitant implication that "realism" is somehow not-modern, and as such is to be consigned to the margin – has a serious consequence. For to do so is to implicitly accept an account of the modernist avant-garde that loses sight of one of its key features, namely its own striving for realism. To accept a limited definition of "realism" as characterized by picturing, by illusionistic imitation, by mimesis, is to lose sight of the central importance to modernism of a sense of the materiality of signification. The sense that how one represents has a determining effect on what one can represent is close to the heart of the modernist enterprise considered in its broadest sense. Restructuring the language of representation to cope with the complexity of the modern reality requiring to be represented is precisely what was being articulated by Brecht when he argued that "reality changes; in order to represent it, modes of representation must also change."[47]

In the wake of cubism, the artistic revolution of the first part of the twentieth century substantially parted company with the political revolution. This fact has some claim to be the cultural–historical tragedy of the twentieth century. Certainly, orthodox socialism became artistically conservative; and orthodox modernism was prone to becoming if not overtly politically conservative then largely quietist. The artistic avant-garde that retained a revolutionary politics, and the revolutionary politics that retained an openness to advanced art, remained very much in a minority. The key period extends approximately from 1914–1917 through to 1968 and its aftermath.

Official socialist realism had a quite specific and circumscribed relationship to "non-Western" cultures. After the promulgation of socialist realism as the exclusive art form of the Soviet Union in the early 1930s the acceptable form and content of art was essentially overseen by politicians: the antithesis of the striving for artistic autonomy in the West. The governing maxim, promulgated at the 16th Party Congress in 1930 was that art should be "socialist in content, national in form."[48] This had an overall impact in ensuring that canons of lifelikeness, narrative legibility, and so forth be adhered to. However, the Soviet Union was made up of several constituent national republics. As a consequence, the further one traveled from Moscow, the more the sense of a permissible national inflection to the acceptable form of art came into play. As Matthew Cullerne Bown, one of the very few to make a serious study of such art, has noted, the notion of a "national form" "retained some real significance" in the republics of central Asia and the Transcaucasia.[49] Yet again, the notion of the "primitive" surfaces. In prerevolutionary Russian modernism, primitivism had played just as important a role as it did in Western Europe, influencing artists as eminent as Kandinsky, Larionov, and Goncharova.[50] In muted form, inflected very much towards the gay and decorative rather than the technically challenging, it continued as a current in the Eastern practice of socialist realism. Bown quotes the artist Aleksandr Volkov, a Russian active in Tashkent in Uzbekistan, as stating: "The painting of the East is built chiefly on the primitive, and on a painterly, decorative beginning." Volkov claimed to base his "depiction of man" on a quasi-geometric basis "elaborating works of primitive flatness."[51]

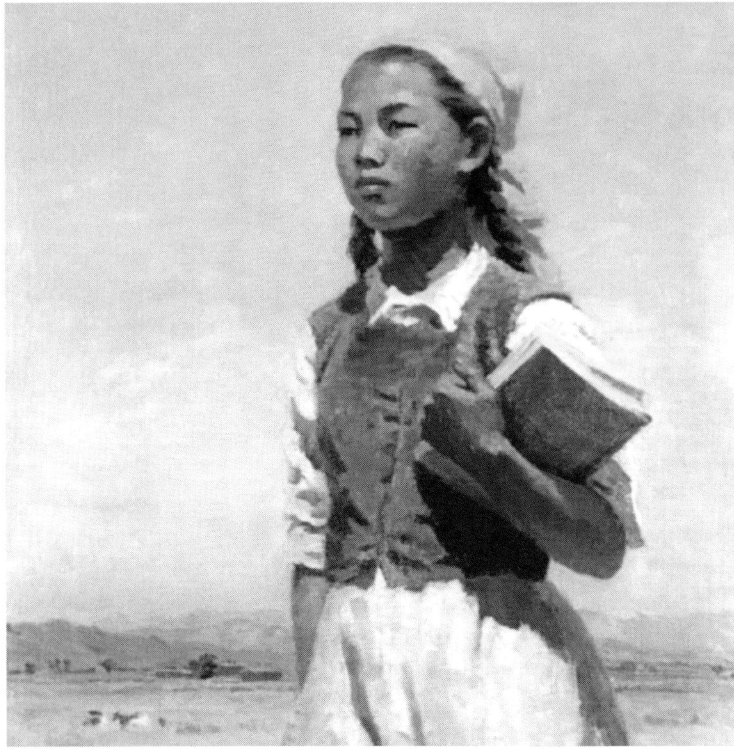

Figure 4.6 Semyon Chuikov, *Daughter of Soviet Kirgizia*, 1950, oil on canvas, 120 × 95 cm. State Tretyakov Gallery, Moscow. © RIA Novosti / Alamy.

This attempt to preserve a "decorative vitality" in the art of the Eastern republics of the Soviet Union had a resurgence after the end of the Second World War when the Stalinist state was once again trying to draw its different nationalities into a united whole. Images of workers on collective farms out on the steppe reading *Pravda* or of women driving modern farming machinery had national success. The icon of this school of Asian socialist realism was Semyon Chuikov's *Daughter of Soviet Kirgizia* of 1950 (Figure 4.6). It shows a Kirghiz schoolgirl carrying her books to school, in Bown's words, "the proud beneficiary of Soviet educational reforms."[52] The striking image, which manages to synthesize the sense of the individual girl's beginning in life and the dawning of a new period for her country, was widely reproduced in posters and books long afterwards as an exemplification of the promise of the soviet way of life.

Such an image, it goes almost without saying, stands in stark contrast to many of the presuppositions we have already encountered under the rubric of a contemporary commitment to a postcolonial identity politics. From this perspective, the Kirghiz schoolgirl is the victim of a form of imperialist oppression, her national identity being subsumed within that of the wider Soviet imperium; just as might be claimed of, say, a Nigerian or a Caribbean schoolgirl in the British Empire. The kinds of contradictions experienced by Aimé Césaire, Léopold Senghor, and others when encountering the reality of the educations they had won in metropolitan

France from Martinique and Senegal, may well have been waiting round the corner for the Kirghiz schoolgirl. Undoubtedly the Soviet image is propagandistic and far from the realities of life in the eastern provinces of the Russian empire. Yet in a world where Taliban militants in Afghanistan and Pakistan are murdering girls who express a desire to receive an education, the official advocacy of a modern secular education does not seem to be wholly devoid of virtue.

Mexico to Michigan

Socially inspired realism was not, of course, confined to the Soviet Union. Despite the silence that has tended to fall over it, the art was practiced all over the world for many decades, from China to Western Europe, in Africa and also in America. It is to America that I now want to turn to look briefly at one of the greatest of all socialist realist projects. It deserves attention in its own right, of course, for what it says about industrial work and modernity (not a common combination within the more normative work of the Western avant-garde). But it also has a claim on our present attention for the connections it draws between modern industry and more distant times and places, for the way it situates modernity in both a history and a geography (Figure 4.7).

In his Detroit mural commission, Diego Rivera is first and foremost representing modern industry.[53] But as we have already seen, in the analyses of Lenin and Trotsky, modern industrial production was inseparable from imperialism. How one conceives Rivera's project has, of course, a lot to do with how one conceives of modernity, and of the artist's role within modernity. Rivera seems to have conceived of his task in a Brechtian way; not that is, to illustrate particular bits of surface reality as such, or at least not solely that, but to reveal the hidden complexes of reality. To achieve this in the Detroit murals he drew on a complex mixture of realism and allegory of a kind seldom seen in modern art. Formalist, aestheticist modernism characteristically eschews allegory as an archaic mode, partly through its advocacy of a notion of psychic union between spectator and symbol but also because of the inescapable dimension of narrative present in allegory. For its part too, normative socialist realism seldom trades in allegory because its artificiality, the conscious layering of codes involved, tends to militate against the illusion of presence that is the central plank of such "realism": the suspension of disbelief that the subject is not really present.

Different parts of the Detroit scheme operate on different levels. In the upper registers, Rivera represents large allegorical figures representing the four "races" of humanity. This is perhaps the closest he comes to primitivism, when he represents idealized figures of each "race" according to skin color – white, yellow, brown, and black. These figures are rooted in Aztec and Toltec Chac Mool figures in the way the body and heads are shifted out of naturalistic positions (a feature which also contributed to their impact on the post-cubist modernist sculptor Henry Moore). They are

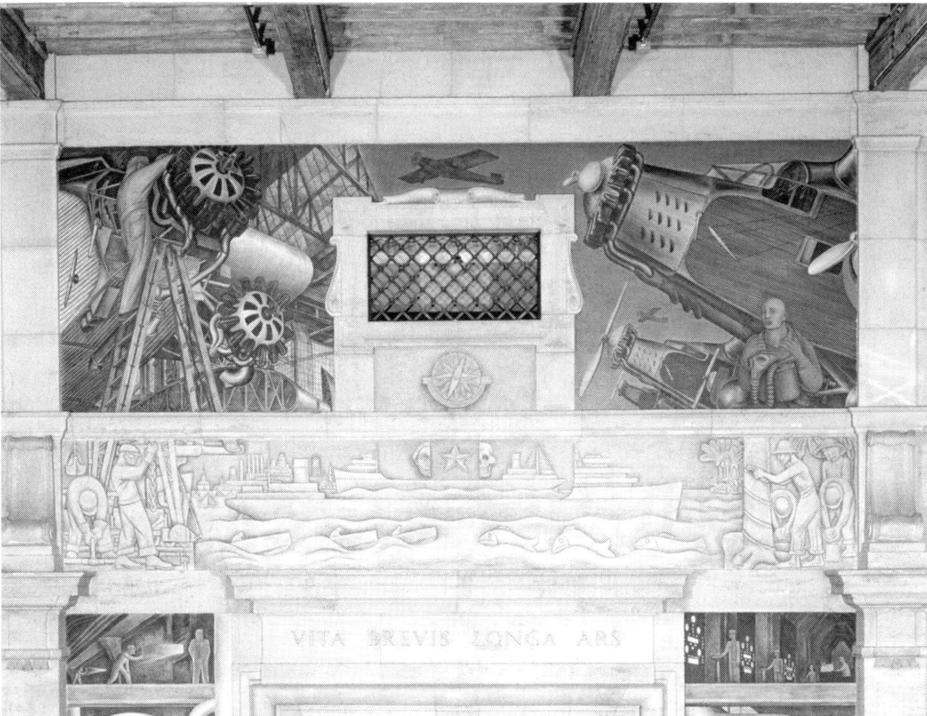

Figure 4.7 Diego Rivera, *Detroit Industry*, detail of west wall showing *Interdependence of North and South*, 1932–1933, fresco. Detroit Institute of Arts, USA / The Bridgeman Art Library. © 2013 Banco de México Diego Rivera Frida Kahlo Museums Trust, Mexico, D.F. / DACS.

furthermore knitted into a more complicated system of equivalents such that each embodies a particular mineral central to the production of iron, examples of which they clutch in their hands, as well as symbolizing all the races present in the Americas. Other registrations of pre-Columbian heritage can be traced in the anthropomorphized rendering of a major piece of modern factory technology – the stamping press – in the image of the Aztec deity Coatlicue. In doing this, Rivera is consciously plugging into an allegorical tradition descending from the European Renaissance, down through eighteenth-century Enlightenment figures such as Tiepolo, but which has been most often seen as unavailable to the modernist artist.

Lower down on the scheme, above the doorway in the west wall, Rivera combines allegorical elements with more straightforwardly realistic ones, again to emphasize the geographical integration of modern industrial production. A painted grisaille panel, intended to simulate sculptural relief, represents the interdependence of North and South America. Freight ships carry ore from the Minnesota Iron Range across the Great Lakes to Detroit. This is flanked on the left by an image of workers in a factory operating equipment used to unload ships. On the right, this is matched by the image of workers in a rubber plantation in South

America, the ultimately doomed "Fordlandia" project in Brazil. The waters in which the ships float are supposed to represent the confluence of the waters of Detroit and the Amazon. This complex interplay of archaic Mexican sources and Western technology, of the North and the South, and of the whole spectrum of humanity producing the modern world, adds up to hugely ambitious project; one in which Western art, for once, does aspire to address the wider world in something like its multifariousness and plenitude, not just its supposed primitive authenticity. That Rivera's work features comparatively little in contemporary accounts of artistic modernism says more about the priorities of those narratives than it does about Rivera's aspirations for a modern realism.

Rivera's whole scheme has a certain ambiguity to it, exemplified by the obvious fact of the communist artist representing the most developed form of capitalist production. But one of the subsidiary elements in the representation is unmistakably to emphasize the international nature of that modern production. In one sense this is a far cry from the overt criticism of imperialism contained in the surrealist opposition to the French Exposition Coloniale. But in another, at exactly the same historical moment in the late 1930s, Breton and Rivera were collaborating with the exiled Trotsky to produce the manifesto "Towards a Free Revolutionary Art." Condemning both the Stalinist regime in the Soviet Union as a "twilight of filth and blood" which had caused its intellectuals and artists to make "servility a career" if they wished to survive *and* the type of modernist "pure art" which in fact "generally serves the extremely impure ends of reaction" they jointly saw "the supreme task of art in our epoch" as being "to take part actively and consciously in the preparation of the revolution."[54] For all their great differences, the surrealist project and Rivera's uncommonly complex version of realism, not to mention Césaire's incendiary *Notebook*, shared this much.

Independence

Such ideas have a problematic status in Western art in the period after the Second World War. In the official accounting, they more or less disappeared, in the celebration of a "free art" centered around the achievement of aesthetic effect and conceived of as autonomous from wider social and political determination. It can be argued, to the contrary, that despite the widespread promulgation of the ideology of an autonomous art, the critical avant-garde never really did disappear. Formations as diverse as Cobra, the Situationist International, Nouveau Réalisme, and Fluxus, as well as minimal art, arte povera, and conceptual art all continued to make a form of realist address to the contradictions of modernity on both sides of the Atlantic and to resist the official culture of the "consumer society."

To the extent that that is true, it must, however, be conceded that despite the momentous changes taking place in the world during that period, in the quarter century from the late 1940s to the early 1970s, an overt address to a world beyond the West remained very much the exception rather than the rule in the heterogeneous practices of the "neo-avant-garde" and its successors. This is not to say that such work lacked a political dimension. But that dimension was, so to speak, compacted into the aesthetic radicalism, *into* the performances, *into* the rejection of the conventions of normative art, *into* the rejection of precious "fine art" materials and the production of finished objects for aesthetic delectation. This was leavened by a growing activism inspired among artists in the late 1960s by the Civil Rights movement and the Vietnam War, as witnessed by the activities of Daniel Buren and others in Paris around May 1968, and the formation of the Art Workers Coalition in New York in 1969. But there was little explicit registration in the work of art itself until the advent of an overtly politicized variant of conceptual art in the early 1970s.

The situation was different outside the West. The relationship of conditions in the world, often the world of newly independent states seeking a postcolonial identity, and the canonical Western tradition, was an inescapable concern for artists. In the case of Nigeria, a colonial art education had been implemented in 1927, largely as a result of pressure from Nigerian artists, especially Aina Onabolu, who had mastered a European illusionistic style of painting. The program of teaching inaugurated by the colonial administration under the leadership of the Englishman Kenneth Murray, however, combined familiarity with European techniques with an unexpected emphasis by Murray on the need to keep sight of African tradition. Nonetheless, teaching staffs remained almost exclusively European, and Western tradition and techniques featured prominently in the course content. By the late 1950s, diploma courses were being offered, and in 1958, in the atmosphere of heightened anticipation building towards the achievement of independence in 1960, an association was formed in the College of Arts, Science and Technology at Zaria in the north of the country dedicated to investigating the requirements for a new, national Nigerian art. As Ola Oloidi put it retrospectively in 1989, to the eight original members of the Zaria Art Society, art was "instrumental both in the winning of independence and in the de-colonialising of the country's environment and cultural heritage."[55]

In an account of the Zaria group, Bruce Onobrakpeya, one of the original members, has emphasized how the "colonial mentality" had eroded people's faith in their own history and traditions, and how as a consequence, art became a central factor in developing a new national consciousness. The key theory here, developed by Uche Okeke, was that of "Natural Synthesis." In Onobrakpeya's formulation, it had two dimensions. On the one hand, there was a re-encounter with tradition: "I seek to go backward in time to rediscover our time-tested values ... Going back in time is progressive rather than regressive." But for Onobrakpeya there was also a second dimension to the synthesis "which combines the best of our values with those from outside." The upshot was "a call to move forward, to explore frontiers with new techniques and ideas, and yet keep faith with the ancestors whose legacy they were reshaping and transforming."[56]

Modern art in the West has been an overwhelmingly secular phenomenon. It has often claimed a powerful spiritual dimension, though this has almost never

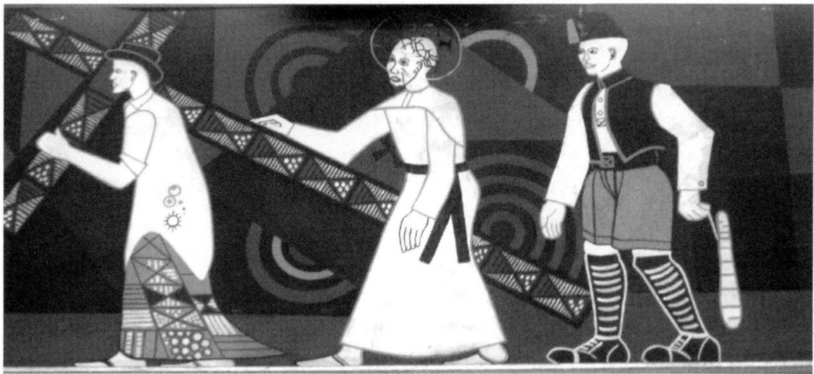

Figure 4.8 Bruce Onobrakpeya, detail from *Stations of the Cross* series, 1967, Church of St Paul, Ebute Metta, Nigeria. Photo: Paul Wood.

been articulated in terms of organized religion. Yet outside the West this is not at all the case. Some of the complexity of the synthesis involved can be seen in the commission, first framed in 1966, for Onobrakpeya to create a series of *Stations of the Cross* for the Church of St Paul in Ebute-Metta in Lagos (Figure 4.8). The museologist and art historian John Picton has subsequently referred to these paintings as the most important works of Nigerian art from the independence period. Completed in October 1967 the series consists of fourteen large panels, each approximately 10 feet wide (122 × 305 cm). Of these and other related series of the time made for both churches and secular sites such as Murtala Mohammed airport, Onobrakpeya has said "The implication of these art works and the use to which they have been addressed is that we have moved forwards towards modernity, carrying with us a spiritual and material identity, our past revealed through art, oral literature, history, folklore, legend and myths."[57]

The distinguishing features of the *Stations of the Cross* series seem to me to be twofold. Onobrakpeya has mentioned the early influence on him, via his pre-independence art education, of Western post-impressionists such as van Gogh and Gauguin. Here he synthesizes elements of their work, "bright with lines defining the flat areas of colours" with indigenous *adire* textiles employing "basic geometric patterns of lines, textures, and bold motifs which very often are abstract or stylised."[58] This synthesis of European avant-garde and native African forms is accompanied by a similar, extraordinary synthesis at the level of content. The traditional sequence of the fourteen "stations" is maintained, but the scenes are taken out of historical context in ancient Roman Palestine and put down in contemporary Africa. The immediately noticeable feature of the series is that Jesus and his followers are Africans, the women in particular wearing brightly colored traditional robes, and even the cross being decorated with geometric *adire* designs. But the real lesson is that Christ's persecutors are not representatives of the Roman Empire but of the British Empire. Interestingly, though, their agents as shown in the pictures are not Europeans. The figures in uniform, nailing Christ to the cross, beating him with truncheons, are Africans, collaborators with the imperial power. This seems to be an instance of what Onobrakpeya had in mind when he retrospectively described his work of this period, including not just these Christian motifs but illustrations accompanying stories by contemporary Yoruba authors including Amos Tutuola and Wole Soyinka as "a new type of realism."[59] As Onobrakpeya relates, at the time this unleashed a "storm of criticisms" from more conservatively minded commentators, but a decade later, at the time of the influential *Festac 77* celebration of Pan-African culture the church became virtually a place of pilgrimage for foreigners visiting Nigeria.[60] Again and again in African work, particularly of the independence period but persisting today, this sense of art having a social role very much in the tradition of early Saint-Simonian definitions of the avant-garde as helping to lead society forwards is evident. As such, this is a quality which marks both a connection with, as well as a significant distinction from, the avant-garde tradition as it developed in the Western metropolitan capitalist nations. It remains a pressing issue in the globalized art world of the present day, in which art all too often becomes a commodity within the culture of the spectacle rather than offering forms of resistance to it.

Since Mid-Century

The Neo-avant-garde

These developments in Nigeria, so briefly touched on here, were being replicated across Africa during the period of independence. As the old European empires retreated and the bi-polar world of the Cold War took over, the search for national cultural identity accompanied movements for political independence across Asia as well as Africa. For Bruce Onobrakpeya, "the struggle for cultural independence" was "more difficult than political independence," and crucial in moving towards the future.[61]

There was a ferment of debate as old ideas were challenged. To take only one example, Franz Fanon, in his address "On National Culture," delivered to the Second Congress of Black Artists and Writers in Rome in 1959, took a stance against "negritude" in favor of an emphatic focus on modernity. "The artist who has decided to illustrate the truths of the nation turns paradoxically towards the past and away from actual events … But the native intellectual who wishes to create an authentic work of art must realize that the truths of the nation are in the first place its realities."[62] The relationship between looking back and moving forwards, balancing the search for cultural heritage with an openness to the modern, exercised artists and writers across Asia, Africa, and the Caribbean.

As far as postwar Western modern art was concerned, these debates might as well have happened on the moon. It is not that Western artists were unaware of the wider world, but it is as if it had no channel into "advanced" art. The beginnings of international air travel and television meant that any sentient being probably had a more powerful sense of the contemporary world than at any time in history. McLuhan's notions of the "global village" and the centrality of the media were ubiquitous by the 1960s.[63] The enormous global photographic exhibition *The Family of Man* (subsequently to be the object of foundational criticism from the radical Left for its bourgeois humanist assumptions) was shown at the Museum of Modern Art in New York as early as 1955. Adorned with quotations from Homer, the Bible, William Blake, and James Joyce, as well as tellingly anonymous phrases from "Sioux Indian" and "Maori," the exhibition was premised on the belief that its five hundred photographs were "a mirror of the essential oneness of mankind throughout the world."[64] That was the problem. To use the language of a later period, the exhibition, and the belief system sustaining it, was oblivious to difference. To an extent, the emerging "neo-avant-garde" was aware of difference, albeit patchily. But even there it was their own differences that exercised them – difference from the dominant culture, difference of sexual orientation (sometimes), difference of gender (perhaps) – rather than cultural difference on a global scale. Along that dimension, something approximating to the normative belief system continued to hold sway.

When Jackson Pollock talked about the idea of an American painting being as absurd as the idea of an American mathematics he was voicing a belief that the problems of painting were the problems of painting wherever they were encountered.[65] The modernist value of the "autonomy" of art feeds into the same belief. So too does Clement Greenberg's remark that "aesthetic value is one, not many." These ideas of universal values are connected to the widespread essentialism of a belief in "human nature" enshrined in projects like The Family of Man but also present as the bedrock that was supposedly dug down to through theories like "primitivism." They were potentially at odds with the much more relativistic temper that was beginning to permeate the heterodox strand of culture labeled the "neo-avant-garde." In the profound conflicts of the late 1960s, cultural and political alike, this latter displaced the former as thoroughly as the former had marginalized its own opponents in the immediate postwar period. That is to say (to put names to faces, so to speak; or journalistic labels to mutable formations …), that once the "neo-avant-garde" mutated into something retrospectively dubbed "conceptualism" it displaced "modernism" as surely as modernism had remaindered the prewar avant-gardes.) In 1952, the once radical, Trotskyist-influenced *Partisan Review* ran a symposium called "Our Country and Our Culture." In their introduction the editors observed that "most writers no longer accept alienation as the artist's fate in America; on the contrary, they want very much to be a part of American life. More and more writers … now believe that their values, if they are to be realized at all, must be realized in America and in relation to the actuality of American life."[66]

Now this is not the sense of American culture that bore down on Allen Ginsberg and Jack Kerouac, on John Cage, maybe on Charlie Parker, nor on Robert Rauschenberg and Jasper Johns. But it shows what they were up against. How could you learn from the rest of the world when everything around you was built on the assumption that it was the business of the rest of the world to learn from *you*, when we are all supposed to be one big potentially happy family once all the bad guys with their guns have been engineered away and everyone can get on with shopping? How do you do that, how do you get out from under? This in the end is what subcultures are for. When you live with the knowledge that the big You is not you at all, you learn to recognize the signs that hint there might be others who feel the same way. For most of the fifties and sixties, Western culture built on Western power was just so *big* that even if you wanted nothing to do with it, you somehow had to tunnel your little nothing underneath all of its big Somethings. You know what I mean …

Relatively little of the wider world comes through into the post-Second World War "neo-avant-garde" on either side of the Atlantic before 1960. Primitivism had been done to death. The idea had lost almost all its historical traction in a world of independent states. Whatever else figures like Mao, Nehru, Nkhruma, Ho Chi Minh, and Sukharno might have meant, they did not signify primitive authenticity. What did retain some currency in the face of the relentless materialism of the American dream was a sense of spiritual refusal. Sometimes this could gain support from alternative strands within the European tradition, as in the case of Ginsberg's visions of William Blake. But the strongest impact on the nascent American counterculture came from the other direction, from across the Pacific, from a continuing sense of the oriental as "Other." The war with Japan and then the Korean War had had the effect of bringing many American servicemen into contact with a very different culture, and this seeped into America when they came home. Gary Snyder had been in Japan in the late 1940s; Sol LeWitt was in Japan and Korea as a soldier in the early fifties. Figures as dissimilar as Jack Kerouac and John Cage were influenced in their thinking by the values they encountered in Zen Buddhism in the late 1940s. Cage was also interested in Indian philosophy and cited the work of Coomaraswamy. None of this was particularly to do with the historical contradictions being experienced by modern Japan or China or India. But once again Western artists were developing the potential for resistance out of their translations from the Orient.

In contrast to the view of art that would distinguish it from all sorts of manifestations of non-art, from politically inspired work to literary narrative to mass culture, and that held a purified aesthetic value to be paramount, Cage had become committed to the idea that "no value judgements are possible because nothing is better than anything else. Art should not be different from life, but an act within life."[67] The point where the acceptance of chance derived from the *I Ching* in Cage's work fused with the slightly different Dadaist acceptance of chance channeled through Marcel Duchamp proved a powerful one for the new avant-garde. In "A Child's History of Fluxus," Dick Higgins wrote of a time "long, long ago, back when the world was young – that is, sometime around the year 1958" when certain artists recognized that "coffee cups can be more beautiful than fancy sculptures," that "the sloshing of my foot in my wet boots sounds more beautiful than fancy organ music." And they "began to ask questions."[68] Around the same time, Allan Kaprow was making the claim that "the young artist of today need no longer say 'I am a painter' or 'a poet' or 'a dancer.' He is simply an 'artist.' All of life will be open to him."[69] What came more and more to be at issue in the art of the 1960s was what that "all of" might mean – in terms of the "when" and the "where" as well as the "what" that might get made and still be art.

A second factor which laid the groundwork for a different order of art to emerge was itself of a very different kind: not the result of heterodox artists seeking alternatives to their own dominant culture but of the global impact of that dominant culture itself. The sheer reach of American power after the Second World War meant that as well as *Coca-Cola*™ and cars, the culture was exported too; and the culture included Art. Both actual exhibitions, as part of a calculated series of interventions designed to export the image of the Free World, and a burgeoning art press, meant that all sorts of new art were being seen more widely than ever before. The impact of this was double-sided. On the one hand it meant that various local clones of American painting and sculpture came into existence in places as far apart as Europe and Australia. On the other hand, it spread the impact of the emergent, heterogeneous, counter-hegemonic avant-garde far and wide too. The former issued in the problem of what came to be called "provincialism." The latter, however, generated a multifarious international avant-garde that for the first time was not just an echo of innovations in the West. Foremost among these were the *Gutai* group, active in Japan from the mid-1950s. But in another manifestation of the cunning of history, the extension of the writ of American power into Europe, especially defeated Germany, meant that the post-Nazi cultural vacuum there was filled not merely by modernist painting but by a healthy dose of the *Fluxus* virus. It is ironic that Germany and Japan, the two countries whose cultural traditions were most devastated by defeat in the world war, should have become hosts to significant manifestations of the counterculture.

By the early 1960s, Yoko Ono from Japan and Nam June Paik from Korea were established figures in Fluxus performances in Europe and America. In often obscure and highly oblique ways, the sense of a wider world which meant something other than materialism and technological progress was making itself felt in the avant-garde. Even so, these remained minority outcrops *alongside* the more widespread critiques of those values emanating from within their heartlands. These latter included some of the less celebratory examples of a "Pop" sensibility by artists as diverse as Warhol and Oldenberg, Hamilton and Paolozzi. The mass of this work focused on the trappings of the consumer society. However, one critical work built on this basis with great economy of means to effectively draw a line under the whole exhausted ideology of primitivism. The French "Nouveau Réalisme" group was formed in 1960, which places it on an approximate timeline with Pop art in American and Britain and other slightly earlier manifestations such as the Independent Group and Rauschenberg's Combines, in taking its critical

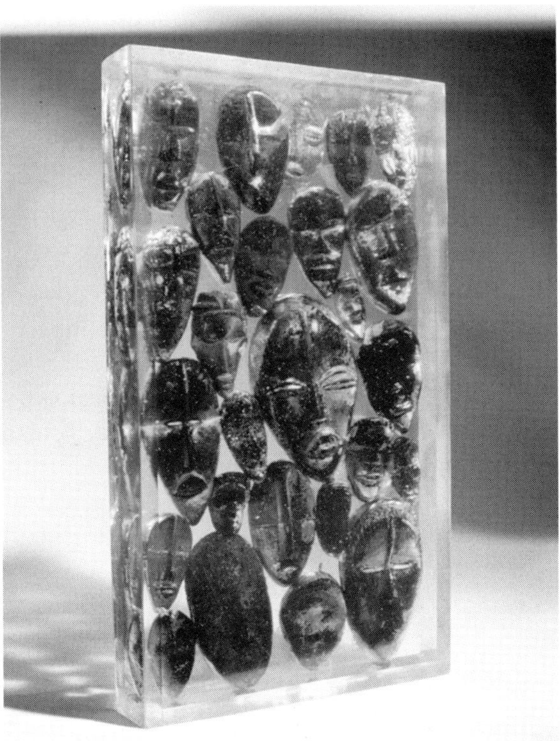

Figure 4.9 Arman, *Accumulation of Souls*, 1972, accumulation of African wood masks embedded in polyester resin, 52 × 29 × 6.5 cm (20½ × 11⅜ × 2½ in). Image courtesy of the Arman Studio Archives New York.

stance in the "gap between art and life." Founder member Arman's tactic was to set overlooked items from the undergrowth of popular culture in slabs of plastic resin. This allowed him to make monuments to ephemera as well as (continuing the Dada tradition noted earlier in the work of Hannah Höch) to draw attention to phenomena such as the construction of femininity in the postwar consumer society. Rather as Höch had done earlier in her ethnographic museum series, picking up on the strange connections between constructions of gender and ethnicity, Arman went on in 1972 to produce the striking *Accumulation of Souls* (Figure 4.9). A set of Dan masks from Africa is memorialized in Arman's trademark plastic. The shift, of course, is that the masks are now less authentic specimens of primitive culture, uncanny evocations of the spirit world, than tokens of the tourist trade. The commodification of ethnicity has taken its place among all the other commodifications that make up modern Western culture. By this time, primitivism, always an ideology, now really was a fraud.

More overtly exotic, and to that extent perhaps less convincing, manifestations of the pressure of the wider world on the borders of the Western avant-garde included Joseph Beuys' *Siberian Symphony* of 1963 in which allegorized tokens of East and

West were unified after a symbolically difficult journey over hard ground. There was, however, nothing obscure or oblique about the Fluxus Manifesto authored by George Maciunas in 1963: "Purge the world of bourgeois sickness, 'intellectual', professional and commercialised culture. Purge the world of dead art, imitation, artificial art, abstract art, illusionistic art … Purge the world of 'Europanism'!"[70]

Across the Atlantic

It would be bizarre not to expect that the Second World War and its aftermath signaled some kind of caesura in European culture's relations with the rest of the world. The barbarism it unleashed holed Europe's claim to civilization below the waterline. For their own part, many advanced American artists were themselves tired of genuflecting to Europe. Not everyone agreed with Clement Greenberg, but he was not wrong when he said that the center of gravity of Western culture shifted after the war. Henceforth, the sense of "Western" art tended to signify America first and the European tradition as something that was now in the past, a kind of ancestor. At least that was the prevailing ideology. The critical edge of European art in the postwar period, not least the continuation of a strong leftist tradition, told a different story. But it was a story that remained largely untold and only patchily understood in the long period of dominance exercised by both American art and American art history that lasted at least until the end of the postwar boom in the mid-1970s.

Nonetheless, there is a gathering sense that by the mid-1960s change was happening. Histories of contemporary art tend to trace themselves back to that moment, to the crisis of canonical modernism that by the end of that decade had become indisputable. A sense of the challenge to established boundaries, a sense that art could be made of anything, indeed *had to be*, if it was to leave its ivory tower and achieve significance in a changing world, was widespread. It was a moment when everything seemed possible, to an almost Wordsworthian extent: "Bliss was it in that dawn to be alive / But to be young was very heaven." The sense of possibility that Wordsworth read into the French Revolution now lived again in the cultural revolution of the 1960s. It definitely seemed so if you were an artist or an art student in certain metropolitan centers in Western Europe and North America. As we have seen, it also seemed to be so if you were an artist in a newly independent country in what was now called the Third World. But the two senses of possibility had little to do with each other. And yet, in the former case, a sense of "the world" (hinted at in a phrase such as Kaprow's "all of life") really did play a part in that sense of release: a sense of the world that promised a reach beyond the traditional centers of high culture, a sense of the world that opened, not so much into contemporary history with all its conflicts and tragedy as into much more abstract stretches of space and time.

George Kubler's *The Shape of Time* was published in 1962.[71] It is in some ways an odd book. Many of its references are to dated, prewar European scholarship, much of it German-language, in fields of anthropology, ethnography, and even mathematics. In a different register, whole passages are touched by the same sensibility that fed into McLuhan, a plethora of references to switches and series and circuits that speak to the impact of contemporary electronics technology, cybernetics, and systems theory. The result was a kind of mystical structuralism, and it had an impact on the avant-garde. Ad Reinhardt knew of it from its first publication. The "marathon slide projections" lasting up to three hours, described by Michael Corris, owed much to Kubler's ideas about form-series. Held at The Club in New York, they involved quickfire formally organized sprints through "up to two thousand slides of art, artefacts or architecture drawn from diverse cultural traditions," many of them taken during his travels in South East Asia. As Corris puts it, "it was as if Reinhardt had conceived of a film of the visual culture of the world and projected it one frame at a time."[72] Robert Morris explicitly referenced the same ideas in his Masters' thesis on "form-classes" in Brancusi's sculpture before turning to address the questions of context that Kubler had sidelined. The book also stands behind Robert Smithson's early breakouts from the confines of the gallery. Kubler was an archaeologist of pre-Columbian Mexico. Smithson's *Incidents of Mirror-Travel in Yucatan* (itself an allusion to John L. Stephens' *Incidents of Travel in Yucatan* of the 1840s) speak to an interest that Kubler's treatment must have stimulated: the point where an encounter with the archaic, fertilized by an encounter with high-powered modern theory, produced the lightning-flash of a new art. You didn't even have to read Kubler all the way through. His first sentence must have stimulated sensibilities open to … well, open to opening. Rosalind Krauss later postulated the concept of the "expanded field" to cope with developments in post-minimalist sculpture. Yet brilliant as this is, it has the air of codifying something that, when it happened, must have had more of the feel of a leap into the air.

Kubler wrote: "Let us suppose that the idea of art can be expanded to embrace the whole range of man-made things, including all tools and writing in addition to the useless, beautiful and poetic things of the world." He continued: "By this view the universe of man-made things simply coincides with the history of art."[73] At a stroke Kubler seemed to have thrown open the doors of academic art history, with its exclusive focus on the Western canon and its obsession with style and biography, and to have opened a vista that stretched all around the world as well as back into deep time. Earlier we noticed how Carl Einstein's formalism shared more with the revolutionary Russian theorists of literary form than it did with the Bloomsbury formalism of Fry and Bell. Kubler's theory was formalist too. And it shared more with contemporary French structuralism than it did with the restrictive formalism of critics like Clement Greenberg that had come to stand in as a sort of label for the actually much more complex project of American modernist art. Kubler's theory involved the working-out of "form-classes." Because of a limited variety of options open to human beings working in particular times and places (in this Kubler differed from the relativists who picked his ideas up and ran with them, and who seem to believe that cultural practice is infinitely malleable), these form series would be worked out over a period, and other options developed. But they could also, so to speak, leap across time. If suitable conditions recurred similar solutions to problems could happen without any intervening causal chain.[74]

It was this kind of possibility that led Robert Morris, then working on his own outdoor earthworks in the early 1970s, to travel to South America and produce the photo-essay "Aligned with Nazca," published in *Artforum* in 1975.[75] The sense of getting away from conventional figure-ground relationships, stimulated by Ehrenzweig's notion of "de-differentiated vision," which had influenced his earlier anti-form pieces consisting of undifferentiated stuff strewn across the gallery floor, now took on vast scale. The sense of constraints on art that had finally crippled modernism and had been gestured against by Fluxus panegyrics to the ordinary, or Kaprow's invocation of 42nd Street as art, were now well and truly transcended. In Morris' view, "Western art" consisted of sets of objects requiring perceptual encounters. Both Renaissance art with its linear perspectival space and impressionist art with its aerial space, for all their differences "were concerned with representing space on a vertical plane. "All twentieth century art" seemed to follow suit. "We expect to encounter objects which will block our vision at relatively close range. Seeing is directed straight out, 90 degrees to the wall or at an object never far from a wall. The pervasive spatial context is one of room space with its strongly accentuated divisions between vertical and horizontal."

It is within such a "context for vision" that the various dichotomies characterizing the Western tradition, "between flat and three-dimensional, marking and making, painting and sculpture" have signified. For Morris, all that was now past. In his view, beginning with the neo-avant-garde of the 1950s a new "episteme" – a term derived from Foucault – had been developing for art, which in its turn had evolved: from a more "objective" space involving "basic rationalised information systems" to "another type of art" whose "mode is not that of the logical icon" but "it is the space of the self which the latter work explores." If by the former Morris means the "minimalist" installation and by the latter he means the kinds of land art practiced by himself, Smithson, and Richard Serra, he seems to be plotting a shift in visual art comparable to the transformation in thought from structuralism to post-structuralism. In conformity with Kubler's thesis about form-series jumping across time, the preoccupations of Morris and his contemporaries making the new art of the seventies found echoes in the Nazca lines in the Peruvian desert, made between 500 BCE and 500 CE. "What one sees on the ground at Nazca has little to do with seeing objects. For if in the urban context space is merely the absence of objects, at Nazca space as distance is rendered visible." For Morris, "whatever the intentions of these forms on the desert, they are morphically related to certain arts we see today."

In such works, as well as Smithson's own slightly earlier *Spiral Jetty*, with their mix of text and image, object and film, their invocations of contemporary theory and ancient myth, the world had come pouring back in to modern Western art. Rosalind Krauss depicted the ideology of modernism as like a series of rooms, *en filade*. Within each room "the individual artist explored, to the limits of his experience and his formal intelligence, the separate constituents of his medium." The result of this was "to open simultaneously the door to the next space, and close out access to the one behind him."[76] The situation of the early 1970s was categorically different. The effect was as if all the doors had simultaneously been blown off and the whole building was now floating on the world's ocean like an ark. Krauss, and many others, went on to call it postmodernism.

"Provincialism"

And yet … and yet … a more critically minded minority were able to perceive the closures which framed this apparently open situation, the underlying currents that determined the flows of this apparently open ocean. In the catalog to Documenta 5, Robert Smithson wrote of a pervasive "cultural confinement." The new avant-garde no less than the old one was an "apparatus." "Some artists imagine they've got a hold on this apparatus, which in fact has got a hold on them. As a result, they end up supporting a cultural prison that is out of their control." Smithson's conclusion, which had profound implications for the new art supposedly liberated from the constraints of modernism, was that "it would be better to disclose confinement rather than make illusions of freedom."[77]

This perception was most fully developed in debates within the New York wing of the Art & Language group, particularly in the contribution of the Australian Ian Burn. In "The Art Market: Affluence and Degradation," published in the mainstream journal *Artforum*, Burn recognized that "while we've been admiring our navels, we have been capitalized and marketed." Burn and others recognized that the newly internationalized art world was a subset of the international capitalist market economy; and it was that market system which increasingly determined the art produced within it, rather than the other way round. Furthermore, this was a system with many different layers: "art criticism, the trade journals, galleries and museums, art schools" all played their part in its reproduction, perhaps most vividly in the "the network of modern art museums which have sprung up like automobile salesrooms throughout the Western world." Taken together, all contributed to the production of an international high culture with its center in New York. The critical bottom line for Burn was that this system, with its rhetoric of free expression and continual innovation, was actually symptomatic of a profoundly *un*equal system of international relations. "The emergence of the international art market along its present lines has been incontestably an arm of a necessary expansion of the whole U.S. neocapitalistic system and consolidation of marketing areas after the Second World War." In the view of its sponsors, this probably felt like a good thing, bringing prosperity and freedom to the world. For Burn and other critics, it was imperialism "in its most despicable state," wherein the "specific character and subjectivity of any one place" was overridden by "New York corporate uniformity."[78]

How to respond to this situation was the key thing. The majority carried on with business as usual. Some, including another Australian within the Art & Language ambit, Terry Smith, expressed a rather toned-down version of Burn's critique of the American-dominated system while hoping that something more egalitarian might emerge: "we should look to the benefits that would accrue to all from acting in a way which projects our own uncertainties and fallibilities," and "value the differences" between variant cultural situations.[79] Burn was less sanguine, and feared that nothing less than "a collapse in the economic structure of this society" would have "any substantial effect on the careening superstructure of modern American art."[80] The eventual global triumph of capitalism after the end of the Cold War led to a situation superficially resembling Smith's vision of difference; albeit with the defining qualification that rather than representing a form of muted dissent from capitalist market relations it stood as the apotheosis of them. Many years before, Clement Greenberg had written that "someday it will have to be told" how the dissenting Trotskyism of the 1930s mutated into the triumphant art for art's sake of American modernism in the postwar period.[81] A similar account remains to be given of how certain radical stances of the 1970s transformed themselves into the cultural management of the global contemporary in the early years of the twenty-first century. Ian Burn, truer to the critical avant-garde tradition from which he wrote, had no such ameliorative vision of an egalitarian art world of the future. Regarding conceptual art as no more than a "transitional practice," Burn for some time turned away from art altogether and served in a more collectively grounded radical cultural practice dedicated to the production of real political change in his native Australia.

These considerations may appear to be, at best, footnotes to the narrative of Western art's changing relationship to the wider world as it entered a new phase in the second half of the twentieth century. They are not. They mark a branching point of considerable significance. The avant-garde tradition had been the place where imperialism had been most critically addressed, and where, in the earlier part of the century, primitivism, the dominant ideology whereby Western art related to the wider world, had been partially contested. From the mid-1970s onwards, the prospect of a radical transformation of the capitalist mode of production, which had underpinned so much avant-garde art, began to recede. In the last quarter of the twentieth century, and with gathering pace after the end of the Cold War, the capitalist system enjoyed a period of unparalleled dominance, ideological as well as economic and political. Even the onset of deep crisis in that system towards the end of the first decade of the twenty-first century has done little to foster the development of credible alternatives. Within that overarching mode, the system of art production has itself become globalized since 1989. This *is* the contemporary situation, and how we got to it, what have been the gains, and what have been the losses, matters. The distinction between "conceptual art" and "conceptualism" bears upon all of this.

Conceptual Art and Conceptualism

The kinds of artwork discussed in the foregoing sections, which go beyond the conventional boundaries of painting and sculpture that have been so central to the Western tradition of art, are now often collectively referred to under the rubric "conceptualism." It is an open question to what extent they can be seen as building upon an earlier tradition of critical avant-garde activity. To put it briefly, in the sense that they mix media and transgress conventional discrete boundaries, both of media and genre, they probably can. In the sense that they are now themselves the globally dominant category of art practice and not a heterodox or oppositional subculture, they probably shouldn't be. However that question is ultimately decided, the fact that such work is widely regarded as standing at the origin of the "contemporary" formation of art means that how it is characterized is a matter of some significance. "Contemporary art" annexes to itself such a panoply of claims for its relevance to the world today, and is itself such an enormous global enterprise with outlets scattered across the entire world, that accounting for what it is and where it comes from is no small matter.

The point at issue is partly that at that time, between the mid-1960s and the mid-1970s, the name "conceptual art" was not the catch-all it has since become. It was one element in a mosaic of practices which attracted rather weak descriptions such as "The New Art" or "The New Avant-Garde."[82] The defining exhibition of the new work was *When Attitudes Become Form*, shown in Switzerland, Germany, and London in 1969. Others included *Op Losse Schroeven* in Holland and, in New York, *Information*. The displays included land art, performance, installation, works using still photography, early video technology, and light, as well as texts. Conceptual art as such tended to be critical of most of these, regarding them, despite the widespread protestations of originality accompanying them, as art world business-as-usual. In its early manifestation, conceptual art drew on analytical philosophy for its critique of modernism and the new avant-garde alike. By the early- to mid-1970s it had turned to Marxism for a critique of the whole institution of art in capitalist society. Given all of this, the question of whether conceptual art was a limited historical episode or whether it can be regarded as something like the hinge between the past and the present is an important one for contemporary art history.

Conceptual art was a long time ago. Yet if conceptual art itself is old, so too are art historical questions about it. They have been raised in both writings and exhibitions. The first major, explicit retrospect on conceptual art came in 1989.

L'art conceptuel: une perspective was shown at the Musée d'Art Moderne in Paris in 1989. The art surveyed in *L'art conceptuel* was quite restricted, and there is a sense in which it could hardly have been otherwise at that time. On a par with 1945 and 1968, 1989 was a charged moment, and with hindsight it can be seen that this exhibition was doing its looking back from within a perspective that was not to last unchallenged for much longer. All the artists represented had been active in the North Atlantic art worlds of the 1960s and 1970s. Only On Kawara, born in Japan, forms a partial exception; but it is partial because his practice was substantially performed across that same transatlantic art world. Another retrospective exhibition followed in 1995. More influential, undoubtedly because it was staged in America and featured the writing of American commentators, *Reconsidering the Object of Art* had a slightly broader remit in terms of the range of art included but not much difference as regards its geography.

Subsequently, there was a positive flurry of retrospective publications on conceptual art around the turn of the century. Anne Rorimer, one of the co-curators of *Reconsidering the Object of Art*, published *New Art in the 60s and 70s*, subtitled *Redefining Reality* in 2001.The book, which achieved considerable status, went over the same basic ground again. All the work discussed emanated from the North American and European transatlantic art world of the period. Newman and Bird's *Rewriting Conceptual Art* was published in 1999. Alberro and Stimson's *Conceptual Art: A Critical Anthology* appeared in 1999. Osborne's large-format survey *Conceptual Art* came out in 2002. My own short study *Conceptual Art* was published in 2002 in the Tate's "Movements in Modern Art" series – evidence of canonicity were it needed – taking its place alongside cubism, expressionism, futurism, pop art, and so on in the Great Chain of Being of the modern Western avant-garde. In each of these treatments an expanded remit can be noted. In addition to the established purview of the Western European and North American avant-gardes, developments in South America, Australia, and Eastern Europe were accorded relatively brief, though significant treatment. But all of this was at bottom redrawing a few of the boundaries of an already well-established map.

The exception to this trend, and in retrospect it was a defining exception, appeared in 1999/2000 in the form of the exhibition *Global Conceptualism* and its accompanying catalog, which bore the subtitle *Points of Origin 1950s – 1980s*. The exhibition originated and was shown only in the United States, and this is telling. But as its title claimed, in a more thoroughgoing fashion than any of the other treatments here mentioned, it sought to redraw the whole map of conceptual art. Using scholars drawn from the areas covered, it encompassed practices in east Asia, including China, Taiwan, Korea, and elsewhere as well as in Japan and Australasia; Eastern Europe and the Soviet Union as well as Western Europe; South America as well as North America; and Africa. And it conferred approximately equal coverage on each area, not privileging North America and Western Europe. Of equal importance, though, in addition to the geographically expanded catchment, there was also a significant theoretical shift. The practices in question are named not as "conceptual art" but as "conceptualism." The difference is important. The idea of "conceptualism" opened up a field far broader than that encompassed not only by *L'art conceptuel* but also by surveys of the art of the 1960s and 1970s, such as Rorimer's *Redefining Reality*.

By 2003, the message of a global conceptualism was driven well and truly home in the self-consciously and ironically titled *How Latitudes Became Form* – again shown only in the United States but aspiring to investigate "the cultural formation of the global subject" and to question "the cultural dominance of Western art and civilization." For participants in the roundtable discussion recorded in the catalog, the original *Attitudes* show of 1969 had been important because it marked "the beginning of [a new phase of] international exhibitions," as well as supposedly embodying some of the spirit of the broader cultural and political radicalism associated with 1968.[83] Less positively, however, it was also regarded as having marked "the peak of Eurocentrism."[84] The most memorable thing about this exhibition was probably its title, but the attitude it evoked was one of increasing significance.

This attitude can be traced, at least for convenience's sake, to 1989. *L'art conceptuel* offered a retrospect on conceptual art. The exhibition *Magiciens de la terre*, also shown in Paris in the same year, represented in one sense at least an impulse quite at odds with conceptual art. The mystical implications of the title, the exoticism with which it seemed to treat the non-Western world, and the romantic valorization of artists as "magicians," all flew in the face of the skepticism and criticality associated with conceptual art and its politicized aftermath. Benjamin Buchloh's interview with the curator Jean-Hubert Martin remains the *locus classicus* of a materialist interrogation of the exhibition's premise.[85]

But for all its faults, *Magiciens de la terre* involved the recognition of something that was not even in the remit of *L'art conceptuel*. Namely that both colonialism and the Cold War were over and globalization was about to take center stage. However globalization is to be conceptualized, positively as the Americans originally did, negatively as most of its victims do now, as an opportunity for multiculturalism or the companion of a new imperialism, there is one thing it has incontrovertibly achieved: it has rendered Eurocentrism parochial. For better or for worse, the *Global Conceptualism* exhibition of 1999/2000 marks the point at which conceptual art was brought into conjunction with the legacy of *Magiciens de la terre*.

It is worth recalling at this point Anne Rorimer's conclusions to her discussion of the "New art of the 60s and 70s" – a discussion which referred exclusively (apart from On Kawara) to American and European art of that period. For her, and indeed for many postmodernist critics and historians, such art had been a key part of a project of "destroying illusion in all of its possible manifestations," offering continuingly relevant "models of resistance to a status quo."[86] This was certainly intended as a reference to an artistic status quo – it goes almost without saying that it evokes Greenbergian modernism. But there is an equally clear sense of a wider culture of "illusion" standing behind this – the implication of museum authorities in class and state power, in ethnic and gender-based discrimination.

Rorimer's sense of conceptualism in a broad sense being part of a wider deconstruction of "illusion," of an "assault on deception," where that "deception" is identified with myths of expressive authorship, a wilful disavowal of framing contexts under the notion of autonomy, and an unwonted restriction on the means and methods available to art under the rubric of medium-specificity, constitutes a powerful roster of what mattered in the art of the 1960s and 1970s. But claims of this sort about the conceptual avant-garde being part of a culture of "resistance to the status quo" are put under tension when they are situated next to those other types of claim made in the *Latitudes* catalog about conceptualism also being part of the "cultural dominance of western art and civilisation" and a partial marker of Eurocentrism. The two claims certainly do not amount to the same thing. Something needs disentangling here.

To be fair to Rorimer, it must be recognized that she twice makes references to issues reaching beyond the central North American / West European purview of her study. In both cases these concern the work of European artists. In the early 1970s, Marcel Broodthaers had mounted various installations dedicated to revealing the way classificatory systems frame the meanings that they circulate; the principal such system with which he was concerned being the museum. In Rorimer's account, his *Jardin d'hiver* of 1974 developed this theme by extending it to the classificatory system of museums bearing on the institution of colonialism, which had of course a special resonance in Belgium because of the Congo. Through Broodthaers' use of various items, including potted palms and old prints showing exotic animals, Rorimer detected a "theme of captivity" "reverberating" through the installation, including "the capturing of other lands in the process of colonisation."[87] That was one work. At the same period, Lothar Baumgarten, who had studied with Joseph Beuys in Düsseldorf, was unusual in establishing an entire body of work which explicitly addressed issues concerning the non-Western world, the history of colonialism, and the effect of industrial expansion across the globe. As early as 1968–1970 he had produced *Unsettled Objects*, a slide presentation of objects in an ethnographic museum context, and subsequently went on to make installation pieces concerned with threatened native society in the Amazon basin and extinction of native American society during the onward march of technological progress in the United States. His *Tropenhaus* of 1974 (Figure 4.10) was commended in Rorimer's account of the contribution of the art of the sixties and seventies to "redefining reality" for being "far-sighted in its global perspective" and envisaging a "more comprehensive, less ethnocentric world view."[88]

Both of these assessments of Broodthaers and Baumgarten are deserved. But at the same time, it doesn't amount to much about the majority world in a 300-page book that makes "resistance to the status quo" the cornerstone of its argument about the importance of the conceptualist art of the 1960s and 1970s. Lost tribes in the Amazon are one thing. Neither would anyone challenge the value of

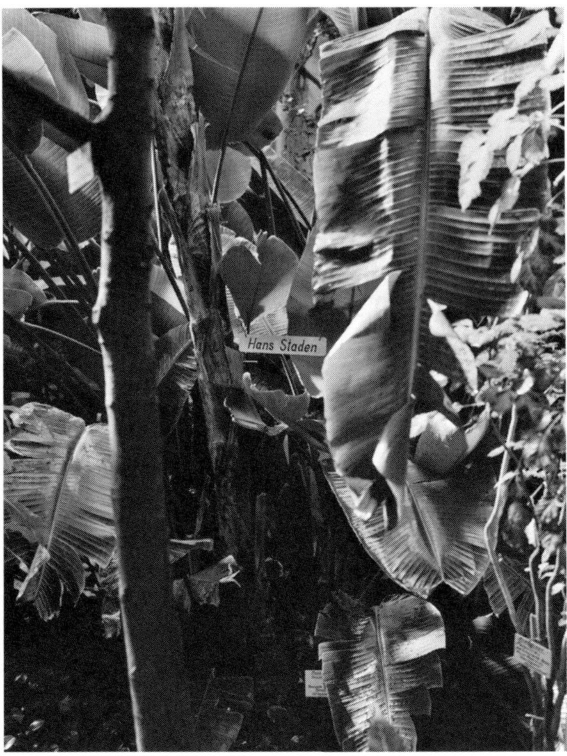

Figure 4.10 Lothar Baumgarten, *Conservatory (Tropenhaus)*, 1972–1974 *Hans Staden* (two trips to Brazil, 1548–1549 and 1550–1555) Hothouse, Botanical Garden, Cologne, 1974. Photo Courtesy of the artist and Marian Goodman Gallery, New York / Paris © DACS 2013.

deconstructing the museum. But of the contemporary world at large, of the end of empire, of independence in Africa and the Caribbean, of the American defeat in Southeast Asia, of the Cold War and the related nuclear threat running through the whole period, there is not a word. It is a strange conception of "destroying illusion" and "modelling resistance" that has so little to say about the actual historical reality whose illusions are being resisted. Two artists who did make reference to that reality were Őyvind Fahlström and Alighiero Boetti, both in the form of world maps; neither fall within the remit of Rorimer's study. Fahlström used a synthesis of medieval map and modern cartoon to highlight the power relations underlying the geography. Boetti traveled to Afghanistan and employed craftswomen to weave maps identifying countries with their national flags (Figure 4.11). Between 1970 and his death in 1994 the maps offered a sort of slow-release record of global change during and after the Cold War.[89] Both projects were exemplary, and both exceptional. Few other artists so tellingly addressed their wider world. The reason we have to keep coming back to these questions about the work of the 1960s and 1970s, and the ways in which it has been interpreted, is because there is so much at stake. The difficulty lies in formulating what that

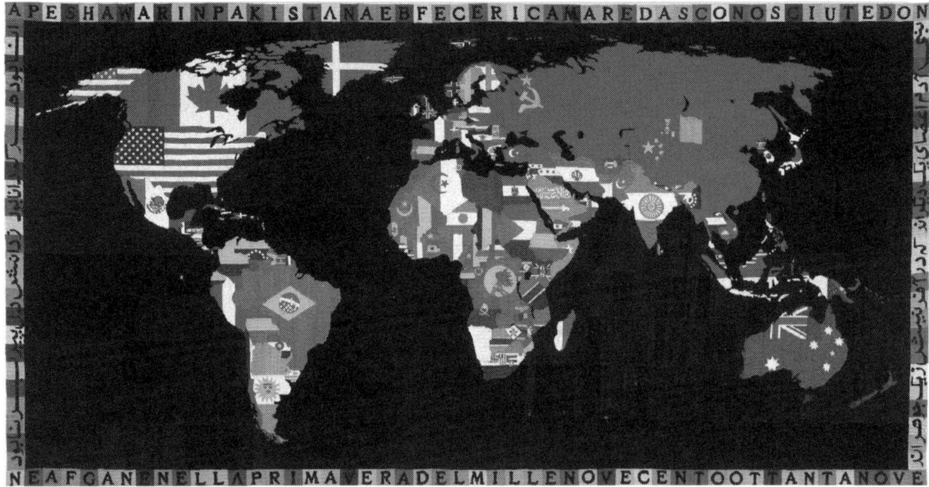

Figure 4.11 Alighiero Boetti, *Map of the World*, embroidery on fabric, 1989, 117.5 × 222.7 cm. New York, Museum of Modern Art (MoMA). Scott Burton Memorial Fund. 1253.1999. Digital image © 2013, The Museum of Modern Art, New York / Scala, Florence. © DACS 2013.

is. I think one way of putting this is to say that what is at stake is the relative implications for art of the legacies of 1968 and 1989.

There are many ways in which historical "conceptual art" can be said to stand at the head of globalized contemporary "conceptualism." The much expanded range of materials and media is the most obvious. But it is quite mistaken to regard this condition as one of ascending progress from the supposed freeing of art from the constraints of modernism towards a completely free aesthetic condition. The most significant freedom the contemporary situation in art mirrors is the freedom of contemporary capital. To regard this conceptualism as the inheritance of historical conceptual art is to misrepresent the latter in respect of its most important feature: not merely its expanded range of aesthetic materials but its critical character, including its often uncertain engagement with the notion of the aesthetic. The majority of contemporary "conceptualism," by contrast, constitutes a hegemonic status quo. Despite appearances, it shares more with the condition of earlier academic art than it does with the historical avant-garde, including conceptual art. The goalposts have moved, but though the values are supposed to be about freedom and openness rather than authority and emulation, an official culture is an official culture: that is why the temples to its worship are so popular, that is why so much money is spent on it.

The question of the legacy of 1968, then, is itself double-edged. It is important to distinguish the iconoclastic, oppositional aspects of sixties conceptual art from the normative status of much contemporary conceptualism. As Rorimer and others have noted, the art of the 1960s and 1970s constituted a profound challenge to all kinds of assumptions about both Western modernism and

Western modernity. But unless that challenge is opened up to an assessment of the consequences of 1989 (by which I mean to include the dual contestation *both* of Western conceptions of modernity *and* the terms of the traditional leftist critique of Western bourgeois modernity), then the advocacy of that art can itself take on an unexpectedly conservative cast. It is a tightrope. Not to neglect the oppositional element of 1968; rather, to open that to subsequent criticism for its (Eurocentric) limitations. Not to accept the self-justifications of the normative contemporary; rather, to acknowledge the genuine openings that have taken place.

Global Conceptualism

Despite the passage of time since the *Global Conceptualism* exhibition in 2000, Stephen Bann's analysis remains much more nuanced and open than many of its successors in its reflections upon the globalized contemporary condition of art. Several of those most closely identified with the theorization of the contemporary condition and the curating of its art are prone to indulge in one-dimensional denunciations of Western modernism. By contrast, Bann argues that "conceptualism ...is both a critique and a continuation of modernism": a critique insofar as it picks up on modernism's "internal inconsistency," that is, on the limitations of the modernist project; a continuation insofar as it maintains and deepens "the critique of the institutions and discourses of Western post-Renaissance art commenced by modernism."[90] This balanced approach contrasts powerfully with the amnesiac claim that there has been an epochal caesura between the modernist and academic Western past on the one side, and on the other, the global contemporary. There has unquestionably been a transformation, indeed Bann tellingly draws out its significance, but it is important not to lose sight of elements of continuity in the drive to celebrate – and arguably to manage – change. Sloughing off the past can seem more attractive than learning from it. But looked at in another way, loss of memory tends to serve the status quo. A key point about Bann's "continuation" argument is that it acknowledges modernism's early status as revolutionary and critical with respect to a dominant culture, and not merely as a dead, restrictive orthodoxy – an insight which has largely been allowed to slip from contemporary debate (and which is, of course, a central element in the argument of the present book).[91] In respect of conceptualism's critique of modernism, Bann draws attention to modernism's evacuation of art's conceptual dimension, to its centering on *material* and (non-cognitive) *feeling* for its criticism of the preceding academic Western canon. By contrast, for Bann conceptualism represents a "return of the repressed" when it reintegrates both language and an accompanying sense of structure (as opposed to modernism's fetishization of the subjective) into the practice of art.[92]

In themselves these are telling insights, but they take on greater significance when applied to the difficult question of accounting for the emergence of conceptualism. The preferred stance of most contemporary thinking on the topic is to reject the "diffusionist" model of artistic innovation, associated in particular with the modernist dyad of "mainstream and provincial" in which artistic initiatives were typically seen as spreading out from very few metropolitan centers. This is replaced in the case of conceptualism with a counterclaim for a series of independently emergent initiatives at various points around the globe. As a result of the case made by projects like *Global Conceptualism* this now seems undeniable. But Bann adds an important qualification. He acknowledges "the many different 'points of origin'" of conceptualism but mitigates the point when he recognizes that the conceptual approach "defined itself against local *as well as* internationally shared conditions"[93] This latter aspect, which is so often neglected in the rush to disparage the Western canon, is crucial. In practically every instance surveyed in *Global Conceptualism* the local generative conditions for the emergence of a heterodox, critical cultural practice – often the deflected consequence of conditions of political repression – were allied with at least some level of awareness of international avant-garde developments. It makes no difference that these occurred mostly through the art press and the mass media; indeed, it is part of the point that they were able to do so, in a McLuhanized world. Some knowledge, some glimpse, of a range of activities from action painting, to Duchamp's Readymade, to Cage's arguments and practice, to Fluxus, invariably leavened the compelling local preconditions and afforded some precedent for going-on as artists in face of them.

To acknowledge this is not to remain in thrall to an outmoded diffusionist perspective but rather to acknowledge something of the intricate interplay of global and local out of which the contemporary is constituted. Looking back from the other side of 1989, it surely has to be accepted that the wider "conceptualist" impulse in the art of the 1960s did indeed have multiple points of origin functioning in a dialectical relationship with key exemplars of the Western avant-garde. This is a relationship quite distinct from the center/periphery, mainstream/provincial logic of canonical modernism. Most commentators on the contemporary have remained content to emphasize the contrast with modernism. However, it is the interplay of contrast and continuity that does justice to the complexity of the situation. This comes out all the more when the longer view is taken, and this is what makes it especially interesting from the perspective of the present study. For modernism itself came at the end of a long history. To the extent that conceptualism marks a move beyond modernism, by the same token it represents a departure, in Bann's words, from "the political economy of centre and periphery which modernism had inherited, ultimately, from Renaissance Europe."[94]

One response to this – the easiest – is to heave a sigh of relief and close the door on the past. Normally when these types of claim are articulated in the contemporary literature of art they are components of a one-dimensional triumphalism that seeks simply to reject Eurocentrism as the principal index of closure and celebrate the liberation of the world from its malign influence. Yet the real lesson requires that we move beyond such sloganeering. From the mid-eighteenth century to the mid-twentieth, burgeoning European power involved industrial development; not developing autarchically, but in symbiosis with empire – using the rest of the world economically in terms of markets for its exported commodities as well as suppliers of raw materials (often at the cost of holding back or even destroying productive capacity elsewhere – the Indian textile industry being a prime example). That is to say, a political economy of center and periphery, of combined and uneven development. In the sphere of art and culture, it can be argued that a similar condition held: wherein chinoiserie, japonisme, and "primitivism" functioned to translate attributes of non-Western cultures into Western terms in order to invigorate a culture perpetually prone to congealing (likewise with the hegemonic European bourgeoisie's internal "Other" of popular culture). In the artistic situation, no less than in the economic, the effect was to marginalize and downgrade not other systems of production as such, but other canons of representation, other systems of art's social signification, relative to the Western model.

The upshot is that there is indeed a case for regarding the academy and subsequently modernism as being implicated in an "economy of center and periphery" throughout the extended modern period. This is not make the reductionist claim that enlightenment was no more than the mask of empire, that modernism was client to capital without remainder. But by the same token it is to recognize the interested nature of the claim that no such connection exists. In standard histories of the socioeconomic sphere, the development of Western industrial capitalism was typically viewed as springing from Western conditions, in the transition from feudalism to capitalism. Nonetheless, more recent globally oriented histories have begun to trace connections rather than assume singularities, to read Western European history throughout the extended modern period from the fifteenth century onwards in terms of its relations with central and eastern Asia, as well as America. Likewise, in the sphere of art and culture, the centrality of the twin pillars of classical antiquity and Christianity to the post-Renaissance Western canon should be beyond dispute. But in more recent work, many instructive and cumulatively crucial exceptions to the rule are now being recovered by art historians after a previous history in which such connections had been largely invisible. The point is to resist the equal and opposite claims that the West was entirely self-propelling, or that it was entirely parasitic, and to investigate the complex interplays that obtained throughout, permitting fluctuating and on-going shifts in the balance of global power: along the twin dimensions of actual material practice in history, and of representational practices in history. Such work is as necessary now, in the face of the increasingly corporate official culture of contemporary art, as it ever was in the face of modernism or its predecessors. Ignorance has never been an ally of freedom.

Consequences

It is no contradiction of that claim to admit, indeed to celebrate, the fact that the relationship of Western art to the wider world has undergone a more profound change since the 1980s than in the previous five hundred years. Terry Smith's compendium *Contemporary Art*, published in 2011, is a valuable illustrated companion to the global range of the new art.[95] In the conclusion to the present book, I disagree with Smith's formulation of a fundamental break between the concerns of contemporary art and the concerns of previous art. I am critical of neophilia, and concerned to resist his one-dimensional rejection of modernism and Marxism. But the sheer mass of illustration he provides offers undeniable evidence of an openness on the part of contemporary artists to a wide range of issues animating contemporary society. This is not to say that interesting subjects of themselves make for good art. But having something to say about things that matter has never been far from the realist project. In times of crisis and contradiction, it seems, realism's capacity to restructure itself comes again to the fore.

Whatever the diversity of tendencies on the contemporary scene, there can be no question, despite the persistence of underlying power structures in the globalized art market, that the historical one-way traffic has been replaced by a more complex circulation. To take only one example from the broad field of American art, as Homi Bhabha has written, the work of Renée Green opened up "an interrogatory, interstitial space" in which "the binary logic through which identities of difference are often constructed – Black/White, Self/Other," are displaced. For Bhabha, in her installations Green allegorized spaces such as "upper" and "lower" rooms, and the liminal passageways between them, in order to "open up the possibility of a cultural hybridity that entertains difference without an assumed or imposed hierarchy." For Bhabha such artwork is one of the key constituents of the postmodern condition, both symptom and cause of a situation in which, increasingly, "the very concepts of homogenous national cultures … are in a profound process of redefinition."[96]

It goes almost without saying that identity politics subtends much, if not most, of the art which seeks to call attention to these questions, as well as to related questions concerning cultural heritage. Arguments about the social construction of identity, made in opposition to the essentialist notions of ethnic or "racial" identity prevalent throughout the colonial period, as well as arguments about the rights to ownership and display of cultural material currently held by major Western museums, stand as a kind of philosophical, political, and legal backdrop to much of the art being made under the contemporary global dispensation. Historians and other cultural commentators working in metropolitan situations and within discourses whose own identity is profoundly inscribed within metropolitan histories, need to tread carefully. And it is right that they should – the present author included. Yet it is also well to remember Suman Gupta's argument that it is possible to retain a conception of identity as socially constructed. That is, it is possible to continue to resist an essentialist politics of identity and yet to reject the type of identity politics that accords absolutely privileged positions to the arguments of ethnic or other minorities and discriminated-against social groups simply on the grounds of membership of such a group, while simultaneously disempowering counterarguments or debating positions solely on the grounds of their speakers' own identity. For Gupta, while the institutionalization of social constructionist identity politics in literary studies and other humanistic and social sciences disciplines "has been an enlightening and expansive process in some respects, it has also emphatically been one that has spread limits and constraints ... curtailing free debate and exchange in significant ways."[97] As a reminder of the risks inherent in such a position, Gupta argues that

> any expression of a political position, however contextualised and particular or however general and acontextualised, is open to critical engagement and debate by anyone, anywhere ... It does not matter *who* (as a gendered body) [and of course this goes also to questions of "race" and ethnicity – P.W.] is articulating or acting in this political arena; all that matters is what basis of integrity, knowledge and understanding, and emotional investment (by a critical and communicative agent) is being brought to the arena.[98]

In England, the "Black British" movement of the 1980s, including figures such as Lubaina Himid and Sonia Boyce, brought questions of gender and diaspora and of the legacy of colonialism into the center of art practice. As Stuart Hall wrote,

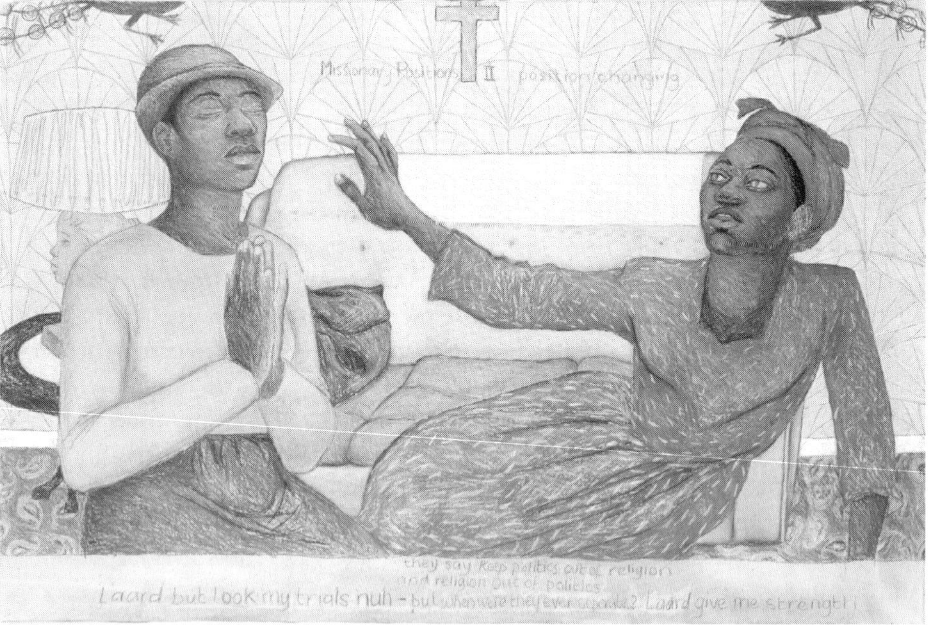

Figure 4.12 Sonia Boyce, *Missionary Position II*, 1985, watercolor, pastel, and crayon on paper, 123.8 × 183 cm. Photo © Tate, London 2013 © Sonia Boyce. All Rights Reserved, DACS 2013.

the late twentieth century had three "general co-ordinates," the first two being the displacement of older European models of high culture and the emergence to dominance of the United Sates. The third was "the decolonisation of the Third World" and the consequent emergence of "decolonised sensibilities."[99] Boyce's picture *Missionary Position II* (Figure 4.12), which bears upon this conjuncture, in fact emerges from it, talks back to the role of religion in maintaining colonial power as well as to its perpetuation within the family in contemporary diasporic contexts. In another response to such contexts, Rasheed Araeen, who came to London from Pakistan in the 1960s, confronted the metropolitan art world with a broad range of work which hybridized Western minimal art and Islamic decorative structures before moving on to a militant form of photo-conceptualism in the 1970s and 1980s. In a long series of works from this period, Araeen combined grid structures with both abstract colors and photographic imagery to make interventions in debates over racism and Islamophobia in contemporary British society (Figure 4.13).

Arguably, however, Araeen's most important contributions came in the related field of exhibition curating and publishing. In 1989, the same year as *Magiciens de la terre*, after a long struggle Araeen finally managed to stage *The Other Story* at the

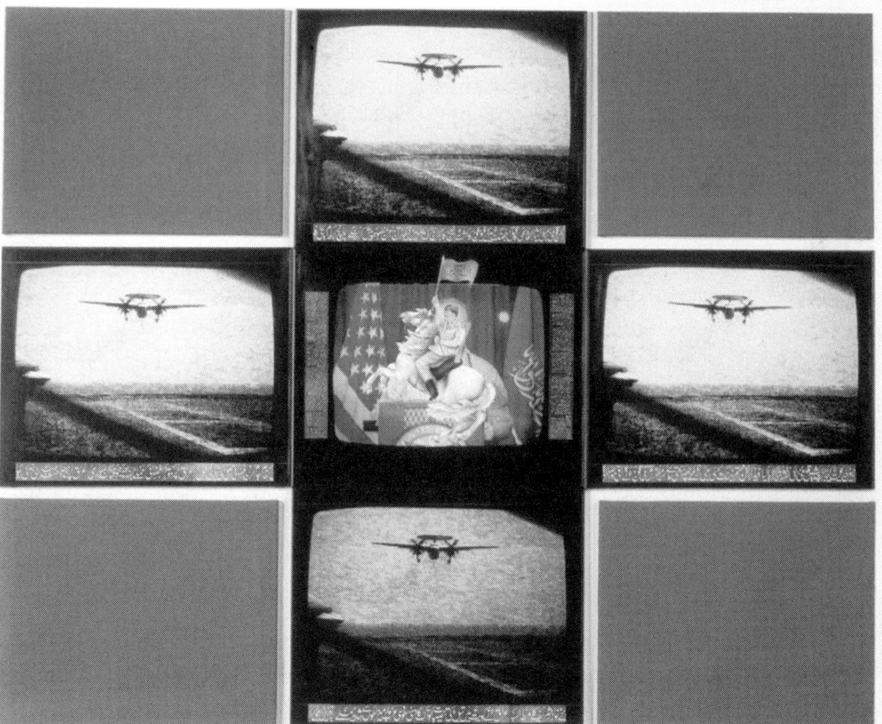

Figure 4.13 Rasheed Araeen, *White Stallion*, 1991, mixed media, 61.5 × 79.5 in. Collection: Imperial War Museum, London. Photograph courtesy of the artist.

Hayward Gallery in London.[100] Featuring the work of artists of African and Asian descent who worked in England, and subjected to an extraordinary barrage of at best Eurocentric and at worst virtually racist criticism, *The Other Story* was a landmark in opening up the exhibition possibilities for black artists in Britain. This was despite itself being subject to criticism for its own exclusions of African and Asian women artists and areas of activity in the supposed "minor" arts, which many were developing at the time. Two years earlier, in 1987, Araeen had launched the journal *Third Text*. Initially subtitled *Third World Perspectives on Contemporary Art and Culture* (subsequently changed to *Critical Perspectives* …), and symbolically bearing on its cover the Behrmann, rather than the Mercator, projection of the world map, *Third Text* continues to run to the present day. Well over a hundred issues have appeared, and it has offered one of the premier forums in world culture for the debate of questions of race and ethnicity, of cultural identity and globalization in relation to art.

On the other side of the world, things were changing no less dramatically. Reading Terry Smith's "Provincialism Problem" essay of 1974 with benefit of hindsight, it is impossible not to notice that all the Australian artists he refers to are white. The left-wing avant-garde of that period was as myopic about issues of racial and ethnic identity as most other sections of Western society. Yet Australia was about to witness an efflorescence of indigenous Aboriginal art which was not only globally unprecedented at that time but has itself gone on to change the conditions of production and reception of art on a worldwide scale. Contemporary Aboriginal art has generated an enormous literature, only a small proportion of which manages to address the manifold complexities of the form. Simultaneously extraordinarily ancient and inescapably a contemporary phenomenon, urban as well as rural, both traditional in its motifs and modern in its media, Aboriginal art continually transgresses normative categories.

Stylistically, Aboriginal art encompasses a spectrum from installation and film to more conventional media such as carved sculptures and paintings. None of these are part of indigenous culture. Traditional visual practices included body painting and designs made on the ground as part of large-scale ceremonial activities, as well as rock art, both painted and engraved, and painting in ochre on tree bark. All of these undergo varieties of transformation into modern formats. Some are closer to traditional types, such as the bark painting carried on in Arnhem Land; others involve the translation of traditional designs onto stretched canvas using acrylic paint. Primitivist myths of authenticity are revealed as just that by contemporary Aboriginal art: ideological constructions born of European prejudice rather than the actualities of indigenous culture.

One of the most challenging types of modern Aboriginal art was also one of the earliest. It was in the 1930s that Albert Namatjira, a ranch-hand at the mission station of Hermannsburg in central Australia, began to make landscape paintings in watercolor based on observations he had made of the Victorian painter Rex Battarbee. These pictures eventually propelled Namatjira to a strange kind of fame which resulted in a clash of cultures that was his tragedy. His pictures for long

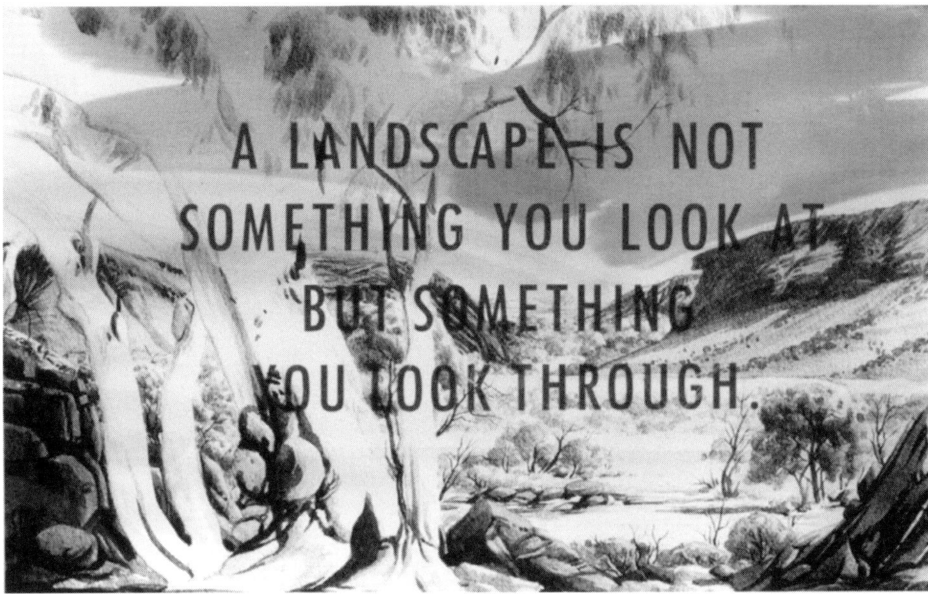

Figure 4.14 Ian Burn, *Homage to Albert (South through Heavitree Gap)*, 1989, watercolor on bromide, plexiglas, wood, 30 × 23 × 10 cm. (Supplied by Ann Stephen) Estate of Ian Burn. Photograph by Paul Green.

existed in a twilight of kitsch, not playing any role in the development of twentieth-century Australian art. It was only after the inception of the modern Aboriginal movement at Papunya in the early 1970s that Namatjira's work was reassessed. In "Namatjira's White Mask" Ian Burn and Ann Stephen advanced the hypothesis that far from simply imitating a European style, Namatjira had been inflecting his work with a specifically Aboriginal apprehension of the landscape: that his works amount to complex, hybrid representations which challenge rather than merely copy the European pictorial relation to the Australian landscape.[101] This text built on work that Burn had done a few years earlier, after he returned to making art at the end of the 1980s. The work grew out of the art historical research Burn had been undertaking into the relationship between Australian life and landscape, which involved coming to an understanding of the difference between Aboriginal and European relationships to land. Returning to the devices of some of his earlier conceptual art involving the layering of texts on transparent or reflective surfaces, in *Homage to Albert (South Through Heavitree Gap)* (Figure 4.14), Burn took a print of one of Namatjira's landscapes of the country around Alice Springs over which was laid a Perspex sheet bearing the legend "A landscape is not something you look at but something you look through." In Aboriginal culture a landscape is not an object entirely separate from the perceiving subject; it is an active constituent of identity.

The question of identity pervades Aboriginal art. Nowhere more so than in the series of prints by Judy Watson made while on a research scholarship to Europe

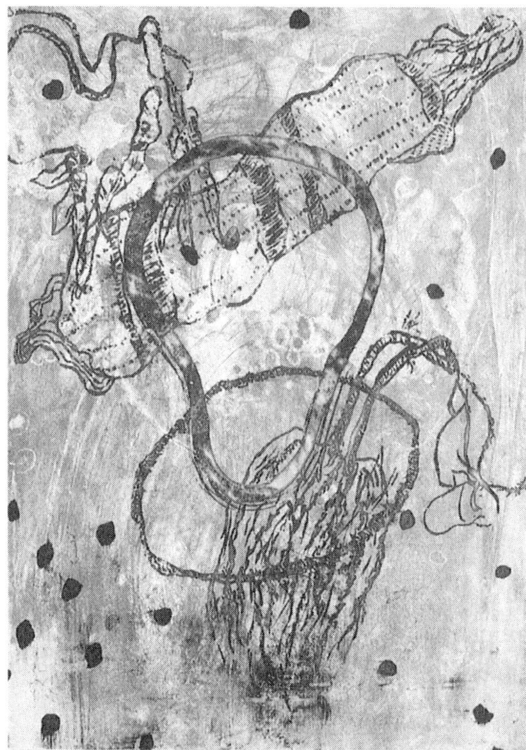

Figure 4.15 Judy Watson, *Our Bones in Your Collections*, 1997. Collection of the artist. © DACS 2013. Image courtesy of Modern Art Oxford / © DACS, London 2013.

(Figure 4.15). Watson researched in the archives of the British Museum and similar institutions to locate cultural material collected from her mother's country in Northern Queensland. These prints also involve the use of layering to achieve a density of meaning as traces of various materials are used as the basis for apparently abstract images. The result is a powerful triptych of prints in which the colonized voice speaks back to the colonizer: *Our Bones in your Collections; Our Hair in your Collections; Our Skin in your Collections*.

This sense of the once-colonized now speaking in their own voice and engaging with the legacy of empire, as well as with other invasive forms of modernity, is pervasive across much international contemporary art. Emanating from areas outside the geographical heartlands of the Western canon, it serves both to assert the independence and centrality of the once-dependent and marginalized and to contest the claim to centrality of the erstwhile "center" itself. Such works of contemporary art are extremely varied in themselves. They range from the work of El Anatsui (once involved along with Bruce Onobrakpeya in the Zaria group articulating a strategy for a post-independence Nigerian art but now operating on an international stage) to the work of George Nuku, of mixed Scottish and Maori descent, now resident in London. El Anatsui uses the detritus of consumer culture, in the form of the metal

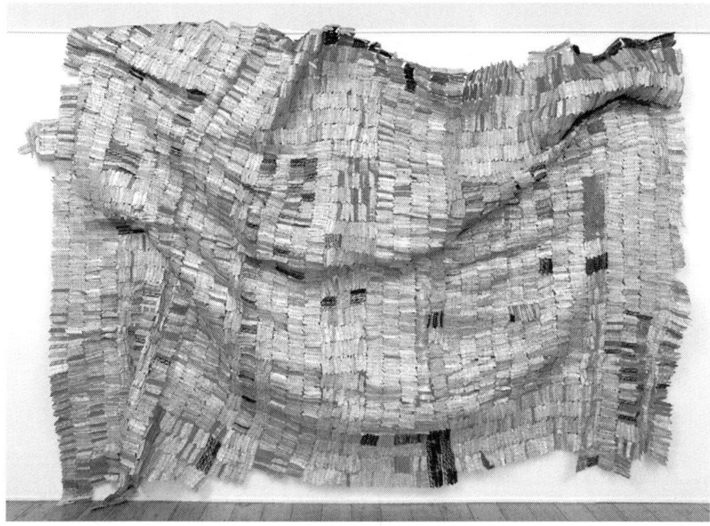

Figure 4.16 El Anatsui, *Man's Cloth*, 2002, aluminium and copper wire, 297 × 374. Collection British Museum. Photo October Gallery, London.

tops of bottles of liquor, themselves redolent of the "triangular trade," initially to construct wall hangings referring to traditional West African robes (Figure 4.16), but subsequently, and not without some irony, to address "universal themes of the kind previously associated with modernist abstraction."[102] Their grand scale and vivid color contrasts transform the negligible and practically valueless into emphatic celebrations of identity, indeed, one might say, of a human dignity itself. Employing a different strategy, Nuku takes motifs from traditional Maori culture, ranging from small *tiki* figures of the kind collected by Cook and Banks and other eighteenth-century European navigators, all the way to complete communal houses with their carved wooden beams and lintels, and recasts them in the quintessentially modern material of transparent plastic (Figure 4.17). This juxtaposition of tradition and modernity positions Nuku's works in a suggestive dialogue between the legacy of colonization and contemporary globalization.

One of the most renowned of such works is *La Bouche du roi* by Romuald Hazoumè of the Republic of Benin in West Africa (Figure 4.18). The title names the place from which African slaves were embarked for shipment across the Atlantic in the eighteenth century as part of the notorious "triangular trade." One of Hazoumè's characteristic forms is the plastic container. Ubiquitous in modern Africa, they are recycled in a thousand and one ways from domestic use to international smuggling. In Hazoumè's work they feature both in sculptural objects, which comment on the motif of the "African mask," and in extensive series of photographs. In these Hazoumè constructs a type of poetic documentary which records the contemporary cross-border smuggling of petrol between Nigeria and Benin as well as investing a more timeless quality on the transient realities of the daily struggle to survive. In *La Bouche du roi* hundreds of Hazoumè's trademark black plastic petrol containers are recycled into

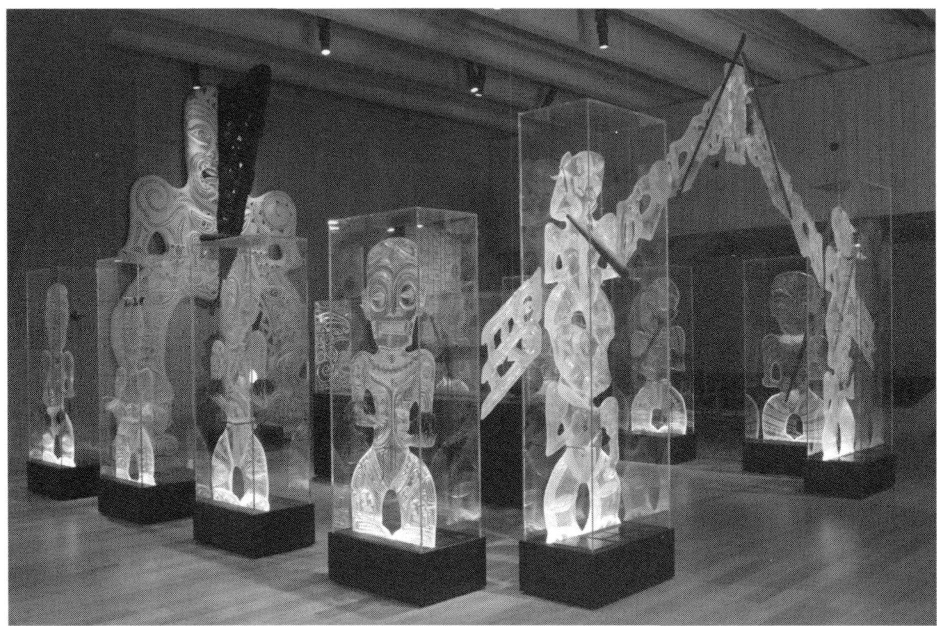

Figure 4.17 George Nuku, *Display of Power* installation, plexiglas and mixed media, 2012, Museum an der Stroom, Antwerp. Photo: Reinhart Cosaert.

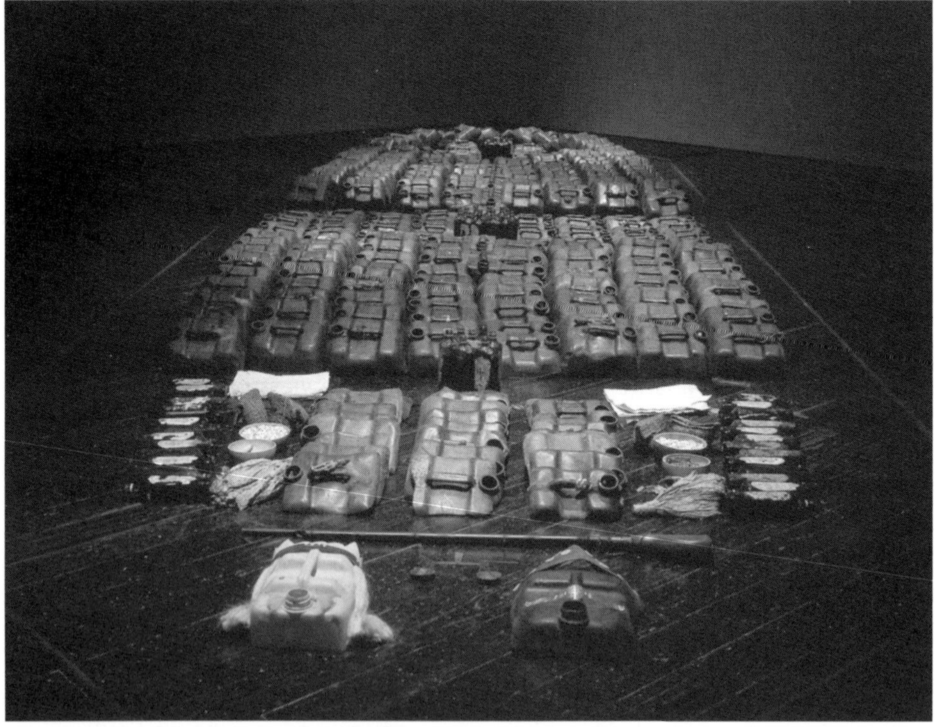

Figure 4.18 Romuald Hazoumè, *La Bouche du roi*, installation piece, 1997–2005. Collection British Museum. © ADAGP, Paris and DACS, London 2013. Photo George D. Hixson / © DACS 2013.

the well-known plan view of the late eighteenth-century slave ship *Brookes*. The installation, which also involves masks, as well as music and even smells, was exhibited at the British Museum in 2007 as part of the commemoration of the bicentenary of the abolition of the transatlantic slave trade. It is a testimony to the complexities of the issues facing the contemporary ethnographic museum that the British Museum subsequently purchased *La Bouche du roi* for its permanent collection.

Display

This raises a related range of questions concerning the display of contemporary art in the global condition. As I said at the beginning of this section, individual cases and generalizations can have a troubled relationship. But provided the generalization is not treated like a Procrustean bed it can provide necessary clarification. In the expanded situation of contemporary non-Western art, two broad tendencies are discernible. On the one hand there is that kind of art which overtly refers to issues at large in the world situation, often taking the form of installations or involving video projections and the like, its forms ultimately derived from the avant-garde, neo-avant-garde, and conceptualist tradition. On the other, there is a kind of art which results from the transformation of indigenous idioms under the impact of a multifarious modernity and which is drawn into the international art world through the globalization of the exhibition and market system.

Although these types of work are equal partners in the field of contemporary world art production, indeed often overlap, there is often a significant difference in the ways they are encountered. The former are likely to be displayed in museums of modern art, and especially in the temporary biennale-type exhibitions which now occur all over the world at frequent intervals. Institutions like Documenta and Tate Modern have no difficulty displaying contemporary art from China or Africa alongside installations of Western equivalents. The latter are relatively seldom seen there, and are more likely to be encountered in the context of the expanded exhibiting policies of ethnographic museums. Thus, to take a single example, in 2012/13 a large display of Aboriginal art was shown at the Musée du Quai Branly in Paris. It was not shown at the Beaubourg. The situation with the display of non-Western pre-modern art is similarly contradictory. The Royal Academy in London regularly hosts temporary exhibitions of non-Western art, including work from Africa, Aztec Mexico, Japan, the Turkish tradition, and others in the same galleries it uses to show modern and contemporary art. But the National Gallery has never exhibited the Benin bronzes as art in a way comparable to its display of art of the European Renaissance period. After considerable controversy, The Louvre does have an annex for the display of some of the most prominent works from the Quai Branly collection, and now has a gallery devoted to the display of Islamic culture. The exception which proves the rule, and it is no accident of course, is Australia, where under pressure from political imperative, the

National Gallery in Canberra prominently features Aboriginal art. Where there's a will, there's a way; and when there appears to be no way, it is usually because of a lack of the corresponding will.

It seems that, set against the grounding context of the evolving discourse of artistic modernism over the last 150 to 200 years, tracing its emergence in the nineteenth century, its establishment in the early twentieth century, and its transformation since the late twentieth century, there have also been three distinct paradigms under which non-Western culture has been received and displayed in the West.[103] The problematic binary here is, of course, a large part of the point at issue: the "non-Western" being received and displayed in the "West." The implicit power relations underpinning that sentence constitute the hidden part of the iceberg of art in modernity.

The first display paradigm was of the object regarded as anthropological artifact. The purpose here is to provide knowledge of exotic or alien ways of life. Such displays are constructed under the sign of "science." They are, or were, intended to communicate knowledge: anthropological or ethnographic knowledge. So long as "art" was identified with classical and post-Renaissance mimesis, these kinds of things were not regarded as art. Repulsive or fascinating, it makes no difference; skillful, ingenious, they may have been, startling examples of "native" craft they may have been, but "fine art" they were not.

The second display paradigm reflects a revolution, namely the revolution of modernism, in which that previous system of values undergoes a transformation. In the words of Meyer Schapiro, "what was once considered monstrous, now became pure form and pure expression."[104] For the avant-garde it was precisely the products of the academic tradition that lost their virtue, became seen as compromised by their complicity in the wider values of bourgeois culture. For them, value migrates to marginalized, disregarded, subordinate practices of representation. These included, as well as the hinterlands of the canon itself, such as Dutch art, and the register of the popular, the representational practices of the rest of the world, including the colonies. Modernism constructs the category "Primitive Art." Resulting displays were organized under the sign of the aesthetic.

However, a third display paradigm duly emerged, under the pressure of broader, world-historical forces, namely decolonization and globalization, as well as more localized pressure. Increasingly, in the last quarter of the twentieth century the translation of the non-Western into the terms of a Western aesthetic under the universalizing rubrics of form and expression, came under attack as part of the wider critical and art-historical move against the precepts of orthodox modernism. In some respects this emergent third paradigm marks the return of the repressed anthropological moment, as it were at a higher level. Here the re-emergence of social–ethnographic considerations marks not a refusal to confer the elevated status of art on the artifacts of exotic cultures but a challenge to the modernist autonomy claim in the name of an expanded field of art activity. From this perspective, the work of art is now regarded less as an object of attention in its own right, as it were an end in itself, and more as a means to the end of engagement with the culture of the Other – other *people*. These displays are constructed under the sign of difference, under the sign of identity politics, wherein it is not aesthetic autonomy that is held to be the governing virtue, but cultural diversity and the relation of art to ways of life.

It is a complicated situation. The British Museum's Sainsbury-sponsored Africa Gallery, which opened in 2001, presents a case in point. Overall the galleries are dedicated to the memory of the English sculptor Henry Moore. A statement by Moore at the entrance commends the "formal distortions" and resulting "expressive power" of "African carvers." As such it represents a paradigmatically modernist reading of African art. Yet in the galleries themselves an installation by Sokari Douglas Camp explicitly seeks to counter a formalist-modernist reading of masks on display nearby and to embed them instead in a more sociological understanding of practices of masquerade. Other parts of the gallery show anonymous objects such as weapons, musical instruments, and utensils, arranged after the manner of a traditional ethnographic display. While yet others display pieces by individual, named contemporary artists including Magdalene Odundo and El Anatsui. The display of the bronze sculptures and plaques from Benin straddles all three modes (Figure 4.19). Some are conventionally displayed in glass cases with

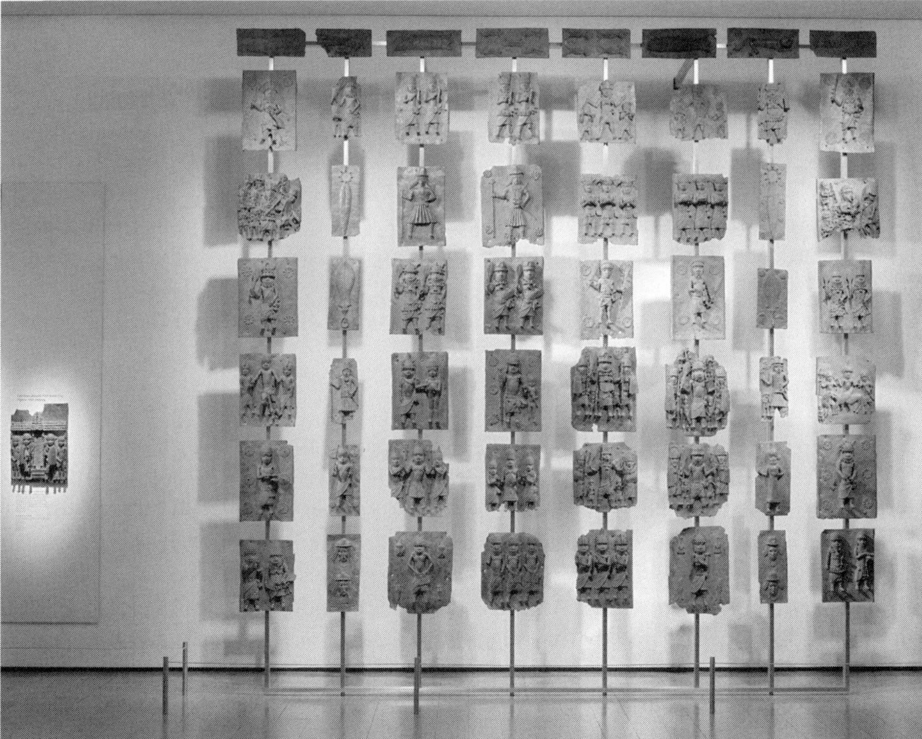

Figure 4.19 Installation view of display of Benin bronzes in the Sainsbury African Galleries, British Museum, c.2000. © The Trustees of the British Museum.

labels. A selection of fifty-six of the two-dimensional plaques are, however, arranged in a grid format, attached to vertical steel poles. As such, the display simultaneously manages to connote a minimalist grid cum contemporary art installation, while yet alluding to the original display of the plaques on the pillars of the Oba's palace in sixteenth-century Benin. The boundaries are fluid, undoubtedly more fluid than they once were, but there is still a sense of boundaries at work as between hitherto "ethnographic" and more purely "aesthetic" contexts and traditions. It is testimony to a complex and unresolved situation that an ethnographic museum such as the British Museum currently displays a more diverse collection of art from around the globe – past and present – than does Tate Modern, flagship of the contemporary, let alone the National Gallery, hallowed site of the Western canon.

Notes

1 Lenin "Imperialism, the Highest Stage of Capitalism" in Lenin 1968, pp. 169–263.
2 Trotsky 1962.
3 Duncan and Radice, eds, 2006.
4 The sole exception of any significance is Italian futurism, whose rejection of the status quo came from the Right, and whose subsequent development in the Italian context was articulated not to revolutionary socialism but to fascism.
5 Bürger 1984 and Cottington 2013.
6 Foster 1985, p. 200.
7 Paul Wood, "Avant-garde and Modern World: Some Aspects of Art in Paris and Beyond *c.* 1850–1914" in Edwards and Wood 2012, pp. 17–50, especially pp. 44–50.
8 Marinetti 1997; the following nine quotations are all from this edition, in order: pp. 8, 33, 16, 154, 146, 33, 184, 38, and 148.
9 Tristan Tzara *"Chanson du Serpent"* and *"Chanson du Cacadou,"*1917 in Stephen, McNamara, and Goad, 2006, pp. 31–36, p. 33.
10 Stephen, McNamara, and Goad, 2006, p. 31.
11 Lavin 1993.
12 I say, "usually translated as," but the key point is that Einstein's work remained little known in English-language art history until relatively recently. The occlusion suffered by the interwar critical, or revolutionary, avant-gardes during the period of the hegemony of formalist modernism extended for even longer in Einstein's case. His work became the subject of scholarly treatment in a special issue of the journal *October* edited by the German scholar Sebastian Zeidler as recently as 2004. This included a translation of the complete text of *Negerplastik*, with an introduction by Zeidler (Einstein 2004).
13 Zeidler, Introduction in Einstein 2004, p. 122.
14 Zeidler, Introduction in Einstein 2004, p. 122.
15 Einstein 2004, p. 132.
16 Einstein 2004, pp. 126–129.

17 Einstein 2004, p. 133.
18 Zeidler, Introduction in Einstein 2004, p. 124.
19 Einstein 2004, all quotations from p. 124.
20 Baines in Schäfer 2002, p. xxi.
21 Interestingly, the two studies appeared within four years of each other; Einstein's, as we have seen, in 1915, Schäfer's *Principles of Egyptian Art* in 1919. Like Einstein, Schäfer also waited a long time for a translator. An English edition did not appear until 1974.
22 Schäfer 2002, p. 80.
23 Emma Brunner-Traut "Aspective" in Schäfer 2002, pp. 421–446, p. 429.
24 Schäfer 2002, p. 81.
25 Schäfer 2002, p. 81.
26 Schäfer 2002, pp. 88–89.
27 Davis 1989, p. 52.
28 John Baines "Theories and universals of representation: Heinrich Schäfer and Egyptian art" 1985, updated in Baines 2007, pp. 207–235.
29 Blake 2002, p. 55.
30 Breton *et al.*, 1931, "Don't Visit the Colonial Exhibition," in Richardson and Fijalkowski, eds, 2001, pp. 183–185.
31 Blake 2002, p. 46.
32 Breton *et al.*, "Murderous Humanitarianism," [1934] in Cunard, ed., 2002, pp. 352–353.
33 Blake 2002, quotations from pp. 55, 56, 40, and 56.
34 Richardson, ed., 1996, p. 24.
35 Clifford "On Ethnographic Surrealism" (1981), in 1988, pp. 117–118.
36 Itself the title of an earlier text by Breton, published in 1926, defending surrealism against criticism by more orthodox representatives of the Communist Party. See Breton 1970, pp. 31–42.
37 "Legitimate Defence" in Richardson and Fijalkowski 2001 pp. 188–190; quotation from p. 190.
38 That said, it has been pointed out that Césaire privileged the African heritage, and "blackness," over other aspects of Caribbean identity in his formulation of the concept of "negritude." See Mireille Rosello, Introduction to Césaire, 1995, p. 27.
39 Suzanne Césaire, "1943: Surrealism and Us" in Richardson 1996, pp. 123–126, quotations from pp. 125 and 123.
40 All quotations from Césaire 1995, in order pp. 73, 75, 81, 87, 91, 93, 125, 99, and 101.
41 See, for example, Partha Mitter 2007
42 Pierre Mabille, "The Jungle" 1945 in Richardson 1996, pp. 199–212; quotation from p. 203.
43 Mabille in Richardson and Fijalkowski 1996, p. 308.
44 A more appropriate comparison might be to Picasso's own *Demoiselles d'Avignon*, to which *The Jungle* so closely approximates in both scale and ambition.
45 Mabille in Richardson and Fijalkowski 1996, pp. 211–212.
46 See Elkins 2007.
47 Brecht, "Popularity and Realism" (1938), in Adorno *et al.*, 1977, pp. 79–85
48 Bown 1991, p. 53.
49 Bown 1998, p. 195.

50 Cf. Alexander Shevchenko, "Neo-Primitivism" in Harrison and Wood 2003, pp. 99–102.
51 Bown 1998, p. 198.
52 Bown 1998, p. 294.
53 Downs 1999.
54 André Breton, Diego Rivera, and Leon Trotsky, "Towards a Free Revolutionary Art" (1938), in Harrison and Wood, 2003, pp. 532–535; quotations from pp. 533, 534, and 535. So much for the surrealists "pledging adherence to Moscow" …
55 Ola Oloidi, "Art and Nationalism in Colonial Nigeria" (1989) in Deliss, ed., 1995, pp. 192–194; quotation from p. 194.
56 Onobrakpeya 1995, pp. 195–197, all quotations from p. 195.
57 Onobrakpeya 1992, p. 20.
58 Onobrakpeya 1992, pp. 31 and 137.
59 Onobrakpeya 1992, p. 113.
60 Onobrakpeya 1992, p. 173.
61 Onobrakpeya in Deliss 1995, p. 197.
62 Fanon, "On National Culture" (1959) in Harrison and Wood, 2003, pp. 710–715; quotation from p. 714; rptd from Fanon 2001.
63 See McLuhan 1967 and Stearn 1968. See also Wood, ed., 2004.
64 Steichen, Edward, Introduction to *The Family of Man*, exhibition catalog, 1955, p. 4.
65 Pollock, "Answers to a Questionnaire," 1944, in Harrison and Wood, 2003, p. 570.
66 Breslin 1983, p. 46.
67 Cage, quoted in Kotz 1990, p. 76.
68 Higgins, "A Child's History of Fluxus" (1979), in Armstrong and Rothfuss 1993.
69 Kaprow 1958.
70 Maciunas, *Fluxus Manifesto*, 1963, illustrated in Paul Wood, "The Neo-avant-garde" in Wood, ed., 2004, p. 309.
71 Kubler 2008.
72 Corris 2008, p. 86. Corris also connects Reinhardt's projections to Malraux's ideas of the "museum without walls."
73 Kubler 2008, p. 1.
74 See Davis 2011.
75 Morris 1975; all the following quotations are taken from this article.
76 Krauss, "A View of Modernism," 1972, in Harrison and Wood 2003, pp. 976–979; quotation from p. 978.
77 Smithson, "Cultural Confinement," 1972, in Harrison and Wood 2003, pp. 970–971.
78 Burn 1975, quotation from p. 35.
79 Smith 1974, quotation from p. 59.
80 Burn 1975, p. 37.
81 Greenberg 1961, quotation from p. 230. This was a revised version of an essay previously published in *Art News* as "New York Painting Only Yesterday" in 1957, itself reprinted in Clement Greenberg, *The Collected Essays and Criticism Volume 4, Modernism with a Vengeance 1957–1969*, edited by John O'Brian, The University of Chicago Press 1993, pp. 19–26. O'Brian adds a footnote quoting the "famous addendum" on p. 19.
82 See, for example, Grégoire Müller, *The New Avant-Garde: Issues for the Art of the Seventies*, Pall Mall Press, London 1972.
83 *How Latitudes Became Form*, exhibition catalog, 2003, p. 19.

84 *How Latitudes Became Form*, exhibition catalog, 2003, p. 130.
85 Buchloh and Martin 1989. See also Steeds *et al.*, 2013.
86 Rorimer, 2001, pp. 273, 275.
87 Rorimer, 2001, pp. 243–245.
88 Rorimer, 2001, p. 273.
89 See Niru Ratnam, "Art and Globalisation" in Perry and Wood, eds., 2004, pp. 276–313; discussion of Fahlström and Boetti pp. 297–8.
90 Bann, Introduction to *Global Conceptualism: Points of Origin 1950s–1980s*, exhibition catalog, 1999, p. 6.
91 See also Wood, ed., 1999.
92 Bann, Introduction to *Global Conceptualism: Points of Origin 1950s–1980s*, exhibition catalog, 1999, p. 6.
93 Bann, Introduction to *Global Conceptualism: Points of Origin 1950s–1980s*, exhibition catalog, 1999, p. 6 (my emphasis).
94 Bann, Introduction to *Global Conceptualism: Points of Origin 1950s–1980s*, exhibition catalog, 1999, p. 6.
95 Smith 2011.
96 Bhabha 1994, Introduction, pp. 5 and 7.
97 Gupta 2007, p. 215.
98 Gupta 2007, pp. 94–5.
99 Hall 1992, quotation from p. 291.
100 Araeen, ed., 1989.
101 Burn and Stephen 1992. This argument has been subjected to criticism (to my mind unconvincingly) by James Elkins in his "Writing About Modernist Painting Outside Western Europe and North America," in Onians 2006, pp. 188–214, especially pp. 190–193.
102 Vogel 2012, especially chapters 7 and 8.
103 See Wood 2012.
104 Schapiro 1978, quotation p. 186.

References

Adorno, Theodor, Walter Benjamin, Bertolt Brecht, and Georg Lukács, 1977, *Aesthetics and Politics: Debates between Bloch, Lukacs, Brecht, Benjamin, Adorno,* with an afterword by Fredric Jameson, Verso, London.

Alberro, Alexander and Blake Stimson, eds, 2000, *Conceptual Art: A Critical Anthology*, new edn, MIT Press, Cambridge, MA and London. First published 1999.

Araeen, Rasheed, ed., 1989, *The Other Story: Afro-Asian Artists in Post-War Britain*, exhibition catalog, Hayward Gallery, London.

Armstrong, E. and J. Rothfuss, 1993, *In The Spirit of Fluxus,* exhibition catalog, Walker Arts Center, Minneapolis.

Baines, John, 2007, *Visual and Written Culture in Ancient Egypt*, Oxford University Press, Oxford.

Bhabha, Homi, 1994, *The Location of Culture*, Routledge, London.

Blake, Jody, 2002, "The truth about the colonies, 1931: *art indigène* in service of the revolution," *Oxford Art Journal* 25 (1): 35–58.

Bown, Matthew Cullerne, 1991, *Art Under Stalin*, Phaidon, Oxford.

Bown, Matthew Cullerne, 1998, *Socialist Realist Painting*, Yale University Press, New Haven and London.

Breslin, James, 1983, *From Modern to Contemporary: American Poetry 1945–65*, The University of Chicago Press, Chicago.

Breton André, 1970, *What is Surrealism? Selected Writings*, ed. with an introduction by Franklin Rosemont, Pluto Press, London.

Buchloh, Benjamin and Jean-Hubert Martin, 1989, "Interview," *Third Text* 3 (6): 19–28.

Bürger, Peter, 1984, *Theory of the Avant-Garde*, trans. Michael Shaw, University of Minnesota Press, Minneapolis. First published as *Theorie der Avantgarde*, 1974.

Burn, Ian, 1975, "The art market: affluence and degredation," *Artforum* 20 (April): 34–37.

Burn, Ian and Ann Stephen, 1992, "Namatjira's white mask," in J. Hardy, V. Megaw, and R. Megaw, eds, *The Heritage of Namatjira*, Heinemann, Melbourne.

Césaire, Aimé, 1995 [1956], *Notebook of a Return to My Native Land*, trans. Mireille Rosello with Annie Pritchard, with an introduction by Mireille Rosello, Bloodaxe Books.

Clifford, James, 1988, "On ethnographic surrealism," in *The Predicament of Culture: Twentieth-Century Ethnography, Literature, and Art*, Harvard University Press Cambridge, MA and London. First published 1981.

Corris, Michael, 2008, *Ad Reinhardt*, Reaktion Books, London.

Cottington, David, 2013, *The Avant-Garde: A Very Short Introduction*, Oxford University Press, Oxford.

Cunard, Nancy, ed., 2002, *Negro: An Anthology*, rptd in abridged form with an introduction by Hugh Ford, Continuum Books, New York and London. First published 1934.

Davis, Whitney, 1989, *The Canonical Tradition in Ancient Egyptian Art*, Cambridge University Press, Cambridge.

Davis, Whitney, 2011, "World series: the unruly orders of world art history," *Third Text* 25 (5) (September): 493–501.

Deliss, Clémentine, ed., 1995, *Seven Stories about Modern Art in Africa*, Flammarion, Paris and New York.

Downs, Linda Bank, 1999, *Diego Rivera: The Detroit Industry Murals*, The Detroit Institute of Arts in association with W. W. Norton & Company, New York and London.

Duncan, Bill and Hugo Radice, eds, 2006, *100 Years of Permanent Revolution: Results and Prospects*, Pluto Press, London and Ann Arbor MI.

Edwards, Steve and Paul Wood, 2012, *Art and Visual Culture 1850–2010: Modernity to Globalisation*, Tate Publishing in association with The Open University.

Einstein, Carl, 2004 [1915], "Negro sculpture," ed. Sebastian Zeidler, special issue *October* 107, (Winter): 122–138. Translation of *Negerplastik*.

Elkins, James, 2007, *Is Art History Global?* Routledge, New York and Abingdon.

Fanon, Frantz, 2001, *The Wretched of the Earth*, trans. Constance Farrington, Penguin Books. First published in translation in 1965; originally published as *Les Damnés de la terre, 1961*.

Foster, Hal, 1985, *Recodings: Art, Spectacle, Cultural Politics*, Bay Press, Seattle, WA.

The Family of Man, exhibition catalog, 1955, Museum of Modern Art, New York.

Global Conceptualism: Points of Origin, 1950s–1980s, exhibition catalog, 1999, Queens Museum of Art, New York.

Greenberg, Clement, 1961, "The Late Thirties in New York," in *Art and Culture*, Beacon Press, Boston 1961, pp. 230–235.

Gupta, Suman, 2007, *Social Constructionist Identity Politics and Literary Studies*, Palgrave Macmillan, Basingstoke, 2007.

Hall, Stuart, 1992, "What is this 'black' in black popular culture?" in Michelle Wallace, ed., *Black Popular Culture*, Bay Press, Seattle, WA.

Harrison, Charles, and Paul Wood, 2003, *Art in Theory 1900–2000: An Anthology of Changing Ideas*, Blackwell, Oxford.

How Latitudes Became Form: Art in a Global Age, exhibition catalog, 2003,Walker Art Center, Minneapolis.

Kaprow, Allan, 1958, "The legacy of Jackson Pollock," *Art News* 57 (6) (October): 56.

Kotz, M.L., 1990, *Rauschenberg / Art and Life*, Harry Abrams, New York.

Kubler, George, 2008, *The Shape of Time*, rev. edn, Yale University Press, New Haven and London. First published 1962.

L'Art conceptuel, une perspective, exhibition catalog, 1989, Musée d'Art Moderne de la Ville de Paris.

Lavin, Maud, 1993, *Cut with the Kitchen Knife: The Weimar Photomontages of Hannah Höch*, Yale University Press, New Haven and London.

Lenin, V.I., 1968, *Selected Works*, Lawrence and Wishart, London.

Magiciens de la terre, exhibition catalog, 1989, Centre Pompidou, Paris.

Marinetti, Filippo-Tommaso, 1997 [1909], *Mafarka the Futurist: An African Novel*, trans. Carol Deithe and Steve Cox, Middlesex University Press. First published as *Mafarka le futuriste: Romaine africaine*.

McLuhan, Marshall, 1967, *The Medium is The Massage*, Penguin, Harmondsworth.

Mitter, Partha, 2007, *The Triumph of Modernism: India's Artists and the Avant-garde 1922–1947*, Reaktion Books, London.

Morris, Robert, 1975, "Aligned with Nazca," *Artforum* 14 (2): 26–39.

Müller, Grégoire, 1972, *The new avant-garde: issues for the art of the seventies*, Pall Mall Press, London.

Newman, Michael and John Bird, eds, 1999, *Rewriting Conceptual Art*, Reaktion Books, London.

Oloidi, Ola, 1995, "Art and nationalism in Colonial Nigeria," in Deliss, Clémentine, ed., *Seven Stories about Modern Art in Africa*, Flammarion, Paris and New York, pp. 192–194. First published in 1989.

Onians, John, ed., 2006, *Compression vs Expression*, Clark Art Institute and Yale University Press, New Haven and London.

Onobrakpeya, Bruce, 1992, *The Spirit in Ascent*, Ovuomararo Gallery, Lagos.

Onobrakpeya, Bruce, 1995, "The Zaria Art Society" in Deliss, Clémentine, ed., *Seven Stories about Modern Art in Africa*, pp. 195–197.

Osborne, Peter, 2002, *Conceptual Art*, Phaidon, London.

Perry, Gill, and Paul Wood, eds., 2004, *Themes in Contemporary Art*, Yale University Press, New Haven and London.

Reconsidering the Object of Art, exhibition catalog, 1995 Los Angeles County Museum of Art.

Richardson, Michael, ed., 1996, *Refusal of the Shadow: Surrealism and the Caribbean*, Verso, London and New York.

Richardson, Michael and Krzysztof Fijalkowski, eds, 2001, *Surrealism against the Current: Tracts and Declarations*, Pluto Press, London and Sterling, VA.

Rorimer, Anne, 2001, *New Art in the 60s and 70s: Redefining Reality*, Thames and Hudson, London and New York.

Schäfer, Heinrich, 2002, *Principles of Egyptian Art*, ed. Emma Brunner-Traut, trans. and ed. John Baines with a forward by E.H. Gombrich, Griffith Institute, Oxford, 2002. First published as *Von ägyptischer Kunst*, 1919.

Schapiro, Meyer, 1978 [1936], "The nature of abstract art," in *Modern Art: 19th and 20th Centuries; Selected papers*, George Braziller, New York, pp. 185–211.

Smith, Terry, 1974, "The provincialism problem," *Artforum* 13 (1) (September): 54–59.

Smith, Terry, 2011, *Contemporary Art: World Currents*, Laurence King Publishing, London.

Stearn, Gerald, 1968, *McLuhan Hot and Cool*, Penguin, Harmondsworth.

Steeds, Lucy, *et al.*, 2013, *Making Art Global (Part 2): Magiciens de la Terre*, Afterall Books, London.

Stephen, Ann, Andrew McNamara, and Philip Goad, 2006, *Modernism and Australia: Documents on Art, Design and Architecture 1917–1967*, The Miegunyah Press.

Trotsky, Leon, 1962 [1930], *The Permanent Revolution: Results and Prospects*, New Park Publications Ltd., London. First published as *Permanentnaya Revolyutsiya*, 1906.

Vogel, Susan Mullin *El Anatsui: Art and Life,* Prestel Verlag, Munich, London and New York, 2012.

When Attitudes Become Form, exhibition catalog, 1969, Institute of Contemporary Arts, London.

Wood, Paul, ed., 1999, *The Challenge of the Avant-Garde*, Yale University Press, New Haven and London.

Wood, Paul, 2002, *Conceptual Art*, Tate Publishing, London.

Wood, Paul, ed., 2004, *Varieties of Modernism*, Yale University Press, New Haven and London.

Wood, Paul, 2012, "Display, restitution and world art history," *Visual Culture in Britain*, 13 (1) (March): 115–137.

5

"World Art History" and "Contemporary Art"

Introduction

The historical material surveyed in the preceding chapters represents an answer to a contemporary question. Or to be more precise, it represents a provisional answer to a question that keeps changing. The question concerns the nature of the historical relation of Western art to the arts of the rest of the world. One of the presuppositions of that question, of course, is the way it places the Western tradition at the center of its narrative. That very fact is sufficient in the eyes of some critics to disqualify it as a proper question to be asking at this time, since it can be interpreted as an attempt to buttress the Western tradition at the very moment when the centrality of the West is being widely questioned in the condition of contemporary globalization. But even if I have not intended such a judgment, even if it has been far from my intention to mount a conservative rearguard action in defense of the Western canon, there is still no doubt about the point of view that the question assumes. It is itself Western, and framed by the assumptions of the Western tradition, artistic and to some extent philosophical.

I do not think this is anything for which I need apologize. To regard the Western artistic tradition solely as the cultural camouflage of imperialism, indeed to regard imperialism itself as a wholly negative historical force, is as simplistic as it would be to view European imperialism and its related culture as an unalloyed force for good. Both positions only have to be stated to be recognized as untenable. To sketch the worldedness, however limited, of a tradition that has until recently tended to regard itself as world-making rather than being made by the world, is in my view, a defensible project. In my own case, it was the response to a first phase of questions raised by the contemporary process of globalization, questions which

Western Art and the Wider World, First Edition. Paul Wood.

were hardly raised at all in art history just a few decades ago but which were beginning to become inescapable by the last decade of the twentieth century. However, as that process itself develops, the question of the relation of Western art to the art, or more broadly, to the visual cultures of the rest of the world, has taken a significantly different turn. It has, so to speak, lost its innocence. Of course, this talk of "phases" is partly a convenience. Different kinds of questions are entwined in a complex present, and while some kinds of answers may be superseded by other types of question, yet still they need to be given. That is the history the previous four chapters have set out to sketch.

As we have seen, throughout the second half of the twentieth century, the normative picture of modernist art as an entirely Euro-American phenomenon occasionally succored by exotic transfusions, was increasingly rendered untenable. Canonical modernist painting and sculpture had, anyway, by the end of the 1960s, effectively faltered as a generative practice. In typical owl of Minerva fashion, the task then fell to a new generation of art historians to re-describe its lineage, in essence to reconnect modernism to modernity rather than police its distinction. But modernism's nemesis, the postwar "neo-avant-garde" and its progeny conceptualism, appeared to know no limits. There was not only a tradition of opposition to mainstream ideology to rediscover and draw upon in contemporary activity, ranging from opposition to the Vietnam War to the varied activities of the Art Workers Coalition; also, whereas modernism in the narrow sense, bedeviled by its hierarchy of "mainstream" and "provincial," seemed able only to generate distant echoes of its metropolitan innovations, conceptualism was almost immediately a dynamic presence across a broad geographical front. Parts of Europe which had played second fiddle to American modernism in the early Cold War years, including Germany, Italy, and Yugoslavia among others, were by the 1960s giving rise to a variety of practices that were no longer especially indebted to New York exemplars. Likewise, hitherto distant places that had now been drawn into the orbit of the Western Cold War polity, most notably Japan and South America, gave rise to avant-garde formations such as Gutai and neo-concretism. Between 1968 and the end of the Cold War twenty years later, a raft of non-medium specific, installation-, performance-, and text-based activities had come to form a much more diversified international status quo, albeit with its economic basis, the market, still anchored in Western Europe and North America.

But even that self-consciously "avant-gardist" or "conceptualist" diversity was only part of the story. In many places the struggle to form a postcolonial identity included a strong emphasis on art and culture and the search for a national form. Sometimes the illusionistic depiction which had formed the pre-modern center ground of Euro-American art continued to be adapted to local needs. Sometimes there were attempts to come to terms with modernist abstraction, especially in respect of its "primitivist" dimension (with its formal debts to the very cultures that were now emerging onto a world stage). This wide range of what was for the most part relatively conservative art from a technical point of view, ranging from

Chinese socialist realism to West African or Indian attempts to incorporate indigenous motifs into a resonant national-contemporary art, remained almost wholly outside the purview of normative art historical accounts.

With the end of the Cold War and the onset of full-blown globalization during the 1990s, the goalposts were well and truly moving. By the first decade of the new century, you could look one way and see the multifarious descendents of the erstwhile international avant-garde exhibited in an apparently endless proliferation of temporary exhibitions from Venice to Shanghai, Rio to Johannesburg, from Sydney to Havana to Istanbul, not to mention remodeled ex-industrial sites in "old" Europe, like Genk and Karlsruhe: a self-avowed and vigorous "global contemporary." Looking in another direction, you could encounter a range of hitherto downgraded practices, either craft-based (and hence challenging the division of the "fine" and "applied" arts and the gender distinctions they so frequently masked) or building on indigenous cultural forms (such as Maori carving or Aboriginal ceremonial), which now also demanded the appellation "Art" on a worldwide stage. Often the two were indistinguishable, or at least they shared the same platform. All represented a challenge to the hegemony of "Art" as it had been conceptualized in the Euro-American "Western" tradition.

A case in point is provided by the *Global Contemporary* exhibition itself (Figure 5.1). Subtitled "Art Worlds After 1989" it was held at the converted munitions factory Zentrum für Kunst und Medientechnologie in Karlsruhe for five months between September 2011 and February 2012 and was jointly curated by an artist, Peter Weibel (himself the Director of ZKM), and an intellectual, the historian and theorist Hans Belting.[1]

Much of the artwork on show was of a piece with what has become standard biennale fare, and was either more or less interesting depending on the individual case. Some pieces reflected on the contemporary global situation: facsimile Bedouin tents decorated with garishly colored images of global tourist destinations, "refunctioned" in various ways: the external escalators of the Centre Pompidou collaged onto a mosque, an onion dome and minaret sprung up on the Guggenheim. Etcetera. Other pieces reflected on the bloated global art market itself: poor people in Eastern Europe bartering chickens and eggs for a Cindy Sherman or an Andy Warhol; a painted, conventionally framed seascape with a slot underneath spewing out ticker tape recording fluctuations in its market price calibrated to how many spectators stopped and looked at it and for how long. Etcetera. But the salient point of the exhibition was how the art was *embedded* in a broader and deeper cultural–political enterprise. Thus the first room introduced the visitor to a hybridized informational / aesthetic presentation: including catalogs of previous "Landmark Exhibitions" beginning with *Magiciens de la terre* in 1989, and strikingly featuring a display of all the issues of *Third Text*, arranged horizontally like colored plaques on a frame which was essentially a re-tread of one of Rasheed Araeen's own early minimalist sculptures: aesthetic and cognitive juxtapositions again. There were displays on the role of auction houses, with their own

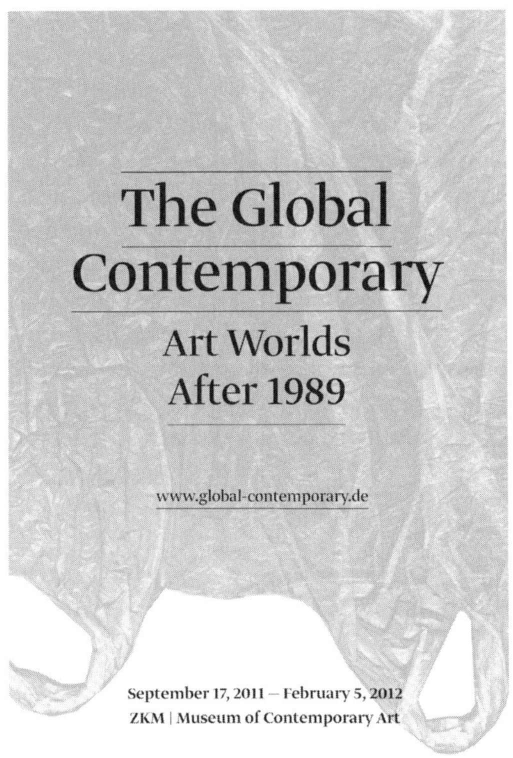

Figure 5.1 Cover of the brochure *The Global Contemporary, Art Worlds After 1989*, exhibition at ZKM | Center for Art and Media Karlsruhe, September 17, 2011 – February 5, 2012, (c) ZKM Karlsruhe

glossy catalogs; displays on the role of language ("Global Village," "Global Warming," "Global Financial Crisis," "Global Surveillance," "Global Positioning System," "Global Terrorism" ...); large wall maps showing the proliferation of biennales. There were high-tech, spectacularly presented displays of the profits turned by art centers around the globe, akin to something one might encounter in a modern stock exchange. There was a continuous program of talks, seminars, and other participatory events lasting through the five months, with the "catalog" coming out not before but after the exhibition in order to incorporate all the discursive events taking place during it. And not one but three accompanying scholarly publications: *Contemporary Art and the Museum: a Global Perspective*; *The Global Art World: Audiences, Markets and Museums*; and *Global Studies: Mapping Contemporary Art and Culture*.[2] I have given this extended description in order to convey a sense of the changed situation. This is no longer an art exhibition as such, certainly not a "modernist" art exhibition; it is a manifestation in which specifically artistic works are embedded as part of, and no more than a part of, an ongoing, collective political–cultural workshop on the question (itself, of course, a political–cultural issue) of the contemporary global condition – informational, financial, military, economic as well as aesthetic.

The terms of the question of the Western tradition's relation to other cultures, as it is currently being discussed, have evolved. A cautious, even negative note has entered the debate, and one constant trope of that debate is how rapidly it is growing and how quickly things change. There are, moreover, two quite distinct aspects to current thought around this question, which, though related, are, perhaps surprisingly (perhaps not), seldom brought together. It is these to which I now finally wish to turn. They concern, respectively, the matter of a "world art history" on the one hand and, on the other, debates over the nature of "contemporary art" in the condition of globalization. I shall discuss particular authors here. I shall express my agreement with some, my disagreement with others. I have my own beliefs and commitments. But I am not a referee. These debates do not take place in Plato's cave. My argument is not with shadows. Neither is it made in some kind of academic common room in the clouds where everyone pretends to be nice to each other. The arguments matter: that is my point. I respect the contribution of all those I discuss, including those I disagree with. I expect to be criticized myself.

These debates are, perforce, academic in the best sense, and this results in a changed balance to this final chapter. I have hitherto sought to embed the discussion of ideas in the discussion of works of art. Now the matter of ideas moves to the fore. I shall, however, briefly return to art as such at the end of this chapter. I would not like to conclude my long discussion of Western art and the wider world with art itself relegated to the background.

"World Art History"

In a basic sense, the emergence of some kind of world art history seems not only inescapable but positively to be desired. So it once seemed to me at any rate, on first looking over the parapet of the Western historical avant-garde and its descendent, conceptual art, and noticing different arts – in my own case, Australian Aboriginal art – in the 1990s. Whether such curiosity and openness can withstand prolonged exposure to the contemporary academic debate on world art history is, sadly, another matter. One of the marked features of the modern university, simultaneously powerful in its focus and conservative in implication – in the humanities at any rate – is its organization around academic specialization. World art history, only a decade or two old in its most recent incarnation, is on its way to becoming just such a specialism. Yet this is not at all what is required. If the promise of some of its aspirations is to be met then a world art history deserving of the name has to advance along a broad front and challenge as much as build upon the received conventions of art historical knowledge. Whether it can in fact hope to achieve this, or whether it remains bounded by the protocols of the Western academy, is one of the key points at issue in the burgeoning literature.

It is useful to acknowledge the prospective impact of this development for the wider field of art history. In one of the earliest interventions, in 1996, John Onians described world art studies as "a new broad discipline" whose initial remit should be "a review of the total potential field" involving "reappraising the full spectrum both of available material and of available approaches." It should be understood at the outset that this was not merely a recommendation to bring the arts of India, China, Africa, and elsewhere into the remit of existing art history. On the contrary, in the case of Europe itself the object of study was to be not canonical High Art but "the complete range of visually interesting material ... from the Paleolithic to the present, from Portugal to the Ukraine, from folk crafts to palace decoration, and from artists' sketchbooks to consumer videos."[3] The initial specification for world art studies envisaged an open situation. It was, presumably, in response to such a prospect, that in 2004 the American art historian James Elkins wrote, in a phrase which has itself already accrued a certain kind of fame, that "far and away the most pressing problem facing the discipline of art history is the prospect of a world art history."[4] Another American scholar, Whitney Davis, sharpened the point, arguing in 2010 that "world art studies is the only possible general frame for art history on a global stage in the next fifteen years or so"; he claims, indeed, that "without world art studies, the discipline of art history has little prospect of maintaining a coherent project as a global enterprise – as practiced and taught throughout the world – in relation to worldwide phenomena of art and visual culture, past and present."[5] It is important here to note the subtle difference between the two central phrases in play: "world art history" and "world art studies." The latter tends to establish distance from the practice of art history as such, and this is something to be kept in mind.

Elkins' comments came in his review of a 700-page book by another American art historian, David Summers. This was the enigmatically titled *Real Spaces* of 2002. Its subtitle, *World Art History and the Rise of Western Modernism*, more accurately described Summers' project. Already, a significant feature is becoming evident, namely the preponderance of American art historians' voices in the debate over a "world art history." Not, of course, that these American accents are exclusive. As already mentioned, the pioneering project of world art studies came from the Englishman John Onians and the department that he organized in the 1990s at the University of East Anglia.[6] More recently, one of the major contributions has been Dutch in origin: the collection *World Art Studies* edited by Kitty Zijlmans and Wilfried van Damme in 2008.

It remains the case, however, that all of these foundational attempts to broach the issue of a widening remit for art history emanate from the broad church of Euro-American art historical scholarship. This is not exclusively so. Both the Zijlmans / van Damme volume and Elkins' wide-ranging collection of audio-recorded debates and linked critical comments, published under the interrogative title *Is Art History Global?* in 2007, sought to draw in as many voices with connections outside the sphere of the Euro-American academy as possible. But even there, most of the contributors speaking from Japanese, or Indian, or African points of view were materially, professionally, part of that same academy, their presence, and ability to speak, frequently conferred by status within it. There are always partial exceptions to this gross rule, but the fact remains that the gravitational pull of debate about the prospects of a world art history or a world art studies emanates from the erstwhile centers of art and its histories anyway, not from the peripheries of the system that the debate in principle seeks to enfranchise. This is a paradox that significantly colors the published debates and inclines to dull the excitement that initially seemed to attach itself to the prospect of greater diversity, complexity, and enrichment of the field.

It is the nature of that "field" itself that is at issue, the constitution of which is quite at odds with Onians' initial prescription for world art studies. Firmly inscribed within the academy, normative art history brings with it a characteristic sociology and a characteristic philosophy. The former is manifest in a structure of university departments, hierarchically organized internally in conformity with wider administrative structures, more informally connected together through a system of publications, conferences, and the like, all increasingly brought into conformity with a system of peer reviewing and quality control on which, ultimately, funding depends. Seen from within, this is simply the way the world of academe is; seen from outside it can also operate as an effective filter for the kinds of thing that are to count as legitimate practice and legitimate knowledge. As for its "philosophy," such institutional norms combine with a set of intellectual protocols which also determine the field, whether the individual researcher be feminist, psychoanalyst, formalist, Marxist, or a traditional empiricist beavering away on reception histories or patronage studies. Central here is a logic of intradisciplinary specialization which often has the effect of rendering general and foundational questions difficult to ask. The widespread result is a more or less invisible reliance on inherited assumptions about ideas as fundamental to the whole enterprise as "art" or indeed "history" themselves. Within the normative field of period-based historical studies – the "modern movement," the "Renaissance," etc. – such ideas provide the framework for scholarship. But as soon as that framework ceases to hold, as arguably seems to be the case for contemporary art and even for its immediate antecedents, the broad range of power relations subtending academic convention themselves enter the field of consideration. The sheer volatility of "art" in the twentieth century within the purview of the Western modernist avant-garde is alone sufficient to challenge implicitly essentialist definitions of the subject area. Extend the purview beyond that Western system and the whole fabric stretches and threatens to tear. In the composition of a would-be world art history, how can the historical Western conception of "art" not become a Procrustean bed into which the diversity of other cultures is forced? And perhaps more challenging still, do fundamental assumptions about space and time, on which the writing of narratives recognizable as "history" depend, survive the acknowledgement of irreducible cultural difference as the condition of the world?

Whatever the validity of such concerns – and we shall return to them – they certainly do not reflect the original intentions of those who became attracted to the idea in the first place: quite the reverse, in fact. If any single motive can be ascribed to those who became interested in the idea of a world art history it has to have been the desire to open up a field that seemed to be developing sclerosis.

Prior to the 1960s, art history presents the appearance of an implicitly conservative field. One only has to write such a sentence, of course, to hear the snorts of derision arising from readers. There were giants, especially in the German tradition, as Michael Podro's *Critical Historians of Art* attests. But Donald Preziosi's reflections, although likewise leaving one in no doubt about the intellectual ambition of the founders of the field, nor about the high stakes involved, nonetheless bring out the religious inflection of "standard art history" as well as its ideological investment in certain notions of civilized humanity.[7] Moreover, in what we might term "traditional art history," the focus was overwhelmingly on the art of the European past rather than the present, on antiquity, the Renaissance, and its immediate successors, with an elucidation of perspectival mimesis at the heart of the matter. It is remarkable how often in the literature on world art history Gombrich's primer *The Story of Art*, which appeared first in 1950, recurs as the negative touchstone for that tradition.[8] This harping on a simplified account does scant justice to Gombrich's achievement, or indeed to the stereotyped "Western art history" for which his *Story* is too often made to stand. But there is no disputing that such an art history was debarred from an adequate address to modernism, just as it was from a serious consideration of non-Western arts, because of its persisting commitment to illusionism as the defining value of Western art.[9] Bounded by the canon to such an extent that the notion of "canon" was invisible, a de facto "nature," and underpinned by a mixture of connoisseurship and formalism that seldom extended into the twentieth century, art history was for the most part a conservative element of a conservative academy.

When it did come to the modern movement, in the Anglophone world at least the dominant account was a development of the older art history's formalism. Dissent from the Left remained marginalized, even when articulated by figures of the stature of Hauser and Schapiro. The radical turn in the academy in the wake of the social upheavals of the late 1960s ended that. With the decisive end of vulgar Marxism as a trap for radical thought, and a greater sensitivity to matters of language and representation, art history suddenly found itself propelled to the cutting edge of a would-be radical academy; part of a newly energized string of activities in the humanities, alongside literature, cultural studies, design history, and others, that looked to a role in the transformation of social inequality rather than the conservation of an elitist heritage.

No doubt, the retreat of the Left in the 1980s and the increasing domination of the radical academy by gender-based critique as part of an overall eclipse of Marxist class analysis by identity politics led to a shift in the terms by which radicalism itself was understood. Far from constraining art history this appeared to stimulate it. As questions of subjectivity, identity, and representation became understood as political from the ground up, art history not only continued to generate significant rereadings of the modern Western canon of art but also came to form part of a widespread critical purchase on prevailing assumptions about the condition of modernity itself. Marxism had always regarded modernization as a virtue. Postcolonial theory was not nearly so sure. This has manifold consequences for the emerging field of world art studies.

The collection *Is Art History Global?* published under the editorship of James Elkins in 2007 brings together thirty-seven voices, ranging in extent from the 50 pages of Elkins' own contributions through Shelley Errington's 35-page afterword to the much shorter written assessments and verbal contributions to a roundtable debate which together constitute the bulk of the volume.[10] It is hard to imagine a more democratically grounded attempt to take the temperature of the field. Yet for all the interest evidenced by the very existence of the project itself, the general drift of the conclusions is pessimistic. One of the clearest statements comes from the Nigerian writer Chika Okeke-Agulu, who writes that "globalism is the pressing issue of art history only if we mean Western art history," and in respect of this latter concludes that "if globalist art history means accepting the standard art history," then "it ought to be resisted."[11] And even Errington, charged in her afterword with the nigh impossible task of summing up the whole sprawling debate, can only conclude that the goal of an art history as "worldwide but neither Eurocentric, essentializing nor reductionist" is "easier said than done, easier proposed than imagined."[12] So is the idea of a world-ranging art history, prompted by cultural and political developments on a global scale which have seemed to render "normal" art history parochial, nonetheless to be pronounced dead on arrival?

It is the alternative that makes one want to say "No": the prospect of packs of specialists, dedicated in the words of Robert Byron to knowing more and more about less and less, burrowing ever deeper into the body of the Western canon in search of undiscovered morsels to feed their PhDs, while the only territory on which thinking about art might continue to mean something vital in a changing world is effectively evacuated. Looked at in this light, world art studies in some form is much to be desired. There is no question, though, that desire will have a price to pay, and there is no knowing, quite, what that price will be. It is only too easy to call airily for transformations in academic disciplines while all the time assuming that business-as-usual will carry on. Little more than a decade separates Onians' outward-looking proclamation of a "new framework" from Elkins' confession, in the wake of the wide-ranging debates that he himself organized, that "art history, as it currently is practiced, is itself certainly an impediment to thinking about worldwide ways of telling art's history."[13] Those who want to develop a world-facing art studies would do well to heed Elkins' skepticism about our ability to negotiate what he calls "the Westerness problem." Existing "methods, concepts and institutions" exert "a tidal pull" on our ability to think about art in history. When it comes to imagining, let alone to practicing, alternatives, "we are not as inventive as we like to think, and we are not as free."[14]

This is a sobering observation, and it involves a realistic assessment of the problems attaching to the project of a world art studies. It also stands as a nice counterweight to some of the attitudes which are visible around that project. Those of us with an interest in a potential world art studies who work in Western academic institutions will all at some time in the relatively recent past have experienced a sort of collective pricking up of ears at the mention of world art history, investigating cross-cultural connections, introducing multicultural elements into courses and the like. There is a ready audience for what is being proposed. Despite appearances, this is not necessarily a good thing. It is certainly something that those with at least one foot outside such institutions are right to be wary of – as Chika Okeke-Agulu's comment has already demonstrated. One of the ways in which capitalism traditionally expanded its remit over the world was to locate new supplies of cheap raw materials, appropriate them, bring them to metropolitan manufacturing centers for processing, and then sell them back at a profit. If the ambition for a world art history works like this, then it is indeed something to be resisted. To take "Aboriginal art" or "Islamic art" and configure it into a new module of an existing course, or a chapter of a book, is not to confront the consequences of cultural difference but to neutralize it. And in so doing to secure ever more profoundly the hegemony of the existing academy, excluding nothing, drawing all within. The ambition to develop the study of art in history on a worldwide basis has to be a radical ambition or it becomes part of the problem rather than the solution. "Radical" in this sense means being directed against at least some of the protocols of the Western academy rather than becoming the agent of its expanded remit.

This is one of the issues Elkins is pointing to: it is easier said than done. Moreover, it is far from clear that Elkins himself would be in sympathy with such a project. One of the salient features of Elkins' own work on the question of a world art history is the way he emphasizes, again and again, the power of that institution of art history as practiced within the Euro-American academy – power which exists both quantitatively in the sense of numbers relative to elsewhere in the world and qualitatively in terms of the power to define what counts as art historical work. Elkins' major interventions in this debate, including *Stories of Art*, *Is Art History Global?* and more recently, *Art and Globalisation*, have been rooted in a sociological-type surveying of the institution internationally: number of departments, number of practitioners, subscriptions to journals, different categories of journals, invitations to conferences, and so forth. This is unglamorous work, but it is useful insofar as it spells out the actual situation of the practice. Where it becomes perhaps less useful is at the point where the positivistic descriptions subtly modulate into prescriptions of what are the boundaries of the sort of practice it might make sense to keep on calling "art history." As has already been observed in the literature, Elkins works with a relatively narrow definition of art history, in the sense both of what the discipline's objects of study are as well as how they are to be studied.[15]

This is clearly in evidence in an essay devoted to the problem of "writing about modernist painting outside Western Europe and North America." Traditionally this was not a problem for modernist historians; the tendency was simply to ignore that which fell outside the modernist mainstream. That mainstream, moreover, was scarcely as broad even as "Western Europe" or "North America," being effectively confined to Paris and New York with a curt nod to early twentieth-century German expressionism. (Ironically, a scarcely less exclusionary policy, admitting only a handful of additions, was maintained by the avowedly "postmodernist" *Art since 1900*.[16]) That which fell outside the geography of the mainstream was termed "provincial" and left to local historians to address. Apart from defensive and largely conservative cultural nationalisms dedicated to preserving the virtues of "British art" (say) in face of an allegedly dehumanized abstract modernism, all ambitious writers wrote about modernist painting in a century-long arc from Manet and Cézanne to Pollock and Rothko. With the subsequent emergence of the neo-avant-garde and conceptual art, back-bearings were taken to admit German Dada and Russian constructivism, but surprisingly little else. The issue only became an issue in the mid-1970s, at the moment of canonical modernism's capsize, when, as we have seen, it was articulated as "The Provincialism Problem" by some Australians active in New York.

Elkins quite correctly identifies four characteristics associated in the modernist paradigm with provincialism (though he himself scarcely employs the term, "provincial," like "primitive," having slipped from polite usage). These are "limited," "uninteresting," "misinformed," and "belated." But surprisingly, this is not a prelude to abandoning such evaluations. Curiously, Elkins seems to get stuck in his sociological sense of the discipline of art history, worrying about the fact that journals like *Art Bulletin* and *Art History* "publish relatively few articles on modernist painting outside the main trajectory" and that histories of the art of individual nations, when they do get written, are "not likely to be widely read in North America and Western Europe." Elkins' problem seems to be that on the one hand he wants to "expand the roster of modernism," which is "important"; but that art outside the mainstream is unlikely to be of "compelling interest" to scholars who "work on the central problems of modernist painting."[17] Yet surely this is itself the problem. To those working within a value system, things falling outside that system cannot be valued within it. The value structure has to be redefined. Yet for Elkins it can't be, because the institutional manifestation of that value system is what academic art history is. Moreover, the system is so bulletproof that any existing alternatives are ruled out in advance. Thus, acknowledging debts to the Western avant-garde merely confirms the "minor," "derivative," "belated," etc. status of the art in question. Conversely, minimizing the relation of the art in question to the Western avant-garde results in accounts of merely local interest that hold together only by turning a blind eye to a key fact about the art. Conversely, again, writing of a different kind, such as responding to the work rather than contextualizing it, falls at another fence. Such writing "is not art history in a full sense."[18] The strongest kind of alternative, manifest in John Clark's innovative *Modern Asian Art*, is damned for being sociological, for not testing its institutional histories against aesthetic judgments. For Elkins, the problem is that the key driver of the modernist avant-garde was "originality." He rules out both the possibility of making originality context-specific and the possibility of sidelining it. As far as he is concerned, the idea "cannot be subtracted away without dismantling the very idea of modernism." If concepts of originality and innovation, on the one side, and dependency or influence, on the other, are suspended, then for Elkins one is left with "a maimed concept of modernism."[19]

These are serious points, and they have to be addressed. Elkins does a convincing job of demonstrating that you cannot eat your axiological cake and continue to have it. You cannot subscribe to the values which put certain works by Cézanne or by Picasso or by Pollock in aesthetic pole position and confer equal value on the work of a Czech cubist or an Australian abstract expressionist. From the point of view of a putative world art studies, I would have to say, "So be it." We seem to have reached a point akin to that reached by the early social history of art in the 1970s whereby materialist explanation has to supervene over the value judgment and, perhaps, the value judgment does indeed have to be rendered context-specific, relativized. The alternative, as Elkins recognizes, is to make exclusions: to deny kitsch in its various manifestations ("debased landscapes offered to tourists on Montmartre, or paintings of jungles and coral reefs on the walls of shopping malls") as well as manifold artistic idiosyncrasies, and to say plainly that such things "do not belong in history." The next question is "insidious and tremendously difficult," namely, "where do I stop?"; "once I begin to exclude certain paintings and types of paintings, there is no way to know how to stop."[20] As Elkins elegantly demonstrates, adhere to those prejudices – if prejudices is what they are – and one finds oneself very rapidly back within the normative judgments of the modernist canon.

It is to Elkins' credit that he articulates these consequences as clearly as he does. But surely, for any aspirant world art studies, the nettle has to be grasped. Yes to the coral reefs and jungles. Yes to Japanese expressionism. Yes to Irish orientalism. Yes to socialist realism, in its various manifestations. Yes to colonial mimesis. Yes to recycled toys … war carpets … fish traps … baskets … computer games … As John Onians said in his original "manifesto," "from folk crafts to palace decorations … to consumer videos"; as Whitney Davis said, "worldwide phenomena of art and visual culture, past and present." If that wave of activities and artifacts washes away the sandcastle of institutionalized art history and its fixation on "fine art," what, really, is it that is being lost?

Elkins' concern is justified. Indeed from the present writer's point of view, both the Western canon of art and much of the scholarship about it is valuable on a world-historic scale. But times change, and development has to happen, never more so than now. It is important, certainly, not to lose the baby with the bathwater. But right now, the alternative seems worse. Gombrich couldn't deal with abstraction. Greenbergian modernism couldn't deal with the readymade. So if the expanded field of art and the equally expanded "new art history" can't deal with all sorts of admixtures and recursions as well as the technologically inspired dissolution of craft, if it cannot tolerate religion and conservatism as well as radical negation, with blurred boundaries across the spectrum of visual activity, then it is just too bad. Art is global now, for better or worse. World art studies has to mirror that and excavate a past that was also always global, even if many of these multifarious pasts and presents lie outside the bounds of Western academic art history as currently practiced.

Nonetheless, despite the implicit optimism of such a program, and even if we conceive it as a challenge to institutionalized art history rather than a potential extension of its writ, there remain serious problems. The main one is that "art" is a specifically Western concept, with an equally specific history. Its presuppositions differ fundamentally from other concepts under which visual culture has been ordered in other societies the world over: Islamic, Chinese, African, Indian, Maori, Aboriginal … the list is as long as there are places and cultures to name. Then there are the various methods which have been brought to the study of art. Formalist, Marxist, psychoanalytic, semiotic … All of these, too, spring from the Western academy.

A kind of fault line can repeatedly be found running through the debates between a commitment to particularism on the one side and a fear of monocausal explanations and universalizing systems on the other. These are seen, it is not overstating it to say, as enemies of difference and are strongly identified with the West. The usual suspects are modernism and Marxism. It hardly needs saying that the majority of perspectives from which these traditions are criticized embrace postcolonialism and identity politics. One of the features which makes David Carrier's *World Art History and its Objects* seem so different from most other contributions to the debate is his embrace of a broadly liberal politics and an intellectual register derived from analytical philosophy rather than deconstruction. His operative theory of art is indebted to Wollheim and Danto, not Said; his view of society is based on Habermas and Rorty, not Foucault and Spivak. It is noteworthy, therefore, that for all the gulf that separates him from postcolonialism and identity politics, Carrier is equally pessimistic about the prospects for a "world art history." Whereas the former fear a covert extension of intellectual imperialism, Carrier fears that it is unlikely there can ever be a "proper history" that is able to situate Chinese, Indian or Islamic art in a developmental tradition because of the combination of too much evidence having been lost (in the way of both artifacts and records) and what in the West has been called art having elsewhere been conceived in different terms.[21] It is worth mentioning also that Carrier's attention is explicitly restricted to those exemplars of what he calls "high art traditions" paralleling that of the West. Africa and Oceania fall entirely outside his discussion. The majority of the world's art eludes the basic requirements of having such a "proper history" written about it. Surely one has to say that the problem here, at the present, lies with the conception of "proper history" rather than with the value or interest of the "arts" in question, if that is what we are committed to calling them.

As we have acknowledged, these are not small problems, particularly when such radically dissonant perspectives raise them. Are there any countervailing arguments to hand with which to underwrite a radically motivated world art studies? For my part, I think there are. But some re-engagement with the terms of the debate is necessary. First among these is the opposition between particularism and universalism. In a postcolonial situation the assertion of radical difference and the incommensurability of cultures is understandable. At its most basic it functions as a line of defense against invasion by powerful forces of the imperium, forces which have become stronger than ever in the condition of globalization, with its unrestricted range of capital flow backed up by modern communication technologies. But the logical consequence of rejecting all forms of cross-cultural generalization because of what they *might* betoken would be a series of cultural autarchies quite remote from the way cultures actually evolve and develop. As Whitney Davis has pointed out, there is a paradox shadowing the "remorselessly emic" bias of so many contributions to the debate on world art studies.[22] Driven by the requirement to address variety, to give difference its due, the result is a rejection of all vestiges of generalization including the very condition of globalization itself, which has brought the debate into existence. It is worth acknowledging explicitly, as Kitty Zijlmans does, that the aspiration to world art studies is a recent phenomenon. This is not an accident. It is not, however, the first time an aspiration to understand the practice of art on a global basis has arisen. There was a previous phase of this in the late nineteenth century, largely though not exclusively in German-language contexts. It is obvious that the emergence of this debate was stimulated by the condition of nineteenth-century imperialism. By the same token, it is evident that the contemporary re-emergence of a concern with the global dimension of cultural practice is itself the result of influences on the academy occasioned by the forces of contemporary politics: in this case, the politics not of imperialism and colonialism but of postcolonialism and resistance to imperialism. To argue that all voices, all intellectual strategies, emanating from the Western academy are *ipso facto* client to colonialism is the barest form of reductionism. Difference and contradiction exist here too. It is quite mistaken to regard the academy as a monolithic threat to virtuous particularity and no more; the academy is itself fissured.

Generalization, comparison, etc. are part of the fabric of research. In intercultural contexts the key motif is translation. This is particularly well articulated by Wilfried van Damme, who acknowledges the position of those whom he defines as "radical relativists" and "extreme particularists." But the consequence of that is the suggestion "that cultures present conceptually and semantically closed universes that are forever inaccessible to cultural outsiders." It is quite true, as van

Damme concedes, that "concepts from a given tradition" will have "their own histories and their own semantic fields"; they will, moreover, be understood by native speakers differently at different points in time. But all of that notwithstanding, for van Damme, evidence from cultures as diverse as Aztec, Yoruba, and English appears to demonstrate "significant semantic overlap" between concepts dealing with the field of the visual arts. Despite the presence of examples of lack of fit, on the whole he argues that "proper elucidation and contextualisation" should enable descriptions and analyses of art made in a language other than that native to the artwork in question to be able to include "key concepts and other crucial terms" to be "retained in their original forms in order for their meanings or semantic resonance to remain intact as much as practically possible."[23]

Van Damme thus holds out at least the possibility of cross-cultural understanding in the field of art. Nonetheless, the question is far from resolved. In his contribution to the *Is Art History Global?* debate, the Japanese speaker Shigemi Inaga points out that "basic terms (in the West) like 'expression' or 'representation' suddenly lose their semantic stability and methodological reliability once they are confronted with other realities constructed with different grammars and syntaxes, and articulated with wholly different vocabularies and taxonomy."[24] No one said it is going to be easy. It is well known that no translation can be transparent, even between relatively closely related languages such as French and English, let alone English and Japanese. But van Damme's openness seems preferable to battened-down autarchy, not least because of what one might call its realism. The problem seems to lie less with the possibility of translation or the provision of collateral information as such than the grounds on which the enterprise is conducted. The world is global whether we like it or not. In terms of production and finance the connectedness is self-evident. That connectedness is enabled by globe-spanning communications media. What irony if the sphere of art, one of the places where a sense of shared humanity might form a point of redress against the depredations of global capital, were to be debarred from making its general case by a misguided commitment to the particular.

Here again there is something to be said. Cross-cultural opacity is real, there is no question about that. Assumptions of transparency are imperialist, or missionary at best. Such assumptions are never abstract; they always emanate from positions of power. It does seem to matter whether the project of a world art studies is regarded as an extension of the Western academy's reach or a fundamental challenge to it. In order to encourage the latter, some contributors to the debate, once again including James Elkins, have suggested a kind of moratorium on the use of Western organizing concepts and methods, a thought experiment to explore the consequences of using, say, Chinese or Indian concepts to write about Western art. Others, including Whitney Davis, have been skeptical. The argument here does go inescapably to the "reach" of Western analytical concepts, and whether or not it is appropriate to regard art, in the words of Zijlmans and van Damme, as "a pan-human phenomenon," a "basic feature of our shared humanity."[25] If radical particularism rejects that, then it is hard to see how one avoids a condition of essentially separate series of inward-looking discourses (none of which would resemble "art history" as we know it). If it is legitimate to speak in that fashion, then there is real traction in the question posed by Davis, "why should we forego theoretical resources" which do indeed try to address art "as a putative human universal"?[26] Indigenous traditions and criteria, local by their very nature, cannot address the global condition of art now; whereas the modern critical tradition can, even as it perhaps cannot describe those local traditions in the plenitude of their own being. If translation and contextualization are permitted, so far so good; if not, any project of generalization crashes and burns. One must, surely, return to the acknowledgment that the contemporary global condition is actual, for better *and* for worse.

One of the projects that is often enlisted to underwrite a rejection of the universalization of methods and concepts from the Western critical tradition is Dipesh Chakrabarty's study of the condition of modernity in contemporary Indian society and culture, *Provincialising Europe*. As we shall see in the next section, the curator Okwui Enwezor explicitly offers it as a model for his own project of "provincialising modernism." But Chakrabarty himself is much more circumspect. It is worth recognizing, incidentally, that Chakrabarty does not address art as such; his project is located within the field of the human sciences, and thus it exhibits a preoccupation with truth and accuracy that all too often seems to seep away from discussion of art. In some respects, Chakrabarty revisits from a globalized, subaltern studies position, the older social science debate concerning the respective viability of concepts of explanation and understanding, the tension between scientific explanation and hermeneutics. He does this by bringing Marx into conjunction with Heidegger under the rubrics *History 1* and *History 2*, respectively, periodizing, aspirantly universalizable "knowledge" and lived experience, "practice." Chakrabarty thus explicitly argues that his "project of provincialising Europe," that is, arguing for the existence of legitimately multiple modernities rather than one modernity existing in Europe which has to be emulated by all other locations, "cannot be a project of cultural relativism." There is no ambiguity about this. For Chakrabarty, his project "does not call for a simplistic out-of-hand rejection of modernity, liberal values, universals, science, reason, grand narratives, totalising explanations and so on." It "cannot originate from a stance that the reason/science/universals that help define Europe as the modern are simply 'culture-specific.'"[27] Chakrabarty's is not an argument for simply replacing *History 1* with a multiplicity of *History 2*s. Rather, he posits Western science as an irreplaceable condition of any kind of searching for social justice *even though* it has to be brought into relation with local, particular experience. In a phrase, European thought for Chakrabarty is "both indispensible and inadequate" to thinking through the problems of localized modernities.[28] In the field of art, then, it is not a matter of setting up the Western canon of art as a standard with which to judge others. It is more a matter of bringing different traditions into facing-relationships with each other. In doing that, concepts and methods drawn from European critical traditions have their part to play, albeit leavened and amplified with translation and contextualization as circumstances require.

Thinking "Contemporary Art"

Debates about a "world art history" or, more defensibly, about a "world art studies" have taken on the importance they have because of changes in the world itself. It is globalization in the here and now that has made it necessary to reconsider narratives of the there and then. As Whitney Davis has put it, that enterprise is best not conceived of as one of getting art history to "go-global," in the sense of extending its normative purview. The task is "less empirical than methodological"; it is a matter of "worlding art" in history, an endeavor, "to put art into new worlds of study."[29] It appears to the present writer that any such "new worlds of study" (such as the leavening of the study of art by archaeology, anthropology, neurology, political economy, or whatever else seems germane), even if their object is the past, have to be animated by the present; perhaps even by a sense of possible futures different from our actual present. As far as I can see, the prospect of a world art studies should not be compartmentalized separately from an engagement with the contemporary in either art or the world. Yet the two discourses tend in practice not to overlap very much. World art studies is almost entirely the creature of the academy, albeit an academy striving to remain awake to the demands of the present. Debate over the nature of contemporary art, by contrast, though by no means absent from the academy, is also much more involved with journalism and the world of practice. In one sense this is to do nothing more than recognize that art history lives in universities whereas art practice lives in the market. But it seems important to keep the channels of communication between the distinctive discourses open.[30] Failure to do so risks antiquarianism on the one hand and amnesia on the other.

Contemporary debate on the globalization of art is already too extensive to permit a comprehensive overview, ranging all the way from supplements in fashion magazines and trade journals through to scholarly periodicals and books, all fuelled by an increasing number of exhibitions either addressing the condition explicitly or assuming it as a kind of ground. All I aim to do here is pick out some of the key preoccupations articulated by leading voices in the debate.

In fact, one of the earliest contributions scarcely addresses globalization as such, though it would be impossible to omit Nicolas Bourriaud's *Relational Aesthetics* from any consideration of the contemporary condition of art. The book was first published in France in 1998, not appearing in English until 2002. It is immediately apparent how much it reflects a period very different from our own. The first decade of the twenty-first century was defined by political and economic crises which at the present time have all the appearance of a permanent condition, at least for the foreseeable future. In February 2012, the Metropolitan Museum of Art in New York hosted a panel discussion aimed at setting cultural production within the broader context of global economics; it carried the heading "Global Economy: Crisis without End. From Europe to Beijing to Washington." The last decade of the twentieth century was not like that – at least, not in the heartlands of Euro-America that still appeared to hold sway over the world a decade after the end of the Cold War and its attendant trumpeting of a global capitalist heaven. In retrospect it is the first Gulf War and the explosion of former Yugoslavia that mark the period, not to mention the asset-stripping of the erstwhile Soviet Union and genocide in Africa. But, on the whole, these things cast no shadow over *Relational Aesthetics*. To the contrary, for Bourriaud it was the previous period, which he identifies with modernism, that was "based on conflict." Whereas, by contrast, "the imaginary of our own day and age is concerned with negotiations, bonds and co-existences." It is strange now to read that "these days we are no longer trying to advance by means of conflictual clashes." The impression of some kind of insulation from the deeper stresses and strains of the time is actually heightened by Bourriaud's insistence on defining his idea of contemporary art *against* utopia. The modernist avant-garde is taken to task for its supposedly idealistic vision of an alternative future, an impossible "golden age on earth," while relational art, by contrast, is seen as "attempting to construct concrete spaces" within a world defined by "fairer social relations."[31]

Bourriaud's argument was very much of its time. But for all that, his project was conceived in radical terms; he explicitly claimed that "relational aesthetics is part of a materialist tradition" and opposed "a return to aesthetic values based on tradition, mastery of technique and respect for historical conventions."[32] In essence, the idea of relational art seems to combine an extreme form of site-specificity with an inverted situationism. However, unlike Debord, who regarded art as an elitist irrelevance at best, or more often an active constituent of ideological mystification, for Bourriaud the "constructed situation" *is* the work of art: "The work that forms a 'relational world,' and a social interstice, updates Situationism and reconciles it … with the art world."[33] Using that notion of the "interstice," which he says Marx employed to describe non-commodity / profit-based forms of community, he holds out the art exhibition itself as providing a model for the possibility of non-instrumental human interaction. Exhibitions provide "free areas" and "time spans whose rhythm contrasts with those structuring everyday life" and help generate "inter-human commerce that differs from the 'communication zones' that are imposed upon us." The vision is one in which "intersubjectivity" becomes not just "the social setting for the reception of art" but itself "the quintessence of artistic practice." For Bourriaud, this is, in and of itself, "a political project," one which turns away from any dream of wholesale transformation and instead seeks to produce "micro-utopias," that is, "interstices opened up in the social corpus."[34]

Admittedly with benefit of hindsight, it is hard now to see this as anything other than a misanalysis: confusing temporary and localized boom conditions in the richest economies of the world for a permanent, universal landscape of peace and prosperity. The bathos really comes out when Bourriaud, in trying to distinguish relational art practice from supposedly discredited previous oppositional forms, avers that the present has still to develop its characteristic oppositional form, one which must be distinct from the soviets, the sit-ins, the demonstrations, the processions, the strikes of an earlier revolutionary culture. Yet all that is on offer is "free parties lasting several days," "computer bugs seizing up thousands of software systems simultaneously" and art exhibitions.[35] Some of this might charitably be regarded as an early perception of the possibilities of hacking and the oppositional use of social media sites, but the rest seems itself to be marked by the very idealism and utopianism it inveighs against. Rather than a serious alternative to the world of instrumental reason, a genuine "invention of models of sociability" and "new life possibilities," Bourriaud's vision looks like a symptom of the concentrated privilege of a stratum within the international art world.[36] There lies the problem, for before it is a research laboratory for new ways of life the art world is a symptom of an existing one. For all the much-vaunted image of the contemporary artist as a "cultural nomad," the figure actually seems to share more with the international businessman. Bourriaud does recognize the charge that relational art merely represents "a phonily utopian pantomime," but he seems seriously to overestimate the potential for his "modelling of forms of sociability" to spread out from the art world to spheres less cushioned by privilege.

Claire Bishop said as much in a critical discussion of Bourriaud's model in 2004, not long after it appeared in English, pointing out "the ease with which the 'laboratory' becomes marketable as a space of leisure and entertainment."[37] In effect, relational art rather than resisting commodification and instrumental reason fitted very well with the latest stage of capitalism, the prioritization of abstracted services over production, and rapid movement of finance on a global scale. As Bishop pointed out, what should be at issue for a putatively radical art is less the generation of intersubjective relations as such than the *kind* of relations that are suggested. "It is no longer enough to say that activating the viewer *tout court* is a democratic act. … The tasks facing us today are to analyse *how* contemporary art addresses the viewer and to assess the quality of the audience relations it produces."[38] The key here is not the production of a specious harmony within the privileged circles of the international art world, much less the implication of potential harmony in the world at large, but the need to address the contradictions and antagonisms that actually constitute social reality in a globalized world.

The tensioned nature of that reality was more forcefully acknowledged in the late 1990s by another leading figure in the debate about contemporary art, the Nigerian-born curator Okwui Enwezor. Already in 1997, in his organization of the 2nd Johannesburg Biennale, the postcolonial condition was for Enwezor the key to the contemporary. Although the biennale ran into criticism for what was perceived as its lack of a relationship to local communities, Enwezor's ambition was to mark a new global situation; one that was "new," moreover, on an epochal scale. For him, the global condition of the late twentieth century marked "the end of a historical phase of modernity." This was more than just the end of the Cold War, which tends to be regarded as the convenient start-date of contemporary globalization. In his view, the phase that was over was the much longer "historical process which began with the expansionist policies of several European countries (Spain, France, Portugal, Holland, England) and early multinationals (the Dutch East India and British East India Companies) from the mid-fifteenth century." For Enwezor, the "phase of modernity" that was ending had a reach of five hundred years, not just fifty. With a disregard for historical specificity that thought nothing of eliding the Renaissance with the Enlightenment, his case was that for the world outside of Europe, the whole long period had been "a negative Age of Decline and Defensiveness."[39] For him, *that* was what was now at stake in characterizations of the "contemporary."

In effect, Enwezor identified the global contemporary with the postcolonial condition. From his perspective, the "postcolonial constellation," as he names it, is the "matrix" that "shapes the ethics of subjectivity and creativity today."[40] A qualification must be entered here, however, for both Enwezor and the other prominent contributor to the debate on contemporary art, the Australian Terry Smith, reserve the term "globalization" to describe the hegemonic power of contemporary global capitalism. Opposed to this are a multiplicity of "transcultural" or "transnational" forces which are interpreted as embodying resistance to the power of globalization as such. It is here that the liberating power of the postcolonial constellation is grounded: in difference.

Though the centering on the postcolonial is particularly Enwezor's stress, Smith just as emphatically sees diversity and difference as the key to the nature of the contemporary situation: "the key characteristic of contemporary art, as it is of contemporary life, in the world today."[41] For both authors, multiplicity and mixing are the hallmarks of the contemporary. Indeed, something of this sort represents common ground across the whole spectrum of debate. This condition is equally conventionally set against the specter of a "universalizing," or "totalizing" perspective which is normally identified with modernism and the avant-garde. There is a pervasive tendency to play fast and loose with these categories, but the upshot is a complex register of positive and negative terms which are always being invoked to mark out the character of the contemporary and the global (or perhaps it would be truer to say the anti-global), on the one hand, from something else which is past, modern(-ist), and Euro-American. Even a cursory review easily generates, for example: universality / multiplicity; totality / diversity; linear / multi-temporal; center / network; global / transnational. In each pairing the former element is coded negative, the latter positive. Moreover, even a hesitant reluctance to accept that structure of values automatically lines you up with the *bad guys*, or – worse – unmasks you as old-fashioned.

From this point of view, modernism's eclipse is now total. Not that this is entirely new. Ever since the neo-avant-garde of the 1950s and the conceptual art of the 1960s, modernism has been critiqued both for its narrowness as art and for its political complicity with a spectrum of class- and gender-based exclusions. But the broadening-out of a sense of the "postcolonial" from the legacy of European empires, from what was once known as the "Third World," to a defining motif of the contemporary global condition writ large has had a further and massively deleterious effect on how modernism is regarded. Now, the arrogation of artistic value to a narrowly conceived "mainstream" emanating from a few highly developed cultural centers in Europe and America seems nothing less than the expression of minority rule at the level of the aesthetic. No doubt, the question of aesthetic value continues to haunt both discourses under discussion here, of "world art studies" and the "global contemporary." (Whether the impulse behind them is deemed imperialist or democratic, neither exhibits any simple fit with questions of aesthetic quality, however that may be articulated.) So, too, does the question of the relation of the Western canon of art (broadly conceived), as well as of the modernist canon (more narrowly conceived), to that same global contemporary. But however those debates play out in the future, in our present, for most contributors to the debate on the nature of the global contemporary, modernism is a thing of the past. In Bourriaud's words, "the principles or the style of twentieth century modernism" are now "far from our preoccupations."[42] For Terry Smith, "contemporary art" is not "simply the latest manifestation of modern art"; it is "different in kind from modern art."[43]

It is worth investigating this because the implications are far-reaching. The attempt to conceptualize contemporary art as a formation distinct from modernism (and, it should be added, from postmodernism) brings along with it another register of problems. These concern the nature of the contemporary itself, the contemporary, that is, understood not just in terms of a range of connected art practices, but as a social and historical condition. Although Bourriaud, Smith, and Enwezor all bring their own priorities and inflections to the argument, there is a fair consensus running through their accounts about the key features of contemporary art.

The most obvious, indeed it is a feature which is incontrovertible, is the much expanded range of materials out of which art is made, or perhaps one should say, the expanded range of materials which artists have employed in their activities, just to emphasize that the production of a finite object is no longer the main point. This is such a central feature of contemporary art that it would be almost trivial to remark it, were it not for the fact that it already has been remarked, long ago, by Rosalind Krauss in her characterization of the "expanded field" of postmodernist art, or even earlier by Allan Kaprow in his descriptions of "environments, assemblages and happenings." Although non-medium-specificity *is* a key characteristic of contemporary art, there is, so to speak, nothing specifically contemporary about it. There *is* a narrower case for the novelty of the variety of electronic media that have flourished in contemporary art since the appearance of the Internet. But the variety of media as such only begins to work as a motif of the specifically "contemporary" if an opposed modernism (medium-specific, formalist, etc.) is aggrandized out of its actual historical orbit to fulfill the role of negative pole against which to define that "contemporary." The more you allow to modernism a degree of complexity, both in its relations with the historical avant-gardes and in its prolonged engagement with representation, the less readily it can be made to serve as a barren and outmoded Aunt Sally against which to celebrate the productive diversity of its successors.

A second feature often taken to be definitive of contemporary art, and which unsurprisingly is emphasized by Bourriaud and Enwezor, both themselves curators, is the increased importance of the curator; especially in the context of the proliferating temporary exhibitions (biennales and similar) which for most people with any interest in such things constitute the key site of encounter with contemporary art. Bourriaud explicitly likens the curator to the film director; and thereby he implicitly relegates the artist-figure to the status of actor in the wider production of which the curator is the real *auteur*. This stance prompts disquiet among some artists. In an *Artforum* debate on the impact of globalization on art and the growth of large-scale temporary exhibitions, Martha Rosler professed herself "perturbed" by what she saw as Enwezor's attempt to "rather decisively elevate the curatorial metadiscourse above the contribution of the artists."[44] Enwezor's response was interesting and ambivalent. While on the one hand rejecting the accusation of "elevating" the curator over the artist he nonetheless constructed an image of "the artist as absolute god," and also of "the false idolatry of the artwork" to which his curatorial practice was opposed.[45] A similar position was also elaborated by Catherine David, curator of *Documenta X* in 1997. For her, the question is not about the artist as such but "about *how* to produce, discuss, debate and circulate to various audiences a certain number of ideas and formal articulations proposed by authors." The further point being that such people – "authors" – "no longer correspond to the economic, social and cultural figure of 'the artist' as it has been constituted in the modern age."[46] Much depends on this and on how the idea is developed. If it points towards the extinction of the modernist artist, and the replacement of that figure by a more reflective, informed, and critical type of cultural producer, well and good. If it points to the increasing remit of pseudo-articulate cultural management, less so.

A third important feature of the contemporary constellation that Smith emphasizes is the recurrent preoccupation in much contemporary art with questions of identity; this can extend all the way from the more psychically inflected register of what Smith calls a preoccupation with "selfhood," to the more socially inflected sense of Enwezor's focus on "the idea of the postnational subject," one who in an age of migration and diaspora comes to constitute "the new global citizen."[47] Once again, though, it would be entirely feasible to claim a preoccupation with identity as characteristic of much of the "postmodernist" art of the last three decades of the twentieth century, not a defining feature of the "contemporary" itself.

A further feature claimed to characterize the transnational contemporary, and which probably can be said to define itself against post-Cold War globalization, is a widespread emphasis on the local. All three authors cast the local against the homogenizing force of globalizing capital through their counter-definitions of the "transnational" (Smith), the "transcultural" (Enwezor), or the "alterglobal" (Bourriaud), all of which are defined by multifarious strategies of resistance to totalization, and hence to an openness to the particular and the local. Once again this is easy to mobilize against the notion of generic formal problems ascribed to modernism. It also has the positive effect of dismantling the center/periphery model associated with modernism while, in aspiration at least, conferring on all localities an equal significance as the generative context for art-making. Among other features, Enwezor and Smith both also emphasize a widespread preoccupation with what Smith describes as a "resistant awareness of the pervasive power of mass and official media."[48]

A final important feature of the contemporary constellation of art practices, rightly noted by both, is the widespread desire of contemporary artists to have an effect on the circumstances in which they intervene, an aspiration as Smith somewhat weakly puts it, to "improve the situation."[49] This stance, which does inform a fair amount of contemporary art, is routinely used to establish distance from modernism in respect of the latter's identification with "autonomy." Autonomy is one of the features of modernism most open to hostile caricature, and this is not the place to debate it. But it is worth establishing what is being claimed of the "contemporary" constellation. Thus Smith argues that contemporary practice involves a "total embrace of everyday life as the domain of affective experience."[50] I take this to be a claim made in opposition to the notion of a distinctive domain of the "aesthetic" separate from the quotidian. Something of the sort does seem to be pervasive, but with what consequences is less easy to determine. And volunteering to save the world, as with many of the other supposedly defining features of contemporary art, also has its longer history.

For better or worse, then, we are left with a consensus. For Smith, place, media, identity, and effect complement Enwezor's emphasis on media, expanded range of materials and types of exhibition, difference, and a blurring of the bounds of economic and cultural effect. It is unlikely that anyone would fundamentally question this phenomenology of contemporary art. The emphases may differ. Enwezor is perennially concerned to keep up the pressure on those forces that seek to maintain business-as-usual, setting his sense of "emergent networks" and "mobile sites of discourse" against "traditional circuits of institutionalized production and reception."[51] Smith, by contrast, is positively starry-eyed, going so far as to believe that contemporary art "can speak to us in some special, direct way, about our experience of living in the present time, of belonging to it, of being contemporary."[52]

This is the crux of the matter. Can a contemporary art constituted along those lines, that is, focused on the effects of mass media, preoccupied with questions of identity and difference, motivated by a conviction of the significance of the local in what Enwezor calls a "tessellated" relationship with the global, deliver a kind of truth about the contemporary situation? Surely the answer has to be a qualified "yes." But in my view, the important point goes to that qualification. An art conceived along those lines can just as easily issue in mystifications of contemporary reality. It is *how* the reality is understood that is at issue, just as much as how the art is understood. It is to the credit of the authors under discussion that wide-ranging accounts of what is distinctive about contemporary art are now so widely available, and broadly speaking so mutually complementary. But the thing to be on guard against here is precisely the risks of such consensus. The unpopular question that needs to be asked is whether we may, in assenting to the characterization of "contemporaneity itself" as "multiple, internally differentiating, category-shifting, shape-changing, unpredictable (that is, diverse),"[53] ourselves be in thrall to one of the most powerful self-images of the age.

All the authors discussed have a highly fluid and mobile conception of the contemporary condition. Multiplicity, plurality, indeterminacy are reiterated over and over again as its defining features, and they are equally often set over against specters of authority and closure: manifest in thought-crimes like "linear" historical thinking, "monocausal" explanations, and "totalizing" accounts of anything. In terms of art, these are identified with modernism (or more generally with the Western canon as a whole); in terms of social theory they are identified with Marxism. Historically, the relation between modernism and Marxism has been complex and open to widely differing interpretations. For some, modernism involved a species of philosophical idealism which merited critique from an historical materialist position. For others, certain forms of artistic modernism were compatible with historical materialist theory and politics. In terms of the debate over contemporaneity, however, this historical complexity is not often encountered. This is partly due to an emphasis on geography rather than history, a tendency to regard contradictions between the West and the majority world as of greater moment than contradictions within Western art and philosophy. It might equally be due to other reasons for downgrading and marginalizing a critical tradition rather than seeking to revise it; reasons involving an unstated rapprochement with the conditions of neoliberal globalization.

Out of the authors discussed here, Bourriaud came closest to some kind of affinity with a Left avant-garde inheritance when he described relational aesthetics as part of a materialist tradition and connected it to the legacy of situationism. But by the time of *Altermodern* in 2009 he was explicitly invoking Lyotard's conception of postmodernism as marking "the end of history considered as a linear narrative." For Bourriaud, "the disappearance of these metanarratives (Marxism in particular)" had ushered in what he called "a culture of improvisation" in which "signs have lost all contact with human history."[54] Analytically, it is hard to see this as more than a rhetorical literary flourish, or a weak apology for the eclecticism exhibited by one strand of postmodernism. But, nonetheless, the invocation of a kind of freewheeling openness to contingency on the one hand and, on the other, an overt identification of Marxism with outmoded "linear" thinking and a false teleology of progress sounds a note which rings through all these theories of the contemporary. The curious thing for Bourriaud, albeit to a degree understandable in a French writer coming from a Left culture dominated by the notoriously Stalinist French Communist Party (the PCF), is that despite his earlier qualified openness to situationism, he now effectively identifies Marxism with the Soviet Union. In a way this is self-fulfilling. If you identify Marxism with a crude and violent bureaucratic politics then of course it is to be shunned. But this is such an impoverished conception that, while one might have come to expect it from the postmodernist theory of the 1980s, to have it reaffirmed so baldly at a relatively late date might actually signify something else. Before discussing that possibility, however, we need briefly to note other characterizations of the contemporary.

Enwezor's commitment to the postcolonial as hallmark of contemporaneity lends a powerful critical dimension to his writing, manifest for example in his justified skepticism about the pieties of Enlightenment. He is impatient with the claim that modernity was a condition restricted to Europe and that it was the function of empire to disseminate it under a rubric of "progress." As he emphasizes, there was an "export" variety whose practice embodied little enough of the "civilizing" theory. But his attitude to Western science, to the Western academy, exhibits little of the complexity of Chakrabarty. Art history, for example, is defined by its "roots in imperial discourse,"[55] and while some such relation is true enough, whether it is so without remainder is another matter entirely. It is not at all so transparently obvious, for example, whether it is adequate to regard contemporary tendencies aiming to broaden art history as nothing more than attempts to assert a "panoptic view of art practice" or to see would-be multicultural curators as "viceroys" charged with "the role of bringing the nonbelievers under the sovereign regard of the great Western tradition."[56] Rhetorical effect is one thing, but it is another simply to massify all currents within multivalent discourses on the grounds of their historical or geographical points of derivation. More troubling still is the way his Foucault-derived desire for "another figure of truth" leads him to conflate hegemonic and counter-hegemonic traditions because of their shared Western-ness. Thus his sought-for "new truth" is explicitly defined in opposition to "two paradigms of totalisation": "capitalism and imperialism" on the one hand and "socialism and totalitarianism" on the other.[57]

Enwezor ends up in the same place as Bourriaud, effectively identifying the principal historical critique of capitalism and imperialism *with it*; he sees their common historical derivation within Western modernity as of more significance than their opposition to each other. This is quite explicit, as when he speaks of the "consensual opposition between the Left and the Right, each pitched in its historical bivouac."[58] Those weasel words, "consensual opposition," take the model of bourgeois parliamentary opposition and expand it to cover the whole spectrum of capitalism and Left opposition, effectively turning the latter into a creature of the former. The upshot is that the postcolonial contemporary is separated from the long historical contention of capitalism and its critique from the Left (a position, incidentally, which one would think does scant justice to many early and mid-twentieth-century national liberation movements themselves).

This is, at best, a long way from Chakrabarty's considered assessment of European science as "inadequate but essential." At its worst it disarms one powerful form of critique of globalism. It can, furthermore, lead to some bizarre positions, as when Enwezor is led to a more or less uncritical panegyric to the neoliberal modernizations of South Korea and China contrasted with a Europe which is in his view "less part of our time," "old and dour" in feeling, and like "a museum of modernity."[59] When a celebration of dynamism involves the acceptance of an almost complete lack of worker representation; of restricted social welfare provision; and a colossal, indeed widening, income gap between the rural and urban poor and an enriched managerial class of the kind that characterizes contemporary China, then one wonders whether being "part of our time" is such a boon at all. If one abandons the formulation of a critique of contemporaneity that seeks to understand it as a "totality" simply because the act of doing so is held to undermine legitimate particularity and be part of a "totalizing" tradition of thought, then surface phenomena risk being misunderstood as definitive of the condition itself. This is, indeed, what happens when contemporaneity is defined as a circumstance of "permanent transition."[60] This is, of course, precisely the way contemporary global capitalism likes to present itself, as resistant to definition, free-floating, improvisatory, open.

In Enwezor's case, because his own work and the art he supports is overtly "resistant to global totalisation,"[61] because his anti-imperialist stance is so strong, and because we are undeniably living through a period of resurgent imperialism, one might see the evocation of "permanent transition" as a relatively harmless by-product of a justified skepticism about the West and an eagerness to leave behind stereotyped oppositions of Left and Right. Yet it is central to Enwezor's position. It is no coincidence that precisely the same figure is also evoked in Terry Smith's writing on the global contemporary. The motif of "permanent transition," it seems, is not a mere figure, a rhetorical gesture, but a key thesis about the nature of the world we are living in and the art it has produced. Ultimately this redounds to the credit neither of the analysis nor of much of the art.

Before trying to draw these conclusions together, let us look at the argument of Terry Smith, among the most prolific of those who have attempted to characterize the contemporary art condition. Smith, like Enwezor, regards "globalizing capitalism" as symbiotic with what he calls "leftism locked into dialectical historicism."[62] This notion of "leftism," it is worth noting, apparently embraces not just the "new" as well as the "old" Lefts of the 1960s and earlier but also contemporary anti-globalization protests. All of which chimes well with Bourriaud's criticism of both conservative (i.e. modernist–aestheticist) responses to contemporaneity and what he called "backward-looking militants."[63] For Smith, the specter of an ever more crushing globalization, combined with a rejection of Left opposition to it under rubrics of totalization and historicism, leads him to apostrophize the need for nothing less than "a different politics, a different ethics and a different imagery."[64] Elsewhere, what appears to be the same idea occurs when living in the present is described as being on the "threshold of large-scale meaning change."[65] Strange, indeed, given this chiliasm, that the Left should be condemned for "utopianism." There is a highly characteristic oscillation between this sense of a need for a new everything and a focus on "modelling the minutiae of the world's processes,"[66] which seems close to Bourriaud's interstitial "microtopias."

An interesting feature of Smith's thinking about the contemporary is that his rejection of what he considers to be universalist, or totalizing, critique (code, in effect, for Marxism) is not matched by an embrace of that emphasis on the irreducibility of difference which is such a marked component of postcolonial debate. In fact, Smith makes a point of distancing his position from both universalizing critique and "singularising particularity."[67] What follows is important, for it goes to one of Smith's two central ideas: "antinomy." What gives the argument its contemporary resonance is that while "universalising critique" and "singularising particularity" are both to be rejected, the desired third way is *not* characterized as a middle way between them. The path that is adopted is to see both as having virtues, albeit as antinomies, and to bring to bear on them an "engaged relativism."[68] Productive work then results in "provisional syntheses" of the existing antinomies against the background of a contemporary condition which, as with Enwezor, is supposedly defined by a state of "permanent transition."[69]

At the risk of laboring the point, I want to try and get clear on the implications of this, because it seems to go to the heart of an important set of now widely publicized positions about the nature of the contemporary world and the role of art in it. The contemporary social/political/economic condition, centrally determined by the fact of "globalization," is repeatedly characterized as a state of "permanent transition." It is sharply distinguished from the previous period, which is named "modernity," which was marked by goals such as "progress" and "improvement." The new condition, the argument goes, requires a new response, quite different from capitalist affirmation (marked by a rhetoric of "freedom," "democracy," and the "market") as well as both main forms of contemporary opposition to it, namely anti-globalization protests and jihad. This desired response, in turn, is couched once again *not* in terms of pursuing a middle course between them but of somehow playing off what are termed the "antinomies" of the current situation (including "overarching explanatory totality" *and* "stand-alone, singularising particularism")[70] and keeping the positive elements of each. Thus: "an appeal for radical particularism to work with and against radical generalization, to treat all the elements in the mix as antinomies."[71] Smith defines this as a strategy of "pluralist relativism" involving "provisional syntheses." I find it difficult to conceive of this as anything more than the elevation of eclecticism to a point of principle, licensed by the twin theses of the total absence of any underlying stability and the definition of the present as a state of permanent transition requiring continually provisional responses.

This is clearly meant as a rejection, albeit an unstated one, of Trotsky's "permanent revolution," reliant as that is on notions of "progress" and historical development. It is also set (this time explicitly) against Baudelaire's theory of modernism, in which he balances the "unchanging and eternal" against the "fleeting and transitory" nature of modernity. The bedrock is now supposedly a thing of the past; everything is now deemed to be in flux, constantly. With both Baudelaire and the compound figure of Marx-Trotsky consigned to the dustbin of history, the way is open for "pluralist relativism" to take the stage as the only proper response to "this utterly changed situation"[72]; this condition of "permanent transition," "which makes us no longer modern."[73] This cluster of ideas is significant. On the one hand, it has some curious bedfellows. Thus, Thomas Laqueur recently characterized "the idea that we are living in a new world that has transcended old constraints" as a key component not of radical but of contemporary neo-conservative thought.[74] On the other hand, it sacrifices the aspiration to a comprehensive analysis of the contemporary condition, in principle. In so doing, the argument privileges the complexities of surface appearance and experience over any sense of underlying developmental logic a priori.

What underwrites this is both an acceptance of the advertising copy of contemporary capitalism itself and a stereotyped rejection of Marxism as one-dimensional as the caricature of modernism noted earlier. Not only is it as though the complexities of the tradition of Western Marxism never existed (everything reduced to a weird amalgam of the Soviet bureaucrat and the utopian *soixante-huitard*) but also, contemporary attempts to elucidate the working of the system are absent from the picture. Yet to take only one prominent example, David Harvey's materialist analysis of contemporary capitalism explicitly proceeds from a rejection of mono-causal explanation – the very charge leveled against Marxism by the theorists of "permanent transition" and "provisional syntheses." Instead, Harvey postulates the interaction of "seven distinctive 'activity spheres' within the evolutionary trajectory of capitalism."[75] These cover technologies, social relations, administrative arrangements, relations of production, relation of humanity to nature, and daily life, as well as "mental conceptions of the world." In contrast to cumbersome and now outmoded base/superstructure metaphors, Harvey is concerned to acknowledge that "no one of the spheres dominates even as none of them are independent of the others. But nor is any one of them determined even collectively by all of the others. Each sphere evolves on its own account but always in dynamic interaction with the others."[76] Proceeding from that kind of starting point, one might hope for more than a floating pluralist relativism, a celebration of superficial diversity. One might hope for an analysis of the forms taken by contemporary art in relation to the forces organizing contemporary globalization, one might begin to see how the globalization of art, not only in a minority of cases, resists, but also in large part serves, those forces. Globalized art production is a part of a neoliberal capitalist formation; it may harbor pockets of resistance within it, but as a system it is not resistant.[77] There are all sorts of contradictions, folds, and prospects for critical traction within the system, but they are to be located despite the system and its managers, not because of them. There is nothing new in that.

From Smith's viewpoint, in a situation deemed to be essentially beyond the reach of systemic analysis, it is Art, and those believed to be capable of grasping its message, that is granted a privileged position when it comes to knowing this situation – since it supposedly replicates in its own diversity the wider contemporary situation. It is "multiple, internally differentiating, category-shifting, shape-changing, unpredictable (that is, diverse) – like contemporaneity itself." As such it is "of our times in some special way."[78] Unblushingly, those tasked with carrying the burden of this "hope-filled enterprise"[79] are the "creative class": none other than "artists, writers, teachers, thinkers, and the many other workers on matters symbolic"; in short, they are "those able to grasp complexity."[80] In an earlier age, this might have been seen as a severe case of the aestheticization of politics, but, thankfully, we have now passed beyond the grip of such totalizing judgments. Instead – if we are carried along by this line of reasoning – we would be happy to believe that contemporary "transnational" art, and its institutional forms, is "reshaping our capacity to grasp the larger forces at work in the world today," and moreover is doing so "more productively than any other communication medium."[81]

By now, to put my cards on the table, what remains of my credulity has evaporated. I cannot see this as anything other than, at best, a form of contemporary idealism that overestimates the role of art in saving the world. The fantasy of a band of international curators, and other art-world *prominenti* obsessed with their iPhones™, riding to the rescue is reminiscent of nothing so much as the cultural project of Diotima and Count Lensdorff in Robert Musil's *Man Without Qualities*: promulgating the forthcoming "Austrian century" on the eve of 1914. Of course, the point then, and perhaps the point now, is that the whole sandcastle was about to be washed away by real historical forces rather than glamorized by wishful thinking.

As Musil saw, "pseudoreality prevails."[82] It is at least arguable that much of contemporary art, "transnational" or otherwise, is not distinctive and special but almost entirely client to the global culture that sustains it and that is in danger of either falling apart or turning "totalitarian" in a real sense. Normative contemporary art is at least as likely to be a mirror reflecting the self-image of the age as a tool for cutting through to the "larger forces at work." None of which is to say that powerful art does not continue to be made – just that it is, as ever, in a minority. Nor indeed that such art, when linked to incisive intellectual critique as in the *Global Contemporary* exhibition, cannot make telling interventions. This remains one of the strangest things about art, that most of the time it doesn't add up to much but that when it does, it does, and that this has always been the case. I think this is my biggest objection to the claim that everything is new, unprecedented, never before beheld. The technology is cleverer. But the connection of significant art to the wider world in which it has its existence, is far from new.

The Wider World Now

In the *Global Contemporary* exhibition itself a multifaceted video piece by the Russian group Chto Delat? ("What Is To Be Done?") took for its target precisely the constellation of forces about which I have been so skeptical here (Figure 5.2). In staged debates about the construction of the Gazprom tower in St Petersburg, based on transcripts of the real thing, the group enact a cabal in which security forces, bureaucrats, "cutting-edge" artists, trendy gallerists, and "critical" intellectuals all conspire together for their mutual benefit. The powers that be, alternately threatening and cajoling, have no trouble enlisting the art-world representatives behind their project: the artist making specious claims for a ridiculously banal golden fish, the intellectuals spouting quotes from Adorno and Badiou. Outside the hothouse atmosphere of the room, in the "real" world, the situation is no better. The "people" are short-sighted, self-seeking, and drained by materialism. The revolutionaries are romantic idiots. There is no way out. In the end, everyone is caught in the tentacles of the system itself. As a convincingly dystopian vision, it has few peers.

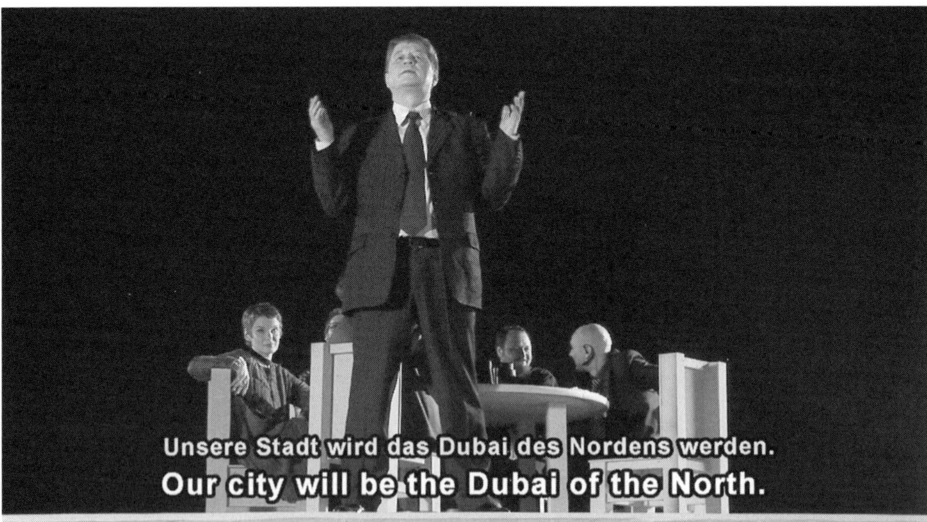

Figure 5.2 Chto Delat, Still from video piece *The Tower: A Songspiel*, 2010, *The Global Contemporary and the Rise of New Art Worlds* exhibition, September 17, 2011–February 5, 2012. Courtesy of Chto Delat and ZKM | Center for Art and Media Karlsruhe.

In a different register, Doris Salcedo's *Shibboleth*, installed at Tate Modern in 2007–2008 makes a comparable, crucial point with startling economy of means. There is a fissure running right through the foundations of the culture. She is right. As John Berryman might once have said, "There is, Mr. Bones, there is." It is a startling juxtaposition, perhaps, but as far as I can see, Salcedo's poetry complements Chto Delat's prose. One of the traditional tasks of art has been to universalize the historical human tragedy. Goya, Manet, Picasso all achieved this out of the raw material of tawdry little skirmishes, imperialist adventurism, and fascist onslaught. Does not Jannis Kounellis achieve a comparable goal for the early twenty-first-century war in Iraq in his 2004 installation in Oxford (Figure 5.3) with its forest of harsh metal crosses marching across a field of brightly colored oriental carpets? Does not the *Aboriginal Memorial*, made by the people of Ramingining in Arnhem Land (Figure 5.4), do the same with its two hundred hollow log coffins, one for every year of the White Australian bicentennial?

As we have seen, many people are rightly wary of the prospect of a world art history, concerned at the damage an uncritical expansion of the protocols of Western academe might do to cultural difference. Similar concerns apply to the notion of a "contemporary art history." In a chilling description, Terry Smith has written of the inaugural meeting of the Society of Contemporary Art Historians at the 2009 College Art Association conference. By his account, the type

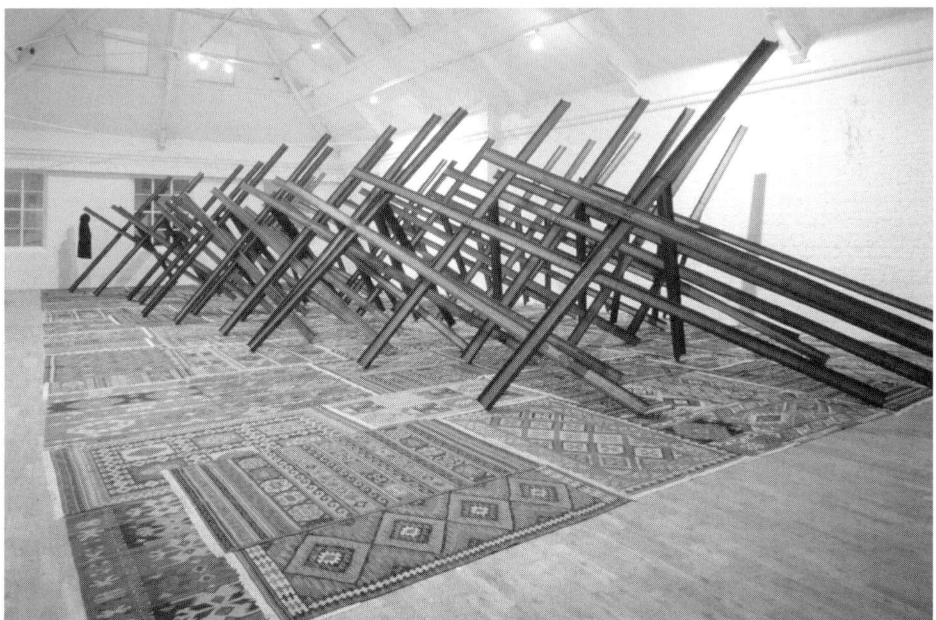

Figure 5.3 Jannis Kounellis, *Untitled*, 2004, installation view, Modern Art Oxford, 15 Dec. 2004–20 March 2005. © DACS 2013. Photography by Manolis Baboussis © Modern Art Oxford / © DACS 2013.

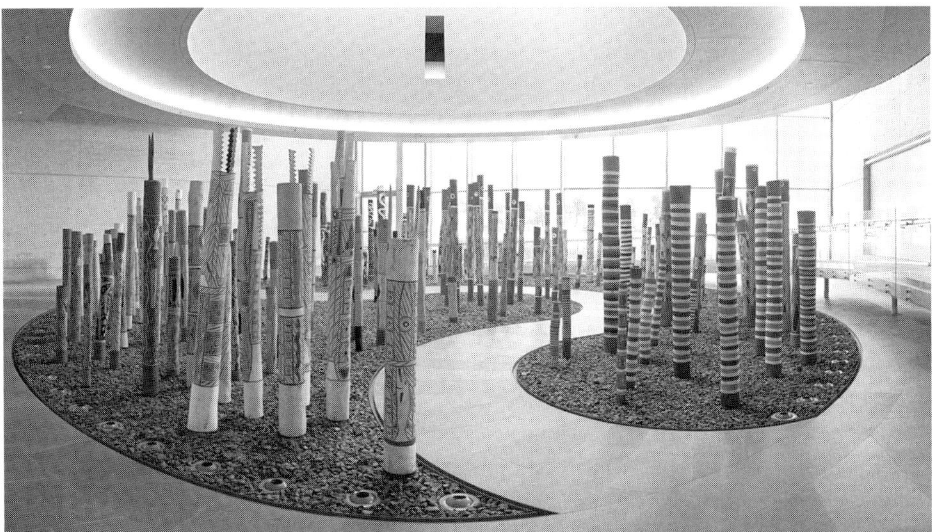

Figure 5.4 Ramingining artists, Ramingining, Northern Territory, Australia, *The Aboriginal Memorial*, 1987–1988 (installation of 200 hollow log bone coffins), natural earth pigments on wood, height (irregular) 327 cm. National Gallery of Australia, Canberra. Purchased with the assistance of funds from National Gallery admission charges and commissioned in 1987. © DACS 2013.

of question which exercised those active in the new field included: "How do I claim a topic before all the others? What if 'my artist' suddenly refuses to co-operate? How do I relate my topic to 'the field'?'"[83] This is the reality. One does not need the x-ray spex of contemporary art to see the "larger forces" at work. They are all too clear: the penetration of scholarship and research by territoriality, careerism – in a word, by the market. What is happening is the commodification of intellectual work, no less so than the commodification of art work on the global market. The suspicion forces itself that what is happening is that a new market is opening up for exploitation, in both art and art history. The impresarios of "contemporary" are making their bids to manage that new market.

A contemporary art worthy of the name surely has to resist this; mutatis mutandis, so too contemporary scholarship in art history. Academic specialism has its place, of course, but it can also deflect attention from larger issues. Being unable to see the wood for the trees is *the* hallmark of the specialist, the one we have met before, who knows more and more about less and less. It is easy, imprisoned within the contemporary hierarchies of academe, to see teaching as the poor relation of research. Yet if a world art studies is going to do any good at all it has to speak to people who are not specialists in the history of art but who are interested in the different cultures of the world, their own and others, past and present: with a view to responding to and indeed producing different ways of being in that world.

The present situation is that the globalization of a relatively autonomous art system has "docked" with the technically radical expanded field to produce an unprecedented state of affairs: an entirely open category, ontologically, historically, and geographically. Art can now be made of anything; or it may not be made at all. It can be made anywhere across the globe, beyond the geographical area where the concept was developed. It can also legitimately be said to have existed in the past, including the deep past, before the concept's actual historical formulation. This does not mean that art is possessed of an unchanging formal essence, to be arrived at by peeling away supposedly cutaneous layers of culturation, as modernist theory would have had it. The understanding of our categories as socially constructed rather than as naturally, let alone supernaturally, ordained, is surely the key theoretical advance of modernity. Yet this is not to deny that forms of enculturation may be perennial, recurrent, and widespread. As long ago as the 1930s, Wittgenstein argued against essentialism and for the notion of the "family resemblance."[84] As Peter Winch and Alastair MacIntyre debated, also a long time ago, the notion of "family resemblance" quickly goes to "forms of life" and relativism opens up.[85] Yet an extreme cultural relativism seems also to have run its course, to have passed the point where it functioned as an emancipatory lever against essentialism, and paradoxically to have elevated difference to the status of an essence of its own. Negating the possibility of translation, obstructing openness, denying permeability, emphasizing one's own difference and complexity, seeing only massification and homogeneity in the other, West, non-West, past, present, good, bad ... it is a counsel of despair. We are, or should be, beyond the point of being deceived by claims about unchanging biological or racial essence. But we are not absolutely free, even given modern advances in genetic research. We do exist within constraints, natural constraints – geological, biological, neurological, and psychological "natures" – dare one say it, "human natures." This is not to suggest the imposition of constraint on art. But it may be that one unexpected effect of the globalization of art in the current period has been to reopen the possibility of regarding art, not as possessed of a formal essence, but not as reduced to an endless series of practices isolated in irreducible cultural specificity either. It may be possible to conceive of art as a socially constructed, internally differentiated human universal, something human beings do; something they do, moreover, in consort with thinking and acting. The old questions have not gone away. The question of the relation not just of aesthetics and politics but of aesthetic activity and ethics, is alive; so too, the question of value.

As I said at the beginning of this chapter, I want to end with art rather than ideas. I have tried to do this with the brief discussion of Chto Delat and Salcedo, Kounellis, and the Ramingining community. But I would like to finish with a discussion of Fiona Tan's *Disorient*, shown at the Venice Biennale in 2009 (Figure 5.5). It allows the narrative to come full circle, back to Venice where we started, and back to Marco Polo. The camera's elegiac movement through a kind of storehouse, or is it an ethnographic museum, or is it a modern cabinet of curiosities? ...

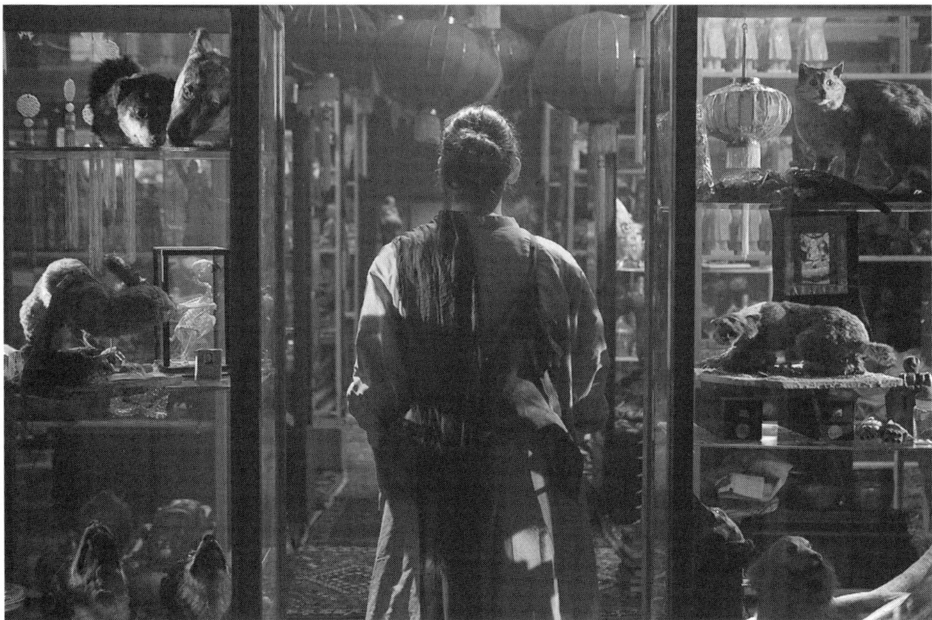

Figure 5.5 Fiona Tan, still photo image (showing back view of figure among museum showcases) from *Disorient*, 2009, twin screen video projection. Courtesy the artist and Frith Street Gallery.

an inchoate array of things "oriental" – porcelain figurines, Buddhas, a statue of Mao, stuffed birds and animals, jumbles of boxes and tins – suggests a reflexiveness about art and culture, its constructed nature yet also its being as material fact. And then there are the words, the quotations from Marco Polo that constitute the sound element of the work, accompanying the visual images. What does that say? Does it imply that the curve of Western domination of the world reaches all the way back, unbroken, to Polo? Some seem to think it does, but I hope not, if only because such a curve does not exist, continuous and unbroken. To establish that has been one of the burdens of this book. Does it speak rather to an unquenchable desire for encounter with the other, a disposition to meet and exchange? I don't know. I would like to think so, but I don't really know.

We don't even really know if Marco Polo did go to China. But we do know that when his book appeared it was called *Description of the World*. Tan's *Disorient* seems to offer another description of a world, a world made out of history and geography, made of difference for sure, but also of passages through difference, of contact and overlap.[86] All of which seems a worthwhile thing for contemporary art to be doing: laying things before us, opening things to view, asking questions, and letting us make our own minds up. Yet this is a critical openness, it seems not to want to let us get away with failing to pay attention, failing to remain alert to the state we are in. This state is undoubtedly complex, we are always being told how complex things now are, how complex is the world. But there is also a certain simplicity to it, not least as far as art is concerned. We now seem to stand at the opposite end of the spectrum from the condition of modernist art. In that condition, art seemed to have become so refined and overspecialized that it had ceased to be about very much beyond contemplation of the aesthetic as such. Whereas now art has merged itself into the world so thoroughly that its own identity has become dissolved into the aestheticization of contingency. Yet the twin poles of a realist address to history *and* a focus upon the aesthetic self-identity of the practice itself continue to bear on art. This is not a new condition. In earlier dark times, Brecht wrote that a realist art had to "discover the causal complexes of society" and "unmask the prevailing view of things as the view of those who are in power." He was not wrong about the task then and he is not wrong now. But neither is the voice from antiquity wrong that recognizes *ars longa, vita brevis*. Art still looks both ways: onto the world around it, the real, mutable, historical world, but also onto a different sense of the world viewed *sub specie aeternae*, onto the aesthetic dimension. The tension between these two continues to constitute the place where art gets made. When either falls from view, something is lost. The contemporary continues to hold within itself the past.

Notes

1 Belting, Buddensieg and Weibel, eds, 2013.
2 Weibel and Buddensieg, eds, 2007; Belting and Buddensieg, eds, 2009; Belting, Birken, Buddensieg, and Weibel, eds, 2011.
3 Onians 1996, p. 206.
4 Elkins 2004, p. 380.
5 Davis 2010, p. 8.
6 See Introduction in Onians 2006. Despite its date of publication, this book was based on the proceedings of a conference titled "Compression vs Expression: Containing and Explaining the World's Art" held at the Clark Institute in April 2000.
7 Preziosi 1989, pp. 102 and 109.
8 Gombrich 1950.
9 For a wittily titled, and persuasively written, contemporary riposte to the Eurocentric bias of normative art history, see Elkins 2002, especially chapters 4 and 5.
10 Elkins, ed., 2007.
11 Okeke-Agulu, in Elkins 2007, p. 205.
12 Errington, in Elkins 2007, p. 434.
13 Elkins 2008, p. 112.
14 Elkins 2008, pp. 115–116.
15 For a postcolonialist critique, see Dave-Mukherji 2005.
16 Foster, *et al.* 2004.
17 Elkins 2006, pp. 189 and 190.
18 Elkins 2006, p. 201.

19 Elkins 2006, pp. 205 and 206.
20 Elkins 2006, p. 211.
21 Carrier, 2008, p. 99.
22 Davis 2010, p. 5.
23 Wilfried van Damme, "Introducing World Art Studies," in Zijlmans and van Damme 2008, pp. 23–61, quotations from pp. 47 and 48.
24 Inaga, in Elkins 2007, p. 278.
25 Zijlmans and van Damme 2008, pp. 7 and 8.
26 Davis 2010, p. 6.
27 Chakrabarty 2008, pp. 42 and 43.
28 Chakrabarty 2008, p. 16.
29 Davis 2010, p. 4.
30 One project which attempts to do this is Elkins, Valiavicharska, and Kim, eds, 2010.
31 Bourriaud 2002, pp. 45 and 46.
32 Bourriaud, 2002, pp. 18 and 84.
33 Bourriaud 2002, p. 85.
34 Bourriaud 2002, pp. 16, 22, and 70.
35 Bourriaud, 2002, p. 83.
36 Bourriaud 2002, pp. 24 and 45.
37 Bishop 2004, p. 52.
38 Bishop 2004, p. 78.
39 Enwezor 1997, pp. 8 and 9.
40 Enwezor 2008, p. 208.
41 Smith 2011, p. 8.
42 Bourriaud, ed., 2009, p. 13.
43 Smith 2011, p. 9.
44 Rosler in *Artforum*, 2003, p. 157.
45 Enwezor in *Artforum*, 2003, p. 157.
46 David in *Artforum*, 2003, p. 158.
47 Enwezor 1997, pp. 10 and 12.
48 Smith 2011, p. 11.
49 Smith 2011, p. 11.
50 Smith 2011, p. 322.
51 Enwezor 2008, p. 228.
52 Smith 2011, p. 9.
53 Smith 2011, p. 9.
54 Bourriaud 2009, p. 18.
55 Enwezor 2008, p. 209.
56 Enwezor 2008, p. 230.
57 Enwezor 2008, p. 231.
58 Enwezor 2008, p. 234.
59 Enwezor 2009, p. 29.
60 Enwezor 2008, p. 222.
61 Enwezor 2008, p. 222.
62 Smith 2010, p. 368.
63 Bourriaud 2002 p. 45.

64 Smith 2010, p. 368.
65 Smith, in Smith, Enwezor and Condee eds., 2008, p. 5.
66 Smith 2006, p. 698.
67 Smith 2006, p. 697.
68 Smith 2006, p. 697.
69 Smith 2006, p. 698; also 2011, p. 12.
70 Smith, Enwezor, and Condee, eds, 2008, p. 9.
71 Smith, Enwezor, and Condee, eds, 2008, p. 9.
72 Smith 2011, p. 316.
73 Smith 2011, p. 12.
74 Lacqueur 2011.
75 Harvey 2010, p. 123.
76 Harvey 2010, p. 123.
77 For a comprehensive elaboration of this point, see Stallabrass 2004.
78 Smith 2011, p. 9.
79 Smith 2011, p. 13.
80 Smith, Enwezor, and Condee, eds, 2008, pp. 1 and 13.
81 Smith 2011, p. 13.
82 Musil 1997, Part II passim.
83 Smith 2010, p. 366.
84 Wittgenstein 2009 [1953], passim.
85 MacIntyre 1970; Winch 1958 and 1964.
86 Fiona Tan, *Disorient*, 2009.

References

Artforum, 2003, "Global tendencies: globalism and the large-scale exhibition," an online debate, November, pp. 152–212.

Belting, Hans, Jacob Birken, Andrea Buddensieg and Peter Weibel, eds, 2011, *Global Studies: Mapping Contemporary Art and Culture,* a ZKM book, Hatje Kantz Verlag, Ostfildern.

Belting, Hans and Andrea Buddensieg, eds, 2009, *The Global Art World: Audiences, Markets and Museums,* a ZKM book, Hatje Kantz Verlag, Ostfildern.

Belting Hans, Andrea Buddensieg, and Peter Weibel, eds, 2013, *The Global Contemporary and the Rise of New Art Worlds*, ZKM Center for Arts and Media Karlsruhe and MIT Press, Cambridge, MA.

Bishop, Claire, 2004, "Antagonism and relational aesthetics," *October* 110 (Fall): 51–79.

Bourriaud, Nicolas, 2002, *Relational Aesthetics*, Les presses du réel. First published in French in 1998 as *Esthétique relationnelle.*

Bourriaud, Nicolas, ed., 2009, *Altermodern*, exhibition catalog, Tate triennial, Tate Publishing, London.

Carrier, David, 2008, *World Art History and its Objects*, Pennsylvania State University Press.

Chakrabarty, Dipesh, 2008, *Provincialising Europe: Postcolonial Thought and Historical Difference*, Princeton University Press First published 2000.

Dave-Mukherji, Parul, 2005, "The other/s' stories of art in the age of multiculturalism," *American Council for Southern Asian Art Newsletter* 64 (Fall/Winter): 10–13.

Davis, Whitney, 2010, "World without art," *Art History* 33: 3–8.

Elkins, James, 2002, *Stories of Art*, Routledge, New York and London.

Elkins, James, 2004,"On David Summers's *Real Spaces*," *Art Bulletin* 86 (2): 373–380. Rptd in Elkins, *Is Art History Global?* pp. 41–71.

Elkins, James, 2006, "Writing about modernist painting outside Western Europe and North America," in Onians *Compression vs Expression*, pp. 188–214.

Elkins, James, ed., 2007, *Is Art History Global?* Routledge, New York and Abingdon.

Elkins, James, 2008, "Can we invent a world art studies?" in Zijlmans and van Damme, *World Art Studies: Exploring Concepts and Approaches*, pp. 107–118.

Elkins, James, Zhivka Valiavicharska, and Alice Kim, eds, 2010, *Art and Globalization*, Pennsylvania State University Press.

Enwezor, Okwui, 1997, *Trade Routes: History and Geography*, exhibition catalog, 2nd Johannesburg Biennale.

Enwezor, Okwui, 2008, "The postcolonial constellation: contemporary art in a state of permanent transition" in Smith, Enwezor and Condee, eds, *Antinomies of Art and Culture: Modernity, Postmodernity and Contemporaneity*, pp. 207–234.

Enwezor, Okwui, 2009, "Modernity and postcolonial ambivalence" in Bourriaud, *Altermodern*, pp. 27–41.

Foster, Hal, Rosalind Krauss, Yve-Alain Bois, and Benjamin H.D. Buchloh, eds, 2004, *Art since 1900: Modernism, Antimodernism, Postmodernism*, Thames and Hudson, London and New York.

Gombrich, Ernst, 1950, *The Story of Art*, Phaidon.

Gupta, Suman, 2007, *Social Constructionist Identity Politics and Literary Studies*, Palgrave Macmillan.

Harvey, David, 2010, *The Enigma of Capital*, Profile Books, London.

Lacqueur, Thomas, 2011, "Review of John Dower, *Cultures of War: Pearl Harbour, Hiroshima, 9-11, Iraq*," *London Review of Books*, August 25, p. 21.

MacIntyre, Alastair, 1970, *Against the Self-Images of the Age*, Duckworth.

Musil, Robert, 1997, *The Man Without Qualities*, new edn, Picador-Macmillan, London. Written c.1919–1938. First published in English in 1995.

October, Responses to a questionnaire on "the contemporary," special issue 130 (Fall) 2009.

Onians, John, 1996, "World art studies and the need for a new natural history of art," *Art Bulletin* 78 (2): 206–209.

Onians, John, ed., 2006, *Compression vs Expression*, Clark Art Institute and Yale University Press, New Haven and London.

Preziosi, Donald, 1989, *Rethinking Art History: Meditations on a Coy Science*, Yale University Press, New Haven and London.

Smith, Terry, 2006, "Contemporary art and contemporaneity" *Critical Inquiry* 32 (Summer): 681–707.

Smith, Terry, 2010, "The state of art history: contemporary art," *Art Bulletin* 92 (4) (December): 366–383.

Smith, Terry, 2011, *Contemporary Art: World Currents*, Laurence King Publishing, London.

Smith, Terry, Okwui Enwezor, and Nancy Condee, eds, 2008, *Antinomies of Art and Culture: Modernity, Postmodernity and Contemporaneity*, Duke University Press, Durham and London.

Stallabrass, Julian, 2004, *Art Incorporated*, Oxford University Press, Oxford.

Tan, Fiona, *et al.*, 2009, *Disorient*, Kehrer Verlag, Heidelberg.

Weibel, Peter and Andrea Buddensieg, eds, 2007, *Contemporary Art and the Museum: A Global Perspective,* a ZKM book, Hatje Kantz Verlag, Ostfildern.

Winch, Peter, 1958, *The Idea of a Social Science and its Relation to Philosophy*, Routledge and Kegan Paul, London.

Winch, Peter, 1964, "Understanding a primitive society," *American Philosophical Quarterly* 1 (4) (October): 307–324.

Wittgenstein, Ludwig 2009 [1953], *Philosophical Investigations*, rev. 4th edn, ed. Peter Hacker and Joachim Schulte, trans. G.E.M. Anscombe, P.M.S. Hacker, and Joachim Schulte, Wiley-Blackwell, Oxford.

Zijlmans, Kitty, and Wilfried van Damme, 2008, *World Art Studies: Exploring Concepts and Approaches*, Valiz, Amsterdam.

Index

Page numbers in *italics* refer to illustrations

Western Art and the Wider World, First Edition. Paul Wood.

Note:

Anna; not restricted to academic orthodoxy specialism –

orthodox academic specialism, p3